THE ROUGH RIDER
AND THE PROFESSOR

THE ROUGH RIDER
AND THE PROFESSOR

Theodore Roosevelt, Henry Cabot Lodge, and
the Friendship that Changed American History

LAURENCE JURDEM

PEGASUS BOOKS
NEW YORK LONDON

THE ROUGH RIDER AND THE PROFESSOR

Pegasus Books, Ltd.
148 West 37th Street, 13th Floor
New York, NY 10018

Copyright © 2023 by Laurence Jurdem

First Pegasus Books cloth edition July 2023

Interior design by Maria Fernandez

Library of Congress Cataloging-in-Publication Data is available.

ISBN: 978-1-63936-441-1

10 9 8 7 6 5 4 3 2 1

Printed in the United States of America
Distributed by Simon & Schuster
www.pegasusbooks.com

For my son, Elliot W. Jurdem, and my father-in-law
George H. Waterman III—a true Rough Rider.

Contents

Cast of Characters

Henry Adams (1838–1918): Historian, friend of Theodore Roosevelt, and mentor to Henry Cabot Lodge; descendant of John Adams and John Quincy Adams

Marian "Clover" Hooper Adams (1843–1885): Wife of Henry Adams; died by suicide in 1885

Margaret Chanler Aldrich (1870–1963): American socialite and philanthropist; friend of Henry Adams, Henry Cabot Lodge, and Theodore Roosevelt

Nelson W. Aldrich (1841–1915): United States senator from Rhode Island (1881–1911); father-in-law of John D. Rockefeller Jr.

Russell A. Alger (1836–1907): Governor of Michigan (1885–1887); secretary of war (1897–1899) under President McKinley; United States senator from Michigan (1902–1907)

Chester Alan Arthur (1829–1886): Chairman of the Republican Party (1879–1881); vice president to James A. Garfield (1881); 21st president of the United States (1881–1885)

Alexander Bannwart (1880–1959): Minor league baseball player; Princeton University graduate; verbally and physically attacked Henry Cabot Lodge over his position on World War I

William Belknap (1829–1890): United States secretary of war (1869–1876) under President Grant

William Sturgis Bigelow (1850–1926): Artistic scholar, Asian art expert, and collector of Japanese art; a close friend of Henry Cabot Lodge

Frank S. Black (1853–1913): Governor of New York (1897–1898); known for the Erie Canal expansion

James Gillespie Blaine (1830–1893): Member of the United States House of Representatives (1863–1876); United States senator from Maine (1876–1881); member of the GOP faction the Half Breeds; GOP presidential candidate (1884); 28th secretary of state (1881) under presidents Garfield and Arthur; 31st secretary of state (1889–1892) under President Harrison

Cornelius Newton Bliss (1833–1911): 21st secretary of the interior (1897–1899) under President McKinley

Benjamin Bristow (1832–1896): 30th secretary of the treasury (1874–1876) under President Grant; 1st solicitor general of the United States (1870–1872) under President Grant

William Jennings Bryan (1860–1925): Nebraska congressman (1891–1895); Democratic/Populist candidate for president (1896, against Republican McKinley); 41st secretary of state (1913–1915) under President Wilson

Archibald (Archie) Willingham DeGraffenreid Clarendon Butt (1865–1912): Military aide to President Roosevelt (1908–1909); secretary to President Taft (1909–1912); died in the sinking of the *Titanic* (1912)

Elizabeth Sherman "Lizzie" Cameron (1857–1944): Washington socialite; niece of General William T. Sherman and Ohio senator John Sherman; wife of Senator Donald Cameron and companion and confidante of Henry Adams

Andrew Carnegie (1935–1919): Founder of Carnegie Steel Company

Venustiano Carranza (1859–1920): 44th president of Mexico (1917–1920); seized power from usurpers after the death of President Francisco Madero

Winthrop Astor Chanler (1863–1926): Friend of Henry Cabot Lodge and Theodore Roosevelt; soldier in the Spanish-American War and World War I; enthusiastic polo player and outdoorsman

John Jay Chapman (1862–1933): Political commentator and reformer; friend of Theodore Roosevelt

Grover Cleveland (1837–1908): Democratic nominee for president (1884); 22nd president of the United States (1885–1889); 24th president of the United States (1893–1897); 28th governor of New York (1882–1885)

Roscoe Conkling (1829–1888): United States senator from New York (1867–1881); member of the GOP faction, the Stalwarts

Elisha Slade Converse (1820–1904): GOP candidate for Massachusetts Congress (1881); founder of the Boston Rubber Shoe Company

CAST OF CHARACTERS

George Cortelyou (1862–1940): Theodore Roosevelt's presidential secretary; chairman of the 1904 Republican National Convention; 44th United States secretary of the treasury (1907–1909) under President Roosevelt

William Cowles (1846–1923): Brother-in-law of Theodore Roosevelt; husband of Anna "Bamie" Roosevelt; rear admiral in the United States Navy; served in the Spanish-American War

Richard Croker (1843–1922): Irish American political boss, Grand Sachem of the New York City Tammany Hall machine (1886–1902)

Leon Czolgosz (1873–1901): Anarchist who shot President McKinley at the Pan American Exposition (1901); sentenced to death

Daisy, Princess of Pless (1873–1943): Born Mary Theresa Olivia née Cornwallis-West; socialite, married to Hans Heinrich XV von Hochberg, 3rd Prince of Pless; close friend of Sir Cecil Spring Rice

Charles Anderson Dana (1819–1897): American journalist, editor, and part owner of the *New York Sun*

Charles Henry Davis (1807–1877): Admiral, served in the Civil War for the Union; father of Anna Cabot Mills Davis Lodge

Cushman K. Davis (1838–1900): United States senator from Minnesota (1887–1900); chairman of the Senate foreign affairs committee (1897–1900)

Harriette Mills Davis (1818–1892): Mother of Anna Cabot Mills Davis Lodge

Mathilda Elizabeth "Bessy" Frelinghuysen Davis (1876–1960): Wife of George Cabot "Bay" Lodge

John Davis (1851–1902): Assistant secretary of state (1882–1885); father of Mathilda

Sarah Helen "Sally" Frelinghuysen Davis (1856–1936): Socialite, mother of "Bessy" Davis; longtime mistress of President Chester Arthur

Eugene V. Debs (1855–1926): Socialist candidate for president (1912)

Commodore George Dewey (1837–1917): Served in the Civil War in the navy; named navy commander of the asiatic squadron (1897)

George F. Edmunds (1828–1919): United States senator from Vermont (1866–1891); Republican

Charles Eliot (1834–1926): President of Harvard University (1869–1909)

William C. Endicott (1826–1900): 36th United States secretary of war (1885–1889)

Joseph B. Foraker (1846–1917): United States senator from Ohio (1897–1909); Republican; governor of Ohio (1886–1890)

Eugene N. Foss (1858–1939): Democratic governor of Massachusetts (1911–1914)

Archduke Franz Ferdinand (1863–1914): Archduke of Austria; assassinated in Sarajevo leading to the start of World War I

Augustus Peabody Gardner (1865–1918): Republican politician serving as a congressman from Massachusetts (1902–1917); husband of Constance Lodge

James A. Garfield (1831–1881): 20th president of the United States (1881); assassinated by Charles J. Guiteau; major general in the United States Army; Ohio congressman (1863–1880)

James R. Garfield (1865–1950): 23rd United States secretary of the interior (1907–1909) under President Roosevelt

Ulysses S. Grant (1822–1885): 18th president of the United States (1869–1877)

Horace Gray (1828–1902): Associate justice of the Supreme Court (1882–1902)

Horace Greeley (1811–1872): Founder and editor of the *New-York Tribune*; GOP presidential candidate (1872)

Charles J. Guiteau (1841–1882): GOP office seeker; assassinated President Garfield; arrested and executed

Winfield Scott Hancock (1824–1886): Democratic candidate for president (1880); major general, served in the Civil War and the Mexican-American War

Marcus A. Hanna (1837–1904): Campaign manager for William McKinley (1896 and 1900); United States senator from Ohio (1897–1904)

Warren Harding (1865–1923): Senator from Ohio (1915–1921); 29th president of the United States (1921–1923)

E. H. Harriman (1848–1909): American financier and railroad titan, chairman of the executive committee of the Union Pacific Railroad (1897–1909)

Clara Stone Hay (1849–1914): Wife of John Hay

John Hay (1838–1905): President Lincoln's private secretary; 12th United States assistant secretary of state (1879–1881) under presidents Hayes and Garfield; 37th United States secretary of state (1898–1905) under presidents McKinley and Roosevelt

Rutherford B. Hayes (1822–1893): Ohioan, 19th president of the United States (1877–1882); abolitionist lawyer; 29th and 32nd governor of Ohio (1868–1872, 1876–1877)

William Randolph Hearst (1863–1951): Owner of the *New York Journal*; New York newspaper baron, purchased several newspapers and magazines across the country; United States congressman (1903–1907)

Henry Lee Higginson (1834–1919): Founder of the Boston Symphony Orchestra; financier and relative of Henry Cabot Lodge

James J. Hill (1838–1916): Chief executive officer of the Great Northern Railway

Garret A. Hobart (1844–1899): Vice president to President McKinley, first term (1897–1899)

Oliver Wendell Holmes Jr. (1841–1935): Lawyer and legal scholar; friend of Henry Cabot Lodge; associate justice of the Supreme Court (1902–1932)

Herbert Hoover (1874–1964): 31st president of the United States (1929–1933); secretary of commerce (1921–1928) under presidents Harding and Coolidge

Victoriano Huerta (1854–1916): Mexican general who appointed himself 39th president of Mexico during a period of instability in 1911

Charles Evans Hughes (1862–1948): Republican governor of New York (1907–1910); 44th United States secretary of state (1921–1925); 11th chief justice of the Supreme Court (1930–1941); Republican presidential candidate (1916)

Andrew Johnson (1808–1875): United States senator from Tennessee (1875); vice president to Abraham Lincoln (1865); 17th president of the United States (1865–1869)

Philander Knox (1853–1921): 44th United States attorney general (1901–1904) under presidents McKinley and Roosevelt; 40th United States secretary of state (1909–1913) under President Taft; United States senator from Pennsylvania (1917–1921)

Robert La Follette (1855–1925): United States senator from Wisconsin (1906–1925); progressive Republican

William Lawrence (1850–1941): Harvard classmate of Henry Cabot Lodge; Episcopal bishop of Massachusetts

George Cabot Lee (1830–1910): Father of Alice Lee; father-in-law of Theodore Roosevelt, relative of Henry Cabot Lodge

Robert E. Lee (1807–1870): Confederate general during the American Civil War

Abraham Lincoln (1809–1865): 16th president of the United States (1861–1865); assassinated by John Wilkes Booth

Anna "Nannie" Cabot Mills Davis Lodge (1851–1915): Henry Cabot Lodge's wife

Constance Davis Lodge (1872–1948): Daughter of Henry Cabot Lodge

George Cabot "Bay" Lodge (1873–1909): Son of Henry Cabot Lodge

John Ellerton Lodge (1807–1862): Father of Henry Cabot Lodge

John E. Lodge (1876–1942): Son of Henry Cabot Lodge

Henry Cabot Lodge (1850–1924): Senator from Massachusetts (1892–1924); close friend of Theodore Roosevelt

Henry Cabot Lodge Jr. (1902–1985): Senator from Massachusetts (1947–1953); Republican vice presidential nominee (1960)

John D. Long (1838–1915): 32nd governor of Massachusetts (1880–1883); 34th United States secretary of the navy (1897–1902) under President McKinley

Alice Roosevelt Longworth (1884–1980): Daughter of Theodore Roosevelt; only child of Alice Hathaway Lee Roosevelt

John R. Lynch (1847–1939): African American congressman from Mississippi (1882–1883)

Hugh McCullough (1808–1895): 27th and 36th United States secretary of the treasury, under presidents Lincoln and Johnson (1865–1869), and Arthur (1884–1885)

William McKinley (1843–1901): Ohio congressman; two-term governor of Ohio; 25th president of the United States (1897–1901); assassinated

Elijah Hunt Mills (1776–1829) and Harriet Blake Mills (1818–1892): Grandparents of Anna Cabot Mills

John Mitchell (1870–1919): President of the United Mine Workers union

J. P. Morgan (1837–1913): Investment banker, head of J. P. Morgan and Co.

Alton B. Parker (1852–1926): Chief judge of the New York Court of Appeals; Democratic presidential nominee (1904)

Lord Julian Pauncefote (1828–1902): British ambassador to the United States (1893–1902)

Herbert H. D. Peirce (1849–1916): United States ambassador to Norway under Theodore Roosevelt

Gifford Pinchot (1865–1946): 4th chief of the Division of Forestry (1898–1905) under presidents McKinley and Roosevelt; first chief of the forest service of the United States (1905–1910) under Theodore Roosevelt

Thomas C. Platt (1833–1910): Republican party machine boss in New York state; senator from New York (1897–1909)

Joseph Pulitzer (1847–1911): Publisher of the *New York World*; congressman from New York (1885–1886)

Lemuel Ely Quigg (1863–1919): Friend of Theodore Roosevelt; journalist and congressman from New York (1894–1899)

Thomas B. Reed (1839–1902): Speaker of the House (1889–1891, 1895–1899); congressman from Maine (1877–1899)

Jacob Riis (1849–1914): Journalist, social reformer, author of *How the Other Half Lives*

Corinne Roosevelt Robinson (1861–1933): Younger sister of Theodore Roosevelt

Douglas Robinson Jr. (1855–1918): Husband of Corinne Roosevelt

Alice Hathaway Lee Roosevelt (1861–1884): American socialite; first wife of Theodore Roosevelt

Anna "Bamie" Roosevelt (1855–1931): Older sister of Theodore Roosevelt

Anna Rebecca Hall Roosevelt (1863–1892): American socialite; wife of Elliott Roosevelt

Edith Carow Roosevelt (1861–1948): Second wife of Theodore Roosevelt

Elliott Bulloch Roosevelt (1860–1894): Younger brother of Theodore Roosevelt

Ethel Roosevelt (1891–1977): Daughter of Theodore Roosevelt

Kermit Roosevelt (1889–1943): Son of Theodore Roosevelt; served in World War I and World War II

Martha Bulloch "Mittie" Roosevelt (1835–1884): Wife of Theodore Roosevelt Sr.

Quentin Roosevelt (1897–1918): Youngest son of Theodore Roosevelt; killed while serving in World War II

Theodore Roosevelt Sr. (1831–1878): Father of Theodore Roosevelt; husband of Mittie Roosevelt

Theodore Roosevelt Jr. (1858–1919): 26th president of the United States; progressive Republican politician

Theodore Roosevelt III (1887–1944): Eldest son of Theodore Roosevelt

Elihu Root (1845–1937): Friend of Theodore Roosevelt; Republican politician and lawyer; 38th secretary of state (1905–1909) under President Roosevelt; 41st secretary of war (1899–1904) under presidents McKinley and Roosevelt

Dwight Sabin (1843–1902): Republican senator from Minnesota (1883–1889), Republican National Committee chairman (1883–1884)

Carl Schurz (1829–1906): Respected liberal member of the GOP; 13th secretary of the interior (1877–1881); senator from Missouri (1869–1875)

Sofie, Duchess of Hohenberg (1868–1914): Wife of Archduke Franz Ferdinand of Austria, assassinated in Sarajevo alongside her husband

Cecil Spring Rice (1859–1918): Ambassador from the Court of St. James to the United States (1912–1918)

William L. Strong (1827–1900): Mayor of New York (1895–1897)

Charles Sumner (1811–1874): Abolitionist; senator from Massachusetts (1851–1874)

Helen "Nellie" Herron Taft (1861–1943): Wife of William Howard Taft

William Howard Taft (1857–1930): 27th president of the United States (1909–1913); chief justice of the United States (1921–1930)

Samuel J. Tilden (1814–1886): Governor of New York (1875–1876); Democratic presidential candidate (1876)

Ben Tillman (1847–1918): Senator from South Carolina (1895–1918)

Augustus Van Wyck (1850–1922): Supreme Court justice of Brooklyn, New York; Democratic nominee for governor of New York (1898)

Francisco "Pancho" Villa (1878–1923): General in the Mexican Revolution, which forced out Mexican president Porfirio Díaz

John Wanamaker (1838–1922): Department store magnate; 35th postmaster general (1889–1893) under President Harrison

Booker T. Washington (1856–1915): African American leader, author, and educator

Thomas Edward Watson (1856–1922): Populist candidate for president (1904)

James B. Weaver (1833–1912): Congressman (1885–1889), populist candidate for president (1892)

Lord Richard Webster (1842–1915): Royal chief justice of England

Henry White (1850–1927): Diplomat, ambassador to Italy (1905) and ambassador to France (1906–1909) under President Roosevelt

General James H. Wilson (1837–1925): Friend of Henry Cabot Lodge; major general in the American Civil War and a brigadier general during the Spanish-American War

Woodrow Wilson (1856–1924): 28th president of the United States (1913–1921)

Edward Wolcott (1848–1905): United States senator from Colorado (1889–1901)

Colonel Leonard Wood (1860–1927): Army major general; commander of Theodore Roosevelt's volunteer Spanish-American War regiment, the First Volunteer Cavalry, aka the Rough Riders

Arthur Von Zimmermann (1864–1940): Secretary of state for foreign affairs of the German empire (1916–1917)

PROLOGUE
Fire and Ice

"[Lodge] was my closest friend personally, politically and
in every other way and occupied toward me a relationship
that no other man has occupied or will occupy."
—Theodore Roosevelt on Henry Cabot Lodge[1]
June 20, 1900, Philadelphia

The entertainment began at eleven o'clock in the morning with a tribute to the music of John Philip Sousa by the Municipal Band of Philadelphia. As the melody echoed through Exposition Auditorium, those who gathered to celebrate the 1900 Republican National Convention eagerly anticipated a memorable afternoon. By the time the Rev. Charles M. Boswell delivered the invocation signifying the opening of the second day's festivities, it was just after 12:30, and few of the 15,000 spectators awaiting the nomination of William McKinley and Theodore Roosevelt for president and vice president of the United States chose to stand. To Boswell's dismay, the delegates seemed to have little taste for religion.[2]

Moments after Boswell left the stage, a procession of fifteen elderly men gathered at the rear of the arena. As "the white-haired patriarchs" proceeded toward the speaker's platform, they carried with them a faded version of the Stars and Stripes. Led by seventy-three-year-old Senator Joseph Hawley of Connecticut, the group symbolized the last remnants of the delegation to the first Republican National Convention, held in Philadelphia forty-four years earlier.[3]

As Hawley and his colleagues stepped to the platform, an enormous roar shook the arena. Gazing out upon the gallery of cheering spectators, the members of that distinguished company who cast their votes more than four decades earlier in favor of the legendary explorer and politician, John C. Frémont, swore their devotion to the vision and values of the Republican Party.[4]

As the ovation continued, the person applauding with the most enthusiasm may have been Theodore Roosevelt. Known for his near obsession with physical activity, the forty-two-year-old governor of New York maintained his conditioning through a regimen of boxing, rowing, and weightlifting. At five foot nine, two hundred and fifty pounds, with a thick neck, barrel chest, and a bushy mustache barely concealing his large white teeth, Roosevelt's spectacle-covered eyes rigorously scanned the building, never wanting to miss a moment of excitement.

A figure with a wide smile and contagious laugh, Roosevelt possessed the ability to be comfortable with people from any walk of life. A natural raconteur, the governor delighted friends and acquaintances with endless stories of his adventures in Cuba during the Spanish-American War or his early days as a rancher in the Badlands of the Dakota Territory. Possessing enormous physical energy and a magnetic personality, Roosevelt enjoyed virtually every task he undertook. Whether enthusiastically smacking supporters on the back while campaigning for office, speaking expansively about the three books he read that day or simply wrestling with his children, many considered Theodore Roosevelt a sheer force of nature.[5]

Born into an elite New York family in 1858, Roosevelt grew up admiring the GOP's most famous standard-bearer, Abraham Lincoln. The man known to his admirers as "the Great Emancipator," believed all individuals regardless of race, color, or creed should have the opportunity to achieve a piece of the American Dream. The governor also shared Lincoln's positions on issues like property rights and the necessity for a protective tariff. Diverging from his political hero on the issue of immigration, Roosevelt believed restrictions were necessary to preserve the economic livelihood of his fellow citizens.[6]

The governor understood his role in the upcoming campaign required praising McKinley's tenure as president, while simultaneously attacking the populism of the likely Democratic challenger, William Jennings Bryan. "The Hero of San Juan Hill" opposed Bryan's economic radicalism. But Roosevelt also remained concerned with the nation's growing economic disparity.[7]

As members of the New York delegation celebrated the party platform of low taxes and limited corporate regulation, more than three-quarters of their fellow citizens lived on the margins of society. The former "Rough Rider" contended these positions were detrimental to the concept of fair play. It was not enough to simply embrace the corporate titans of the new industrial era. The leadership of the GOP needed to advocate for policies that once again welcomed those willing to strive, take risks, and engage in what Roosevelt referred to as "the strenuous life."[8]

A short distance away sat Roosevelt's dearest friend, Senator Henry Cabot Lodge of Massachusetts. An imposing and intimidating man at six foot two, Lodge, stoic and cerebral, maintained his slim, athletic frame through fox hunting, tennis, and frequent rides with Roosevelt through Washington, DC's Rock Creek Park. Renowned for his natty style of dress, Lodge's "finely chiseled features, [hazel] eyes," and "closely cropped iron gray beard" gave the Bay State Republican every inch the image of elegance and dignity.[9]

A skilled debater and superb parliamentarian, Lodge, born in 1850 and descended from one of the premier families in Massachusetts, exhibited little humor or warmth. When, however, he was in the presence of his vivacious wife, Anna Cabot Mills Davis Lodge, known affectionately as "Nannie," intimate friends like Roosevelt, his elegant but overprotective wife Edith, or the engaging British diplomat Cecil Spring Rice, Lodge was an engaging conversationalist known for quoting Shakespeare and other forms of literature.[10]

Possessing strong personal loyalty, professional integrity, and moral character, Lodge also had an unpredictable temperament which could erupt at any moment. When one of his own constituents accused the senator of moral cowardice, Lodge, despite being in his middle sixties, punched the man in the face.[11]

Throughout their careers in public life, Lodge and Roosevelt encouraged one another to mine the greatness that resided within each of them. In that regard, the New York patrician looked forward to hearing Lodge address the delegates in his role as permanent chairman of the convention. A staunch party man, who believed the only good Democrat was a "politically dead one," the senator's remarks were expected to highlight the accomplishments of President McKinley and his administration over the last four years.[12]

Concerned with the rapid "consolidation of industry" Roosevelt and Lodge each contended that those like McKinley and his premier adviser, Senator Mark Hanna of Ohio, were too sympathetic to the interests of American business. The 1900 presidential nominee and his colleagues favored policies that allowed financial speculation to flourish. Roosevelt and Lodge believed that the only way all Americans could thrive economically was through the application of government power to constrain the financial inequalities they believed responsible for the country's social instability and moral decay.[13]

Known as one of the most erudite men in the nation's capital, many admired Lodge's intelligence and devotion to duty. But Lodge was no orator. In fact, the former Harvard professor's speaking style was so tedious someone once "compared it to the tearing of a bed sheet." Roosevelt, however, eagerly anticipated Lodge's remarks, describing him to a friend as one who possessed not only a "delightful, big-boyish personage," but someone he admired with reverence and respect.[14]

As the applause honoring Hawley and his colleagues subsided, Senator Edward Wolcott of Colorado, the convention's temporary chairman, announced that Roosevelt would be part of a small committee selected to escort Lodge to the forefront of the arena. A popular figure on the Washington social scene, with a taste for faro and other games of chance, Wolcott was an ardent supporter of the party's vice-presidential nominee.[15]

Roosevelt, dressed in a dark suit and trademark Rough Rider hat, always enjoyed being at the center of attention. The *Washington Post* noted, however, that despite the strong ovation, the governor of New York "made no effort to conceal the annoyance he felt at thus being dragged into view." That expression of irritability was due to Roosevelt's conflicting emotions over his decision to serve as McKinley's running mate, an issue he had struggled with from the moment Lodge first raised the idea in the summer of 1899.[16]

Following Wolcott's introduction, Roosevelt, accompanied by Governor Leslie Shaw of Iowa, guided Lodge to the convention platform. The senator, who stood ramrod straight and whose voice "showed splendid carrying power," praised the achievements of the current occupant of the White House, for "promises kept" and "work done." Throughout the address, as applause interrupted Lodge's remarks, Roosevelt could not help but realize how far the two men had come in their personal and professional lives.[17]

In 1884 Roosevelt and Lodge faced political ostracism following their failed effort to topple the nomination of GOP presidential candidate James G. Blaine. Out of that experience, the two forged a friendship of more than thirty years that in time proved responsible for changing the course of the history of the United States. That relationship not only accelerated the rise of Theodore Roosevelt but played a significant part in the nation gaining a prominent position in world affairs.

Proponents of American exceptionalism, Roosevelt and Lodge believed the ideas encapsulated in the Declaration of Independence of 1776 and the Constitution of 1787 represented something entirely unique in human history. The two politicians contended the country could only achieve its destiny by achieving its rightful place on the international stage. In 1898, Lodge and Roosevelt waged a strategic campaign to acquire key territories in the Pacific theater. Both men believed these expansionist objectives not only enhanced the country's national interests but provided a means of invigorating the nation's character during a period of drift and division.[18]

On more than one occasion, the friendship between the two came under strain. Following Roosevelt's succession to the presidency in 1901, Lodge, always the more successful of the two, suddenly saw his protégé at the top of the political pyramid. Despite the sudden shift in their relationship, Lodge's admiration for Roosevelt never wavered. But during Roosevelt's tenure in the White House, his desire to ideologically expand the Republican Party caused the president to embrace a series of progressive reforms contrary to his mentor's conservative point of view.[19]

In 1912, the tensions between the two exploded for all to see. With the objective of securing a third presidential term, Roosevelt bolted from the Republican Party in favor of a populist agenda. That path, one that Lodge had warned Roosevelt never to choose, created serious differences between the two men. The senator believed Roosevelt's support of positions like the recall of judges and the direct election of senators not only endangered the fortunes of the Republican Party but threatened the foundations of the nation's democratic system.[20]

Following the defeat of Roosevelt's independent drive for the presidency, the two men reunited over their mutual disdain for the personality and policies of Woodrow Wilson. Both believed Wilson's foolish idealism and weak character placed the greatness of the United States in jeopardy. The relationship between Lodge and Roosevelt endured many twists and turns, including the tragic deaths of friends and family. Despite these traumatic moments, the personal conviviality between Roosevelt and Lodge continued until the former president took his final breath in January 1919.

Theodore Roosevelt viewed Henry Cabot Lodge as "his closest friend, personally, politically and in every other way." Lodge, in turn, believed Roosevelt to be "one of the most loveable as well as one of the cleverest and most darling men I have ever known." The two men "complemented each other perfectly." They shared an interest in sports, history, literature, and living well. Most important, they possessed a common vision of the United States as a force for good in the world. Along with their wives, they were as close as any two people could be.[21]

While the two men occasionally differed in their political views, their upbringing and education were almost identical. Having each lost fathers, at the ages of eleven and nineteen respectively, neither Lodge nor Roosevelt had a strong role model to ground or guide them as they reached adulthood. Raised with a much older sister and doted on by his mother Anna, Lodge developed a wide array of acquaintances but very few friends. While many of Lodge's contemporaries enjoyed glamorous evenings or summers in Newport, Rhode Island, the senator preferred reading or writing in the isolated beauty of his family home overlooking the sea on the Eastern shore of Massachusetts.[22]

Roosevelt, ill for much of his childhood, also spent considerable time alone. Surrounded by books on history, literature, and the natural world, Roosevelt had little connection with other children except for his three siblings. Once close with his brother Elliott, the two siblings slowly drifted apart as the younger Roosevelt succumbed to mental illness, exacerbated by a long struggle with alcoholism. While T. R. adored the company of people, the two-term president had few he relied on for consistent advice and counsel.[23]

Over time Lodge became Roosevelt's confidant, the only person other than his wife and two sisters with whom he believed he could share his deepest thoughts or feelings. In a friendship of more than thirty years, each treated the other as a member of their extended family. It was a relationship Roosevelt grew to value. "[Y]ou two are really the only people for whom I genuinely care," Theodore confessed to Nannie Lodge in 1886.[24]

Without question, Roosevelt's tremendous personal gifts would one day have made him a contender for the presidency. That sudden surge of upward mobility when Roosevelt rose from state assemblyman to president in just over sixteen years would never have occurred if not for the acumen and connections of Henry Cabot Lodge.

Over the course of their decades-long friendship, the two exchanged more than twenty-five hundred letters, and wrote about one another's attitudes and activities in correspondence with family and close friends. It is no surprise numerous historians describe the friendship between Roosevelt and Lodge as "one of the greatest in United States history."[25]

※

The debate around the legacy of Theodore Roosevelt continues to remain relevant more than a century after his passing. Many of the issues confronting the country today also dominated the headlines during the era of these two prominent political figures.

These issues included: the debate over how to curb the influence of corporations, the scale and scope of government power, the continuing shift of demographics due to widespread immigration, the question of whether tariffs are positive solutions for economic growth, and the United States' role within the international arena. As in the time of Roosevelt and Lodge, many Americans continue to feel displaced as they struggle to adapt to the country's shifting economy due to the impact of globalization and the dominant influence of technology.[26]

Both Roosevelt and Lodge criticized the influence of big business in the economy as well as the ethical and moral toll it took on society. Each despised the excesses of materialism, believing it responsible for a loss of focus on faith and family.[27]

For all of Roosevelt's fiery rhetoric, however, he believed in incrementalism to construct a more perfect union. Lodge shared Roosevelt's gradualist instincts. The Bostonian, however, also concerned himself in employing whatever strategy necessary to keep his party in power.[28]

The book analyzes how Lodge and Roosevelt viewed and addressed the domestic and international issues that polarized their era. The narrative also demonstrates that the tensions confronting the GOP during the late nineteenth and early twentieth century were not unique to their own time, but are issues that remain at the forefront of the politics of the twenty-first century.[29]

PART ONE
THE SEARCH FOR ORDER

ONE
A Common Code

"My father was the finest man I ever knew."
—Theodore Roosevelt

L ate in the evening, on Tuesday April 18, 1865, a delegation gathered on the third floor of the United States Treasury building in Washington, DC, a short distance from the Executive Mansion at 1600 Pennsylvania Avenue. Greeted by Treasury Secretary Hugh McCullough, the group, which included the prominent financier George Cabot Ward and the founder of the Illinois Central Railroad, Jonathan Sturges, had traveled from New York City's Union League Club to pay their respects to the late president, Abraham Lincoln.[1]

As the men spoke with the secretary, they were surrounded by a suite of heavy oak furniture, sweeping green and yellow curtains, and a large, gilded chandelier. The room, immersed in black cloth, symbolized the beginning of a period of national mourning for the beloved statesman from Illinois.[2]

Shortly after McCullough entered the room, President Andrew Johnson joined them. Upon arriving, the always elegantly attired former senator from Tennessee made remarks promising to continue to pursue the policies and objectives of the nation's eighteenth president.[3]

Among those standing nearby was the handsome and commanding figure of Theodore Roosevelt Sr. Tall, with piercing eyes, and a dark, heavy beard, the thirty-three-year-old philanthropist wore a dark three-piece suit, starched white shirt, light blue tie, with a yellow centifolia rose anchored within his vest buttonhole. The man who his sister-in-law referred to as "Great Heart," had become an acquaintance of Lincoln's through the president's private secretary, John Hay.[4]

A stout moralist, and ardent nationalist, Roosevelt had expected to participate in the Civil War. But Roosevelt's wife, the frail and beautiful Martha Bulloch, objected. With numerous members of her family fighting for the Confederate States of America, "Mittie Roosevelt," was convinced that a confrontation between her husband and one of her relatives was inevitable. To ease her anxieties, Roosevelt chose to hire two substitutes to take his place on the battlefield. Despite agreeing to his wife's wishes, T. R. Sr. remained determined to support the war effort any way he could.[5]

Working with Hay and several others, the senior Roosevelt developed a government initiative known as the allotment system. Riding long distances from one disease-infested Union camp to another, Roosevelt Sr. and other allotment commissioners attempted to convince members of the army to send their pay home to their families rather than waste it on gambling, alcohol, or other useless endeavors.[6]

Roosevelt Sr.'s interest in trying to reform those susceptible to being lured into a life of sin was an issue that had preoccupied him for years. Following a dissatisfying period working for his family's import business, he decided to employ his sizeable financial resources to improve the lives of New York City's less fortunate. That philanthropy, which included funding organizations like the Children's Aid Society and the New York Dispensary Hospital, made T. R. Sr. a prominent figure among an elite group of New Yorkers trying to eradicate poverty throughout Manhattan.[7]

When Roosevelt Sr. visited the nation's capital, he enjoyed the company of John Hay. Indulging in the generous menu at the sprawling Willard Hotel, the two men discussed the progress of the war and which military man had the ear of the president. More than once, while sitting with Hay in Lincoln's pew during services at St. John's Episcopal Church, Roosevelt Sr.'s tall frame and dark continence caused him to be mistaken for the nation's chief executive.[8]

The story was one that delighted Roosevelt Sr.'s young son and namesake, Theodore. The second of Roosevelt's four children, the boy loved that his father was friendly with the president of the United States. The child was even more delighted that senior had helped the first lady, Mary Todd Lincoln, select a bonnet for a Washington garden party. These delightful anecdotes made young Theodore a passionate admirer of the former country lawyer from Springfield for the rest of his life.[9]

A commitment to family and patriotism also resonated within the character of John Ellerton Lodge. Tall, classically handsome, and of significant means, Lodge possessed a "stern" and "demanding" temperament that drove him mercilessly in the development of his merchant shipping business. With a thick, tousled head of reddish brown hair and a dark, thin beard extending from the periphery of one jawline to the other, Lodge worked long hours in an office just off the confines of Boston Harbor. With colorful names like the *Argonaut*, the *Storm King*, and *Don Quixote*, Lodge's ships traveled between North America and Asia in search of silks, spices, and other items difficult to obtain in the United States.[10]

Fascinated by world affairs, Lodge had little interest in politics. The one exception was his outspoken opposition to slavery.

Conducting business in New Orleans during one stage of his career, the New Englander had experienced firsthand the harshness of what Southerners referred to as "the peculiar institution." A member of the Republican Party and a close friend of the Massachusetts abolitionist senator Charles Sumner, John Lodge, like Theodore Roosevelt Sr., became determined to fight for the Union cause when hostilities began on April 12, 1861.[11]

Unfortunately, due to a knee injury suffered in a riding accident years earlier, Lodge was unable to exercise his right to fight for the North. Unwilling to stand by while others prepared to fight and die for a cause greater than themselves, Lodge focused his attention on raising money and enlisting those interested in volunteering for the war effort. While neither Lodge nor Roosevelt Sr. served their respective states on the field of battle, each believed that honor, courage, and responsibility mattered. These were lessons both men imparted to their children and ones that Henry Cabot Lodge and Theodore Roosevelt Jr. never forgot.[12]

Residing in spacious and elegant homes with high ceilings and "large bay windows" on Beacon Street in Boston and Gramercy Park in New York, Lodge and Roosevelt Sr. adored their children and were revered by them in return. In an autobiography published in 1913, the former president described his father as "the finest man I ever knew." Henry Cabot Lodge, known as Cabot, viewed his father in a similar manner. In a memoir of his early life published the same year as Roosevelt's, the senator described the elder Lodge as "perfect company to a child." With such descriptions as these, it is no surprise that each boy viewed their father as the center of their world.[13]

Coming of age in these Eastern cities during the late nineteenth century, Henry Cabot Lodge and Theodore Roosevelt Jr. embraced their respective father's interests as well as their values. In the narrative, *Early Memories*, Lodge recalled being enthralled by everything that involved the business of shipping and the sea. Gazing out the window of his father's "counting-room," the young boy watched as the large clipper ships sailed off into the horizon bound for Africa, Asia, and other destinations. That moment and many others caused the young man to develop a lifelong love of maritime history and nautical affairs.[14]

As Lodge became inspired by his father's love of the sea, young Theodore Roosevelt was drawn to his own father's efforts to improve life for those not blessed by his family's good fortune. A man of great physicality, Roosevelt Sr. believed that one's spiritual strength evolved through building one's body in the service of God. That philosophy encouraged action and self-reliance while discouraging idleness and complacency. "Man was never intended to become an oyster," the elder Roosevelt wrote to a member of his extended family. These traits of character were reinforced as the junior Roosevelt spent hours watching his father expound upon the importance of moral uplift to those who resided in homes for impoverished newsboys, scattered throughout lower Manhattan.[15]

As Roosevelt and his father grew closer, the future president absorbed several critical principles. These core beliefs embraced the ideas that one had a solemn duty to set a standard of behavior for their fellow citizens, care for the less fortunate, and lead an ordered and moral life. That mantra became a fundamental part of Roosevelt Jr.'s identity and played a critical role in the decisions he made in and out of office.[16]

In Boston, John E. Lodge brought the same disciplined, but loving persona to his own son. During frequent fourteen-mile horse and buggy rides to the family's large villa on the Eastern shore of Massachusetts, the boy absorbed the senior Lodge's advice about how to make one's way in society. "Only the idlers of the world [have] no time," John E. Lodge firmly instructed his son. In watching both their fathers engage in the spirit of noblesse oblige, Lodge and Roosevelt Jr. came to understand that their privileged position presented them with a responsibility to set an example their contemporaries could follow.[17]

With an emphasis on a strong work ethic, as well as being instructed in the importance of leading a life of morality and faith, the two boys grew up in a disciplined and formal world reflective of the Puritan values of the period. Despite stringent upbringings, each found time for sport and outdoor activities. Neither was a natural athlete, but Lodge and Roosevelt Jr. enjoyed the thrill of attempting to master a particular skill.[18]

Isolated for extensive periods of time due to chronic asthma, T. R. Jr. was determined to participate in his family's fondness for competition and camaraderie. Attempting to keep up with his siblings as they ran, swam, and climbed trees, the son emulated his father's advice about the importance of physical engagement.[19]

Lodge, in turn, learned horseback riding, swimming, and sailing all from an early age. Most of these activities occurred at the family's vacation home in the seaside community of Nahant. Located on twelve acres and surrounded by weeping willow trees, the boy delighted in the sounds of the ocean lashing across the cliffs of his family's estate. It was a world he frequently returned to and one he found far more comfortable and ideal than his native Boston.[20]

Athletics held an important place within each family's environment. However, it was the life of the mind that from an early age captivated Lodge's and Roosevelt's two young sons. In their initial contact with literature, it was the tall tales of writers like Sir Walter Scott and James Fenimore Cooper that engaged the boys' imaginations. Due to their father's influence, Lodge and Roosevelt Jr. also became admirers of the dramatist William Shakespeare and the poet Alexander Pope.[21]

Love of Shakespeare's writings so resonated with Lodge that for the rest of his life the senator was known for carrying a volume of the Bard's work in his coat pocket. Following his father's death, Roosevelt also remained an admirer of these early literary influences. For both figures, their early encounters with stories of courage, honor, and service embedded those qualities within each man's worldview.[22]

These heroic traits portrayed in stories of high adventure were on full display during the Civil War. Even with neither of their fathers participating, the conflict had an enormous impact on the life experience of Lodge's and Roosevelt Sr.'s two young sons. "The war pervaded everything," Senator Lodge wrote in describing the effect of the hostilities on his early life.[23]

Just eleven years old when the war began, the conflict left a significant impression on Lodge's state of mind. For young Roosevelt, barely more than three, "the war was the first news from the world outside to penetrate the secure haven of home and family." In observing the conflict on their respective communities, the atmosphere instilled within each boy an admiration for courage and patriotism neither ever lost.[24]

Too young to understand the intellectual complexities behind the war, the two young men grasped the intensity of emotion experienced by each side. The tensions were seen in microcosm within the Roosevelt household. Mittie Roosevelt, despite being married to one of New York City's prominent citizens, remained committed to her Southern relatives fighting for the Confederacy.[25]

The younger Roosevelt noticed his mother's passion but preferred to support the position of his father and the president he served. T. R. Jr.'s strong support for the Union was seen by his frequent appearance in an outfit resembling those worn by one of the New York regiments. In addition, when saying his evening prayers, he asked God to grind Robert E. Lee and the Army of Northern Virginia into rubble.[26]

Following the Union victory in 1865, the Roosevelts' second son remained ambivalent that his father had missed the opportunity to display his courage during a monumental moment in history. Keeping his father's decision to decline military service out of his autobiography, Roosevelt Jr. compensated by touting his own battle-field experience. "I did not intend to have to hire somebody else to do my shooting for me," he recalled in describing his participation in the Spanish-American War more than three decades later. For the remainder of his life, Theodore Roosevelt believed experiencing the sting of battle was not only an opportunity for glory, but one of the few ways in which a man's character was measured.[27]

Swept up by the excitement of the war, the young Lodge aspired to enlist as a drummer boy, a wish immediately dismissed by his parents. Attending the Dixwell Latin School in Boston, Lodge and his class-mates were expected to participate in extensive military drills, with the daunting possibility they might one day participate in the conflict.[28]

As hostilities progressed, the Lodge family experienced feelings of loss endured by many across the country. The long casualty lists of those who perished in campaigns at Fredericksburg, Virginia, or Vicksburg, Mississippi, made a powerful impact on the young man. "This reading the death-roll and scanning bulletins to see how many men you have known and cared for, whose people are your people . . . have been killed is not an experience that one ever forgets," Lodge recalled decades later.[29]

The emotion over the war paled to the moment in 1862 when John E. Lodge collapsed and died from a heart attack at age fifty-two. For the son, the loss of his closest companion "felt like a bolt of lightning." Despite experiencing pride at the number of people who attended the funeral, Lodge was "overwhelmed with grief." Eventually recovering, the senator later confessed that his father's untimely passing left him with a void that was never filled.[30]

Following the Civil War, Lodge and Roosevelt Jr. read, studied, and traveled extensively. Lodge attended Harvard from 1867–1871 followed by Roosevelt Jr., whose tenure at the college lasted from 1876–1880.[31]

Reflecting on the collegiate experience, Lodge described his years in Cambridge as "Singularly devoid of either distinction or interest." A future doctor of philosophy, Lodge did little to extend himself academically. Rather than devoting countless hours to study, Lodge preferred to spend time attending plays at the Hasty Pudding Club or wiling away the evenings in the large library of the Porcellian Club.

Even with little focus and poor discipline, Lodge managed to graduate near the upper middle of his class. In the years to come, however, the New Englander remained ambivalent about his college experience. Involved with Harvard for much of his life, Lodge viewed his college career as representative of missed opportunity and wasted potential.[32]

Theodore Roosevelt Jr's. college experience was not dissimilar to Lodge's. "I thoroughly enjoyed Harvard," Roosevelt wrote in his autobiography. However, on more detailed reflection the future president concluded, "there was very little . . . which helped me in after life." Roosevelt's Harvard contemporary and early biographer William Roscoe Thayer disagreed. The author argued that through T. R.'s display of physical and intellectual energy, after years of illness and isolation, the once weak asthmatic proved to his classmates and most important himself that academically and socially, he truly did belong.[33]

As the adolescent Roosevelt grew accustomed to college life, his father's career shifted from preaching about reform to being presented with an opportunity to craft policy. In 1877, the nation's new president, Rutherford B. Hayes, impressed with the elder Roosevelt's reform activities, nominated him for the position of collector of customs to the port of New York. Hayes's decision to name a high-minded figure like Roosevelt Sr. to administer the custom house sent a strong message to the nation that corruption within the administration was unacceptable.

With the customs house known as a lucrative source of patronage, no one was more outraged by the president's decision than the powerful New York senator, Roscoe Conkling. Known for his flamboyant style of dress, colorful umbrellas, and charismatic personality, Conkling used his powerful network to undermine Theodore Sr.'s confirmation. As the president's nominee waited for the legislative process to proceed, he urged politicians of both parties to develop a civil service law that reformed how individuals were selected for government positions. T. R. Sr.'s campaign made little headway and he was forced to endure day after day of political bickering among those in the Senate.[34]

The lengthy delays soon began to take their toll on the once seemingly indestructible patriarch. In the days before Christmas 1877, Theodore Sr. collapsed. Deeply concerned over the state of his father's health, the junior Roosevelt rushed home from Harvard to discover that senior was recovering well. While the developments led to a festive holiday season, the episode left the once dynamic "Great Heart" a shadow of his former self. With winter break concluded, Roosevelt Jr. returned to Cambridge, believing his father would want nothing to distract his son from his social and academic commitments.[35]

Concluding his sophomore year, Theodore Jr. tried to use social outings as a distraction from his father's illness. Even with the best of care, however, the senior Roosevelt's condition deteriorated. Succumbing to bowel cancer in February 1878, no one was more affected by Theodore Roosevelt Sr.'s death than his second child.[36]

As Roosevelt recovered from the loss of his father, he was offered the opportunity to join several prominent clubs. One of these invitations was from the Porcellian. It was during a visit to the club's location on Harvard Street that Roosevelt first met Henry Cabot Lodge. In a memo written in 1908 about their association, Roosevelt recalled briefly meeting the young professor, but the two never knew one another until their involvement in Republican politics years later.[37]

Reaching the conclusion of their respective Harvard careers, Henry Cabot Lodge and Theodore Roosevelt each remained uncertain about the road ahead. Raised in luxury and comfort, both men had gained an appreciation for sports, literature, history, and a respect for family and service. In losing their fathers early in life both men never forgot the lesson that with privilege came responsibility.

In addition to the loss of their paternal influences, Roosevelt and Lodge saw their worlds altered by a shift in the societal tone and industrial fabric of their respective communities. These changes were not only responsible for the direction of each man's career but drove the decisions each made in their desire to restore a sense of order for themselves and their nation.

TWO
Irreversible Change

"They seem to think that money warrants everything . . .
and that nothing must be allowed to stand in the way of
what money wants."

—Henry Cabot Lodge

On July 1, 1869, Anna Lodge asked her son to greet a distant relative arriving at the Lynn, Massachusetts, train station. Lodge, a tall, thin, finely featured nineteen-year-old with curly dark hair, hazel eyes, and prominent chin, had recently completed his junior year at Harvard. Making the four-mile trip from the family residence at Nahant, Lodge was scheduled to meet a distant cousin, Anna Cabot Mills Davis. The eighteen-year-old Davis had accepted an invitation from Lodge's mother to visit the family at the Massachusetts seashore. Cabot had little memory of Davis. The two had not seen one another since they were children.[1]

The young woman who emerged from the train that bright, summer day, was later described by Theodore Roosevelt as one who "looked as queens ought to look, but as no queen I have ever seen does look . . ." Anna Davis was elegant and willowy, with dark, blond hair and striking violet eyes that one friend described as "the color of the sky when stars began to twinkle." Known to her friends and family as "Nannie," Davis was the daughter of Admiral Charles Henry

Davis, and the beautiful, well-read Harriette Mills of Northampton, Massachusetts.[2]

A prominent naval figure who saw extensive combat during the Civil War, Charles Davis had served with distinction at the Battle of Vicksburg. Returning to Washington a decorated officer, Davis served as a pallbearer for his good friend, Abraham Lincoln, following the president's assassination in 1865.[3]

Nannie Davis possessed great beauty and poise. She was, however, far more than one of the many delicate swans floating around the debutante balls of Boston or New York. From an early age, Harriette Davis emphasized to her six children the importance of education.

That lesson was not lost on Nannie. An avid reader of Shakespeare and other prominent literary figures of the period, Davis had a near photographic memory. By the age of sixteen she had memorized an extensive amount of poetry and other verse. A graduate of Wellesley College, her maternal grandmother, the wife of Massachusetts senator Elijah Hunt Mills, instilled in Davis the importance of public service and proper etiquette in public life.[4]

Nannie also possessed a rapier-like wit and a wonderful sense of humor. It is unsurprising that Henry Cabot Lodge was captivated by Admiral Davis's daughter when she appeared on the Lynn station platform. Lodge found Nannie Davis enchanting not only for her exquisite features and lithe frame, but the fact she was holding a book containing James Boswell's *Life of Samuel Johnson*, one of the most important works of British literature.[5]

The two became inseparable. When Nannie returned to Washington, Lodge wrote to her daily. Anna Lodge was delighted with the match, describing it to a friend as "a love-poem in real life."[6]

Following Lodge's graduation from Harvard, he and Nannie were married on June 29, 1871 at Boston's Christ Church. Lodge was filled with pride. He had won the hand of a beautiful and cultivated woman, who adored words and ideas, just as he did.

Following the wedding, the newlyweds departed on a two-year European honeymoon. Their adventure began with a transatlantic crossing on a German steamer. Above deck the voyage experienced little turbulence. Below was another matter. As Lodge biographer John Garraty estimates, Nannie was in the first weeks of pregnancy when the couple arrived on the continent that September.[7]

Visiting Paris shortly after the Franco-Prussian War, Lodge escorted his new bride on a grand excursion through the City of Light. With the French capital still recovering from the conflict, the new Mrs. Lodge had a memorable experience. "Cabot treated Venus of Milo like an old friend," Nannie wrote her mother-in-law. The future politician delighted in exhibiting his knowledge of European art and sculpture to his new bride and looked forward to their life ahead.[8]

Taking advantage of the high rate of the American dollar, Nannie explored the dynamic European fashions on the Champs-Élysées and Avenue Montaigne. When her friend, Amelia Sargent, questioned the purchase of several outfits, the new bride replied, "if my dresses suited me and were the thing in Paris, I shouldn't much care how they were received in Boston." That moment was one of many when Nannie Lodge had little difficulty speaking her mind. It was a quality that her husband respected but did not always appreciate.[9]

The Lodges decided to extend their stay in Paris due to the delicate nature of Nannie's condition. While most women might be apprehensive in the months leading to the birth of their first child, Mrs. Lodge showed little concern. As the moment of delivery approached, and dressed in formal eveningwear, she insisted they finish dinner before admitting the baby's arrival was imminent.[10]

At 1:00 in the morning, on April 5, 1872, Nannie gave birth to a daughter, who the couple named Constance. Both parents were emotional. Describing his wife's bravery in a letter to his mother, Lodge was overwhelmed by the experience. That tender display of emotion represented a side of Henry Cabot Lodge few saw. On that glorious morning in Paris, it was not the cold, Machiavellian figure that sat at his wife's bedside, but a proud twenty-one-year-old father wondering what the future held for him and his new family.[11]

In October 1878, Theodore Roosevelt was looking forward to a weekend away from Cambridge at the home of his close friend Richard Saltonstall. A scion of one of the elite families in Massachusetts, the Saltonstalls resided in the community of Chestnut Hill, a short carriage ride from Cambridge.[12]

The Victorian mansion Roosevelt visited was located on a sizeable piece of property less than thirty yards from another grand home, occupied by George Cabot Lee. A Harvard graduate, a member of the prominent banking house Lee, Higginson & Co., and the father of six children, Roosevelt's future bride, Alice Hathaway Lee was the second of the family's five daughters.[13]

The story of the courtship between Theodore Roosevelt and Alice Lee is well known. Alice, like Nannie Lodge was considered one of the great beauties of her era. Tall and athletic, at five foot seven, with blond hair and blue eyes, the first Mrs. Roosevelt possessed what T. R. described as a "bewitching" sense of humor. Based on these descriptions it was no surprise that Alice was one of the most eligible young ladies in the country.[14]

Throughout his tenure at Harvard Roosevelt continued to aggressively court Alice Lee. When his first proposal was declined in the summer of 1879, Roosevelt remained determined to win the hand of his elusive quarry. "She won't have me, but I am going to have her," he declared to a friend during a Hasty Pudding event. As Roosevelt pursued his studies and other activities, the Lees' daughter remained at the forefront of his mind.[15]

After an ardent courtship Alice agreed to marry. The engagement became official on Valentine's Day 1880. The wedding was held eight months later, on October 27, the same day as Roosevelt's twenty-second birthday.[16]

Following nuptials at Brookline's Unitarian church the newly-weds decided to have a pre-honeymoon at the Roosevelts' home, named Tranquility, in Oyster Bay, New York. Returning to Manhattan the couple began their married life in a brownstone on East 57th Street. In considering a profession, the recent college graduate had decided to study law with the idea of one day pursuing a career in politics.[17]

Throughout their European trip in 1872, Henry Cabot Lodge remained uncertain about his professional future. During a visit to Rome, he encountered a former classmate, Michael Henry Simpson. With Lodge's wife home with their newborn, the two young men immersed themselves in the art and history of the ancient city.[18]

As Lodge and Simpson sat on the Spanish Steps or admired the architectural marvels of the Roman Forum, Simpson discussed his plans following a return to the United States. The young man shared Lodge's father's belief that complacency and idleness were no way to spend one's life.[19]

The two had grown up with enormous opportunity, and Lodge's friend argued that men of their economic and social background had an obligation to engage in an occupation that involved politics, public service, or the crafting of ideas. Lodge had never considered any of these possibilities, but Simpson's argument altered his friend's frame of mind.[20]

During the rest of his stay in Europe, Lodge became determined to find a career that matched his abilities. Considering a variety of options, Lodge looked forward to more conversations with Simpson about the future. As the Lodges prepared to return to the United States, they were shocked to hear of Simpson's untimely death. On holiday in Florence, the twenty-six-year-old had passed away following a severe case of typhoid fever. As Lodge and his young family sailed for home the Bostonian realized he had to look elsewhere for professional guidance.[21]

Returning to Massachusetts, Lodge sought advice from his former history instructor, Henry Adams. A grandson and great grandson of two American presidents, Adams had begun teaching medieval history at Harvard in 1870. Anti-Semitic and contemptuous of those who did not meet his social or intellectual criteria, Adams's friends and acquaintances numbered some of the most prominent members in society and politics.[22]

Uninterested in traditional teaching methods, Adams dismissed the memorization of dates and basic historical facts. When confronted with a question he could not answer, Adams had no difficulty admitting his shortcomings. "Good heavens!" he frequently shouted at a trembling undergraduate, "How should I know. Look it up!"[23]

The former journalist was an eccentric figure around Harvard yard. With his bald head, thick gray mustache, and Vandyke beard, the commentator was a popular professor on campus. Tall and thin, Adams was a man of refined taste and immaculate dress. Wearing distinctive white linen outfits from head to foot in summer or dark wool suits when a chill entered the air, the commentator and historian represented the epitome of Eastern elitism.[24]

It was no surprise that Adams found a kindred spirit in Henry Cabot Lodge. During Lodge's honeymoon the two had exchanged letters discussing the future. In one of their correspondences, Adams advised his former pupil to focus on history and literature as the foundations for a career as a writer or academic.[25]

Following Adams's counsel, Lodge began preparing for advanced degrees in history and law. The young patrician also assisted his new mentor in managing the *North American Review*, an academic journal containing essays on the latest books in history and literature. The young man was elated at receiving such a wonderful opportunity. "Nothing has ever come to me which gave me such joy as that offer from Henry Adams," Lodge recalled years later.[26]

With Lodge having no paternal influence, Adams's decision to introduce his protégé to the salons of academia was instrumental in allowing the young man to gain a sense of direction and purpose. As Lodge adapted to the joys and challenges of fatherhood (a son, George Cabot, nicknamed "Bay," was born in October 1873 and another son, John, was born in 1876), Adams was also responsible for giving Lodge his first taste of the combative world of Republican politics.[27]

Since before the conclusion of the Civil War in 1865, the Republican Party had considered itself an advocate of equal rights for all. Supporters of the GOP had enjoyed proclaiming they were responsible for defending the nation from the Democratic message of subversion and secession. Unlike those of the opposing party who were wary of any sort of action that increased the role of government, Republicans favored employing federal power to enhance economic prosperity.[28]

Through monetary reform and land distribution these economic policies also included the application of tariffs. With a significant import tax on foreign goods, Republicans believed they protected the interests of the American labor class while simultaneously burgeoning the nation's industrial growth.[29]

The other large portion of the GOP platform concerned individual morality and honest government. Members of the Republican Party prided themselves on political integrity as well as proclaiming their abstinence from alcohol, gambling, and prostitution. More important, individual voting habits reflected the nation's political character.[30]

During the Gilded Age political parties dominated American life. Regionalism, religious affiliation, and family background frequently dictated one's voting record. While one had the impression that the party's supporters chose the candidate on the ballot that was not entirely correct.

The public may have voted for the nominee of their respective party. However, most of those placed on the ballot were selected by a hierarchy of state and city bureaucrats who had the ability to make or break those who aspired for higher office. With bossism dominating the political landscape, those like Henry Adams and other Republican liberals aspired to give the American people a candidate unafraid of disrupting the status quo.[31]

Following the election of Ulysses S. Grant in 1868 divisions within the Republican Party began to develop. Tariffs, a lack of progress on civil service reform, and opposition to the use of federal power in the implementation of Reconstruction policies in the former Confederate states caused liberals to split from Republican regulars. Refusing to support an administration they believed inherently corrupt, liberals and others nominated Horace Greeley, the outspoken founder and editor of the *New York Tribune*, for president in 1872. Hoping to capitalize on the anti-Grant movement Democrats also selected the contrarian newspaperman as their choice to replace the decorated former general in the Executive Mansion.[32]

Adams was no fan of Greeley. Believing parties and patronage were responsible for the erosion of the Republic's intellect and virtue, the historian concluded that Greeley lacked the temperament necessary for the presidency. "If the Gods insist on making Mr. Greeley our President, I give it up," Adams wrote in a letter to one of his many friends.[33]

There was little reason for Adams to worry. President Grant easily won another four years in office. But throughout Grant's second term the liberal and moderate wing of the GOP remained unhappy.[34]

As the president's tenure continued, his administration was battered by financial scandals, leading to resignations by the secretary of the treasury, Benjamin Bristow, in 1875 and the secretary of war, William Belknap, in 1876. These controversies not only damaged Grant's credibility but caused voters to question the GOP image as the party of morality and honest government.[35]

The party's reputation for transparency was not the only portion of the GOP brand in crisis. Initially grateful for the bustling economy, the agricultural community and working class saw their fortunes disrupted during the financial Panic of 1873. The depression that began in European markets culminated with a massive economic downturn in the United States. The overinvestment by several American banks in the burgeoning railroad industry resulted in numerous bankruptcies and massive unemployment. When the economy stabilized six years later, many Americans blamed the nation's financial instability on the Grant administration.[36]

In addition, voters also criticized Republicans for relying on gold rather than silver as the nation's coinage of choice. Members of the small business community believed that silver, less expensive and recently discovered in abundance on the Western frontier, would expand the nation's money supply, making loans easier to obtain. That controversy made it difficult for the GOP to present itself as the party of integrity and prosperity. The effects of the nation's disapproval of Republican stewardship resulted in the Democrats regaining control of the House of Representatives during the off year elections in 1874.[37]

Adams remained disturbed by the scandals that scarred Grant's second term. Monitoring the president's activities, the historian believed the man from Ohio had betrayed the nation's founders by failing to employ the powers of the executive branch to end political patronage. To confront the corruptive influences within the GOP, Adams created a reformist organization, with the objective of influencing the selection of the two parties' presidential candidates for the election of 1876.[38]

Adams, Lodge, and others were part of a group of Eastern, Harvard elites who hoped to set a new tone for the GOP. Adams and his colleagues hoped to break the control the bosses had over the party and elevate leaders who believed in integrity and diverse points of view.[39]

Many of these figures favored eliminating tariffs as barriers to free trade and implementing a nonpartisan civil service to end the corruptive spoils system in government. Considered by some as custodians of the public trust, these GOP liberals believed it was their duty to alert their fellow Republicans to the dangers of selecting a candidate whose motives and virtues were morally and ethically suspect. Lodge in his early twenties became immersed in the process of finding prominent political personalities willing to support an alternative to the nation's two major political organizations.[40]

As Lodge surveyed members of the business and governing establishment, a pattern began to emerge. Those who wrote positive replies for such a movement were primarily professionals concerned with political reform and good government. Members of the political class who responded believed it impossible to achieve any kind of change outside the two-party system. It was a lesson Lodge took to heart and one he employed repeatedly as his political career developed. [41]

Adams was impressed with his former pupil's passion. At the same time the commentator worried about Lodge's attraction to the unsavory world of running for office. "I have never known a young man to go into politics who was not the worse for it," Adams had written Lodge three years earlier. Having watched many politicians come and go, Adams believed that those who spent too much of their lives in pursuit of power rapidly lost their integrity and self-respect. Adams feared that by exposing Lodge to the competitive atmosphere of the political arena he had set his young friend on a course that could only lead to ruin. [42]

Disappointed in the results of his research, Lodge remained committed to Adams and other liberals in their objective to select a reformer as their 1876 nominee. In the hopes of reviving the trust of many within the party, Republicans nominated the scandal-free, three-time governor of Ohio, Rutherford B. Hayes. The Democrats, attempting to capitalize on the recent Republican scandals selected the intellectually serious governor of New York Samuel J. Tilden. [43]

A prominent lawyer, Tilden had achieved a reputation for battling the corruption of the political machine run by William M. ("Boss") Tweed. Despite each nominee offering aspects of reform as part of their governing agenda, Lodge found both candidates uninspiring, with neither possessing the qualities that entitled them to the presidency. [44]

On Election Day, Lodge viewed the Democrat as the lesser of two evils and cast an unhappy vote for Tilden. Reflecting decades later about his first encounter with civic affairs, the senator recalled, "I withdrew from politics, determined if I went in again to go in a party & do the best I could there." Initially disgusted by the political process; Lodge nonetheless became absorbed by the profession and the power that came with it. [45]

Even with Tilden's reputation as a staunch reformer, the New York came up short by one electoral college vote. Following accusations of ballot tampering, Congress created an interparty commission to decide the disputed votes of three states. After lengthy negotiations between members of Congress, the panel declared Hayes the winner.[46]

With both sides committing fraud in their attempts to win the presidency, Democrats believed big business had helped push Hayes over the top. As political tensions reached a breaking point, the new president did his best to placate both parties.[47]

Appointing a Democrat as postmaster general, the man from the Buckeye State also refused to continue to employ the military to support unpopular Republican governments in the South. These bipartisan gestures did little to resolve the doubts many had about the integrity of the new president as well as whether the affairs of government were being conducted honestly.[48]

The belief that corporate interests had a stranglehold on the nation's leadership resulted in a national strike by railroad workers in 1877. Hayes's decision to deploy the military to end the work stoppage caused only greater suspicion among voters that the president was in the pocket of the railroad and other corporate interests. In the elections of 1879, anger over the "Great Fraud of 1876," caused Republicans to lose the United States Senate, leaving the party in the congressional minority for the first time since the Civil War.[49]

By 1880, the dissention within the GOP had resulted in the development of two factions. One segment known as "Stalwarts," led by Senator Roscoe Conkling hoped to nominate President Grant for a third term. Conkling and his followers also favored a pro-business agenda, with a desire to maintain the patronage system.[50]

The other portion of the party, known as "Half-Breeds," were led by the presidential hopeful, Congressman James G. Blaine. With a goal of expanding the party into the solidly Democratic South, the group proposed more pragmatic and progressive legislation. These proposals included the sharing of tariff revenue among the states, implementation of civil service reform, and government funding of education for whites and African Americans. With the nation remaining polarized by the results of the 1876 election, Hayes declared he would vacate the presidency after one term. [51]

In the fall of 1880, following a two-week honeymoon in Oyster Bay, Theodore Roosevelt returned to a life packed with activity. As the new family patriarch, Roosevelt had assumed the responsibilities of the many charitable organizations affiliated with his late father. These included participation at the Newsboys' Lodging House dinner and election as a trustee of several medical institutions focused on the care of infants. [52]

Besides looking after the interests of his mother and siblings, Roosevelt continued studying at Columbia Law School. Following a regimen of morning legal training at the institution's run-down building in lower Manhattan, T. R. rushed over to the Astor Library on Lafayette Place. Surrounded by 80,000 books, the young law student devoted the remainder of his day to an analysis of American naval strategy during the War of 1812. [53]

As Roosevelt filled his days with law and other intellectual pursuits, his evenings were just as busy. One of the more prominent couples in the city, Theodore and Alice Lee mingled with the Astors, Vanderbilts, and other members of New York society. Despite finding the glamour and gossip initially entertaining, Roosevelt soon became bored with the vacuous conversation. [54]

Besides being unhappy with the excessive displays of wealth as well as the immoral behavior occurring around him, Roosevelt began questioning his choice of a legal career. Continuing his daily walks from his home to the law school on Great Jones Street, T. R. vacillated about his decision to pursue a life as an attorney.[55]

A man of enormous drive, Roosevelt remained determined to find a profession he could truly call his own. Business, law, philanthropy—those were the standard occupations of men of "cultivated taste" who wanted to live an "easy life." Roosevelt wanted to craft his own destiny and achieve success based entirely on his own merits. Unexpectedly, he soon found that opportunity in the decidedly uncultivated world of New York state politics.[56]

As the Roosevelts ran from one glamorous engagement to the next, Theodore began frequenting the Twenty-first Congressional District Republican Association. Located above a saloon, the space was filled by men with strong Irish brogues who smoked cigars and spat into spittoons. Dressed in a stiff collar and white tie, the law student resembled someone from another world.[57]

After becoming a fixture within the Republican clubhouse, Roosevelt assisted the organization by working on several campaigns and delivering a series of speeches. One discourse involved favoring a nonpartisan street cleaning initiative advocated by the state legislature. Another was a powerful attack against a machine candidate who hoped to return to the state assembly. The latter remarks caught the eye of political organizer Joe Murray, who aspired to seize control of the Republican club from its longstanding chairman, Jacob Hess.[58]

Murray nominated Roosevelt for the assembly against a candidate favored by the district's leader. Flattered by the confidence of the garrulous Republican, Roosevelt initially had no intention of running for office. Always a lover of competition and a believer in public service, T. R. agreed to take up the challenge. Imbued with the philanthropic qualities of his father, Roosevelt was also drawn to the idea of using his charismatic personality and intellectual ability to make a difference in the community.[59]

Running on a platform of "clean streets and clean politics," the novice candidate won his first political victory by more than one thousand votes. Proud of his accomplishment, Roosevelt had the opportunity to put his passion for reform to the test. As he prepared to enter the viper-filled world of legislative politics, Roosevelt realized there was no occupation that was more alien to his way of life than the one he had just chosen.[60]

Following Henry Cabot Lodge's disillusioning experience in the campaign of 1876, the recently minted Harvard PhD focused his attentions on scholarly interests. It was of little surprise that Lodge was drawn to history. Growing up, he was surrounded by many of the renowned academics of the day. It was not uncommon for Harvard historians like Francis Parkman or George Bancroft to dine with John Lodge and his family on a frequent basis.[61]

Assigned to teach a course on American colonial history to Harvard's undergraduates, Lodge was a challenging professor. In his first class, the young academic saw his attendance decline from fifty students to three. When Henry Adams resigned from the college to focus on his own scholarship in 1877, Lodge added his mentor's seminar on Anglo-Saxon law to his course schedule.[62]

That same year, Lodge published his first work of history. *Life and Letters of George Cabot* was a portrait of the family's distinguished ancestor, the first senator from Massachusetts and ally of Alexander Hamilton. Even as some reviewers including Henry Adams, characterized Lodge's work as partisan, the narrative, filled with an abundance of unpublished documents, sold well.[63]

As Lodge devoted himself to scholarly affairs, he was unable to remove current events from coloring his perspective on the past. The historian viewed his ancestor and other members of the Founding Fathers' generation as men of exceptional character. Writing about the morals and manners of the Federalist era with a certain wistfulness, Lodge's tone was a reaction to the rapid industrial growth experienced by the nation following the Civil War.[64]

With the nation's massive expansion, a transformation of the country's economic infrastructure was rapidly occurring. As businesses developed and the public welcomed new inventions like Montgomery Ward's mail-order catalog, local markets became irrelevant.[65]

These industrial changes resulted in an influx of immigration from Eastern and Western Europe, transforming Massachusetts into the most diverse state of the nineteenth century. Beginning in 1846, thousands of Irish, Italian, and Polish immigrants flooded the Port of Boston. These developments transformed the once sedate New England community into a bustling center of commercial activity.[66]

As a historian, Lodge understood that economic and cultural shifts were inevitable. But the professor was unhappy with the emotional and financial toll these changes took on the lives of his friends and neighbors. Many of these families "had fought in the Revolution," achieving social and economic success in law or business.[67]

As these changes accelerated, many individuals found themselves "pushed out of sight," or "driven against the conventional wall," by events they were unable to control or comprehend. "Nowhere in America was society so complex or change so rapid as in Massachusetts," Henry Adams wrote, describing the changes shaping the Bay State.[68]

It was not only the mass immigration and the industrial shifts that Lodge found unsettling. The Bostonian was also troubled by the gross display of wealth and immorality, epitomized by "the new rich."

The future senator held a dim view of those like Cornelius Vanderbilt, Jay Gould, and others, whose garish escapades were vividly captured in the nation's press.[69]

In Lodge's view, the group that had seized the country's industrial mantle represented a dark stain on the nation he revered. "They seem to think that money warrants everything . . . and that nothing must be allowed to stand in the way of what money wants," Lodge wrote of the new and disturbing trend.[70]

Lodge was not alone in these opinions. As members of Boston's elite saw their positions of authority erode, Lodge's friend, the Harvard academic Barrett Wendell, spoke for many when he wrote, "We are vanishing into perpetual obscurity . . . America has swept from our grasp. The future is beyond us."[71]

Lodge did not share his friend's apocalyptic view. As a student of his family's history Lodge understood that his ancestors were committed to playing a significant role in the life of their times. Lodge was determined to emulate that tradition.[72]

The decision to refocus his attentions on political affairs reflected Lodge's desire to follow the path of public service and statesmanship blazed by George Cabot and other members of the founding era. Simultaneously, the historian shared the belief of his fellow Bostonian Henry Adams that "America had passed irrevocably away from him." Instead of pushing back against these tides of change, Adams had chosen to cloister himself within his home in Washington, writing tomes about the history of the nation. Dismissing that idea, Lodge decided to employ his abilities to contain the changes occurring around him.[73]

Ingratiating himself with the Massachusetts Republican Party, Lodge won his first campaign for the state legislature in 1879. With some in his district viewing Lodge as an out of touch dilettante, the newly minted state representative showed the voters he was engaged with the issues. More important, Lodge demonstrated to those who controlled the political fate of Massachusetts his organizational and burgeoning political talents were skills to be reckoned with.[74]

❧

Roosevelt served three one-year terms in the New York Assembly, from 1882–1884. During his tenure in the state's lower house, Theodore sought to shine a spotlight on those who cared little for the average New Yorker. Working tirelessly, T. R. initiated legislation and demanded investigations when he believed the public was at risk. These actions included bills addressing the purification of the state's water supply, while also banning the manufacturing of cigars in tenements that housed the city's most impoverished citizens.[75]

As Roosevelt focused more attention on his reform agenda, he bristled at the insensitive behavior of the wealthy industrialists arriving in New York. Encouraged by Alice Lee to run with the smart set, T. R. kept his opinions to himself. The aspiring legislator had once looked forward to the lavish affairs that dominated his and his wife's social life. Over time, however, these evenings had begun to wear on him. "I am not very fond of going out," he wrote disagreeably in his journal following a particularly tedious evening.[76]

For the young assemblyman there was more to one's existence than a life of hedonistic excess. Watching his brother Elliott, increasingly addicted to alcohol and other narcotics, Roosevelt recalled the lessons of his father. Theodore Sr. believed life was about the pleasures of hard work, rising to a challenge, and seizing a moment. His son shared those beliefs and viewed men who attempted to stifle the politics of reform as the same people responsible for the corruptive practices polluting American society.[77]

Returning to his duties in Albany, Roosevelt came to realize he could not carry his crusade for change alone. The assemblyman's initial tenure in the statehouse was that of an abrasive and outspoken legislator. To succeed, the New Yorker understood he needed a coalition who favored the goals he sought to accomplish. It was a valuable lesson in the art of politics and one that Roosevelt attempted to employ as he gained more influence.[78]

During his second term in 1883, Roosevelt caught the eye of the state's new Democratic governor, Grover Cleveland. The three-hundred-pound former mayor of Buffalo and the fitness-crazed state legislator shared similar views. Both men were elected with the promise of ending corruption and encouraging political reform. The two politicians bonded on their desire to replace the spoils system with a civil service program, appointing people to government positions based on competence and merit, rather than party loyalty.[79]

In spring of 1883, the New York governor, with aspirations of running for president the following year, partnered with Roosevelt to achieve passage of a civil service reform bill. It was a glorious moment for T. R., who was hailed by the press and many of his colleagues as a catalyst for change. Roosevelt had another reason for jubilation. Alice had announced that she was pregnant.[80]

T. R. was delighted with the idea of being a father. He loved children and hoped to have a large family. Returning to Albany in the winter of 1884, the first-time father-to-be remained apprehensive about his wife's condition. Distracting himself, Roosevelt hired a boxing coach and focused his energies on the civil service reform bill scheduled to go before the legislature in the second week of February.

Roosevelt thought his anxieties were relieved when on February 12, 1884, Alice delivered a baby girl. Thrilled at the joyous event, he celebrated with his friends in the assembly. Even as T. R. handed out cigars to colleagues, events at home were taking a dreadful turn. The following day the assemblyman received a telegram alerting him that his wife was experiencing postpartum complications. In addition, Mittie Roosevelt had fallen ill and was bedridden with a high fever. Racing to the train, Roosevelt attempted to reach home as soon as possible. But the lengthy journey down the Hudson caused him to arrive in New York as his wife and his mother were slipping away. [81]

The deaths of Alice Lee from Bright's disease and Mittie Roosevelt from typhoid, all within twenty-four hours, devastated Theodore Roosevelt. News of the unspeakable tragedy stunned Roosevelt's fellow Republicans. Many wondered how someone could recover from such an ordeal.[82]

Lodge enjoyed his introduction to electoral politics, serving two terms in the state legislature from 1880–1882. Positioning himself as a reformer, Lodge's great achievement was strengthening the state election laws. Without possessing a dynamic personality, Lodge was an effective networker, rapidly making contacts within the state Republican machine. The legislator charmed his new colleagues with invitations to his home for intimate receptions and dinners all meticulously managed under Nannie's discerning eye. In time the Lodges' charm offensive began to produce opportunities for greater leadership within the Massachusetts GOP.[83]

In June 1880, these new relationships assisted Lodge in winning appointment as a delegate to the Republican Convention in Chicago. The achievement, combined with his rising reputation, caused the young legislator to become even more committed to a political career.

"I am a Republican and propose to remain so," Lodge wrote Massachusetts political manager Joseph Wilson. As Lodge became more attracted to the idea of obtaining political power, he remained determined to select a leader of the nation based not simply on knowledge and experience, but character and integrity.[84]

Arriving in the Windy City, Lodge was conflicted between the party's two top contenders, President Ulysses S. Grant and Senator James G. Blaine of Maine. As secretary for the state delegation Lodge found himself leaning toward an alternative, Vermont senator George F. Edmunds.[85]

A colorless and uninspiring figure, the Vermonter had a spotless reputation, a commitment to good government, and was an advocate of civil service reform. Political insiders knew Edmunds stood little chance. Lodge and others, however, hoped enough delegates would support the senator to cause a convention deadlock, leading to the selection of an alternative candidate.[86]

Over the next few days, the delegates were unable to resolve their differences. Finally, on the thirty-sixth ballot, the convention chose Ohio congressman James A. Garfield. Lodge was pleased. The nominee had a sparkling Civil War record and held moderate positions on many issues including transparency in government and rights for people of color. To pacify "the Stalwarts," delegates also selected the inexperienced, but politically well-connected New Yorker Chester A. Arthur to serve as Garfield's vice president. "Massachusetts came here to beat Grant and Blaine, having done so the delegation ought to be satisfied," Lodge commented to the *Boston Evening Transcript* following Garfield's nomination.[87]

Lodge returned to Boston filled with confidence. Retaining his seat in the legislature, the legislator ran and lost the 1881 election for State Senate. Months later, a redistricting opportunity allowed him to seek a seat in Congress. Lodge did his utmost to overwhelm the other contenders but failed to win the nomination. Following the loss, Lodge ingratiated himself with GOP regulars by campaigning for the party's candidate, Elisha S. Converse.[88]

When Converse was defeated, Lodge was unsurprised. He had a low opinion of the shoe manufacturer, viewing him as a man of garish taste with little political aptitude. One cannot be surprised by Lodge's opinion.[89]

The Bostonian was a highly competitive person and one who had no issue baring his teeth during a fight. A figure of great pride, any loss Lodge suffered, no matter how trivial, was deeply upsetting. "No healthy thinking animal likes to grow old," Cabot wrote as he ruminated on his political future.[90]

Lodge had underestimated his popularity. Even with a defeat on his record the Bostonian emerged with a devoted following. Not long after losing the nomination for Congress, Cabot was elected chairman of the state Republican Party's central committee. The honor was one of the few positive spots for the Massachusetts GOP during the 1882 elections. Suffering losses across the state, Lodge concluded that a new strategy was required. "There are no great issues," Lodge wrote in his journal, as he observed the political terrain. "Therefore, politics in the future will be necessarily a question of the men who [the people] on the whole think are the best." It was a fitting comment since Lodge considered himself one of those who would soon occupy the upper echelons of Massachusetts politics.[91]

The conclusion was not one based purely on ego. Lodge understood he was a rising political star. The former academic was becoming more confident with the workings of politics, and many were gaining more respect for his oratory and diligent work ethic. "I am not going to stop here but propose next time to win," Lodge wrote Civil War veteran James H. Wilson. Those comments proved fortuitous as Lodge spent much of his career walking the delicate line of trying to keep his party in power while remaining faithful to his principles of incremental change.[92]

With Lodge's future within the GOP looking brighter, the tur-moil that had destabilized the party over the last few years seemed to have finally subsided. In November 1880, Garfield narrowly pre-vailed over his charismatic Democratic challenger, General Winfield Scott Hancock. Helped by the popularity of the tariff, the GOP also regained control of both branches of Congress. Arriving in office, the new president aspired to expand the nation's interests in the Western hemisphere through economic inroads in Latin America. Garfield's ambitions came to naught. On July 2, 1881, while standing at the Washington train station, the president was shot and mortally wounded by deranged GOP office seeker Charles J. Guiteau.[93]

Succeeding to the presidency in September 1881, Chester A. Arthur proved to be a more effective chief executive than anticipated. In May 1882, with the objective of containing the mass numbers of immigrants flowing into the United States, Arthur placed his sig-nature on the Chinese Exclusion Act, which stopped those seeking to exchange a life of toil in the Asian nation for one of opportunity in the United States. Two years later, the president also fulfilled his predecessor's promise by signing a civil service law known as the Pendleton Act. The favorable response of these policies caused many Republicans to anticipate Arthur's reelection as the 1884 convention approached.[94]

As the country moved toward the next presidential campaign Theodore Roosevelt and Henry Cabot Lodge committed them-selves to climbing the political ladder of their respective states. Enduring personal loss and political defeat, each man remained determined to battle the corruption and immorality swirling around them. While those objectives remained important, both came to the realization that allies and coalitions were necessary if one hoped to rule.

As the two Harvard men gazed out at the political horizons from their perches in Massachusetts and New York, neither realized that the time to choose between the politics of realism and the politics of idealism was rapidly approaching.

THREE
Valley of Decision

"Unquestionably, Blaine is our greatest danger."
—Theodore Roosevelt

Following the deaths of Roosevelt's wife and mother, the state legislator worked like a demon. Whether it was fighting for the passage of a bill championing the rights of orphans of color or investigating corruption within the New York State Department of Corrections, the assemblyman was determined to accomplish it all. "[T]here is now nothing left for me except to try to so live as not to dishonor the memory of those I loved who have gone before me," Roosevelt wrote a friend, shortly before returning to complete his final term in the legislature.[1]

In the last week of April 1884 Roosevelt traveled to the State Republican convention in Utica, New York. Political professionals were gathering at the community's opulent opera house to select the delegates for that year's GOP national convention.

Unhappy with party favorites, Senator James G. Blaine and President Chester A. Arthur, Roosevelt managed to get himself and three other independent Republicans chosen to represent New York at the proceedings that June in Chicago. The Independents favored the gray-bearded, contrarian Vermont senator, George F. Edmunds, the same figure Lodge had tried and failed to nominate four years earlier.[2]

With his wife deceased and his baby daughter in the capable hands of his sister, Bamie, T. R. returned to Albany. Roosevelt viewed the upcoming Republican convention as his final act in public life. "I have very little expectation of being able to keep on in politics," the assemblyman wrote the editor of the *Utica Morning Herald* as he contemplated the end of the legislative session.[3]

T. R. had found the activities in the Mohawk Valley arduous. Attempting to expand the current slate of Republican candidates, Roosevelt was attacked by opponents with what he described to the editor as "venomous hatred." The constant animosity he had experienced during his tenure in the assembly was more than he could bear. "I will not stay in public life unless I can do so on my own terms, and my ideal, whether lived up to or not, is rather a high one," the outgoing state representative wrote.[4]

Between personal sadness and professional frustration, Roosevelt looked forward to relaxing beneath the sun-drenched landscapes of the Dakota Territory. Nature had always revived his spirits. Roosevelt believed experiencing the rustic atmosphere of the Badlands would renew his energy in preparation for the road ahead. Five days later, while perusing the mail and planning for his visit to Chicago, Roosevelt opened a letter from fellow Porcellian Club member Henry Cabot Lodge.[5]

Theodore was familiar with the New Englander's reputation. At the time, Lodge was not only receiving praise for his published works of history but had gained notoriety for organizing the 1883 campaign that defeated Massachusetts's unpopular governor, Benjamin F. Butler. While both men had attended Harvard and shared similar political opinions, each had also received a nomination to represent their respective states in Chicago. Roosevelt had just begun putting pen to paper to congratulate his GOP colleague when he opened a letter containing a greeting from the thirty-four-year-old Bostonian.[6]

Always keeping abreast of political developments, Lodge was aware of Roosevelt's burgeoning reputation as a reformer. Familiar with the latest literature in US History, Lodge would have read Roosevelt's study analyzing American naval strategy during the War of 1812. With so much in common, it is surprising the two young dudes had not begun corresponding earlier.[7]

Lodge and Roosevelt also shared a mutual frustration with the state of the Republican Party. Unhappy with the choices of Arthur and Blaine, Lodge inquired about T. R.'s interest in traveling to Washington to ascertain whether Senator Edmunds or Secretary of War Robert T. Lincoln was willing to consider being a candidate for the nomination. More important, Lodge wanted to see if support existed for any alternatives other than the two GOP favorites. "Unquestionably, Blaine is our greatest danger," Roosevelt wrote in a reply to Lodge on May 5. "We who stand against both must be organized and . . . *must* select our candidate with the greatest care." Delighted by Lodge's inquiry, Roosevelt invited him to spend the evening in New York, with plans to travel by train to Washington the following day.[8]

As Chester A. Arthur's term neared its conclusion in 1884, the president's supporters believed the administration's record made him a favorite to win reelection. Alternatively, following failures in 1876 and 1880, Senator James G. Blaine was seen by many as finally having the opportunity to win the office that had eluded him. Unbeknownst to their supporters, neither Arthur nor Blaine had any interest in claiming the party mantle.[9]

In 1884, James G. Blaine was one of the nation's brightest political stars. Tall, elegant, with dark eyes, a large nose and a striking white beard, the politician from Maine was partial to gold-buttoned blue and black swallow-tail coats with striped trousers. As one who enjoyed an affluent lifestyle Blaine lived in a large Victorian mansion just across from the Maine statehouse. A great political tactician, with a strong partisan edge, the senator had built his reputation as an electrifying performer by preparing meticulously for each public address.[10]

But beneath the confident exterior, Blaine was a moody, insecure man, desperate for approval. Having lost the presidency on two successive occasions, the "Plumed Knight" believed the fates had aligned against him. The fact that Blaine was standing right near President Garfield when he was assassinated, did little to calm the Maine politician's hypochondriacal and fatalistic personality. Between these issues and unproven accusations that he had accepted bribes of railroad stock while speaker of the House of Representatives, Blaine grew uninterested in competing a third time for the presidency.[11]

With Blaine preferring to remain in retirement following a brief stint as Garfield's secretary of state, President Arthur also had little interest in returning to the Executive Mansion. Following a term in office that received little approval, Arthur had lost interest in representing his party on the national stage. Never terribly ambitious, and still recovering from the loss of his wife four years earlier, the president was also secretly suffering from Bright's disease and did not have long to live. In the end, it was an appeal to each man's vanity that convinced Arthur and Blaine to stand for the nomination.[12]

Lodge and Roosevelt enjoyed their conversation on the trip to the nation's capital. The New York legislator found his new friend impressive. Just eight years older, Lodge had written numerous articles, published five books, and was rapidly moving up the ladder of the Massachusetts Republican Party. The professor really was a "scholar in politics." The idea of having a foot in scholarly pursuits and another in public life appealed to all of Roosevelt's interests. Over the course of the lengthy railroad journey, the younger man realized he had found the perfect model in the flinty New Englander.[13]

Lodge also found himself impressed with his younger companion. Serious and highly reserved, the academic admired Roosevelt's gregarious nature, superb intellect, and driving ambition. While the two enjoyed history and sports, each had grown up with a strong work ethic, and a determination to achieve something of significance in life. In pursuing a political career, both had selected an occupation outside their comfort zones and beyond the status quo of their culture and class.[14]

The visit to Washington proved disappointing. When it came to gathering support for a potential Edmunds nomination, Roosevelt and Lodge were disheartened to discover none existed. Following their travels, the two men returned to their respective cities with anticipation of meeting again in Chicago during the first week of June.[15]

As the convention approached, Lodge and Roosevelt continued to correspond. Boarding their respective trains for the convention, the two men remained committed to blocking Blaine's presidential ambitions. In the final analysis, each had decided to support whoever the party chose for its nominee. Until that time came, the two men were determined to prevent the Maine politician from becoming the party's next standard-bearer.[16]

As Roosevelt continued to criticize Blaine, the New Yorker also tried to push Lodge to convince Bay state delegates to remain independent from both candidates. "For Heaven's sake," Theodore wrote earnestly on May 26, "don't let the Massachusetts delegation commit any such act of suicidal folly as (from panic merely) supporting Arthur would be." Roosevelt considered the current president "the very weakest candidate we could nominate," and one who "would be beaten out of sight" if he was selected by the convention.[17]

Blaine's "mottled record" and unscrupulous reputation, however, represented everything Roosevelt despised about the state of politics. In letters to Lodge, T. R. referred to the presidential candidate as "our greatest danger," "a dangerous man," and a "devil." Lodge concurred with his friend but believed Blaine's nomination was virtually assured.[18]

Traveling by private railroad car on the *Sunset Limited*, Roosevelt reached Chicago on May 31. Collecting his bags, the independent delegate soon arrived at the 60,000-square-foot Grand Pacific Hotel. The establishment, located at the center of the city's commercial district, had opened nine years earlier to great fanfare.

Claiming to have the largest dining room in the country, the hotel dominated an entire city block. Boasting oak paneling, broad staircases, billiard rooms, and offices, the Grand Pacific also played host to some of the trendiest shops in the city. Wearing a "chipper" straw hat with the "underside in bright blue," a new pair of "French calf, low-cut shoes," and carrying an elegant cane, Roosevelt's appearance energized the patrons entering and exiting the hotel's bright, skylit lobby.[19]

Lodge, having arrived on the same day, stayed at the more understated Leland House. Renovated in 1881, the hotel had become known for its elegant marble interiors, fine food, and lively music. Upon checking in the Massachusetts Republican went to the hotel's second floor and entered a large suite reserved for the Bay State delegation. After greeting those in attendance, the Massachusetts politician began considering measures necessary to stop "the Blaine train" from reaching its destination.[20]

Lodge and Roosevelt realized there were not enough reform votes for an outright Edmunds nomination. The Independents, however, had the potential to block both leading candidates, forcing the convention to make a compromise as it had four and eight years earlier.

Roosevelt remained committed to the Edmunds candidacy. If, however, the senator went down in defeat, the New Yorker would support whichever candidate the convention chose. With the proceedings set to convene in two days, Roosevelt remained determined to find an alternative candidate to challenge the Democrats in November.[21]

Theodore Roosevelt and Henry Cabot Lodge arose on the morning of June 3, 1884 to a city bathed in sunlight. As their respective delegations prepared to depart for Exposition Auditorium, they were greeted by thousands of spectators lining the streets holding multicolored placards, indicating their candidate of choice. Walking east, Roosevelt and his colleagues crossed the wide, wooden boulevard of Michigan Avenue, as the red roof of the convention center glistened in the distance.[22]

Built following the Great Fire of 1871, the arena, with its two-hundred-foot arches and green interiors surrounded by an array of glass, bore a resemblance to New York's Grand Central Station. The arena, decorated by flags celebrating the gathering of Republicans from across the nation, was soon filled by 10,000 political officials and members of the press. Located at the far end of the venue, the convention platform, described as being equal in size to New York's Metropolitan Opera stage, was tastefully decorated by "a gilt eagle," with shades of red, white, and blue representing the flag of the Republic. Lastly, a portrait of the assassinated President Garfield gazed out upon the mass number of chairs emblazoned with names and numbers of the nation's thirty-eight states.[23]

As the delegation from the Empire State, wearing white and gold badges, entered the auditorium a local band played Gilbert and Sullivan's popular tune, "When I First Put This Uniform On." Roosevelt, displaying his usual ebullient behavior, bounded over several rows of chairs until finally reaching his seat near the front of the arena. Before the proceedings even began Lodge, described "as tall with crisp short hair," and "full beard," remained certain there was little chance of Blaine losing the nomination.[24]

For the Independents, the question remained the strength of Blaine's support. Roosevelt, Lodge, and their colleagues decided to test that commitment by challenging the Blaine campaign's choice of Powell Clayton as temporary chairman of the convention. Clayton was a former governor and senator from Arkansas, who attempted to enhance his reputation by falsely claiming he had lost an arm during the Civil War. The Arkansan, prepared to do whatever was necessary to obtain a position in the next administration, had initially promised Arthur's campaign eighteen electoral votes from Arkansas and Texas in exchange for a cabinet post.[25]

When the president's advisers declined the offer, the former governor became an ardent Blaine supporter. Hearing of these unscrupulous activities, Lodge was livid. "I will move to put someone in over Clayton if I have to do it and vote for it alone!" the Bostonian declared to Roosevelt. Others used stronger language to describe Clayton's behavior. "This blank Clayton ought to have his head blown off!" an Arthur delegate exclaimed. Following Lodge's comments, Roosevelt happily chose to support his new friend.[26]

Conferring until late Monday evening, the Independents decided that Lodge would contend the delegates had the right to select their own temporary chairman. With the hope that those opposed to Blaine would support them, the group decided to designate African American congressman, John R. Lynch from Mississippi as temporary chairman. When Lynch declined the opportunity, Roosevelt and his allies convinced the mustached and goateed delegate it was his "patriotic duty" to accept the honorary position. The fact that members of Blaine's campaign tried to intimidate Lynch inspired the talented legislator to side with Roosevelt and his colleagues.[27]

The decision to select Lynch had nothing do with Lodge and Roosevelt's views on race. Both men had a low opinion of Black people's intellectual capabilities and little confidence they had the ability to govern themselves. Lodge equated race with one's destiny. While Lynch appeared to represent an exception, the Bostonian believed that the characteristics emblematic of each person's racial identity represented an "indestructible stock of ideas, traditions, sentiments, modes of thought . . . upon which argument has no effect."[28]

Roosevelt's racial opinions were more nuanced than his fellow delegate. Possessed with a strong sense of empathy, fairness, and a driving curiosity, T. R. contended that the qualities that defined an individual were not finite. Motivated by one's desire for self-improvement, T. R. believed one's characteristics could change over time based on environmental circumstances. Even with their racial prejudices Lodge and Roosevelt shared the belief that African Americans were imperative to the success of the Republican Party and had earned the right of American citizenship.[29]

While some opposed the idea of an African American as temporary chairman, Roosevelt believed, "it was a fitting thing for us to choose to preside over this convention one of that race whose right to sit within these walls is due to the blood and treasure so lavishly spent by the founders of the Republican Party." The Independents' strategy in selecting Lynch was also political in nature. By putting a Black man in a place of prominence, Lodge and Roosevelt believed the move might galvanize those who were discontented with the convention's choice of nominees.[30]

The time was approaching 12:30 in the afternoon when Republican chairman Senator Dwight Sabin of Minnesota, his brown hair parted to the left (and wearing a droopy mustache resembling that of the infamous sheriff Wyatt Earp), called for Clayton's nomination. No sooner had Sabin finished his remarks when Lodge stepped on a chair and in a high-pitched voice asked for Lynch to also be considered by the delegates. The New Englander referred to the Mississippian as a man of "courage and character" whose wide reputation throughout the South enhanced the party of Lincoln. As the crowd displayed little reaction Lodge demanded a roll call to approve Lynch's selection.[31]

After several delegates disagreed, Roosevelt, determined to get the attention of the convention, climbed on to a chair as well. In an animated delivery with a voice like a foghorn and a hand on his hip, the New York delegate highlighted the American tradition of self-government, guaranteeing the right of the people to make their own choice in who should serve as their representative.[32]

Roosevelt stated that calling for a majority vote to decide the temporary chairmanship was nothing more than a lesson in American democracy. With the former assemblyman's remarks interrupted six times by applause, T. R. also endured catcalls, demanding he return to his seat.[33]

Other speeches favoring and opposing Lynch's nomination followed. While some delegates completed their remarks, other members of the convention found themselves shouted down. As the process continued, the arena grew progressively rowdier, as spectators began ordering sandwiches, as well as beer and other alcoholic beverages.[34]

As the arguments continued, chants of "No No No!" or "Vote Vote Vote!" filled the packed auditorium. Finally, with the attendees near exhaustion, the roll call began. When the delegates from Wisconsin announced their votes giving Lynch the victory, 484–384, Roosevelt's supporters showered him with congratulations. It was the New Yorker's first speech on the national stage. The reaction sent a powerful message to Republicans across the country that a new star had emerged from within the party ranks.[35]

The confrontation over Powell Clayton became the shining moment of the convention for Roosevelt and Lodge. Over the next few days, as his independent colleagues grew frustrated, Roosevelt employed every ounce of energy on behalf of the Edmunds candidacy. Many admired the New Yorker's passion, but political insiders knew Blaine's nomination was inevitable. The only hope to stop him was for a coalition of Independents, Arthur delegates, and others unhappy with Blaine to put forward a compromise candidate.[36]

The talks between the Independents and the Arthur campaign came to nothing. As the two sides discussed different individuals, neither group was able to find a name with enough influence to challenge Blaine's popularity. That reality did not stop Lodge from giving the impression that an air of uncertainty remained over the Republican choice. "I do not think Blaine can now be nominated," Lodge told the *Boston Globe*.[37]

On June 6 the final roll call began. With 411 votes needed to make the Blaine nomination official, Roosevelt and the other Independents raced around the arena seeking to delay the Mainer's coronation. When the convention reached the third round of voting, George William Curtis, the white-haired political editor of *Harper's Weekly* sought to delay the balloting until the following day.[38]

As Curtis's request was dismissed Roosevelt stood, waved his arms, and demanded a point of order. Shouted down by a rabid pro-Blaine crowd, T. R. raged at the podium. "Sit down and stop your noise," the chief delegate at large from New Jersey yelled. Having reached a boiling point, Roosevelt exploded. "Shut up your own head, you damned scoundrel you!" For Roosevelt, the outburst was more in frustration than anger. With Blaine's nomination succeeding on the fourth ballot the Independents realized their greatest fear had come to fruition. "I was at the birth of the Republican Party and I fear I am to witness its death," the elderly Curtis commented.[39]

As the Blaine chants spread through the arena, the heavy frame of Congressman William McKinley lumbered toward the New York delegation. Finding Roosevelt despondent, the genial politician asked him to make Blaine's nomination unanimous. Without even a passing glance, Roosevelt shook his head. Then silently exited the auditorium.[40]

Physically depleted, his thoughts swimming in emotion, Roosevelt walked slowly toward his hotel. Moments later he was confronted by a reporter for the *New York World*. Asked if he planned on supporting Blaine during the campaign, Roosevelt, his "eyes flashing with indignation," refused to disclose his intentions. When the journalist inquired about Roosevelt campaigning for the GOP ticket, the New Yorker replied that he was planning on ranching in the Dakota territory for the rest of the summer.[41]

Even with all his energy and strength of will, T. R. realized he had failed to prevent the party from making an enormous mistake. It was surprising that Roosevelt held his tongue with the journalist. During moments of anger and stress, when Roosevelt's temperament grew dark and his tone loud, there was no telling what could occur.[42]

While Lodge was also disapointed, he had nonetheless emerged from the convention as a figure of note. The Massachusetts legislator was complimented for his staunch work ethic and determination, and was mentioned as one whose political career was on the rise.[43]

At midnight, restless and still smoldering with frustration, Roosevelt entered the suite formally reserved for independent candidates. Other than Horace White, assistant editor of the *New York Evening Post*, the room was deserted. White, a seasoned journalist, had become acquainted with Abraham Lincoln in 1854 as he spoke against the Kansas-Nebraska Act. Four years later White encountered the future president again. Working for the *Chicago*

Tribune White chronicled Lincoln's famous campaign for Senate against Stephen Douglas in 1858.[44]

Roosevelt found the reporter for the anti-Blaine publication rapidly scribbling a telegram, detailing how the paper should describe the attitude of Independent Republicans. Roosevelt informed the journalist that if he had editorial control the telegram would read, "Any proper Democratic nomination would have our [the independents'] hearty support." By "proper Democrat," T. R. meant the party's nominee Grover Cleveland. Thinking nothing of what he just told a veteran reporter, Roosevelt returned to his room, with anticipation of escaping West the following day.[45]

On the morning of June 7, Roosevelt happily departed on a train from Chicago to St. Paul, Minnesota. Arriving in the "Saintly City" two days later, Roosevelt was approached by a reporter from the *Pioneer Press*, a publication favorable to the Blaine campaign.[46]

When asked if he planned on leaving the party over his objections to the senator's nomination, Roosevelt's mind seemed to have calmed. "I shall bolt the nomination of the convention by no means," Roosevelt replied. In addition, Roosevelt informed the journalist he believed Blaine would triumph in the West, the middle of the country, and in the East.[47]

Even as he spoke optimistically about Blaine's success, Roosevelt could not contain his disapproval of the Mainer's nomination. In addition, Roosevelt not only communicated his displeasure about the party's choice, he also implied that a large portion of the convention shared his point of view.[48]

As Roosevelt prepared to board the train, he wondered if it was the end of his political career. Despite that concern the aspiring reformer remained upbeat about what he and Lodge had accomplished. "I am glad to have been present at the convention, and to have taken part in its proceedings," Roosevelt wrote his sister Bamie.[49]

Concluding his letter Roosevelt stepped onto the train and disappeared into the confines of the great Northwest. After the most difficult year of his life, Roosevelt was happy to head into isolation, grateful to travel far away from anyone or anything that could remind him of what he had experienced. When Roosevelt would reemerge and what path he would take remained an open question.[50]

As Theodore Roosevelt stood down from the tension-filled world of politics, Henry Cabot Lodge stood up. Preparing for his return to Boston, Lodge understood that in a national election, personalities rather than issues would tun the tide. Regardless of Blaine's wild popularity, Lodge believed the GOP nominee had little chance of success. "Why, he couldn't carry Massachusetts," Lodge said, taking a jab at the party's standard-bearer.[51]

No matter how the Bostonian analyzed the political dynamics, the Mainer's nomination was difficult to reconcile. "It was the bitterest thing I ever had to do in my life," Lodge later wrote in his decision to support Blaine. "To bolt would have been the easiest thing in the world and the pleasantest, but in my eyes, it was dishonorable." Lodge was right on both counts.[52]

As an elected member of the Massachusetts delegation, the chairman of the state GOP was duty bound to support the convention's choice. On the other hand, during the 1880 campaign Lodge had declared that if the nominee went counter to one's principles, one had a duty to follow their conscience. In 1884, however, Lodge chose politics over principle.[53]

For all of Lodge's soul-searching his motive for remaining in politics was simple. From the moment he became involved in his first campaign, Lodge relished the cut and thrust of political debate, loved the admiration of his fellow citizens, and enjoyed the cachet of being at the center of attention.

Most important, Lodge began to enjoy the trappings of political power and was interested in learning how to manipulate it to suit his own ends. The aspiring congressman understood that to further his ambition, he needed to maintain his relationship with regulars within the Republican Party. "No man should be in politics unless he would honestly rather not be there," Henry Adams had told his protégé. Boarding a train for home, Lodge wanted to remain the "scholar in politics," flying as high as his energy and intellect could take him.[54]

1884 was a significant year for Roosevelt and Lodge. Despite the GOP selecting a figure each found objectionable, the two friends found themselves on the cusp of political stardom. As Roosevelt remained conflicted about his own future, Lodge, uncertain of how supporting Blaine would affect him politically, remained committed to enhancing his position within the Republican Party. While Roosevelt temporarily turned away from public life to immerse himself in the natural world, Lodge focused his energies on continuing his drive for political glory. As both men took stock of their situations, neither realized that their decisions during the summer of 1884 would haunt their political careers far more than they ever anticipated.

FOUR
Guiding the Rocket

"I have felt that you were one of the very few men whom
I really desired to know as a *friend*."

—Theodore Roosevelt

A t three in the morning on September 7, 1884, Theodore Roosevelt arrived at a deserted railroad trestle on the Western
plains. The depot, recently changed from "Little Missouri," to
"Medora," was in a dusty, unexplored portion of the Dakota territory.
As Roosevelt began to disembark, the only light available was a dim
lantern displayed by the train's sleepy conductor. Stepping down on
to the worn platform, the New Yorker found himself surrounded
by darkness with nothing but the sound of a railroad whistle fading
distantly into the cool fall air.[1]

Roosevelt's spirits were revived during his time in the West.
Enjoying the rough and wild country, the former assemblyman
hunted antelope and buffalo, participated in cattle roundups, and
spent numerous hours enjoying the vivid colors of the skyline.
Focusing on his burgeoning ranching activities, Roosevelt tried to
erase the depressing moments in Chicago from his thoughts.[2]

The events of the convention continued to reverberate. In the days
following the aspiring rancher's arrival in Medora, his comments
to the *Pioneer Press* had caused an uproar among GOP officials.

Roosevelt's interview created such controversy that the *New York Evening Post* sent a telegram asking him to clarify his statement about Blaine's nomination. Hoping to solve the problem, Roosevelt made the mistake of denying the conversation even occurred. "To my knowledge had no interview for publication . . . May have said I opposed Blaine for public reasons, not personal to myself." T. R.'s confusing reply simply caused him more negative publicity.[3]

Roosevelt was in a difficult situation. Blaine's attitudes were contrary to every political value he stood for. The former assemblyman understood, however, that any hope he had for a political career was in vain if he did not display some support for the party's choice. In a brief note to Lodge, during the second week of June, Roosevelt believed the two needed to discuss their next steps. Unbeknownst to Roosevelt, Lodge's actions in Chicago had resulted in major social repercussions.[4]

Returning to Boston, Lodge was attacked over his decision to support the GOP nominee. Many who occupied the rarefied atmosphere of Boston's Beacon Hill were enraged over Blaine's candidacy. Unwilling to support a man with a soiled reputation, many of the city's Back Bay aristocracy decided to cast their vote for the Democratic nominee, Grover Cleveland. While many among the New England elite begrudgingly accepted the changing times, watching the cheapening of the nation's leadership was not a development they were willing to accept.[5]

Following the conclusion of the convention, the Massachusetts Reform Club, a bastion of Liberal Republicanism, condemned Lodge and his fellow delegates for supporting the national ticket. Additionally, members of the organization outraged by Blaine's nomination formed a coalition, determined to defeat the Mainer in the fall. The membership included Harvard president Charles Eliot and the unitarian minister and Lodge relative Thomas W. Higginson, as well as Lodge's old friend, the attorney Moorfield Storey. Once praised for his political acumen and eloquence, Lodge found himself labeled a traitor to his class, and a man who had sold his soul in the name of political ambition.[6]

Boston society ostracized Lodge. Men he had lunched with since 1871 at the exclusive Somerset Club no longer spoke with him. The mantel in the Lodges' library, once filled with invitations to evenings on Beacon Hill, stood bare. Henry Adams, who had introduced Lodge to Republican politics, was devastated by his former student's decision. Remaining devoted to Nannie and the Lodge children, the warm feelings Adams once held for his protégé never returned. "The hostility of those persons in Boston and Massachusetts who had bolted from the Republican Party concentrated itself in large measure upon my devoted head," Lodge recalled in 1908.[7]

The most stinging rebuke came from Lodge's cousin and Roosevelt's former father-in-law, George Cabot Lee. When the banker learned of the two men's choice to support Blaine, he responded by saying, "as for Cabot Lodge, nobody's surprised at him; but you can tell that young whipper-snapper [Roosevelt] in New York from me that his independence was the only thing in him we cared for . . ." Lodge tried to explain to Lee and others his decision was a matter of "principle," but no one believed him.[8]

For Lodge, Boston became a different world. On the few occasions friends invited him and Nannie to their homes, the couple were uncertain whether to attend. Even at their residence on Nahant the Lodges preferred to keep out of public view.[9]

Nevertheless, a select few of those on Beacon Hill still welcomed Lodge's company. When one old friend asked the couple to dine with his family, Lodge was overwhelmed. "It is very kind of your father and mother to ask us to dinner. People in Boston would not do that." To those few who still sought his friendship, like the artistic scholar William Sturgis Bigelow, author Lucius Sargent, and lawyer Oliver Wendell Holmes Jr., the Bostonian remained unfailingly loyal. "For all people who stood by me then I have felt a gratitude ever since which nothing can efface," he wrote decades later.[10]

Those who found Lodge arrogant and unpleasant were unsurprised by his decision to follow the politically pragmatic path. Harvard classmate William Lawrence, the Episcopal Bishop of Massachusetts, admitted Lodge's endorsement of Blaine caused him to lose respect for his old chum. "I had no use for Cabot politically for years after. I felt that he had traduced his cause, and his personal ambition to go to Congress was mixed up with his action," the clergyman recalled in a biographical sketch of the senator published in 1925.[11]

Lodge's combative attitude did not make life any easier. Rather than trying to consider the opinion of those who disagreed, the aspiring politician dismissed his friends as "arrogant and short sighted." There is no doubt that Lodge allowed ambition to get the better of him. One, however, can also understand the pain he experienced as so many chose to dismiss the New Englander and his wife from their lives.[12]

Seething with indignation, Lodge determined to persevere. "If I am to be banned because I vote according to what I believe . . . I will fight against such treatment with all my strength," Lodge lamented to his former reform colleague Carl Schurz. Schurz, a widely respected liberal member of the GOP, tried to convince Lodge to rescind his support of Blaine. The older man's request went for naught. For all of Schurz's efforts to explain his reasoning, Lodge remained bitter at those who had judged him so harshly. "I have grown callous to the abuse & slander which have been poured out on me at home because I ventured to go my own way," he wrote in his journal in 1890.[13]

Henry Adams once described Lodge as being "unmitigated Boston." Sadly, the community once the epicenter of Lodge's existence no longer welcomed him. Lodge may have resented the treatment by his friends and neighbors, but his decision to support Blaine symbolized that of a pragmatic politician focused on professional rather than social success.

In time, as Lodge's career gained more prestige, the anger against him cooled. However, there were always those who viewed Lodge with suspicion, believing he had sold his soul in the name of political power.[14]

Lodge's decision to side with Republican regulars was understandable. Achieving success in the state party required him to associate with those who controlled the organizations inner workings. The vindictiveness, however, with which Lodge's friends attacked him was unreasonable and counterproductive. Liberal Republicans like Henry Adams may have preached the philosophy of good government, but Lodge was prepared to make the choices necessary to achieve his larger goal.

For Adams and others, the compromises of character necessary to climb the political ladder were simply too great a sacrifice. Lodge's and Roosevelt's good friend, socialite Margaret Chanler, once referred to the Bostonian as a "militant politician." There is certainly some truth to that characterization but it is not entirely accurate. Even as a staunch supporter of the Republican Party, Lodge always understood that compromise was often critical to achieve the greater good.[15]

Many viewed Lodge's new associations with GOP professionals as another example of his raw ambition. Lodge, however, saw working within the party structure as the only way to get anything accomplished. "I learned . . . that things political are only to be brought about by cooperation, or in other words, by organized parties," he wrote years later, "where you act together because you agree in the main and submit to much you do not like in order to advance the larger principles of greater importance." Lodge possessed a desire to achieve something long lasting. That motivation was primarily driven by the commitment to fulfill the tradition of his ancestors, whose record of accomplishment had stood the test of time.[16]

In June 1884 Roosevelt boarded a train for the East. With the growing controversy surrounding his support of Blaine and concern for the health of his baby daughter, the rancher returned to New York. Whether or not politics remained in his future, Roosevelt believed that standing with the Republican Party was the correct decision.[17]

Weeks before departing for home, T. R. wrote Lodge encouraging his friend not to allow the insults he was receiving from the Boston liberals to undermine his focus on the campaign for his election to Massachusetts's sixth congressional district. "I do not know a man in the country whose future I regard as so promising as is yours," Roosevelt wrote from his ranch at "Little Missouri."[18]

As each experienced his share of peaks and valleys Roosevelt and Lodge stood shoulder to shoulder. Throughout 1884, Roosevelt, a widower and uncertain of what lay ahead, desperately needed someone with whom he could confide. T. R. was grateful for Lodge's kind advice and thoughtful counsel. "I have rarely been more pleased by anything than I was by your pleasant words of friendship for me; for two or three years I have felt you were one of the very few men whom I really desired to have as a *friend*," Roosevelt wrote as Lodge fervently campaigned for the House of Representatives.[19]

Following a visit with his daughter, Alice, at the Roosevelt brownstone on Madison Avenue, T. R. looked forward to a relaxing visit with Lodge at Nahant. Studying the political news, Roosevelt was not surprised to see many of those he had worked with in Chicago bolting the party in favor of Grover Cleveland. The *New York Herald*, the *New York Times*, and other publications of note also departed the Republican fold. Arriving at the Lodge's home, Roosevelt found his friend in a foul mood. Enjoying the late-night sea air, the two men talked of their current predicament. For all their disappointment with the nomination of Blaine, both believed there was nothing that could be done but support the ticket.[20]

On July 19, 1884, Roosevelt arranged a meeting with the *Boston Herald*. Over the course of the interview, T. R. stated that he planned to vote the Republican slate in November.

"A man cannot act both without and within the party; he can do either, but he cannot possibly do both," the former assemblyman told the newspaper. Roosevelt contended Blaine was the unquestionable choice of the party. As head of his respective delegation, he had a duty to abide by the wishes of the convention. "I went in with my eyes open . . . I did my best and got beaten, and I propose to stand by the result," T. R. told the reporter in a brusque manner.[21]

These comments were nothing new. Before the convention Lodge and Roosevelt had agreed to support the wishes of the delegates regardless of the nominee. Still in Dakota, on June 18 Roosevelt wrote Lodge saying plainly, "We can take part in no bolt." Following the interview, Roosevelt felt satisfied he had informed the public of his intention.[22]

When Roosevelt's comments became public many accused T. R. of being under the control of the "evil genius," Cabot Lodge. That charge made for some much-needed levity. "Scandalous disclosure! The True Reason for an alleged reformer's support of Blaine! The infamous Roosevelt bribed by the notorious Lodge! He sells his birthright for a mere hairbrush! Decent citizens disgusted!" Roosevelt wrote gleefully to Nannie Lodge, turning a portion of his letter into a tabloid headline.[23]

Attacked by the editors of the *Evening Post* and *The Nation*, T. R. responded in kind.

"I have received shoals of letters, pathetic and abusive to which I have replied with vivacity or ferocity, according to the circumstances of the case," Roosevelt informed Lodge shortly before he returned West. The scholar thought the whole idea that he held a Svengali-like influence over Roosevelt was ridiculous. "No man ever lived who could have influenced, still less controlled, Theodore Roosevelt on such a question as this," Lodge wrote, in an undated memo about the 1884 election.[24]

As the nation began to focus on the fall campaign, Roosevelt told Lodge he was determined "to be on hand to do what I can, on the stump or otherwise." Roosevelt looked forward to assisting Lodge in his race for Congress. With his own chances to return to the political stage still unknown, the opportunity of playing an active role in the campaign remained an attractive opportunity.[25]

Arriving in New York that October, Bamie was glad her brother had returned to the house on Madison Avenue. Afflicted with a form of tuberculosis, T. R.'s sister did not allow the illness to deter her from enjoying a full life of entertainment, travel, and conversation. Not blessed with her mother's looks, Bamie possessed her father's dynamic personality that made her a popular hostess and astute political observer. Throughout Roosevelt's life he frequently relied on his sister for advice and emotional support.[26]

Sympathetic to her brother's frustration with the Republican Party, Bamie believed politics was the ideal career for her younger sibling. "Theodore would not be happy out of public affairs," she told Lodge, with whom she had a lifelong correspondence.[27]

Roosevelt then departed for speaking engagements to assist candidates running for office that fall. Following an appearance before a Young Republican organization across the river in Brooklyn, T. R. then headed to Massachusetts. Accepting the Lodges' hospitality on Nahant he prepared to join the congressional candidate on several stops around the state.[28]

Before heading off on the hustings, the couple gave Roosevelt a dinner to celebrate his twenty-sixth birthday. Knowing their friend's fondness for men of letters, the couple invited the popular author William Dean Howells, the *Atlantic Monthly* editor Thomas Bailey Aldrich, and legal scholar Oliver Wendell Holmes Jr. Roosevelt was delighted. "I do not know when I have enjoyed a dinner so much," he commented to Bamie. Roosevelt then left Nahant looking forward to assisting Lodge in winning his first major campaign. During an event at Boston's Faneuil Hall, the New Yorker praised Lodge's ability and character, while also taking great joy in bashing the sanctimonious attitude of his former liberal allies.[29]

Lodge appreciated Roosevelt's comments. As the media wrote about Blaine's sordid business dealings or Cleveland's illegitimate child, Lodge decided to follow T. R.'s counsel to work hard for the party and speak as little as possible about the GOP nominee. Throughout the campaign, the candidate employed the tenacity and grit that numerous opponents experienced throughout his political career. Displaying his knowledge of legislative detail Lodge communicated his passion for civil service reform, and a strong tariff.[30]

In the hopes of placating those opposed to his embracing the national ticket, Lodge focused little on Blaine. That strategy collapsed on the eve of the election. At a Massachusetts Republican fundraising dinner at Boston's Brunswick Hotel, Lodge was designated to introduce Blaine as required by his duties as chairman of the state's Republican committee.[31]

Arriving in the dining room, with the Mainer's hand resting on Lodge's arm, Lodge sat uncomfortably at the candidate's side. The evening was not Lodge's finest hour. Awkward and uncertain, Lodge did his best to praise the guest of honor for instilling enthusiasm among the Republican faithful.[32]

As applause filled the room, Lodge was unable to escape. Following the dinner, Blaine remained glued to Lodge's side as the two attended a torchlit parade scheduled in honor of the Republican nominee. Watching the procession from a reviewing stand surrounded by thousands of spectators, one wonders what Lodge was thinking. Days later when recording the event in his journal, all Lodge could write was "Alas, Alas." The glum comment was just the beginning of a depressing election day.[33]

No one who followed the campaign was surprised by the results of the voting. Even with personal scandals, Cleveland managed to win the election with 282 electoral votes to Blaine's 219 votes. While the GOP nominee won Massachusetts, Republicans witnessed a decline of their formidable power across the Northeast.

Narrow victories in New York and Connecticut as well as the solid Democratic South provided Cleveland with significant advantage. The geographical shift combined with Henry Adams's and other liberals' decisions to bolt from the the party gave Democrats the presidency for the first time in more than two decades.[34]

More important, Lodge lost his congressional race by a margin of less than three hundred votes. It was a difficult ordeal for the politician to bear. "I was defeated by 265 in a vote of over 30,000 & my political career & hope came to an end," the defeated candidate lamented following the election.[35]

Other than the support of his wife and family Roosevelt's gesture of friendship cheered Lodge the most. Knowing that both men were swimming against the tide of their chosen profession, T. R.'s strong encouragement for Lodge to remain in the battle brightened the Bostonian's hopes for the future. "Of course, there seems no use of saying anything in the way of consolation; and probably you feel as if your career had ended; *that is not so*," Roosevelt wrote from his home in New York.[36]

Roosevelt did not shy away from the fact that his friend's defeat was significant. He also knew that Lodge was a man of indomitable spirit who had developed an enormous following among Republicans in Massachusetts. "They will never forget you and come back in time you must and will," T. R. wrote. Lodge was overwhelmed with Roosevelt's support. "The more I see him . . . the more and more I love him," the Republican wrote in the spring of 1885.[37]

As Roosevelt offered Lodge an optimistic point of view, he remained dismayed over the state of the socioeconomic landscape. Based on the recent election results T. R. believed his political prospects looked grim. Roosevelt had positioned himself as a reformer during his time in the legislature. However, he believed he had undone much of that reputation by supporting Blaine for president. "Blaine's nomination meant to me pretty sure political death," he wrote Lodge on November 10.[38]

As gloom settled over the Republican Party following the election, Roosevelt found little to say except believing both he and Lodge had done their best. "I have stood a great deal; and now that the throw has been against me, I shall certainly not complain." Despite these brave words, Roosevelt saw little reason for optimism. "I have not believed and do not believe that I shall ever be likely to come back into political life," the former legislator commented to Lodge.[39]

Depressive tendencies may have caused Roosevelt to exaggerate his own political demise. The New Yorker, however, was also not an entrenched figure within the state's political machine. That knowledge was responsible for enhancing his appeal among Empire State voters. In addition, the former legislative reformer appealed to the average

New Yorker for his ability to fight graft and corruption responsible for undercutting so many people's confidence in government.

While T. R. may have lost the support of New York Independents, the group represented a narrow minority within the state Republican Party. In time, Roosevelt realized Lodge was right. The public had a short memory. Voters were concerned about the candidate's natural abilities, and his political vision, not simply where he stood on one issue.[40]

Following the events of 1884, many in and out of the Republican Party viewed Roosevelt as just another slimy politician looking to capitalize on a particular moment. Ironically, Blaine's defeat allowed Roosevelt to wash his hands of the tedious senator, freeing him to search for a government opportunity that suited his abilities and attitudes.[41]

With the conclusion of the campaign, Roosevelt returned to Medora. During his visit several prominent citizens of the territory approached T. R. about being a candidate for Congress. Since statehood was more than five years away, the opportunity, while flattering, did not serve Roosevelt's purpose. The offer did enhance Roosevelt's confidence, giving him a positive view of his future political prospects.[42]

Following the loss of the congressional election Lodge returned to his literary pursuits. Renewing his interest in the Federalist Era, the historian filled his days by embarking on the lengthy project of editing the writings of Alexander Hamilton. Lodge also socialized and networked, building relationships within Massachusetts politics that might allow a different result when he ran for office again.[43]

As the year came to an end, Lodge and Roosevelt found themselves dismissed by their contemporaries as shallow opportunists. Focusing on other interests, each man distracted himself from his respective defeats and disappointments. While Lodge returned to scholarly pursuits, politics remained at the forefront of his imagination.

Roosevelt attempted to put his political misfortunes behind him by returning to the serenity of the frontier. Engaging in roundups and cattle drives, T. R. wondered if his decision to support James Blaine had doomed his chances for success in public life. Despite their mutual disappointments the two men could take comfort in their growing friendship with one another. That relationship, begun only months earlier, soon proved mutually fruitful in the revival of each man's political fortunes.

FIVE

From Outsiders to Insiders

"I am always willing to pay the piper when I have had a
good dance."

—Theodore Roosevelt

I n August 1885, Theodore Roosevelt returned to New York for an
eight-week visit to the East. Overseeing construction of a home
near the small hamlet of Oyster Bay, T. R. soon departed Long
Island for a few days with the Lodges at their compound on Nahant.
Lodge and Roosevelt were avid horsemen. Enjoying spirited gallops
around the Lodge estate at East Point, T. R. accepted the Bostonian's
invitation to ride his majestic black hunter, Toronto. With his mind
drifting to his affairs in the West, Roosevelt enjoyed relaxing with
the couple on their large veranda, discussing Shakespeare and other
works of literature.[1]

Shortly before departing New York for a return to the West,
Roosevelt commented on the new government in Washington. Both
he and Lodge believed President Grover Cleveland was an honorable
man. While those he had appointed were not of the highest caliber,
neither man believed the new cabinet was a danger to the country.[2]

The two friends were anxious to return to politics. With the
election having just concluded there was little either could do except
wait for the next opportunity. Determined to run for Congress in

1886, Lodge retained his position as head of the Massachusetts GOP. Roosevelt, with a similar goal in mind, spent the fall of 1885 working on his own political return by campaigning for gubernatorial hopeful Ira Davenport and other New York Republican candidates.[3]

On October 17, 1885, T. R. shared the stage with Lodge as the two participated in a rally for the New York Republican slate at Brooklyn's Flatbush Music Hall. The party faithful greeted each man's remarks warmly. Lodge, who spoke only briefly, had attended with the objective of supporting his friend's reentry into the political arena. As Lodge sat on the dais, one foot methodically swinging back and forth, T. R. received an ovation of such intensity that a Brooklyn newspaper reported that the foundations of the building trembled.[4]

Roosevelt enjoyed his return to the campaign trail. Being in front of a crowd energized him almost as much as his time in the West. Filled with renewed vigor, Roosevelt hammered away at his Democratic opponents while touting his favorite issue: civil service reform.[5]

When not on the campaign trail, Roosevelt exercised and indulged in his newfound passion, fox hunting. The sport was a favorite of Lodge's, and Roosevelt loved the speed and the competition associated with it. Always trying to impress his older friend with his horsemanship, Roosevelt frequently wrote Lodge of his adventures in the saddle. Riding for exercise was never enough. The idea was to test one's fitness and manly skill, and for Roosevelt, the more dangerous that test the better.[6]

On one occasion during the latter part of October, T. R. described an incident that occurred on a hunt in Meadowbrook, New York. Following the refusal of his horse to jump a five-foot fence, Roosevelt's mount tumbled to the ground. The fall left Roosevelt with a crushed arm and a severely scraped face. The scope of the disaster might have caused most men to retire from the sport. The idea never entered

Roosevelt's mind. "I am always willing to pay the piper when I have had a good dance;" he wrote Lodge following the accident.[7]

The physical exercise and campaigning for the New York state ticket was not the only activity engaging Roosevelt's interest. Visiting the family home on Madison Avenue earlier in the month, T. R. encountered his sister Corinne's close friend, Edith Carow. Elegant and highly reserved, with alabaster skin and wavy dark hair, the two had known each other since childhood. Reaching their formative years, the deep friendship blossomed into romance. However, in the summer of 1878, after rejecting Roosevelt's multiple proposals of marriage, an argument erupted between the two that ruptured the relationship.[8]

Neither party revealed the details of the dispute. Many believed Roosevelt's family disapproved of the marriage. Once a wealthy and prominent family, Edith's father's poor business acumen and severe alcoholism had left the Carows virtually destitute.[9]

Even as Roosevelt eventually courted and married Alice Lee, he occasionally inquired about Edith through his sister Bamie. Following Alice's untimely death, the two reunited. As his love for Edith returned, Roosevelt remained torn. Vowing never to marry again, he soon rationalized that since he had considered marrying Edith years earlier it was acceptable to change his mind.[10]

Roosevelt had made the right decision. Needy, with an inability to spend long periods of time alone, Edith possessed qualities that complemented many of his own. The future second Mrs. Roosevelt was a curious, well-read woman who could engage her future husband intellectually. T. R. also wanted more children. Edith had the capacity to fulfill those requirements and more.[11]

Following Roosevelt's fox hunting accident, he escorted Edith to the Meadowbrook Hunt Ball held at his recently completed home at Sagamore Hill. Three weeks later, on November 17, 1885, Roosevelt proposed and Edith accepted. Concerned about the impact their engagement might have on Roosevelt's family as well as the couple's position in society, the announcement was kept private.[12]

Romantic turmoil in his personal life did not deter Roosevelt from focusing on his next opportunity. "I will be delighted when I get settled down to work of some sort again," T. R. wrote Lodge following the Bostonian's visit to New York in the first week of February 1886, "To be a man of the world is *not* my strong point." During that winter Lodge had recommended to historian John T. Morse Jr. that he commission Roosevelt to write a biography of the Missouri senator Thomas Hart Benton. The rugged and charismatic Midwesterner was the type of figure that had always engaged Roosevelt's interest.[13]

Preparing to return West that spring, Roosevelt questioned whether the book would be a success. Always in competition with Lodge, Roosevelt was envious of the historian's literary achievements. Since the loss of his election for Congress, Lodge had continued to publish while also remaining engaged with the Massachusetts Republican Party.[14]

In addition, Lodge had raised his political profile by taking a financial interest in the *Boston Daily Advertiser.* Turning the publication into a powerful organ of the Massachusetts GOP allowed Cabot to employ the paper as a political platform in preparation for a congressional run the following year.[15]

Along with these activities Lodge was forging ahead on a biography of George Washington. "I trust that you won't entirely forget your somewhat happy-go-lucky friend," Roosevelt wrote in a self-deprecating yet insecure tone.[16]

In March Roosevelt headed back to Dakota, while Edith and her family prepared to set sail for Europe the following month. The couple believed remaining separate until the announcement of their engagement was the correct procedure. During his time in the West,

T. R. could not resist boasting to Lodge of his cowboy adventures. "I got . . . three horse thieves in fine style," he bragged, as he attended to matters at his Elkhorn Ranch. Struggling with the biography of Benton, T. R. glanced over his shoulder at Lodge's own professional progress. "Have you begun on your Washington yet? And do you really intend to run for Congress this fall," Roosevelt wrote from Medora in late March 1886.[17]

Lodge enjoyed the verbal sparring, but he also stood ready to assist Roosevelt in any way possible. "Would it be too infernal a nuisance for you to hire one of your minions on the *Advertiser* (of course at my expense) to look up [Benton's] life after he left the Senate in 1850," T. R. asked Lodge in June of 1886. The historian was happy to help.[18]

In July Roosevelt sent the manuscript off to the publisher. "I hope [Benton] is decent, but lately I have been troubled with dreadful misgivings," T. R. wrote Lodge following the book's completion. At the same time Roosevelt remained frustrated. Writing was not enough. He wanted work that would allow him to return to public life.[19]

Months earlier Roosevelt had discussed becoming president of the New York Board of Health. Lodge thought the idea a nonstarter and beneath Roosevelt's ability. In the end the opportunity never developed. While Roosevelt looked forward to marrying Edith in Europe at the end of the year T. R. remained discouraged about his professional prospects.[20]

Roosevelt obsessively searched for a public issue to vault him back into prominence. In August, he asked Lodge to keep him appraised of any rumblings of trouble along the border between Mexico and the United States. "Will you telegraph me at once if war becomes inevitable," T. R. wrote, hoping to raise a company of riflemen composed of his friends in the West. The settling of the border dispute caused Roosevelt to wonder if his opportunity for political advancement was gone for good.[21]

In the meantime, Lodge's aspirations of returning to office progressed. In the fall of 1886, the rank and file renominated him for Congress. Once again, Lodge employed his organizational and networking resources that saw him vigorously campaign throughout the hamlets of Lynn and Nahant. At the same time Roosevelt's political career also appeared on the cusp of revival.[22]

On October 21, 1886, days before Lodge received the nomination for his second campaign for Congress, his friend accepted the opportunity to become the Republican nominee for mayor of New York City. Roosevelt admitted to Lodge that with three weeks remaining until election day he was doubtful of any chance of success. Secretly, Roosevelt was thrilled with the nomination. While he had given the impression the offer was unexpected, that was not entirely true.[23]

Roosevelt had attended the New York State convention in Utica, New York, with an eye on who the GOP might nominate for the city's mayoralty. The political gathering allowed Roosevelt to not only renew acquaintances with the party's local representatives but give notice to the press that he was hoping to return to the center of the action.[24]

The mayoral race featured Roosevelt, the United Labor Party's Henry George, and the wealthy Democratic former congressman, Abram S. Hewitt. George was an economist and journalist whose 1879 book, *Progress and Poverty*, which advocated for a single tax on land, had taken the nation by storm. The George candidacy also resonated with many unhappy over the growing disparity of wealth occurring across the nation.[25]

Roosevelt believed his chances for victory were bleak and Lodge agreed. But the mayoral opportunity allowed T. R. to lead a unified Republican organization. Composed of members of the GOP machine under the party boss Thomas Platt, and the patrician reform class under the command of corporate lawyer Elihu Root, the situation gave Roosevelt the opportunity to become a major presence within the GOP structure.[26]

T. R. had learned from Lodge that political success could only be achieved by working within the party system. The two friends had tried to upset that process in 1884 and paid dearly for their mistake. Lodge lost his first campaign for Congress, but in going down in defeat, he had strengthened his bonds within the party. Roosevelt realized he needed to do the same. Remaining uncertain, T. R. asked Lodge if he could schedule some time to discuss the matter as he prepared to jump into the campaign.[27]

In Massachusetts, Lodge's nomination for Congress was not viewed favorably by all members of the party. Boston's liberal Republicans belittled the candidate, never forgiving him for supporting James Blaine two years earlier. Lodge's opponents were so incensed by his candidacy, rumors began circulating in the city's newspapers that the congressional hopeful had asked the GOP's former standard-bearer to make an appearance on his behalf. For Lodge the race was an arduous experience due to his ongoing conflict with Boston's liberal upper class.[28]

The Mugwumps (as the congressional hopeful described the liberals) "pursued me with a vindictive malice for which I was not prepared," Lodge wrote during the campaign. The Bostonian also contended with attacks from members of the press. The *Boston Globe* described the candidate as "fidgeting about in a Beacon Hill cradle, his only aspiration being to get his big toe into his mouth." Money also remained an important factor. Lodge and his opponent, Henry B. Lovering, each relied on their financial resources to gain an advantage. When the numbers were tallied Lodge had won his quest for a congressional seat by just over seven hundred votes.[29]

As Lodge headed toward victory, Roosevelt attempted to make a strong showing out of an unwinnable mayoral contest. Despite the fates not being in his favor, T. R. showed the powers within the state's GOP that he possessed an extraordinary drive and capacity for work. Dashing from one campaign appearance to another, Roosevelt endured eighteen-hour days with his usual energy and optimism.[30]

Roosevelt also experienced the wrath of the Independents. The small group composing the city's elites had not forgotten T. R.'s support for the GOP nominee in the last presidential election. "Three cheers for James G. Blaine," one heckler yelled at a Roosevelt campaign event. The mayoral hopeful, dismissing the Mugwumps as amateurish and soft, remained determined to persevere.[31]

Roosevelt was able to do little to change the inevitable. Finishing behind Hewitt and George with just over 60,000 votes, Roosevelt believed his future was damaged irreparably. Happy for Lodge's success, T. R. wired his friend about his recent loss. "Am badly defeated. Worse even than I feared," he alerted Lodge via telegram. Lodge rushed to New York where he did his best to encourage his friend that a bright future remained ahead.[32]

Despite the painful loss, the election allowed Roosevelt to return to the Republican fold. Throughout the campaign T. R. had reacquainted voters with his positions as a reformer determined to clean up the corruption that permeated the Empire City. Most important, he had shown his willingness to do what was necessary to help the GOP. With the mayoral campaign behind him, Roosevelt focused his attention on his upcoming wedding to Edith. Despite doing the utmost to keep the engagement secret, news of the Roosevelt-Carow nuptials appeared in the society section of the *New York Times*.[33]

The possibility of negative reaction to the engagement had so concerned Roosevelt that he did not inform the Lodges of his plans until five days before he sailed for Europe. Remaining uncertain if the engagement to Edith was an honorable choice, T. R. communicated his decision in a revealing missive to Nannie Lodge. "I do wish I could only see you face-to-face, there are so many things to tell you which I cannot put on paper," T. R. wrote.[34]

Describing his plans to marry Edith in England, Roosevelt explained how important it was that the Lodges "like Edith and receive her warmly . . ." Roosevelt then asked Nannie to not breathe a word of the upcoming nuptials to anyone. "[N]ot a soul is to know but you two and my own family," Roosevelt wrote.[35]

Even as T. R. prepared to travel abroad he remained conflicted over the upcoming marriage. The loss of Alice had overwhelmed him. In addition, the late Mrs. Roosevelt was also a relation of Lodge's, making the letter to the couple even more awkward. "Now, dear Nannie you and Cabot are more to me than any other people outside of my own family," T. R. wrote, emphasizing the importance of their relationship.[36]

The earnestness of the note reflected the reverence Roosevelt held toward Nannie Lodge. Besides possessing an intellect second to none, Nannie's background as the daughter of a navy admiral gave her the ability to discuss maritime affairs in extraordinary detail. Though far more glamorous than Edith, both were bright, strong-willed women who had little problem putting their respective husbands in their place. On one occasion while visiting the Roosevelts in Oyster Bay, Nannie had not taken kindly to her host encouraging her to race him down a steep hill known as Cooper's Bluff. "Nobody who heard her would ever again have accused her of possessing a timid or irresolute character," Roosevelt wrote Lodge following his wife's staunch refusal to participate in the playful exercise.[37]

Traveling on the Cunard Line's RMS *Etruria*, Roosevelt and Bamie busied themselves with last-minute wedding details. In the first few days of their voyage, a distinguished-looking man with thinning hair and a well-manicured goatee approached them. The gentleman was Cecil Spring Rice, a British foreign service officer returning to London following a visit to Canada. A master networker, "Springy," as he was known, had somehow arranged a letter of introduction to Bamie upon learning she and her brother had booked passage on the transatlantic journey to Liverpool.[38]

A graduate of Eaton and Oxford with "a genius for friendships" and an eye for the fairer sex, Spring Rice was preparing for a career in diplomacy. Urbane and athletic, with a keen curiosity and a love of conversation, T. R. and "Springy" immediately bonded over a variety of interests. Not having any friends in London, Roosevelt asked Spring Rice to serve as his best man, an offer which the Englishman eagerly accepted.[39]

Arriving in London, T. R. checked into a lavish suite at Brown's Hotel. With the help of Spring Rice, Roosevelt rapidly made connections among London society. "Mr. Roosevelt's table . . . is covered with invitations to four times as many dinners as he can eat," one correspondent observed. With time to spare before taking his second trip down the aisle, Roosevelt did his best to take advantage of every social opportunity at his disposal. "I have been treated like a prince," he wrote joyously to Lodge during his stay in London.[40]

Spring Rice introduced his new friend to intellectuals across the social spectrum. These included the playwright George Bernard Shaw, the historian James Bryce, and the politician and journalist John Morley. Never wanting to miss a chance at physical activity, Roosevelt took advantage of the opportunity to exercise his passion for hunting and shooting whenever the moment presented itself. "The ground was so soft I was hardly even jarred," T. R. wrote Lodge as he described another encounter with an uncooperative horse.[41]

Roosevelt and Edith married on a cold and overcast day on December 2, 1886. On the afternoon of the wedding, absorbed in conversation, Roosevelt and Spring Rice lost track of time. En route to St. George's Church in Hanover Square, the diplomat ordered the horse cab to suddenly stop. Jumping out, "Springy" ran into a small shop and emerged with a pair of bright orange gloves, which he convinced T. R. to wear during the ceremony.[42]

Following a fifteen-week honeymoon in England, France, and Italy, the Roosevelts returned to New York at the end of March 1887. Meeting Bamie at her apartment on Madison Avenue, the newlyweds were joined by Lodge and Spring Rice. The Englishman had met Lodge in Washington while serving as secretary to the British legation. Since both men were socially well-connected, enjoyed reading history, and discussing international affairs it was no surprise the congressman and the diplomat had met one another.[43]

Edith was well acquainted with Spring Rice, but that afternoon was her first meeting with Lodge. Initially, the New Englander's formal disposition caused Edith to view him with some intimidation. Still, the new Mrs. Roosevelt was soon relieved to discover the two shared a strong knowledge of literature. Over the next few years, Lodge came to value Edith's advice and judgment. The feeling was mutual. Roosevelt's new wife held the future senator in such high regard, she informed her husband that if something were to happen to him, Lodge was the only person she would want to deliver the news.[44]

Lodge had plenty of time to visit with Roosevelt and Spring Rice. The new session of Congress did not begin until the end of 1887. That fall, the family rented a house on Nineteenth Street and Jefferson Place. The dreary furnishings made Lodge unhappy, but his wife did her best to make the home habitable. "Nannie . . . is fast giving it the peculiar look of comfort & refinement which follows her footsteps even in the most uncompromising of hired houses," Lodge commented to his mother.[45]

Other than forging a friendship with rising Ohio congressman William McKinley, Lodge accomplished little during his initial term in Congress. With Grover Cleveland in the White House and the House of Representatives under Democratic control, Lodge could do little but learn the legislative process. The freshman congressman had shown himself to possess strong organizational and networking skills. Lodge came to realize, however, he had little knowledge of how the business of politics was conducted in the District of Columbia.[46]

Requiring a seasoned adviser to guide him through the complexities of the nation's lower house, the congressman recruited E. B. Hayes, a calculating Bay State politician and mayor of Lynn, Massachusetts. Aside from legislative strategies, Hayes instructed the new congressman in the importance of distributing government jobs to deserving supporters. The Bay State politico understood that as a supporter of a civil service code, Lodge disliked the patronage system, believing it responsible for much of the corruption that consumed public life. "I have always trembled for you in this appointment business," Hayes wrote Lodge of the many uncomfortable realities required for political success.[47]

With little to do during the initial congressional session, the Lodges filled that void by pursuing an active social life. Less entrenched in formality and tradition than cities like Boston or New York, Washington during the late nineteenth century was exciting and vibrant. Following their arrival, the couple received invitations to dinners and other gatherings, many lasting until two or three o'clock in the morning.[48]

Not surprisingly, Nannie Lodge was often the most elegant woman in attendance. Dressed in gowns of flowing silk, the congressman's wife was never without a signature "velvet or pearl band" encircling her neck. Lodge was delighted that his bride was frequently "the belle of the ball," captivating everyone she met with her vitality and effusive sense of humor.[49]

It was easy for the Lodges to integrate themselves into the Washington social scene. Having spent time with Nannie's father, Admiral Davis, during his tenure as manager of the Naval Observatory, the couple were familiar with numerous members of the city's political class and diplomatic corps. Also present were old friends like Henry Adams, Secretary of War William C. Endicott, and Harvard historian George Bancroft, all of whom the Lodges had known in Boston.[50]

Through Adams the couple encountered the luminous Washington socialite Elizabeth Sherman Cameron. A magnetic and stylish brunette, "Lizzie" was the niece of General William T. Sherman and his younger brother, Ohio senator John Sherman. Obsessed with wealth and social position, the family demanded Lizzie marry someone of influence and means.[51]

Lizzie settled on the Pennsylvania senator J. Donald Cameron. Ill-tempered, alcoholic, and more than two decades older than his bride, the twenty-year-old Mrs. Cameron tolerated the Pennsylvanian, not only because of his political position but because he also possessed a significant fortune. "He is very nice about it all and keeps away from me except when I tell him he can come," Lizzie wrote to her mother in describing her and the senator's relationship. As the marriage became one of convenience, Lizzie became the muse and confidante of Henry Adams, whose wife Clover had committed suicide in 1885.[52]

Adams also introduced the Lodges to the highly talented John Hay. Following his service as President Lincoln's secretary, Hay had served as assistant secretary of state under fellow Ohioan Rutherford B. Hayes before resigning to pursue his own journalistic and literary efforts. When the Lodges encountered Hay, the erudite writer and diplomat was married to Clara Stone, the strong-willed, pious, and overweight daughter of a wealthy railroad executive.[53]

In becoming acquainted with the Camerons, Hays, and other prominent members of the Washington community, Lodge used his home to network and socialize as he had in Boston. The congressman was happy to have departed the city on the Charles. In Boston Lodge had to concern himself with personal slights by the Beacon Hill set. In the Federal City, filled with politicians of all stripes, Lodge was simply another ambitious legislator on the rise.

As Nannie oversaw the couple's social schedule she also served as her husband's most important adviser. When Lodge wrote a speech or historical essay, Nannie was the first to review it. One evening Lodge asked his wife for her thoughts about an address he was scheduled to deliver at a Massachusetts rally. Nannie's kind but critical remarks forced the congressman to rewrite the speech three times before she gave it her seal of approval.

A selfless personality, Lodge's wife believed she had little to do with her husband's success. "You exaggerate any part I may have played in Cabot's career. He is a man who would always have worked & succeeded," Nannie wrote to Roosevelt's sister, Corrine. While Nannie was raised with the belief that education was important, she believed her first duty was as wife, mother, and helpmate to her husband.[54]

The congressman adored Nannie and his children. Lodge was also often cold and short-tempered. That quality was highlighted when Henry Adams and Lizzie Cameron visited the couple on Nahant. "I wonder how you endured the noise and violence of them all last summer," Lizzie inquired following their stay at the Lodges' seaside retreat. "I never heard such wrangling and Nannie's worn face is now explicable," Cameron wrote in describing the unsettling events.[55]

On December 6, 1887, President Cleveland delivered his annual message to Congress. The former governor surprised many political observers when he demanded reform of the nation's tariff system. A growing federal surplus over the last eight years had motivated the president to call for the revision of the national economic legislation. Cleveland requested that Congress eliminate import taxes on a variety of foreign goods while limiting duties on others. With that declaration, the president gave the impression to his party he was an advocate of free trade.[56]

The issue of the tariff remained one of the central issues for the Republican Party. Not only did it remain highly favorable with the nation's business sector, but it also resonated with members of the labor class. The party's outspokenness on the issue led many wealthy conservatives, like department store magnate John Wanamaker, to raise large amounts of money to promote the tariff among the Republican faithful.[57]

Cleveland's controversial remarks gave many Republicans hope that their party could reclaim the presidency in the 1888 election. That year the GOP nominated Benjamin Harrison. A lawyer and former one-term senator from Indiana, Harrison had served as a general during the Civil War. As one of the shorter party standard-bearers, Harrison, at five foot six and known as "Little Ben," was popular with the public for his thoughtful oratory and restrained demeanor.[58]

Roosevelt was eager to become involved in the upcoming election campaign. In October 1888, T. R. decided to highlight Harrison's candidacy during a whistle-stop tour through Michigan, Minnesota, and Illinois. The adulation he received along the way filled Roosevelt with joy.[59]

The trip's success made Roosevelt hope that the positive reviews he received would gain him notoriety among Harrison's intimates. Still, T. R. remained uncertain if fate would allow him another chance at public service. "Of late years I have been out in my political prophesies . . . so I have some hesitancy in trying my hand again," T. R. wrote Lodge, as the congressman campaigned for reelection.[60]

On election day, the controversy over the tariff cost the Democrats while paying dividends for Republicans. Despite losing the popular vote to President Cleveland, Harrison won the election by obtaining a majority within the Electoral College. Not only did the GOP succeed in winning the presidency but it also regained control of the House of Representatives.

With Massachusetts remaining staunchly Republican, Lodge was delighted when he learned of his reelection. The other figure who had reason to smile was James G. Blaine. Having chosen not to seek the nomination, the senator decided to focus his energies on Harrison's campaign. Following the election, the new president named the former GOP standard-bearer as his secretary of state.[61]

Lodge and Blaine's relationship had improved since the election of 1884. But the congressman had never warmed to the former presidential hopeful. One of the reasons the two men's relationship had become more congenial was Blaine's high opinion of Nannie Lodge.

The secretary, like many in Washington, was captivated by Nannie's charm and beauty but also respected her intellect and counsel. On March 19, 1889, Blaine asked the congressman's wife for advice on a candidate to serve as assistant secretary of state. "Do you happen to know a young gentleman—gentleman strongly accented . . . not over forty-five, well-educated, speaking French well, preferably German also?" Blaine inquired.[62]

The description of the position listed the requirements and salary. It further stated the appointee would have the opportunity to experience a nice office with an ideal view. Reading Blaine's missive, Nannie Lodge concluded that Theodore Roosevelt was the ideal choice.[63]

Ordinarily, Lodge would have found it humiliating to ask his former nemesis for a favor. But the congressman desperately wished to see Roosevelt back in public office. Interested in international affairs, T. R.'s education and background made him more than prepared for the opportunity.

Blaine had no interest in giving Roosevelt the position. The Maine politician had not forgotten T. R.'s behavior at the 1884 convention. The new secretary also had other concerns.

"My real trouble in regard to Mr. Roosevelt is that I fear he lacks the repose and patient endurance required in an assistant secretary of state," Blaine commented to Nannie.[64]

The former senator was also wary of the friction Roosevelt's independence could create during his occasional vacations. "I do somehow fear that my sleep at Augusta or Bar Harbor would not be quite so easy and refreshing if so brilliant and aggressive a man had hold of the helm," Blaine wrote following his meeting with Congressman Lodge.[65]

With one opportunity closed, Lodge networked with intimates of President Harrison. Despite T. R.'s political setbacks, the congressman had not lost the belief that his friend was a figure of destiny. Roosevelt appreciated Lodge's efforts in cultivating members of the new administration. "You are certainly the most loyal friend that ever breathed," T. R. wrote in March 1889.[66]

Roosevelt, however, expected little from Lodge's lobbying campaign. With a desire "above all things to go into politics," Roosevelt realized that his independent spirit for disturbing the status quo was not a quality political professionals found appealing. During the presidential campaign T. R. had remained an outspoken critic of the Republican Party. Roosevelt had favored civil service reform while also contending that the tariff policy required revision.[67]

Lodge was not deterred. Knowing that the best way to accomplish anything was to go to the top, the resourceful politician met with the new president to convince him that Roosevelt could serve as an asset to the administration. Believing more pressure was required, the congressman also requested that speaker of the house Thomas B. Reed bend Harrison's ear on Theodore's behalf.[68]

Well over six feet in stature and weighing more than three hundred pounds, the future speaker of the House of Representatives was a voracious reader whose home in Washington contained a library with thousands of books. Highly guarded and wary of the Washington press corps, Reed kept a diary of his most intimate thoughts written entirely in French. An exceptional debater, Reed's encyclopedic memory and his ability to cut his opponent to ribbons on the House floor frequently left Lodge and Roosevelt speechless.[69]

Employing his friendship with Reed, Lodge asked the congressman to use his influence with the Executive Mansion to secure Roosevelt a spot on the Civil Service Commission. Refusing to sit idle, Lodge also paid a call to President Harrison's secretary Elijah W. Halford to express his desire that Roosevelt be considered for the government position. Following a conversation between the president and his secretary, T. R. was invited for an interview. After a brief exchange, Harrison offered Roosevelt the position.[70]

Delighted, Lodge informed Roosevelt of the news at an event celebrating the centennial of George Washington's inauguration. The festivities were highlighted by a seated dinner for eight hundred dignitaries, industrialists, and other luminaries at New York's Metropolitan Opera. As the dignitaries dined on Atlantic salmon with hollandaise, sweetbreads, and filet of beef, Lodge informed his friend of the new opportunity.[71]

The congressman was uncertain if Roosevelt was willing to leave his growing family. The position was neither powerful nor lucrative. Roosevelt was unconcerned. Even with financial difficulties, he happily accepted his new role.[72]

Roosevelt and Lodge had come a long way since the disaster of 1884. The congressman's counsel, and use of his large political network, had helped Roosevelt return to the political arena. Lodge also had another reason to celebrate. After being excoriated by his own class, the Bostonian had persevered in not allowing those he viewed as self-serving amateurs to interfere with his goal of winning higher office.

The next few years saw Roosevelt and Lodge relying on their individual abilities to obtain greater political influence. During their time in the nation's capital, both men and their families developed a close relationship. As T. R. employed his role on the Civil Service Commission to root out those he believed were using their positions to abuse the public trust, Lodge offered Roosevelt a steady hand, with the intention of helping prepare his friend for greater success in the years ahead.

SIX

Climbing the Greasy Pole

"I would literally have given my right arm to make the race."

—Theodore Roosevelt

Shortly before 10:00 A.M. on May 13, 1889, Theodore Roosevelt, dressed in a Brooks Brothers suit with a pair of "gold rimmed" spectacles clinging to the bridge of his nose, dashed up the stairs of Washington's stately City Hall. Roosevelt's destination was the United States Civil Service Commission. In a sedate environment of well-manicured lawns, the small department gave the illusion of being far larger because of its high ceilings and bay windows.

"I am the new civil service commissioner, Theodore Roosevelt of New York," T. R. declared to the bemusement of the office's employees. With an overwhelming presence, President Harrison's new appointee showed his colleagues he was ready to devote his full energies to pursuing corruption in government no matter where it led.[1]

Over the last few years Roosevelt had enjoyed the writing and ranching life. However, it was politics that remained the new commissioner's true passion. In preparation for his tenure in the Federal City, Lodge had offered T. R. his rented townhouse on Connecticut Avenue. Grateful for his friend's generosity, Roosevelt intended to spend most of his time traveling on government business or spending evenings in the office.[2]

The Lodges would not abide their friend sitting home alone. Determined to make Roosevelt's time in the nation's capital enjoyable, Nannie made introductions to several couples who invited the new commissioner to dinner. During these first few months Roosevelt also became better acquainted with Henry Adams. The historian thought the new civil service commissioner was making a mistake for accepting the government oversight position. The observation reflected the commentator's deep cynicism about public service and the challenges of navigating the corruptive influences inhabiting the capital.[3]

T. R. did occasionally indulge in the clubby life that encompassed Washington society. Work, however remained his priority. In June 1890, after holding the position for barely a month, Roosevelt began making large claims about his performance. "I have made this Commission a living force," the Washington bureaucrat bragged to Lodge. These dramatic attitudes frequently caused the new commissioner to give the impression that his professional struggles were far more challenging than they were. Throughout his public career, the boisterous patrician loved to give the impression he was consistently under siege, battling against sinister forces determined to prevent him from fulfilling his mission.[4]

Early in Roosevelt's tenure, the new commissioner and his colleagues traveled around the country investigating civil service violations among the nation's political appointees. On one occasion, the commission began scrutinizing William Wallace, President Harrison's former law partner and Indiana's current postmaster. The investigators found no malfeasance implicating Wallace.[5]

But during the inquiry the agency did succeed in recommending the termination of several government employees. The findings and the resulting embarrassing publicity gave Indiana Republicans a view of Roosevelt and his fellow commissioners that was far from favorable.[6]

The new commissioner understood that investigating associates of the president would cause the administration to view him with distrust. Harrison's advisers had requested Roosevelt to apply the law "Rigidly . . . where people will stand it, and handled gingerly elsewhere." Roosevelt viewed the request as cheap favoritism and refused to abide by the Executive Mansion's request. "I am a great believer in practical politics; but when my duty is to enforce a law, that law is surely going to be enforced without fear or favor," he wrote Lodge shortly after beginning the position.[7]

As the trip through the Midwest progressed, Roosevelt became the public face of the organization. Throughout the young commissioner's travels, newspapers followed Roosevelt's every move. Editors enjoyed T. R.'s provocative statements, particularly those that criticized his fellow Republicans over the issue of patronage.[8]

State and party officials did not view these comments favorably. "It seems to me that [Roosevelt] should be given to understand that it would be well for him to have less to say to newspapers," Indiana's attorney general, Louis Michener, wrote in a note to Harrison's advisers.[9]

Writing Lodge in the first week of July 1890, Roosevelt informed the congressman he was not tone deaf to the knowledge that "for the last week my party friends in Washington have evidently felt a little shaky." Despite criticism from members of the GOP, Roosevelt's popularity with the press enhanced the commissions exposure, improving its legitimacy among the press and the public.[10]

Always concerned with unrest within Republican ranks, Congressman Lodge became uncomfortable with Roosevelt's outspoken criticism. Throughout T. R.'s career Lodge, along with Edith Roosevelt, had the difficult task of moderating Roosevelt's vocal outbursts.

It was a challenge, particularly with someone who enjoyed the sound of their own voice.[11]

Always thinking about Roosevelt's long-term political prospects, Lodge knew his friend's critical statements were unwise. In a letter to the congressman a week later, Roosevelt got the message.

"I cry peccavi and will assume a statesmanlike reserve of manner whenever reporters come near me," T. R. wrote, following a letter from the Bostonian asking him to tone down the rhetoric.[12]

During Lodge's time in Congress, the New Englander worked in conjunction with Roosevelt to press for reforms within the Civil Service Administration. Lodge found the idea of political patronage repugnant, believing it was a practice that enhanced greed and corruption. Still, for those opportunities that did not fall under the auspices of the government agency, Lodge believed it was his job to appoint honorable individuals who deserved professional opportunities.[13]

Working with his colleagues from the Bay State, Lodge made political appointments to the Charlestown Navy Yard, the Port of Boston, and other Massachusetts-based institutions. Simultaneously the congressman also lobbied the Harrison Administration to broaden the authority of the Civil Service Commission by placing those and other state positions under its purview.[14]

As Lodge enhanced his network throughout the nation's capital, he focused his energies on developing a bill allowing the federal government to oversee the integrity of congressional elections. Since representatives of a particular state were based on population, T. R. and Lodge considered it unfair that Southern Democrats were denying Black voters their right to vote under the Fourteenth and Fifteenth Amendments to the United States Constitution.[15]

The legislation known as the "Lodge Bill" was introduced on June 26, 1890. The bill provided that following a disputed election a judge was given the authority to appoint supervisors to ensure the ballots

THE ROUGH RIDER AND THE PROFESSOR

were properly calculated. If the monitors believed irregularities had occurred, the federal government assigned canvassers to arbitrate the dispute. If neither party was willing to abide by the decision, the judiciary was designated to decide the election. If the losing candidate refused to abide by the verdict, Congress was empowered with the authority to void the electoral results.[16]

Lodge's views were admirable but a political rationale also lay behind his reasoning. The congressman (as well as Roosevelt and others) felt frustrated that the Democratic Party dominated the southern part of the country. A measure to federalize congressional elections was a powerful strategy to dislodge the party's grip on that portion of the nation.[17]

Lodge raised the issue of the legislation's necessity in an articulate speech on the floor of Congress in the last week of June 1890. Most likely dressed in a tailored suit, with "pockets foppishly cut on the horizontal" and a gold watch chain dangling from his vest, the New Englander stood in the well of the House of Representatives declaring that as citizens, the United States government bore the responsibility to protect the African American right to vote.[18]

In response Democrats labeled Lodge's legislation the "Force Bill" and accused the Republican of engaging in a massive legislative overreach. Roosevelt supported Lodge's action declaring no one had the right to prevent African Americans from exercising their constitutional rights.[19]

The bill passed the House by a slim party vote. When it reached the Senate, the legislation was overwhelmed by the reality of Republican priorities. For all the party rhetoric about the importance of upholding the rights of the franchise for Black Americans, the GOP chose to focus its coalition on the party's economic program by putting its resources behind the passage of a tariff proposed by Ohio congressman William McKinley.[20]

Lodge was devastated by the bill's defeat. The congressman had done the utmost to argue for his position, with clear evidence and strong reasoning. Failure was always difficult for the politician to grasp. Rather than accepting defeat and analyzing what he could have done to improve his argument, Lodge looked with dismissiveness and contempt upon those who had opposed him.[21]

The frustration may also have emerged from Lodge's growing boredom over his duties in the House of Representatives. The position was respectable, but the size of the institution limited Lodge's ability to expand his power. Seniority was the coin of the realm and if Lodge wanted to rise, he needed to acquire a significant period of service. Having an eye on a seat in the Senate, Lodge was determined to seize it sooner rather than later.[22]

As Lodge battled for civil service reform and electoral integrity in Congress, Roosevelt discovered his position within the Civil Service Commission gave him little authority to create meaningful change. The commission investigation of the nation's Midwestern postmasters had caused outrage among party stalwarts including President Harrison's postmaster general, John Wanamaker.[23]

From the moment Harrison appointed Wanamaker to his cabinet, the businessman ordered his staff to replace the entire postal bureaucracy. When Roosevelt asked the department store magnate to slow the process, Wanamaker dismissed the request. Roosevelt alerted Harrison of his cabinet secretary's actions. "Little Ben" was uninterested.[24]

Lodge tried to calm his friend's temperament. "I am sure the President means to stand by you," Lodge wrote, following a two-hour train ride with Harrison. "You must not be impatient if he does not move as fast as you would like." Lodge's words did little to ease Roosevelt's frustrations.[25]

The commissioner loathed Wanamaker. Throughout his dealings with the nation's postmaster, Roosevelt referred to the department store magnate as "outrageously disagreeable," an "ill-conditioned creature," and "[A] hypocritical haberdasher." Harrison's refusal to offer guidance gave Roosevelt little confidence in the president's administration. "I do wish he would give us a *little* more active support," T. R. wrote Lodge. Despite cringing at every criticism Roosevelt made of the president Lodge remained unsurprised by his friend's blunt point of view.[26]

Between T. R.'s confrontations with Wanamaker, the commissioner also battled members of both parties opposed to the approval of the agency's budget. Even while experiencing disappointment, Roosevelt tried to remain optimistic. Enjoying the attention of the press as well as antagonizing many within the GOP, Roosevelt was delighted to have the job.[27]

During that same period Edith Roosevelt arrived in Washington. Having given birth to the couple's second child, Kermit, in October 1889, Roosevelt was delighted to be reunited with his family. The commissioner introduced his wife to capitol society by escorting her to a New Year's Day reception with President Harrison in the Blue Room of the Executive Mansion.[28]

While Edith appreciated the event, she hoped her stabilizing influence might provide her husband emotional relief. Even with his wife by his side Roosevelt was unable to relax. In addition to the pressures of his civil service duties, Roosevelt also had an expanding family to consider. In need of additional money T. R. supplemented his income by researching and writing a narrative on the history of New York State.[29]

Despite financial limitations the Roosevelts enjoyed the city's social season as the nation entered 1890. One of Edith's favorite occasions was dining with Henry Adams. A seat at the historian's table in his exquisite townhouse on Lafayette Square was one of society's most sought-after invitations. Overlooking the president's residence,

Adams's home was filled with an enormous variety of books and works of art. During these occasions T. R. and Edith enjoyed the company of John and Clara Hay. The couple were frequent visitors and lived in an identical home next to Adams on an adjoining piece of property. [30]

Roosevelt initially thought Hay was an entertaining figure. When T. R. realized the former diplomat was not enamored by his encyclopedic intellect, Roosevelt changed his opinion by characterizing Hay as condescending and long-winded. The journalist respected Roosevelt's intelligence and scholarship but found his habit of dominating a conversation boorish and egotistical. [31]

Mingling with Elizabeth and Donald Cameron, the couple thought Lizzie a pleasant personality, unaware of the senator's wife's unique ability of "liking people on the surface while despising them underneath." The point was illustrated by Lizzie's backbiting comments about Edith having too many children while being married to a man of limited means. [32]

For all his personal enjoyment, Roosevelt remained frustrated over what he believed was a lack of progress in his professional role. When T. R. accepted the government oversight opportunity, he believed his commitment would allow him to use the role as a stepping stone to higher office. But many Washington insiders including Lodge had warned Roosevelt the commission was a position of limited authority as well as being an office that offered little future opportunity. [33]

As time went on T. R.'s hope of upward progress began to wane. Growing disillusioned with Harrison, Roosevelt lashed out at the president, describing him in letters to Lodge as "narrow minded," "obstinate," and "a little gray cold blooded toad." As the summer heat consumed Washington the commissioner looked forward to exchanging the humidity of the nation's capital for the more pleasant climate of his ranch near Medora. [34]

In September 1890 following a brief stop in Dakota, the Roosevelts with Bamie, Corinne, and her husband Douglas Robinson
traveled to Yellowstone National Park. Accompanying the family was
the Lodges' sixteen-year-old son, "Bay." Raised among some of the
most prominent intellectuals of the period, the young man was nur-
tured by such figures as Henry Adams and William Sturgis Bigelow,
who tutored the boy in art, literature, and history.[35]

Unlike his father the younger Lodge did not possess the New Englander's singlemindedness and ambition. "His tendency is to neglect
study," Lodge said of Bay in a letter to Anna Lodge. Concerned about
the boy's direction, the Lodges decided to allow their son to delay his
freshman year at Harvard to travel on the excursion to Yellowstone.[36]

The trip proved challenging. Inclement weather made the conditions muddy and difficult. Bay found the travel invigorating.
However, Roosevelt believed the rigorous hikes overwhelmed the
young man and throughout the journey he worried about Lodge's
son's health.[37]

Following the trip, the younger Lodge and Roosevelt began corresponding. After concluding a disastrous freshman year at Harvard
which resulted in the young man being placed on academic probation,
T. R. encouraged Lodge's son to keep his spirits up. "I went through
practically the same experience myself," Roosevelt wrote Bay.[38]

Roosevelt was never in any danger of faltering academically. Bay,
however, came from a family that had high expectations for their son's
success. Knowing the pressure Bay experienced, Roosevelt embel-
lished his academic performance, to provide him some comfort and
reassurance.[39]

Bay's scholastic improvements were not enough to prevent his
father's discouragement. When his son was again placed on academic probation, the congressman was devastated. "I do not know
what to make of [Bay]," Lodge wrote Henry Adams. Despite the

son possessing intelligence and ability, one of Lodge's biographers concludes that he was intimidated by the congressman's accomplishments. "I sometimes wish I did not have such a bright father because I am expected to do so much better than I am able," Bay lamented to Nannie Lodge.[40]

A poor performance at Harvard had not prevented Bay from showing an aptitude for literature. Following graduation, the young man focused his energies on becoming a successful essayist and poet. Believing Bay possessed genuine literary talent, T. R. decided to help him succeed.[41]

Roosevelt acted as his young friend's patron. Using his vast array of contacts at *Harper's Magazine*, the *Atlantic Monthly*, and other publications, T. R. did his utmost to help Bay obtain publishing opportunities. Lodge's best biographer, John Garraty, argues that the congressman and his powerful friends did the young man a disservice. Bay Lodge had progressed since his days as an undisciplined Harvard undergraduate, but he possessed little talent to become one of the great poets of the day. Relying on Roosevelt and others to call in favors from their friends gave the young man the false impression that his work had significant merit.[42]

Remaining frustrated over his son's future, the congressman also lamented the failure of the federal election bill. On the positive side, even with the bill's disappointing results, the controversial nature of the legislation raised Lodge's profile. In 1890, a combination of name recognition, strong canvassing and meticulous organizational skills allowed Lodge to secure a third term in the House of Representatives. Lodge's victory was a small patch of sunlight in an otherwise gloomy election for the GOP.[43]

Putting their majority behind the McKinley tariff, the Republicans framed their support of the issue as improving wages for the American worker. Democrats accused Republicans of being more focused on enhancing the profits of big business than on concern for the average citizen. On election day, voters unhappy with the nation's rising inflation returned the Democrats to the majority in the House of Representatives.[44]

Lodge's increasing anger over the challenging political environment for the Republican Party made life increasingly difficult for his wife. Other than her busy social schedule and serving as Henry Adams's escort to events at the Executive Mansion, Nannie began finding pleasant distraction in the company of John Hay. At five foot eight, Hay radiated charisma. Always perfectly dressed, with wavy brown hair, dark eyes, and a well-manicured beard displaying wisps of gray, the former diplomat and newspaperman was a lover of conversation, art, and a "master in the science of human relationships."[45]

From the moment Henry Adams introduced Hay to Nannie Lodge, the author was captivated by the congressman's beautiful and engaging wife. As the diplomat and his former colleague, John G. Nicolay, progressed on their ten-volume biography of Abraham Lincoln, Hay's mind harkened back to the woman with blue eyes and a beautifully sculpted neck. Vivacious, glamorous, a superb piano player, and a witty conversationalist, Nannie was everything the plump and introverted Clara Hay was not.[46]

A marvelous raconteur who had traveled extensively and spoke four languages, Hay relished entertaining the political elite of Washington. Renowned for hosting dinners at his large redbrick three-story home, with its high gold leafed ceilings and stained glass windows, the former under secretary of state was celebrated for serving the finest food and wine to the most stylish men and women in the capital.[47]

Known for having expensive tastes, Hay had a restless nature and a wandering eye. Over the course of seventeen years of marriage, the man who so loved good times had grown frustrated with his wife's serious demeanor and increasing weight. Even when Hay attempted to placate Clara with a trip to an exciting destination, his bride's attitude remained unchanged.[48]

In the spring of 1890, while romancing Lizzie Cameron, Hay began focusing his attentions on Nannie Lodge. As her husband grew absorbed with his reelection campaign, Nannie and Hay began enjoying one another's company. Under the auspices of Lizzie Cameron and Henry Adams the two were rarely alone. While Hay and Nannie enjoyed many evenings together, the secretary of state's biographer John Taliaferro reached no conclusion on how intimate the relationship became.[49]

Washington society seemed oblivious to Nannie and Hay's liaison. The situation was different in Clara Hay's hometown of Cleveland, Ohio. On one occasion when traveling to the Cleveland suburb of Mansfield, Lizzie found that the gossip about the couple was all the rage. "I hate to hear it here in Mrs. Hay's home," Lizzie wrote Adams while paying a visit to her family in the Ohio suburbs.[50]

Throughout 1890, Hay escorted Nannie to museums and invited her to intimate recitals at his home. Dining together frequently in the company of Adams and Cameron, the two also continued their romance outside the Federal City. "Nanny and Cabot go to New York on the 10th. It is rather a coincidence that Mr. Hay must start on the same day," Lizzie slyly observed in a letter to Adams.[51]

Upon hearing that the Lodges intended to extend their stay to view the New York Horse Show, Hay decided to continue his visit as well. It was an interesting coincidence. As historian Patricia O'Toole comments, while Lodge adored horses and was an avid rider, Hay had never shown any affinity for the subject.[52]

Hay also managed to spend time with Nannie in Boston and at the Lodge home on Nahant. Bundling his wife and family off to New Hampshire's Lake Sunapee, the diplomat, with Lizzie Cameron in tow, traveled to the New England seashore. "John and Nannie got a little walk together but, on the whole behaved extremely well," Lizzie wrote gleefully while Adams was traveling to Hawaii with artist John La Farge.[53]

The attention from Hay and her position of prominence as the wife of one of Washington's rising stars should have filled Nannie with joy. But Nannie Lodge possessed an insecurity few realized. Beneath her confident and elegant exterior, Henry Cabot Lodge's wife was not only jealous of Lizzie Cameron but also wary of the other "bright young things" that roamed the salons of Washington. Many had the perception of the Lodges as one of the most social and outgoing couples in the capital. Both, however, were highly private, and preferred the company of intimate friends to the large and lavish dinner parties and receptions they frequently attended.[54]

As with so many other aspects of Hay's life, his interest in Nannie soon began to fade. There is little doubt that the diplomat found Lodge's wife engaging company, but it was Lizzie Cameron who remained Hay's obsession. Even with his attraction to Lizzie, Hay remained devoted to his wife and children. His ambitious personage would never jeopardize the familial or social position he had so carefully built with a marital scandal that had the potential to destroy it all.[55]

In spring 1891, with their relationship at an end, Nannie Lodge turned her attentions to her family. There is no doubt Lodge was a difficult man. But the congressman worshipped his wife and adored their children. Nannie Lodge also enjoyed being the wife of a rising politician and the prestige that came with it.[56]

When Roosevelt met with Lodge in January 1890 Cabot remained in a surly mood over the defeat of his election bill. The congressman was in such poor temper he even refused T. R.'s request to consider speaking at an event for Roosevelt's good friend, the journalist James Brander Matthews. Lodge remained so furious about the issue the idea of even discussing any subject touching on elections or the South put him in a disagreeable frame of mind.[57]

Roosevelt was unhappy as well, due to his struggles at the Civil Service Commission. With his career at a standstill, T. R. focused his energies on investigating officials he believed responsible for violating their oath of office. For all of Roosevelt's commitment to help the federal government improve transparency the commissioner believed his efforts made little impact.[58]

Concerned with his professional and financial future, T. R. became even more distracted following ongoing difficulties with his brother, Elliott. Once seen as a person of great promise, Elliott Roosevelt's drinking, opioid use, and womanizing had caused his family increasing embarrassment. When Elliott married the beautiful but emotionally fragile Anna Hall in 1883, T. R. and his sisters hoped the responsibility of a new family would cause their brother to reassess his priorities.[59]

Sadly, even with a new wife and children, Elliott's behavior grew more erratic. In 1890 the family became embroiled in scandal when one of Elliott's maids brought a paternity suit claiming he had fathered her illegitimate child.[60]

The situation filled Roosevelt with anxiety. As Elliott's use of alcohol worsened, he grew increasingly unstable. Unpredictable mood swings and emotional outbursts caused Bamie and Corrine to fear for Elliott's wife's safety. "I literally do not know what depths of horror may not be before him—and us," Roosevelt concluded in a cryptic letter to Lodge, in late summer 1891.[61]

Roosevelt also remained worried that Harrison had tired of his commissioner's excessive complaining over a lack of moral support.

Writing Lodge in October to congratulate him on the engagement of his daughter Constance to wealthy polo player, Augustus Peabody Gardner, Roosevelt unburdened himself to his friend about the troubles plaguing him professionally and personally. "The horror about poor Elliott makes me all the less able to take with equanimity the irritating uncertainty as to my tenure and positions under the administration," Roosevelt wrote.[62]

As Harrison prepared to campaign against former president Grover Cleveland in the upcoming 1892 election, Lodge positioned himself for the opportunity to become the next senator from Massachusetts. Shortly after being reelected to the House of Representatives, Lodge had made his aspirations known in a note to a local newspaper editor. The congressman made clear that "if all goes well between now and then" he expected to run for the seat being vacated by the retiring senator, Henry L. Dawes.[63]

In the months leading up to the election, Massachusetts politicians approached Lodge about running for governor. Roosevelt encouraged the congressman to focus on the Senate. The commissioner advised his friend to inform key personnel of his future political plans. Unbeknownst to Roosevelt, Lodge and his allies already had a stranglehold on the party nomination.[64]

To increase his chances of victory, Lodge presided over the Massachusetts state convention. The senatorial hopeful may have had differences with President Harrison, but the ambitious Bostonian was not going to allow his opinion of the commander in chief's performance to interfere with his drive for greater political influence. Roosevelt was pleased with Lodge's progress and encouraged his friend to continue his campaign for the party nomination.[65]

Lodge's campaign coincided with the presidential race of 1892. Following the loss by the GOP of the House of Representatives two years earlier, Harrison remained an unpopular figure. Hoping to prevent the incumbent from being nominated, Republicans planned to name James Blaine as the party's standard-bearer. Pleased with his position as secretary of state, Blaine refused his party's draft, leaving Harrison as the only viable choice. While the president carried the nomination, delegates left the convention in Minneapolis angry and divided as the nation headed into the fall campaign.[66]

The Republican insiders' view of the president also reflected the opinion of the nation at large. A cold, reserved figure, overwhelmed with worry over the condition of his beloved wife, who was ill with tuberculosis, Harrison put little effort into the race. On November 3 Grover Cleveland became the first president to achieve two nonconsecutive terms.[67]

Roosevelt was indifferent following Cleveland's defeat of Harrison. Not surprised by the Republican's loss of the presidency, T. R. was more concerned with the strong performance of populist candidate James Weaver, who received more than a million votes. The former congressman's strong showing illustrated that the public's anger over the issue of income inequality was not only resonating in the West but gaining momentum throughout the nation.[68]

With the Democrats regaining control of all three branches of government, the Massachusetts legislature had remained in the hands of the GOP. When the state held its caucus to decide the next senator, the speaker of the Massachusetts State Senate declared Lodge the winner 147–130. Being elected to the United States Senate was an enormous victory. Without a dynamic nature or the oratorical talents of a natural politician, Lodge, at age forty-three, had used his grit and persistence to persevere in the hardscrabble world of Massachusetts politics.[69]

Even with the Republican Party's loss of the presidency, Lodge's political organization and acumen had allowed the pragmatic former academic to prosper, while Roosevelt's career appeared at a standstill.

"Poor Cabot *must* be successful, while Teddy is happiest when he conquers but quite happy if he only fights," Cecil Spring Rice wrote Lizzie Cameron in an accurate depiction of the two men.[70]

As the Lodges celebrated, Roosevelt reached out to prominent Republican liberal Carl Schurz. With money tight and no opportunity awaiting him in New York, Roosevelt requested that the prominent liberal ask the president about T. R. remaining with the Civil Service Commission. Following a brief meeting in April 1893, Cleveland asked Roosevelt to continue in his position.[71]

Roosevelt hoped the new president's offer to extend his tenure might signal an interest in making civil service reform a priority. Sadly, little changed. Favoritism and patronage dominated the political landscape. Struggling professionally, and with Elliott descending deeper into paranoia, Roosevelt grew more despondent.[72]

On August 14, 1894, Elliott Roosevelt's life of pain and unrealized potential came to an abrupt end. Following an attempt to jump from his apartment window, Theodore's brother collapsed and died of a sudden and violent seizure. The loss left his older brother heartbroken. "It was far the better that the end should come," Roosevelt wrote Lodge following Elliott's passing. For all T. R.'s bravado, he was not shy to admit the pain he felt following the passing of his once beloved sibling. "I confess I felt more broken than I had thought," Roosevelt wrote to the senator.[73]

Following Elliott's death, Roosevelt's financial life, always an issue of concern, experienced a tragic blow. In May 1893 the nation's banks, over-leveraged due to excessive borrowing by businessmen hoping to capitalize on the burgeoning railroad industry, led to the collapse of the New York Stock Exchange. Known as the Panic of 1893, 360 banks located throughout the Midwest and the South were forced to close. Steel plants and other businesses shuttered their doors, leaving nearly 25 percent of the nation unemployed.[74]

Roosevelt's investments, which had suffered enormously when his cattle ranch was crippled by the severe winter of 1886–1887, incurred even greater losses. Analyzing their investment portfolio, the Roosevelts realized the economic downturn had resulted in the loss of millions of dollars. The sale of some property near the family home in Oyster Bay replenished a portion of those funds, but with the two significant financial misfortunes the family's finances were in a precarious condition.[75]

Roosevelt lamented his inability to care for his burgeoning family. Lodge, always a reliable friend, had invited T. R. to stay with him when Edith returned to Sagamore Hill. With frustration in his personal and his professional life the commissioner more than appreciated the companionship.[76]

At the time of the financial crisis Lodge was renovating his new home in Washington at 1765 Massachusetts Avenue. A large portion of the senator's income came from stock in General Electric. When the stock exchange collapsed the company suspended dividends, money necessary for Lodge to complete the construction. The additions included a spacious library as well as a series of stables that allowed Lodge to indulge in his love of riding. The senator's housing problems were only temporary. Anna Lodge happily gave her son $50,000 to complete the family's new residence.[77]

Henry Adams, returning to the United States that July, could not help but gloat over his former pupil's misfortune. From his stateroom aboard the Cunard Line's RMS *Umbria*, with its "bad food and impossible neighbors," the commentator was only too happy to spread the word of Lodge's financial difficulties. "[T]he failure-impending-of the General Electric Company . . . will smash Boston flat, and I fear will stop Cabot Lodge's little building plans," Adams happily wrote Lizzie Cameron.[78]

The Adams family was not spared from the financial turmoil. Days before departing on the transatlantic crossing, Adams received a letter from his brother, Charles Francis, alerting him to the frightful news of the family's trust being severely impacted by the collapse. To make matters worse, Adams's elder brother John, who oversaw the Adams assets had grown so agitated he suffered a nervous breakdown.[79]

In the summer of 1894, as T. R. grinded away at his job with the commission, he was approached by an old friend Lemuel Quigg about running again for mayor of New York. The elegantly dressed former journalist and political operative was looking for a popular Republican reformer to lead the city's fusion ticket. Quigg thought Roosevelt the ideal candidate.[80]

Edith was opposed to her husband jumping into another political campaign. Understanding his wife's concern over their precarious financial situation, Roosevelt declined the opportunity. Following a brief visit to Medora, T. R. remained bitter over his lost opportunity. "I would literally have given my right arm to have made the race, win or lose. It was the one golden chance which never returns," he wrote Lodge. Knowing he couldn't risk his family's future for his own political gain, Roosevelt remained in Washington.[81]

In November, the new mayor of New York, Republican William F. Strong, contacted Roosevelt about a position as commissioner of street cleaning. For all of T. R.'s interests in finding a fresh opportunity, removing trash and refuse from the city's streets did not fill him with excitement. In addition, Lodge told him not to take the position. "Cabot has felt that I was a brand snatched from the burning, in the street cleaning matter, and has kept a close eye on all my movements," Roosevelt told Bamie. From his new seat in the Senate, Lodge encouraged the commissioner to forgo local politics and focus his energies on becoming involved in the 1896 campaign.[82]

Lodge more than anyone understood Roosevelt's drive to remain relevant. For the moment, few options existed. Always fascinated by the greatness of the American experience, the two authored a book for boys highlighting some of their favorite historical figures and moments from the nation's past. Published in the spring of 1895, *Hero Tales from American History* contained twenty-six essays, which included vignettes on Daniel Boone, George Washington, and the Battle of New Orleans.[83]

While satisfying, the book was not enough to fulfill Roosevelt's boundless desire for activity. As the year continued, the commissioner grew agitated and argumentative. Having turned down the street cleaning opportunity, T. R. remained interested in becoming a part of the mayor's administration. At the same time, the delicate condition of his family's finances made Roosevelt apprehensive about taking a position below his current salary.[84]

Strong may have thought Roosevelt ideal for the street cleaning opportunity. Edith disagreed. Seeking Lodge's advice, T. R.'s wife inquired about a potential role as one of three police commissioners in the new administration. Unbeknownst to Roosevelt the senator headed to New York to investigate the matter.[85]

In March 1895, following Lodge's conversations with Mayor Strong, T. R. was surprised to receive a letter from Quigg about an opportunity as a member of the New York City Police Board. While interested, Roosevelt remained uncertain. "A year hence I would like to take an active part in the presidential campaign, and I could not well do that as Police Commissioner," Roosevelt wrote the Congressman.[86]

Roosevelt asked Lodge to address the issue with Strong's team. "[Y]ou feel as much as I do, the arguments for and against my being Police Commissioner," Roosevelt wrote on April 3. "You are on the ground and do talk it over with Douglas [Robinson, T. R.'s brother-in-law] and the Mayor; it is an important thing for me and if I ought to take it I must do so soon. It is very puzzling." Following his communication, Roosevelt grew impatient. Less than twenty-four hours later, he informed Quigg that Lodge was prepared to discuss final arrangements about the position.[87]

By the mid-1890s, Henry Cabot Lodge had used his guile and organizational ability to become the most powerful personality in Massachusetts politics. The senator also continued to guide Roosevelt with the goal of helping him achieve greater professional success. Despite T. R. suffering turmoil within his personal life and uncertainty in his career, he believed political administration was the occupation he enjoyed more than any other. At age thirty-three, T. R. was still looking for a position on which to exert his full energies and ambitions. As he prepared to depart Washington for New York, Roosevelt hoped the new opportunity with the Police Board was the one that would finally allow him to make his mark.

SEVEN
Forging an Agenda

"Oh, how glad I am to be an American!"

—Henry Cabot Lodge

several months after the collapse of the nation's economy in August 1893, Henry Cabot Lodge arrived in the United States Senate. As many citizens remained uncertain about their financial future, the junior senator from Massachusetts's investments remained secure. With most of the funds under the control of his mother, in addition to his $5,000 annual salary, Lodge expanded his writing commitments to gain even greater economic freedom. "I not only write pot boilers but would gladly write more, for I am having hard sledding in these times," Lodge complained to Anna Lodge.[1]

Thrilled to work in the same room as his heroes Cabot and Sumner, Lodge focused on his new role with energy and discipline. Working late into the night in his large library, the senator walked the floor until two or three o'clock in the morning revising remarks for his latest speech. A great instability existed in the country. With a Democrat occupying the presidency Lodge realized solutions to revive the nation's economy would not be easy.[2]

The gentleman from Massachusetts was viewed by his colleagues as "the most scholarly man in the Senate." But Senator Joseph Foraker of Ohio thought Lodge's attitude "was too scholarly . . . for personal comfort." At times Lodge's condescending and aloof personality grated on his fellow legislators.[3]

Always meticulously prepared, Lodge took his role of representing his state very seriously. Others within the legislative body were not so diligent. "Bad grammar, whether spoken or written, always annoyed him . . . A split infinitive gave him positive pain, no matter who split it," the Ohio Republican recalled in his memoir.[4]

One of the first issues Lodge faced was the question of repealing the Sherman Silver Purchase Act. In 1890 as part of the GOP compromise to win passage of the McKinley tariff, President Benjamin Harrison arranged for the US Treasury to purchase over four million ounces of silver a month. The gesture was made to appease congressmen from the western states, who wanted to make it less complicated for their constituents to borrow funds from banks.[5]

The shift in monetary policy unnerved international investors. Concerned about the devaluation of the dollar, financiers in Europe sold off large quantities of American currency. These transactions along with several other factors caused the nation's gold supply to plunge, resulting in the implosion of the nation's financial system. As the crisis deepened, J. P. Morgan and other prominent men on Wall Street called for Congress to repeal the silver legislation.[6]

Lodge had unhappily supported the Sherman Act while a member of the House of Representatives. As silver fell out of favor with European governments, the senator realized his decision to vote in favor of the legislation was a mistake. "I will not again, if I can possibly avoid it, vote for any compromises with free silver," Lodge commented to a friend.[7]

Following Cleveland's special message calling for the repeal of the Silver Act in August 1893, Lodge decided to support the president's position. It was one of the few occasions in Lodge's thirty-six-year congressional career when he favored legislation advocated by the opposition party.[8]

Lodge also addressed another domestic issue: immigration. On February 19, 1891, then-Congressman Lodge had expressed concern about the large numbers of Eastern Europeans flooding American shores. "We are certainly in no present danger of being overcrowded by desirable immigrants, but we are at this moment overcrowded with undesirable immigrants," Lodge stated on the chamber floor. In a detailed reading of the American founding, the former academic concluded "it is on the moral qualities of the English-speaking race that our history, our victories, and all our future rest." Lodge understood that a nation based on principles of individual freedom and personal liberty would attract those from other nations.[9]

The New Englander also believed, however, those permitted to emigrate should descend from societies whose fundamental ideas and customs were associated with the American tradition. While a portion of Lodge's reasoning for immigration restriction was based on lineage, an important political element was also responsible for the senator's motivation.[10]

Throughout the first half of the nineteenth century, the tariff remained responsible for Republicans maintaining the favor of working-class voters. By the late 1880s the presence of immigrant contract workers in the railroad and mining industries created considerable resentment on the part of American workers. In a poll taken by the Wisconsin Bureau of Labor between 1887–1888, 60 percent of native-born Americans stated immigrant labor was responsible for diminishing their wages and employment opportunities.[11]

Developing a strategy to protect the job security of the American worker in 1895, Lodge proposed a bill banning those immigrants unable to read or write from entering the United States. The senator believed a literacy test would appeal to those voters tired of competing with immigrants for jobs. The legislation also favored members of the middle class, who viewed many immigrants from eastern and southern Europe as burdens to the nation's resources due to their inability to contribute to the economic growth of the country.[12]

Lodge emphasized that his legislation helped the workers of Massachusetts as well as the rest of the nation. In addition, the senator believed restricting illiterate persons from invading the nation's shores prevented the country from descending into economic and moral chaos. "Dangerous and undesirable immigration is certain to affect . . . the quality of our citizenship and I know that it will injure the wages of our workingmen," Lodge declared as he campaigned for the Senate in 1892.[13]

Despite narrowly passing the Congress on March 2, 1897, the president vetoed the Immigration Literacy Test. President Cleveland believed that excluding someone because of illiteracy was not an accurate measurement of determining if they had the capacity to be a productive member of the nation.[14]

Lodge was surprised by the president's decision. "The veto did no harm to us politically nor to me personally," Lodge commented to Roosevelt. "I was disappointed because I wanted this great piece of useful legislation upon the statute books." If the immigration bill's defeat discouraged the senator, he had little to worry about. An astute politician, Lodge realized the political climate regarding the issue had begun to shift in his favor.[15]

In New York, Roosevelt immersed himself in his role on the Police Commission. Ensconced in his headquarters at 300 Mulberry Street in Lower Manhattan the new commissioner devoted forty hours a week to his new role. "I have had more work on my hands than you can imagine," Roosevelt wrote Lodge in the middle of May 1895.[16]

Fascinated with his new opportunity, Roosevelt refused to lose sight of his goal for a career in national politics. "So that in a couple of years or less," he informed Lodge, "I shall have finished the work here . . . I shall then be quite ready to take up a new job, if I think I can do it better, or can accomplish more in it." As Roosevelt alerted the senator of his plans, the new commissioner faced the dilemma of reforming one of the most dysfunctional and corrupt police departments in the nation.[17]

Roosevelt had no illusions about the challenges ahead. Being chairman of the Police Board was a title in name only. The 1895 state Bipartisan Police Act gave T. R. no additional authority over his other three colleagues. "I have got to move against the scandals in this Department, if my work is to be at all thorough, but my hands have been tied in a large measure, thanks to the action of the legislature," T. R. wrote Lodge that spring.[18]

The new commissioner used what power he had to reform the department. Applying the same enthusiasm he exercised during his days as a civil service commissioner, Roosevelt began cracking down on the corruption and dysfunction plaguing the police force. During his tenure the commissioner awarded medals for courageous behavior, created an elite bicycle patrol squad, and enforced codes for proficiency with firearms. [19]

When Roosevelt was not improving the internal working of the police department, he and his old friend, journalist Jacob Riis, walked the streets of lower Manhattan in search of vice and other examples of illegality. Riis was the author of the groundbreaking book, *How the Other Half Lives*. The narrative highlighted conditions of poverty endured by countless numbers of the city's downtrodden. Emerging late in the evening, wrapped in a black cloak, and accompanied by several journalists, Roosevelt patrolled some of Lower Manhattan's most decrepit tenements. The commissioner found it incomprehensible that so many immigrants lived in such squalor, with no apparent possibility of a better future.[20]

Happy to try to cleanse the city of immoral activity, in June 1895 Roosevelt was ordered to enforce a thirty-eight-year-old regulation prohibiting saloons from opening on Sundays. The commissioner disagreed with the statute. Many of the city's occupants were of European descent and viewed drinking as a natural part of their heritage, an argument Roosevelt agreed with.[21]

The commissioner was unsurprised by the negative response to the law. Attacked by the city's German press over the issue, an unhappy T. R. told Lodge he planned to do his duty. Even with the city in the control of a Republican mayor, the enforcement campaign left Roosevelt open to criticism from the local GOP leadership. New York City's large German population traditionally voted Republican. Watching the group's growing alienation over the law caused many to blame Roosevelt for jeopardizing an important constituency.[22]

Enduring the attacks from the press and other opponents with his usual fighting spirit, Roosevelt enjoyed his role on the police commission. Writing Lodge in July 1895 as the senator and his family vacationed in London, Roosevelt kidded his friend about each other's activities. "While you are engaged in a round of reckless dissipation with the English aristocracy, I intend . . . to inflict on you accounts of the work we hot and groveling practical politicians of the baser sort are doing as our summer work in New York." Lodge, also traveling with Cecil Spring Rice and Henry Adams, was delighted to hear how Roosevelt was adjusting to his new challenge.[23]

Perusing the London papers, the senator noted his friend's actions as police commissioner had generated extensive publicity. "In the *Morning Post* . . . the other day was a column and a half from another correspondent, an Englishman, all about the Police . . . So you see your fame spreads far." Reading of Roosevelt's activities, Lodge had no doubt his friend's actions would enhance his future career prospects.[24]

Roosevelt viewed his role on the commission as more than just personal advancement. Always the moralist, the commissioner recalled his father employing his powerful personality to preach to impoverished newspaper boys the merits of eliminating corruptive influences from their daily lives. Roosevelt aspired to use his role in law enforcement with the objective of achieving societal reform on a much broader scale.[25]

As T. R. spent his days locked in his office on Mulberry Street and his nights prowling the city's lower regions, he remained envious of Lodge's adventures in London. With Henry Adams shaking his bald head as his traveling companions entertained themselves by "flopping on royalty and following the servile steps of the heathen," Lodge also spent several days meeting the elite figures in British politics and foreign affairs. Since the days of the senator's boyhood watching the great ships depart from the port of Boston, the senator never lost his fascination with what lay beyond the oceans of North America.[26]

Lodge was delighted that so many viewed the United States as a burgeoning influence on the world stage. "The thing that has most impressed me here," he wrote Roosevelt that July, "is the growth of the United States—you feel it here better than at home—and oh, how glad I am to be an American!" During conversations with British politicians Lodge concluded the United States' burgeoning economy needed to walk hand in hand with what he believed was the nation's expansionist tradition.[27]

For the country to become a leading international power, Lodge contended it was necessary to update its maritime fleet. The senator's thoughts gained greater clarity following his reading of Captain

Alfred T. Mahan's 1890 analysis, *The Influence of Sea Power Upon History 1660–1783*.[28]

Studying Mahan's positions, Lodge realized he was reading one of the great books on naval strategy. The two historians shared several interests. Both men had admired the stories of James Fenimore Cooper and other tales of adventure. More important, each adored the sea and found themselves fascinated by the influence it held in enhancing a nation's military power.[29]

In the first months of 1895, Lodge employed Mahan's arguments to condemn President Cleveland's "miserable and grotesque" management of American foreign affairs. The commentaries emerged following Cleveland's decision to cancel the planned annexation of Hawaii by the United States. Lodge and other imperialists believed the president's pronouncements jeopardized the nation's access to the Pacific. The senator further accused Cleveland of undermining the nation's strength in the region following an order withdrawing naval vessels from Hawaii's perimeter.[30]

In Lodge's view, the acquisition of the islands allowed the United States to increase its international commercial interests. By not acquiring Hawaii, Lodge believed Cleveland had missed the opportunity to gain advantage over European nations seeking an upper hand in the Pacific. In addition to favoring the acquisition of the islands, the senator touted the idea of Washington spreading its influence into the Southern Hemisphere. Lodge's strategy, known in political circles as the "Large Policy," began with the United States obtaining control of the island of Cuba and culminated with connecting the Atlantic and Pacific oceans in the construction of a canal across the isthmus of Central America.[31]

The senator believed the individuals and ideas responsible for the creation of the United States were exceptional in nature. In that respect, those who had inherited the American tradition of republican government had a responsibility to serve as an example for the rest of the world. Lodge concluded that if Washington could spread these principles of liberty and personal freedom to less sophisticated nations, the world could become a more stable and harmonious place.[32]

The senator believed the other issue that ruled foreign policy was the issue of self-interest. France, Great Britain, and Spain were global superpowers that had managed to enhance their empires through the creation of a sizeable navy. At the same time, those countries used their military power to deter other nations from interfering in their affairs. "The great nations are absorbing for their future expansion and their present defense . . . As one of the great nations of the world, the United States must not fall out of the line of march," Lodge wrote in the Forum during the spring of 1895.[33]

While Lodge enjoyed Mahan's analysis, Roosevelt devoured it. Writing to the navy man in 1890, the police commissioner praised the author for his analysis and foresight. Roosevelt's comments were not the first correspondence with Mahan. Three years earlier, the strategist had invited T. R. to lecture at the Naval War College on his analysis of the War of 1812. The men had remained in touch and following publication of Mahan's narrative, Theodore promoted his friend's treatise to everyone he knew.[34]

T. R. shared Lodge's belief that those Western Europeans who had settled the United States were men of vision and character. As T. R. developed his multivolume history, The Winning of the West, the author argued that boundless expansion was the dominant theme that had shaped the American experience.[35]

While Roosevelt was outraged over Cleveland's foreign policy, matters in New York required his attention. Forced to endure criticism over his campaign to enforce the Sunday shutdown of the city saloons, Republicans in the Empire State grew increasingly upset about the political fate of their party.[36]

As the November elections approached, Mayor William Strong and other New York Republicans distanced themselves from Roosevelt's enforcement of the legislation. Those included Lemuel Quigg who had played an instrumental role in helping Roosevelt gain his position on the police board. With political boss Thomas Platt and other city politicians growing increasingly concerned, Quigg tore into Roosevelt, accusing his friend of an utter lack of gratitude. The criticism failed to impress the police commissioner, with T. R. dismissing Quigg's comments as an example of men more concerned with their political future than upholding the letter of the law.[37]

Lodge continued to stand with Roosevelt as he monitored his friend's predicament in New York. "I do not see that any course can be pursued at present except the one you are following," the senator commented to his friend in February 1896. Roosevelt appreciated Lodge's optimistic response but remained concerned that a potential landslide by Tammany Hall in the upcoming city elections could damage his reputation with New York voters.[38]

Realizing the political winds had turned against Roosevelt, the senator understood politics was a profession requiring perseverance and grit. But Lodge also understood the trials his friend was experiencing. "I am glad that I have known you long and loved you well," Lodge wrote affectionately in February 1896.[39]

Lodge also realized that Roosevelt's refusal to follow the instruction of the party leadership was problematic. Despite the commissioner's popularity with the public many within the GOP believed Roosevelt was not reliable when pragmatic choices were required. The situation was made worse by Roosevelt's frequent appearances in the press. Lodge advised T. R. to stay out of the headlines and only use formal speaking opportunities to comment on local or national issues. While a prudent suggestion, T. R.'s addiction to the limelight made it challenging to follow his friend's advice.[40]

As he encountered one difficulty after another many worried that reforming the department was taking a toll on Roosevelt's health. A figure of endless energy, the commissioner appeared "worn and tired." Lodge and T. R.'s mutual friend William Sturgis Bigelow speculated that the commissioner was on the cusp of a nervous collapse. "It is only a question of time when he has a breakdown, and when he does it will be a bad one." Lodge did not disagree.[41]

Confiding to Bamie, Lodge commented that "I am anxious about him, not from physical but from mental signs." Edith worried most of all. Since her husband had been put in charge of the Police Board, conditions had improved. But the bureaucratic infighting that made these changes possible left her husband more agitated than ever before.[42]

The achievements did nothing to lessen Roosevelt's depression. Concerned about his friend's mental state, the senator encouraged Roosevelt to consider future opportunities. "You have won a following, a big one . . . You only need to use these advantages politically . . . [Y]ou can force the machine to give you what you want," Lodge wrote from Paris in the fall of 1895.[43]

Lodge's comments about Roosevelt's growing political power proved premature. In September 1895, during New York State's Republican convention, the GOP hierarchy did everything it could to distance itself from the committed reformer.[44]

Roosevelt believed Thomas C. Platt, the powerful head of the state Republican machine, was attempting to damage his political viability for higher office. Labeled the "Easy Boss," Platt's courtly attitude and stooped arthritic appearance belied a figure who ruled the party with an iron hand. T. R. complained to Lodge that the boss's influence was so pervasive it had prevented him being selected as a delegate to the 1896 national convention in St. Louis, Missouri.[45]

The senator refused to allow Roosevelt to remain downhearted about his predicament. Believing that his friend remained a formidable political figure, Lodge advised Roosevelt to build a base of support by traveling through the areas of the state where he was viewed favorably. "They must see you and get to know you," Lodge wrote.[46]

Lodge believed that strategy would allow T. R. to develop a base of support that would carry him into the US Senate. "I can judge of your standing and reputation better than you," Lodge wrote. The senator emphasized that his friend's degree of success as commissioner was enough to make him a major political force. "You will pardon all this advice but I am sure I am right as I was about your taking this place," Lodge wrote, in September 1895. The senator also stated a belief he had possessed from the moment he first met Roosevelt. "I do not say you are to be president tomorrow. I do not say it will be—I am sure it may and can be," Lodge wrote in the same letter.[47]

Lodge's encouragement did little to lift Theodore's spirits. As the 1895 elections approached the commissioner saw nothing but failure ahead. "Now it seems to me as though, through no fault of mine, we are to meet defeat in this city." Dismissing the upcoming vote by stating he could care less about the results, Roosevelt preferred to dwell on his resentment toward the Republican hierarchy.[48]

Frustrated at being used as a scapegoat to distract the public from the party's incompetent management of the campaign, Roosevelt was determined to complete his tenure as commissioner. With the New York GOP's inability to embrace Roosevelt's administrative success, the senator believed Platt and his colleagues were employing a losing strategy. "Anything more idiotic I have never seen," Lodge commented as he monitored the poorly developed New York campaign.[49]

Roosevelt also informed Lodge that he was prepared to go on the offensive against state Republican officials as soon as he had the opportunity. The senator attempted to dissuade him from saying anything he might regret. "I know how trying it all is, I know how stupidly and outrageously they have behaved but to come out and denounce Platt is simply to play Platt's game." Lodge believed if Roosevelt lost his temper, the enemy had won the day. "They can't get you out. You can only do that yourself," Lodge wrote. [50]

Edith also employed Lodge's advice to calm her husband's temper. "I do believe that next to myself [Cabot] cares more for you than any one else in the world," she said. Following pressure from the two most important people in his life, Roosevelt promised to heed the senator's advice. "All right! I won't attack any one," Roosevelt informed Lodge.[51]

Supporting the party was not the only issue the commissioner faced. Roosevelt was perceived by many within the GOP as a lightning rod. Platt and others within the party viewed T. R.'s ideological inconsistencies and unpredictable rhetoric as dangerous liabilities. For all Roosevelt's dislike of those who controlled the state organization, the commissioner realized fruitless disputes did nothing to enhance his chances for higher office.

Roosevelt proved correct in his electoral prediction. Despite Republicans holding the upper portions of the state, Tammany swept the city elections. The saloon closures had a significant impact on the voting. The once reliable German American constituency—outraged by Roosevelt's actions—switched their votes to the Democratic Party by a margin of more than 80 percent.[52]

The commissioner had done his best to uphold the saloon closure statute. Roosevelt had also surprised many observers in using administrative skill to update and reform one of the most corrupt police departments in the nation. T. R. took little satisfaction in the goodwill his achievements generated from friends and family. All the commissioner could see was the unfair treatment he had received from those within the Republican leadership.[53]

As Roosevelt lamented his poor fortunes, Lodge turned his attention to the election of 1896. With the economy in poor condition many speculated the Republicans had a chance to reclaim the presidency. Two candidates dominated the GOP landscape. William McKinley, the genial politician from Ohio, and the erudite speaker of the House of Representatives, Thomas B. Reed. Both men possessed a variety of strengths that many believed made each ideal as chief executive.[54]

Lodge had known Reed since their days in Congress. The senator considered his friend far superior in knowledge and experience to the upbeat two-term governor of Ohio. "It will be a great misfortune to have McKinley nominated, a much wider misfortune than anything else," Lodge wrote T. R. in late February 1896.[55]

Senator Lodge's unflattering opinion of McKinley was due to the governor's unfavorable view of Lodge's and Roosevelt's expansionist foreign policy. McKinley, who had witnessed death during the Civil War's Battle of Antietam in 1862, preferred focusing on the nation's affairs at home rather than any military adventurism by the United States.[56]

For all Reed's knowledge and oratorical flair, the Speaker had little taste for the favors required to become the party nominee. At odds with many Westerners over the silver issue, Reed also disagreed with the agenda of the imperialists within the GOP. The speaker shared McKinley's concern about the condition of the economy, along with the belief that American intervention in foreign affairs did nothing but cause unnecessary instability. As Reed showed little interest in the expansionists' vision, Roosevelt concluded an investment in the man from Maine's candidacy was counterproductive.[57]

Roosevelt had little time to ponder Reed's presidential fate. Still disappointed over the recent New York elections, T. R. believed his days as police commissioner were numbered. Frustrated by the controversy over the saloon closures, Boss Platt blamed the commissioner for the poor results of Republican candidates throughout the city.[58]

Never one to lose composure, the Easy Boss summoned Roosevelt to a meeting in his suite at New York's cavernous Fifth Avenue Hotel. The commissioner expected the conference with Platt to result in the termination of his law enforcement career.[59]

Roosevelt and Platt were a study in contrasts. During their conversation on January 19, 1896, the knickerbocker's tired and drawn appearance eclipsed that of the Easy Boss.

At sixty-three, Platt appeared far older. Thin, frail, and barely able to stand or speak above a whisper, Platt displayed none of T. R.'s vigorous physicality. Following the meeting Roosevelt concluded that, despite Platt's infirmities, his mental acuity for bending politicians to his will was as formidable as ever.[60]

Platt informed Roosevelt that over the next few months he was going to arrange for the legislature to dissolve the Police Board. The commissioner was unsurprised by the outcome of the conversation. With his job coming to an end and the Republicans favored for the presidency, Roosevelt had little to gain by creating more animosity within New York's Republican ranks.[61]

T. R.'s political future and a growing Cuban rebellion for independence from Spain were both potential topics of conversation when the Roosevelts stayed with the Lodges in Washington during January 1896. As Theodore approached his final months on the Police Commission, he was desperate for advice about what road to pursue. The visit was enjoyable for Roosevelt as he gathered with friends from his days as civil service commissioner.[62]

Following the commissioner's return to his office in Lower Manhattan, Roosevelt yearned to return to Washington. "There is no society in New York which makes up in any way for the circle of friends whom I found so congenial here," he had written Bamie during his visit. More important, Washington was never boring. Roosevelt hoped with a potential shift from one party to another new opportunities would arise, giving him the chance to reach the next level of political power.[63]

As Roosevelt maintained his fragile position in City government, Lodge focused on determining the 1896 Republican nominee. Despite the senator's efforts, Reed's campaign had failed to catch the imagination of the party faithful. The political void was filled by Governor McKinley and his campaign manager, Marcus A. Hanna. While Reed thought asking anyone for political donations a mortal sin, Hanna believed big money drove the political process. "There are two things that are important in politics. The first one is money, and I can't remember what the second one is," the future senator from Ohio said in 1895.[64]

With the tariff remaining popular within the GOP, McKinley vowed to return the nation to prosperity. The "Major," as Hanna called him, also declared his refusal to allow the nation's Republican political bosses to control his agenda. The latter statement did not sit well with those like New York's Thomas Platt. However, by the time the party delegates assembled in St. Louis, the team from Ohio had assured themselves of the nomination.[65]

Roosevelt and Lodge remained disappointed by Reed's inability to become the party's standard-bearer. Both men realized that with the Democrats nominating the charismatic Nebraska congressman, William Jennings Bryan, McKinley was the only person that stood between a return to economic prosperity or another fiscal collapse. Referring to the Democratic Convention as "a witches' sabbath," Roosevelt contended it was vital that the Republicans win the election. "[W]e have never had, save only during the Civil War, a party whose success at the national election would have argued so ill for national welfare," Roosevelt commented about the state of the Democratic ticket.[66]

Roosevelt and Lodge realized they needed to make a strong effort to ensure a McKinley victory. T. R. also understood that the governor's success was also vital for his own political future. Believing that Lodge's wide network and wise counsel could bring benefits to the McKinley campaign, Roosevelt encouraged the senator to build an alliance with McKinley's staunchest ally.[67]

Commenting on Hanna in a note to Lodge, Roosevelt described the strategist as "a good natured, well-meaning, coarse man, shrewd and hardheaded but neither very farsighted nor very broad-minded." T. R. also characterized McKinley's deputy as "imperious" and one who needed "to be handled with some care." Roosevelt made it clear to Lodge that Hanna understood McKinley had a difficult campaign and that the senator's access to northeastern money would appeal to the former Cleveland businessman.[68]

In the latter part of June following the conclusion of the convention, Lodge convinced Roosevelt to serve as an advocate for the McKinley campaign. "Now don't say you can't or talk Police. This is more important than Police," Cabot commented to his friend in August. T. R.'s initial speeches were so popular GOP officials asked him to travel with Lodge on a five-day late September tour of New York State. The two had enjoyable experiences as they bashed Bryan's candidacy at every turn.[69]

The two wrapped up their campaign swing with a brief visit to Canton, Ohio, where McKinley was applying all his energy to win the presidency from his front porch. Meeting with the party nominee the senator enjoyed the governor's quiet confidence. Roosevelt thought meeting the GOP nominee a pleasant experience. If the Ohioan won in November, T. R. hoped his whistle-stop tours would improve the chances of obtaining a position in the new administration.[70]

In the latter part of September Roosevelt departed on a speaking tour of the Midwest in support of the Republican ticket. Delighted by the size of the crowds, T. R. enjoyed interacting with the audiences that greeted him during visits to Chicago and Detroit. The trip filled Roosevelt with enthusiasm, and he predicted that McKinley would win the West and have a strong performance in the East.[71]

On November 3, 1896, the former governor of Ohio defeated Bryan by 600,000 votes. It was the largest victory by a presidential candidate in a quarter of a century. But Bryan had struck a chord. Even those who were pleased by McKinley's victory could not help but admire the presidential candidate's charm and charisma.[72]

One of those impressed by the youthful Democrat was Nannie Lodge. "That man fought such a fight that even those in the East can call him a crusader, an inspired fanatic—a prophet! It has been marvelous," Nannie wrote in her description of the campaign to Cecil Spring Rice.[73]

Roosevelt had done the utmost to place himself in the position for an opportunity with the new administration. He had served as a valuable ally for McKinley and convinced many of his wealthy friends to contribute to the new president's war chest. However, the outgoing New York police commissioner was not an intimate of anyone within the new president's inner circle. In addition, Roosevelt's support of Tom Reed was potentially problematic for one hoping for a position as part of the new Republican order.

By 1897 Roosevelt had achieved a significant accomplishment in reforming the New York Police Department. Despite the success, T. R. remained in search of an opportunity to make an impact on the nation's domestic or foreign policy. Lodge, in the Senate since 1893, had become a formidable personality through his outspoken comments about immigration and a greater international role for the United States.

The senator also remained committed to enhancing the influence of the Republican Party. As the public prepared for a new man in the Executive Mansion, Roosevelt and Lodge not only hoped McKinley's leadership would result in greater individual opportunities, but also a chance for the United States to achieve its destiny of greatness on the world stage.

EIGHT
First among Nations

"Of course, it was Lodge who engineered it, at the end as at the beginning."

—Theodore Roosevelt

I n December of 1896, Theodore Roosevelt aspired to obtain a position in the new Republican administration. "I don't wish to go to Canton unless McKinley sends for me," Roosevelt commented to a friend. "He already knows me, and does not need to find out anything by personal investigation." Lodge wanted T. R. back in Washington. More important, the senator hoped to have his friend serve in a position that furthered their mutual interest of expanding the nation's foreign policy.[1]

A month earlier, the senator's commitment to that goal had caused him to arrange another meeting with the president-elect. Lunching with McKinley on November 29, the senator informed the governor of the need to acquire Hawaii and the growing tensions between Spain and Cuba. Lodge also made a strong case for Roosevelt to receive a position in the administration. The governor found the idea appealing. "[McKinley] spoke of you with great regard for your character and your services and he would like to have you in Washington," Lodge wrote Roosevelt.[2]

Even during his conversations with the new president, Lodge employed additional methods to get Roosevelt his next position. The senator wrote to Cincinnati lawyer Bellamy Storer, asking him to use his influence with McKinley to get their mutual friend a role with the Navy Department.[3]

In New York, T. R. was thrilled with Lodge's efforts. While McKinley appeared amenable to Roosevelt being part of the administration, the governor had concerns. The new president remained wary of T. R.'s desire to follow his own agenda. When Lodge related that concern, Roosevelt attempted to put the senator's mind at ease. "Of course I have no preconceived policy of any kind which I wish to push through, and I think he would find that I would not be in any way a marplot or agitator," Roosevelt wrote in response to the president's apprehensions.[4]

Lodge called in favors for Roosevelt with other members of his network as well. In the first week of December 1897, the senator reached out to his colleagues Senator Edward Wolcott of Colorado and Senator Cushman K. Davis from Minnesota. The senator also scheduled a dinner with Mark Hanna with the objective of convincing him of the advantages Roosevelt could bring to the administration.[5]

Lodge even went as far as to discuss Roosevelt's professional future with New York's Boss Platt. The Easy Boss remained uncertain about assisting Roosevelt, but Lodge encouraged T. R. to meet with the Republican kingmaker. Roosevelt was happy to meet with Platt or anyone else who could further his cause. The head of the New York political machine had grown tired of his skirmishes with Roosevelt, and Platt was more than happy to get the publicity-hungry commissioner out of New York [6]

As McKinley considered the composition of his administration, Lodge positioned Roosevelt as a candidate for assistant secretary of the navy. Besides Roosevelt's interest in returning to government,

T. R. also emphasized his other desire: to return to the nation's capital to renew the joy he took in being "near you and Nannie, the only people for whom I really care outside my own family."[7]

As the first month of the new year came and went Roosevelt remained at Sagamore Hill. With many government positions remaining unfilled, Lodge explained that McKinley was taking his time organizing his cabinet. In the last week of January Lodge speculated that the president-elect might consider former Massachusetts governor John D. Long as secretary of the navy. If the president chose Long, Lodge believed that his friend's appointment was all but assured.[8]

As Roosevelt waited for word from Canton, Lodge had powerful allies lobby T. R.'s case. The senator called on John Hay and Speaker Reed to tout Roosevelt's abilities to McKinley and his colleagues. Believing these assets were not enough, Lodge also recruited T. R.'s friend, Ohio judge William Howard Taft, as well as Secretary of the Interior Cornelius Bliss to wield their influence with the president. Even new vice president, Garret Hobart, was asked by the senator to work on Roosevelt's behalf.[9]

Still Roosevelt waited. For all those prominent figures campaigning for him others were working to get him blackballed from the administration. "[T]here is a fear that you will want to fight somebody at once," Lodge stated. But the senator reassured Roosevelt that his moment would come.[10]

On March 5, 1897, McKinley named Long as secretary of the navy. Upon being informed, Roosevelt promised Lodge he would work diligently to accomplish any task no matter how menial. "[M]y aim should be solely to make his administration a success," Roosevelt wrote on March 22.[11]

Long, a soft-spoken, slow-moving Bay Stater, remained concerned about T. R.'s frenetic nature and habit for dominating every role he was given. Still Lodge convinced the new secretary that Roosevelt was a good man to have on staff. T. R. was overwhelmed when he heard of the appointment. "I do think you are the staunchest and most loyal friend in the world," he wrote Lodge on March 10th.[12]

The praise was not insincere. Roosevelt was grateful for what the senator had accomplished, and not shy about admitting it to others. "Of course it was Lodge who engineered it, at the end as at the beginning," T. R. wrote of his new position to the diplomat Henry White.[13]

Lodge was thrilled with Roosevelt's return to Washington. Having his friend in the capital gave him enormous joy. When Roosevelt had completed his tenure with the Civil Service Commission Lodge had written his mother that he had felt "a terrible loss . . . to have his daily companionship for six years come to an end." Upon hearing Theodore was returning to the capital city, the Lodges had a special door added to the ground floor of their home on Massachusetts Avenue. That entrance, leading directly into the senator's library, allowed Roosevelt to come and go whenever he pleased.[14]

Their mutual friend Sturgis Bigelow was delighted as well. "I have an almost superstitious feeling about [Roosevelt], that he has a great deal depending on him . . . There is nobody else just like him above the horizon," the Asian art expert wrote to Lodge. The senator realized that Long did not possess Roosevelt's passion for a modern navy. But Lodge hoped the new assistant secretary's knowledge and enthusiasm would instill in the older gentleman the importance of strengthening the nation's maritime defenses.[15]

Roosevelt received formal notification of his new position on April 19, 1897. Writing a telegram to Lodge, Long's new deputy declared his return to the capital city by announcing that "Sinbad has evidently landed the old man of the sea." Roosevelt looked forward to his return to the Washington social life he had so enjoyed during his time with the Civil Service Commission.[16]

With Edith, again pregnant, Roosevelt returned to the nation's capital. Renting a home for his family across the street from the British Embassy, T. R. decided to stay with the Lodges until after Edith's delivery. Most days when not engaged in business at the Navy Department, Roosevelt discussed strategy and politics with Lodge and other like-minded imperialists in the dining room of Washington's Metropolitan Club. As Roosevelt dined on pork chops, potatoes, and beer, the new assistant secretary along with fellow club members Colonel Leonard Wood and Commodore George Dewey analyzed the state of the nation's foreign policy.[17]

One of the issues at the forefront of their conversations was the growing instability in Cuba. With an insurrection against Spain begun in 1895, many in Congress believed the United States needed to intervene to protect its business interests. With a large expat presence, the island was also a frequent travel destination for Americans involved in the lucrative sugar trade.[18]

In turn, Cuban exports to the United States amounted to 87 percent of all exports. Poor management of the nation's economy had created animosity against the Spanish, leading to an insurrection that spread throughout the island province. The violence also caught the eye of numerous Cuban Americans who raised money and created publicity for an independence movement they hoped would grow in popularity.[19]

Lodge believed that an American seizure of Cuba would demonstrate to the rest of the world that the United States was an expanding international power. The senator stood behind the Monroe Doctrine, contending the United States was within its rights to intervene in the island's affairs. The imperialist also believed that coming to the aid of the Cuban people gave the United States the opportunity to portray itself as a beacon of freedom to nations around the world.[20]

Lodge also believed bringing the spirit of liberty to a nation seeking independence against a European power would resonate with the public. "Americans must make up our minds whether we are to be dominant in the Western Hemisphere and keep it free from foreign invasion or whether we are to stand aside and let it be seized as Africa has been," the senator wrote to Henry Higginson in the spring of 1896. [21]

As Congress became more involved in the Latin American conflict, the Senate leadership named Lodge to the Cuban Affairs Committee. Lodge's contention that the nation should support Cuba proved controversial. The declaration put the senator at odds with many businessmen concerned that a war would play havoc with their investments and create economic turmoil.[22]

The senator disagreed with those who believed the United States should remain focused on affairs at home. "The issues of war and peace, like the duty of this great country on the Cuban question must be decided on higher and broader grounds than business considerations," Lodge wrote one of his supporters. Lodge also contended that even if the United States chose to ignore the instability on the island, he believed that until the Cuban issue was resolved it would continue to dominate the national news, playing havoc with the nation's financial markets.[23]

While Roosevelt publicly curbed his language over events in Cuba, in private he shared Lodge's opinion about the United States expanding abroad. "I do feel that it would be everything for us to take firm action on behalf of the wretched Cubans," T. R. told Lodge in the late summer of 1897.[24]

Roosevelt also did his utmost to keep the Cuban issue on McKinley's agenda. Cultivating his relationship with the president, T. R. submitted a memo expressing the importance of a modern navy. "No nation can hold its place in the world . . . unless it stands ready to guard its rights with an armed hand," Roosevelt said during a speech at Newport, Rhode Island's Naval War College, in June 1897. McKinley, reading an account of the assistant secretary's comments, agreed with the position.[25]

While Lodge did not yearn for war, the senator believed a conflict would allow the American people to unite in a patriotic effort. Watching the development of the nation over the last few years, Lodge and Roosevelt believed that many of their fellow citizens had become focused on the objectives of monetary and material success. The two men contended that that crisis of character had made much of the public complacent, uninterested in emulating the pioneer spirit that once symbolized the expansionist tradition.[26]

Refusing to lose sight of the need for military preparedness Roosevelt pushed Secretary Long to update the nation's maritime defenses. With his usual ingenuity, the assistant secretary compiled a list of comments by former presidents about the necessity of expanding the navy with the idea of distributing them to Congress. Lodge appreciated Roosevelt's efforts but advised him to present the idea to McKinley and Long before taking the initiative.[27]

Lodge was concerned that without following proper channels T. R. would confirm his opponents' fears of being unwilling to follow the chain of command. In June 1897, Roosevelt and Lodge convinced President McKinley to submit a treaty to the Senate calling for the annexation of Hawaii. The treaty, not ratified until the following year, provided the United States a foothold in the Pacific.[28]

That September, as tensions between Cuba and Spain increased, the president asked Roosevelt to accompany him on a ride around Washington. In addition to praising the assistant secretary's administrative abilities, McKinley informed Roosevelt he favored the addition of battleships and torpedo boats to the nation's fleet. Praising

McKinley's decision, Roosevelt believed preparedness remained critical as the specter of war appeared on the horizon.[29]

Roosevelt wondered if he was overstepping his authority by discussing his ideas directly with McKinley. Raising the issue with Long, Lodge informed T. R. that the president "was entirely satisfied with all you had done and praised in the highest the work and service you were doing for the Navy." A week later the senator again informed T. R. that Long remained pleased in his deputy's administration of the department and encouraged Roosevelt to continue the good work.[30]

Roosevelt's position in the Navy Department also gave Lodge the benefits of arranging promotions for his constituents at the Charlestown Navy Yard. "When the state of work requires the appointment of foremen or painters," the senator wrote Roosevelt on September 28, 1897, "I want Hiram Edgerly, who is now in charge there to be promoted to the foreman's place." Lodge understood that if employing occasional favor helped him remain in office, so be it.[31]

In early November, Roosevelt informed Lodge that he had convinced Secretary Long of the importance of preparedness in the face of growing hostilities between Spain and Cuba. The conversation resulted in Long's decision to authorize the construction of a battleship, as well as additional torpedo boats. While not an enthusiast of the imperialist agenda, Long was a patriot who cared for the safety of the nation above all else.[32]

In January 1898, as Roosevelt was at home with his family in Washington, disturbances broke out across Cuba. Concerned for the safety of the American contingent, the Navy Department authorized the battleship USS *Maine* to deploy to Havana harbor. When the disturbances came to nothing Lodge wondered if that moment was but a prelude to a general revolution.[33]

On February 15 the USS *Maine* exploded. With no obvious culprit, Long convened a board of inquiry. Media outlets such as

Joseph Pulitzer's *New York World* and William Randolph Hearst's *New York Journal* chose not to wait for the commission's conclusions. The tabloids, known for their support of the beleaguered Cubans, immediately accused the Spanish government of the attack on the American vessel.[34]

Much of the public blamed Madrid as well. Lodge believed that no hostilities should be initiated until the navy revealed the results of its investigation. However, the senator contended that Spain was at fault. Roosevelt was in full agreement with his friend. "The Maine was sunk by an act of dirty treachery on the part of the Spaniards," the assistant secretary said.[35]

As Lodge awaited the results of the inquiry, he paid a visit to Roosevelt at the Navy Department. With Secretary Long suffering from insomnia and other ailments, the assistant secretary was overwhelmed with work. The senator watched in wonder as Roosevelt issued orders to members of the American fleet, examined nautical charts, and prepared requests for Congress, all the while monitoring the growing conflict on the Latin American island less than five hundred miles from the nation's shores.[36]

The most important order Roosevelt issued that day was a dispatch sent to Commodore George Dewey. If war was declared Roosevelt ordered Dewey to engage the Spanish fleet that surrounded the Philippines. Lodge's biographer John Garraty makes clear that while the senator approved of Roosevelt's decision, he was purely an observer and had nothing to do with authorizing the order.[37]

On March 21, 1898, a panel of naval experts led by gunnery officer William T. Sampson concluded the destruction of the USS *Maine* was not caused by any kind of malfunction aboard ship. With the cause inconclusive, many believed the explosion was caused by a foreign agent. Following the report's publication, Roosevelt tried to convince McKinley that war with Spain was the only solution. "I have advised the President in the presence of his cabinet . . . as strongly as I know how, to settle the matter instantly by armed intervention," T. R. wrote his brother-in-law William Cowles. Roosevelt believed a lack of a response was a violation of the nation's national honor and a disservice to the Cuban people.[38]

The assistant secretary may have yearned for war, but Lodge remained cautious. Other than quietly visiting with constituents the senator made no statements to the press nor delivered any comments on the Senate floor. As the tabloid press stirred the public toward a confrontation with Madrid, Lodge tried to calm the tempers of his fellow senators.

Lodge believed McKinley a thoughtful leader and one prepared to look at all the specifics before the nation decided to act. At the same time, the senator warned the president that a firm decision was required. "It is equally true that this unanimity of support, so freely & patriotically given, would disintegrate in a day if there were to be hesitation or weakness shown in dealing with the Maine incident or the Cuban question at large . . ." Lodge wrote the president following the release of the investigation.[39]

Eight days later, McKinley, who hated the idea of going to war, prepared to call the Congress to request the deployment of military forces. The threat appeared viable enough to cause the Spanish government to cease their hostilities against the island. Neither McKinley, Roosevelt nor Lodge, who referred to Madrid's temporary cease fire as "a humbug armistice," took the Spanish decision seriously.[40]

Believing a unified front remained critical, Lodge worked within the Senate to develop a joint resolution that garnered majority approval. On April 13, standing in the well of the nation's upper house, Lodge declared his support for intervention in Cuba. "We are face-to-face with Spain today in fulfillment of a great movement which has run through the centuries," Lodge declared in emphasizing the tradition of American expansionism. On April 19, 1898, at three o'clock in the morning, the resolution was approved. Following its passage Spain severed diplomatic relations with the United States.[41]

With declaration of hostilities between the United States and the Spanish Empire, Theodore Roosevelt jumped into the fight. When the assistant secretary resigned his position and decided to enlist in the army, Roosevelt's friends and acquaintances thought his decision ridiculous. "What on earth is this report of Roosevelt's resignation? Is his wife dead? Has he quarreled with everybody? Is he quite mad?" Henry Adams inquired of Lizzie Cameron while visiting Constantinople on May 1.[42]

Roosevelt's decision to organize a regiment composed of his friends from around the country caused Lodge and T. R.'s mutual friend Winthrop Chanler to declare that Roosevelt was "going mad." The polo-playing aristocrat found Roosevelt's decision to forgo his position not only depressing, but in concurrence with Lodge detrimental to his political career. Writing in his journal, Secretary Long believed that his deputy had "lost his head" to a conflict he believed was an enormous mistake.[43]

Lodge was unhappy with Roosevelt's decision to leave Washington and head for Cuba. More important, the senator was concerned for his son-in-law, Augustus Gardner, and his eldest son Bay, both of whom were determined to enlist in the conflict. "They go for their country. There can be no higher duty," Lodge wrote his mother in May 1898.[44]

Over the last few years, Lodge had become pleased with Bay's progress. The young man had succeeded in publishing several poems in prominent publications like *The Atlantic Monthly* and *Scribner's Magazine*. Much of Bay's success was due to Roosevelt's editorial connections. T. R. thought Bay's talent exceptional and believed his writings deserved wide circulation.[45]

Roosevelt was happy to submit young Lodge's writings for publication. "I rather hesitate to tell you how much I think of your poetry for fear I should make you conceited," T. R. wrote Bay in February 1896. A month later Bay wrote the poem "The Wave." Roosevelt was emphatic about the work and engaged his many editorial contacts to have it published as soon as possible.[46]

Beginning in October 1896, Bay moved to the nation's capital to serve as his father's aide. The decision to retain his son was one the senator did not make lightly. Roosevelt exchanged several lengthy correspondences with Lodge over the issue. The senator was concerned that hiring Bay as part of his staff violated his ethical code and gave the impression of impropriety.[47]

After considerable thought Bay was hired. Roosevelt believed the controversy would rapidly fade from the public mind. When the United States went to war against Spain, Bay served as a gunnery officer on his uncle Charles Henry Davis's cruiser, the USS *Dixie*. Meanwhile, the navy placed Lodge's son-in-law on the staff of the senator's friend General James H. Wilson.[48]

Roosevelt believed the only contribution he could make to the war was to serve in battle. With the assistance of Secretary of War Russell A. Alger, Roosevelt was offered command of a volunteer regiment. Knowing he did not have the experience, T. R. gave command to Alger's physician and longtime military man Colonel Leonard Wood. The senator, unable to fight in the conflict, made his own contribution by loaning his home on Nahant to the miliary in support of the war effort.[49]

Under the leadership of Wood and Roosevelt, the First Volunteer Cavalry (or Rough Riders) resembled a unique group. The regiment was not only composed of hard men from the West but those from prominent Eastern families who were members of the Union League and Knickerbocker Clubs as well as graduates of Ivy League universities. While each volunteer possessed a different pedigree, everyone in the unit was an accomplished rider and marksman.[50]

Deployed to San Antonio, Texas, Roosevelt and Wood worked rapidly to get the regiment prepared. T. R. kept Lodge informed of his activities as he described the unit as composed of many men "who do not look at life in the spirit of decorum." Roosevelt enjoyed the camaraderie that pervaded the group. "You would be amused to see three Knickerbocker Club men cooking and washing dishes for one of the New Mexico companies," Roosevelt wrote Lodge on May 19.[51]

The senator followed news of the Rough Riders' preparations with great interest. "Unless I am utterly and profoundly mistaken the Administration is now fully committed to the large policy that we both desire," Lodge wrote Roosevelt. The senator urged Roosevelt not to rush his regiment's training, concerned that many of the men did not possess the proper equipment for a successful military campaign.[52]

Lodge informed Roosevelt that the McKinley Administration had decided to win the war in rapid fashion by deploying 100,000 men into Cuba. Sitting in his office in Washington the senator was anxious about all his friends and loved ones recently placed in harm's way. Lodge hoped that Roosevelt as well as the other members of his regiment were properly prepared when the battle finally commenced.[53]

The principal Rough Rider desperately wanted to get the regiment to Cuba. Roosevelt attempted to lobby the senator to get his men sent to the island as early as possible. While the secretary of war decided to order T. R.'s unit to Tampa, Florida, Alger declined Roosevelt's request to allow his men to bring their horses on the journey. "It is a little bit rough to make us fight on foot with only two-thirds of our strength," T. R. complained to Lodge following the group's arrival in Tampa.[54]

Arriving in Florida, the poor conditions of the American training facility stunned Roosevelt and Wood. "No words could describe to you the confusion and lack of system and the general mismanagement of affairs here," Roosevelt wrote Lodge on June 10.[55]

The lack of general preparedness outraged Roosevelt. Accustomed to events running at breakneck speed, the former police commissioner expressed concern that the inferior facility would endanger the success of the operation.[56]

Roosevelt and Wood believed the unsanitary environment of the camp presented a national scandal. T. R. believed the situation so severe that it required McKinley and Alger's attention. "I wonder if it would be possible for you to tell . . . the President, and if necessary, the Secretary of War, just what is going on here and the damage that is being done," Roosevelt wrote Lodge on June 12.[57]

Roosevelt's description of the conditions confirmed Lodge's worst fears. "I knew pretty well what a state of things existed at Tampa," the senator wrote three days later. Lodge admitted the government was "entirely unprepared and the disorganization is something frightful." Frustrated in his inability to engage the War Department, the senator promised Roosevelt he would do his best to try to improve the situation as the regiment prepared to begin its campaign against the Spanish Army.[58]

Roosevelt's regiment was thrilled upon its arrival in Cuba. Testing his courage under fire was a lifelong dream and the former assistant secretary was fully prepared to accept his fate whether for good or ill. "Well, whatever comes I shall feel contented with having left the Navy Department to go into the army for the war," Theodore commented as he and his troops prepared for battle.[59]

Roosevelt's decision to leave civilian life to serve in the Spanish-American War generated massive publicity. Much of the press celebrated the Rough Riders' success following a skirmish against the Spanish by declaring T. R. be nominated for governor of New York. Lodge believed if Roosevelt should survive the conflict, he would have the world at his feet. "I have not the least doubt that you can go to Congress, if you want to," the senator wrote on June 29.[60]

For Roosevelt and Lodge 1898 was a moment of celebration. For several years the two men had discussed the idea of expanding the presence of the United States abroad. With Roosevelt in the Navy Department and Lodge attempting to influence the nation's foreign affairs from the Senate, the two friends had each played a part in helping the United States expand its control over the Western Hemisphere.

During 1897–1898 no one's career shone more brightly than Roosevelt's. With Lodge's contacts and his stealth networking the senator remained Theodore's most effective patron. With success in the Navy Department and Roosevelt's newfound celebrity on the battlefield, Lodge had no doubt that his friend's star was finally on the rise.[61]

NINE
To the Top of the Pyramid

"I can put it most tersely by saying that if I were a candidate for the Presidency I would take the Vice-Presidency in a minute at this juncture."

—Henry Cabot Lodge

Henry Cabot Lodge reveled in Theodore Roosevelt's military success. Having admired physical courage since he was a boy, Lodge sat in his Washington townhouse riveted by Roosevelt's exploits during the Battle of San Juan Hill. "You are one of the popular persons of the war and deserve to be. Pray God you come out all right," Lodge wrote July 4, 1898.[1]

Two days later, Lodge wrote Roosevelt again. On that occasion the senator discussed T. R.'s political prospects. "I hear talk all the time about your being run for Governor and Congressman, and at this moment you could have pretty much anything you wanted." What Lodge wanted was Roosevelt to serve alongside him in the United States Senate.[2]

Days later, as Roosevelt and his band of Rough Riders found themselves immersed in an epidemic of yellow fever, Lodge attended a meeting with the heavily bearded owner of the *New York Sun*, Charles A. Dana, and his soft-spoken publisher William Laffan. The men were strong supporters of Roosevelt with extensive contacts in the New York State Republican Party, and Lodge expressed interest in their views on Roosevelt's political opportunities once he returned to the United States.[3]

Understanding New York's governorship was a subject of popular speculation. Lodge did not think the Albany statehouse was a good idea. Having already alienated numerous members of the state GOP, Lodge believed Roosevelt's energy and curiosity required a national stage. In the New England legislator's opinion, along with those of Dana and Laffan, the Senate represented the quickest way to the presidency. However, the more Lodge listened to his friends from the *Sun,* he realized a sizeable amount of momentum had already developed around a Roosevelt candidacy for governor.[4]

Lodge left the meeting with little concern. Even with the Senate out of reach, the Bostonian understood Roosevelt's enormous celebrity presented him with an array of prospects. "You must not think that I am dreaming about these things because you can have no idea of your popularity here," Lodge wrote Roosevelt on July 12.[5]

Appreciative of Lodge's note, Roosevelt was not unaware of the excitement his military exploits had generated among voters in the Empire State. "The good people in New York . . . seem . . . crazy over me," Roosevelt wrote Lodge in the latter part of July. In that same letter, however, T. R. reflected Lodge's concerns about his ambivalence toward the state Republican political machine. "I don't know how to get on with the New York politicians," Roosevelt complained as he and his troops languished in Cuba awaiting orders from the War Department.[6]

Having enjoyed his first taste of military adventure, Roosevelt looked forward to another opportunity to test his mettle on the battlefield. But the "Colonel" as he was known by his men was disappointed. Two weeks later, with hostilities between Spain and the United States nearly concluded, the Rough Riders boarded the troop ship *Miami* from Santiago de Cuba bound for the shores of North America. After a week's journey, the ship dropped anchor three miles off New York's Montauk Point, a short distance from Roosevelt's home at Oyster Bay.[7]

As the Rough Riders stepped down the gangplank on August 16, 1898, Colonel Roosevelt looked fitter and trimmer than he had in months. Pressed to comment about his potential candidacy for governor of New York, Roosevelt dismissed the question with a hearty laugh, looking amused each time the subject was broached. Roosevelt, who loved sparring with the media, had no interest in revealing any news about the future until the details were fully arranged.[8]

Following Roosevelt's landing on Long Island, Lodge, ensconced in his home on Nahant, was relieved to read of Roosevelt's safe return. "I will run down to Oyster Bay and see you," Lodge wrote. Reading of Roosevelt's coy response to reporter's questions about his political future, the senator knew there was no time to waste. "I have so many things to say to you that can be better said than written," the senator confided while gazing out at the waters of the Atlantic.[9]

Based on Lodge's conversation with his contacts at the *Sun*, one would have thought Roosevelt's Republican nomination for governor a foregone conclusion. But any political decision made in New York needed the approval of Theodore's old opponent Thomas Platt. Elected to the Senate in 1897, the white-haired politician was enjoying the summer at the Oriental Hotel, overlooking Brooklyn's Sheepshead Bay. Platt had thought little of the outspoken patrician since his departure as New York City's police commissioner several years earlier.[10]

Aware of T. R.'s recent notoriety, the senator expressed little enthusiasm at the prospect of the outspoken reformer occupying the state's Executive Mansion. A political pragmatist whose primary goal was maintaining Republican power, Platt understood a Roosevelt governorship presented its own series of challenges. However, Platt came to the realization that the Rough Rider's candidacy might present a solution to a dilemma he and his colleagues had hoped to solve for some time.[11]

The situation involved New York's incumbent governor Frank S. Black. A lawyer and popular upstate figure from Troy, New York, Black, nicknamed "the Judge," had a reputation for his serious demeanor and no-nonsense manner. A longstanding friend and protégé of Platt's, the governor had fallen under scrutiny following the results of an investigation into the expansion of the Erie Canal. The project, which cost nine million dollars, had received considerable criticism due to countless delays. In addition, Black's aide, George Aldridge, was unable to account for the disappearance of one million dollars earmarked for the canal improvement project.[12]

Despite Black not being directly implicated, Platt concluded that the growing scandal had irreparably damaged his friend's prospects for reelection. With Roosevelt's strong reputation for integrity and his recent heroism in the war with Spain, the Easy Boss believed the former police commissioner represented an ideal solution for keeping the Democrats at bay.[13]

As Platt considered his options, another party expressed interest in Roosevelt serving as the state's chief executive of New York. John Jay Chapman, a political commentator, reformer, and old friend of Roosevelt's believed the man he affectionately called "Teddy" represented an ideal choice as the Independent party's nominee for the Albany statehouse. Even as Roosevelt remained skeptical of good government types, the colonel chose to attend a meeting with Chapman and his colleagues just three days after his return from Cuba.[14]

Roosevelt had not forgotten the uproar created among New York's "silk-stocking" set following his decision to support James Blaine in 1884. But Chapman had intrigued Roosevelt with the idea of being at the top of a ticket surrounded by young men of independent integrity. Knowing that Lodge had a dim view of Liberal Republicans, Roosevelt decided to keep his options open.

As Roosevelt considered Chapman's offer, the colonel received a visit from his old friend and Platt intermediary Lemuel E. Quigg. Viewing the war veteran as a promising candidate, Quigg remained concerned with T. R.'s ability to work with the Republican machine. Roosevelt convinced Quigg that his rebellious nature was under control. "I said that I should not make war on Mr. Platt or anybody else if war could be avoided; that what I wanted was to be Governor and not a faction leader," Roosevelt recalled in describing the meeting years later.[15]

In demand by GOP regulars and liberal reformers Roosevelt remained insecure about his political prospects. "If the popular feeling is strong enough . . . I shall be nominated and elected. . . if I am not nominated, I shall take the result with . . . a certain sense of relief," Roosevelt wrote Lodge on September 4, 1898. On the surface, one might have viewed Roosevelt's tone as simply another sign of distrust toward Platt and the state GOP. Lodge knew Roosevelt well enough to realize there was much more involved. [16]

Roosevelt possessed tremendous mental and physical vitality. That all-consuming energy allowed him an enormous capacity for work and play. That frenetic nature, however, could also result in severe anxiety, causing T. R. to believe on multiple occasions that his career was at an end.[17]

When Lodge saw signs of Roosevelt's "black care," the senator knew a reinforcement of confidence was called for. "Everything seems to be going right . . . in New York," Lodge wrote days later, "and I should say from this point of view that your nomination and election were assured." The senator, always believing Roosevelt possessed a unique political ability, refused to allow petty flaws to undermine his friend's future.[18]

Lodge's prediction of Roosevelt's success was confirmed when the colonel attended a meeting with Senator Platt during the second week of September. On a Saturday afternoon, dressed in a conservative dark suit and military hat, Roosevelt quietly entered the ladies' entrance of the white marbled Fifth Avenue Hotel in downtown New York. The building not only served as the center of Republican party activity, but Platt's residence when not in Albany or Washington.[19]

During a conversation in Platt's suite, the two settled their past differences. If elected, Roosevelt repeated his pledge to consult with the Easy Boss and other party leaders on personnel and legislative matters. As the conversation concluded, however, Platt made clear that Roosevelt needed to sever his relationship with Chapman and the other reformers. Roosevelt understood the political reality. A nomination by the Independents was counterproductive. "I cannot accept the so-called independent nomination and keep good faith with the other men on the Republican ticket," he wrote Lodge on September 19.[20]

Chapman and his fellow reformers were T. R.'s ideal constituency. But Roosevelt realized embracing that side of the party extinguished any possibility of election. Lodge, who never forgot his own mistreatment by the Mugwump side of the GOP was in strong agreement. "You are absolutely right in refusing that independent nomination," he commented to Roosevelt on September 23.[21]

Lodge may have encouraged Roosevelt's effort to return to Albany, but he reiterated his belief that the Senate was preferable to the "cut-throat" world of local politics. In arguing that the nation's capital served as a better political platform, the senator was also considering his own self-interest. Lodge deeply missed his personal interaction with Roosevelt. The idea of playing tennis, horseback riding, or simply sitting and exchanging idle gossip seemed preferable to visits between New York and Washington.[22]

Days before the state nominating convention a supporter of Governor Black and a member of the New York machine leaked an affidavit to the press stating that Roosevelt remained a resident of Washington, DC. Under state law, candidates for governor were required to have a residency in New York for at least five years. A complicated tax situation involving the home in Oyster Bay had caused Roosevelt to try to remain a DC resident for as long as possible. As a lifelong New Yorker, T. R. was devastated when the state's newspapers accused him of poor judgment. "I hated to have any combination of incidents make me look for a moment as if I were doing something shifty," Roosevelt wrote Lodge.[23]

As the controversy escalated, Roosevelt offered to drop out of the race. The Easy Boss, having seen more than his share of political shenanigans, called on GOP wise man Elihu Root. Through Root and Platt's legal maneuvering, Roosevelt easily won the nomination over the incumbent governor 753–218.[24]

In winning the nomination, Roosevelt knew he needed to focus his energies on a campaign issue that would appeal to the emotions of the voters. The Republicans had little to offer. Between the disagreeable issue of the Erie Canal, the problematic nature of the war with Spain, and the pervasive nature of big business in state affairs, Roosevelt was uncertain if victory was possible.[25]

Unable to find an issue to galvanize the public, T. R. employed his recent military celebrity as a means of generating support. During one of his early speeches at New York's Carnegie Hall, the colonel called upon his audience to embrace a new role for the United States, as a shining beacon of international power encircling the globe. While Lodge thought the speech was a success, those in the audience representing the Albany machine concluded the opposite. A strong opponent of the war, Platt became so outraged by Roosevelt's imperialistic rhetoric he arranged for the nominee to be sent home to Oyster Bay until further notice.[26]

As Theodore sat in his home on Long Island awaiting Platt's decision about the status of the campaign, he grew progressively angrier over the GOP boss's ideological rigidity. "Lord! How I would like to live in a civilized community . . . Here I press them just as far as I possibly can, but it is astonishing how little they will stand," Roosevelt wrote Lodge, lamenting the provinciality of Platt and his colleagues. The New York boss and his colleagues realized their apprehensions of being unable to control the outspoken candidate were coming to fruition. The relationship between Platt and T. R. was a marriage of convenience. But those within the Republican hierarchy worried that the rift developing between the two could cost their party the election.[27]

It was Governor Black who offered to calm the situation. He suggested the candidate deliver a speech in Black's hometown of Troy, New York. Roosevelt begrudgingly agreed. Arriving at his destination, T. R. was greeted by pouring rain and an underwhelming reception of four hundred drenched supporters.[28]

During Roosevelt's appearance upstate he stumbled upon an issue to employ against the Democrats. As head of the Tammany machine, former steamboat engineer and amateur boxer Richard Croker had decided not to renominate a Democratic justice, Joseph Daly, to the State Supreme Court. A respected jurist, Daly had come to Croker's attention following his refusal to select a member of the Democratic machine as his court clerk.[29]

Employing the strategy that Tammany was attempting to manipulate the state's judiciary, Roosevelt targeted the Democratic nominee, Brooklyn Supreme Court judge Augustus Van Wyck, as being an enabler of Tammany's corrupt activities.[30]

In the latter part of October, Lodge, campaigning for his own reelection to the Senate, rushed down to New York to make an appearance on Roosevelt's behalf at New York's Cooper Union.

Touting his friend's administrative abilities, integrity, and commitment to public service, Lodge exclaimed that his audience could do no better than elect Roosevelt governor.[31]

Traveling near Niagara Falls, the nominee called the senator's remarks "the best speech in my entire campaign." Lodge was pleased with Roosevelt's progress but expressed trepidation as election day approached. "I am so anxious about the result, more anxious than I have ever been about any election contest in my life," Lodge exclaimed. When the ballots were counted the colonel defeated Van Wyck by just over 18,000 votes.[32]

During the latter part of 1898, Lodge hoped that the Senate would ratify the treaty officially ending hostilities between the United States and Spain. The terms of the negotiation not only gave the United States the Philippines at a cost of twenty million dollars, but the islands of Guam and Puerto Rico. Delighted with the terms, Lodge remained concerned that those opposed to his imperialistic vision, including his senatorial colleague George F. Hoar, would block the agreement's ratification.[33]

Lodge made the treaty and McKinley's record as president the centerpieces of his drive for a second term in the Senate. Reelected easily due to an overwhelmingly Republican legislature, the Bostonian contended that problems over the treaty's ratification were inevitable. Hoping to find a solution he discussed the matter with John Hay, who McKinley had named secretary of state in September 1898.[34]

As the Senate debated the treaty, Hay and Lodge negotiated the issue under the eyes of a silently irritated Henry Adams. "For an hour they talked Senate and Treaty and dreary Senatorial drivel," Adams commented to Lizzie Cameron. For all his contrarian attitude, Adams supported Lodge's imperialistic views. "Our country has asserted its right and power even more emphatically than I tried to assert it," he wrote his muse during the first week of December 1898.[35]

After considerable debate and a well-developed strategy coordinated between Lodge and Senator Nelson Aldrich of Rhode Island, the Senate ratified the treaty 57–27. Lodge felt gratified by the victory but exhausted by the effort. "I felt exactly as if I had been struggling up the side of a mountain and as if there was not an ounce more of exertion left in any muscle of my body," the senator wrote Roosevelt following the vote.[36]

Pleased to return to the Congress's upper house for another six years and content with the state of the country both domestically and internationally, Lodge had little to criticize. "Cabot smiles because he has got his reelection, and all the world feels how great and good he is, but the others smile because they know no better," Henry Adams wrote snidely to Lizzie Cameron in the last days of February.[37]

When Roosevelt moved into the governor's mansion in Albany in the first week of January 1899, he did so with mixed emotions. After being a subordinate for so many years he was thrilled to finally possess real power. "I have worked hard all my life and have never been particularly lucky, but this summer I *was* lucky, and I am enjoying it to the full," he wrote Cecil Spring Rice.[38]

Despite Platt's age and ill health, the New York senator had no intention of allowing the new governor to do as he pleased. The GOP boss commented that he liked Roosevelt, but T. R. informed Lodge he expected a great deal of criticism over his management, understanding that the New York political machine remained ambivalent about his reform instincts.[39]

Initially Roosevelt did his best to consult Platt on appointments to his administration. However, the two soon clashed when the New York boss expressed his desire to appoint a director of public works over the governor's objections. "[G]ood work cannot be done by the ordinary party hack, even of the best type; and the really high-class men will not take it," Roosevelt wrote Lodge, days away from taking the oath of office.[40]

Lodge believed antagonizing Platt was counterproductive. The senator urged his friend not to look at every disagreement as a battle to be fought. "Do not get worried over the Superintendent of Public Works and do not be hurried . . . let the thing run along until you are able to secure a Superintendent who is exactly to your mind," the senator wrote Roosevelt on the last day of 1898.[41]

The governor did his best to follow Lodge's advice. Roosevelt kept the New York senator informed through weekly breakfast meetings in Platt's hotel suite. But T. R. remained determined to be his own man by pursuing policies that benefited all New Yorkers.[42]

Roosevelt began his term as governor with a powerful series of legislative actions. The governor called on the state assembly to authorize measures focusing on tax and civil service reform, allowing women the right to vote, and regulating work hours for women and children. At the same time T. R. followed Lodge's counsel by keeping disputes with Platt to a minimum. Governor Roosevelt realized that the voters had not elected him as an agent of dramatic change, but one who possessed a passion for integrity with the ability to contend with the Albany machine.[43]

One of the issues that the governor first confronted concerned corporations that received the rights to supply gas, electricity, and other utilities to the state. Executives who controlled these lucrative franchises showed their debt to politicians like Platt by pouring an exorbitant amount of money into the Republican treasury. The governor, viewing the process as blatant acts of patronage, contended that these earnings should no longer remain tax free. "This is all wrong," Roosevelt wrote of the problematic situation, as Lodge and his family prepared for a six-month vacation to France and Italy.[44]

Platt was not pleased by Roosevelt's decision to make the state GOP's wealthy donors pay a price for the lucrative corporative practice. The senator concluded the legislation would not only hurt the party but damage the governor's future. "If that becomes a law no corporation will ever again contribute a dollar to any campaign fund when you are a candidate," Platt told Roosevelt. Undeterred, T. R.'s extensive lobbying, as well as large public and media support, led to the passage of the 1899 Franchise Tax Bill with two days remaining in the legislative session.[45]

Pleased with his initial period as governor, Roosevelt expressed his gratification with the appointments made and the legislation produced. In addition to the environmental and labor policies, T. R. had signed legislation giving state employees an eight-hour workday while raising salaries for the state's schoolteachers. "I think I may say I have come out all right," Roosevelt wrote Lodge on April 27, 1899.[46]

Refusing to rest on his laurels, Roosevelt recognized that the political winds steering his future remained unpredictable. "18 months hence I may be so much out of kilter with the machine that there will be no possibility of my renomination," he wrote Lodge. As the nation prepared for the election of 1900 Roosevelt and Lodge focused their attention on the political dynamics shaping the country.[47]

Since William Jennings Bryan's defeat three years earlier the powerful orator had only grown in popularity. Bryan's dynamism caused T. R. to believe that the populist would present a difficult challenge to the administration. "Of course, McKinley must be renominated; so the success of the Republican party depends upon him," the governor commented to Lodge, traveling in Rome.[48]

The Lodges' trip to Europe was not all swims in the Mediterranean and walks in the sunshine. A year earlier Nannie had developed trouble with one of her heart valves. In organizing the six-month trip, the senator hoped time away from the chaos of the capitol city would give his wife the rest she needed.[49]

Lodge also had his mind on politics. Believing the strong economy would help the president win reelection, the senator remained concerned about the violence and instability plaguing the Philippines since the first week of February 1899.[50]

Days before the Senate ratified the treaty ending the Spanish-American War, trouble arose throughout the country. Determined to prevent their nation from being dominated by another foreign power, violence developed between Filipinos and American troops. Despite the conflict, Lodge believed the United States' acquisitions in the Pacific had put the nation on a path to becoming one of the globe's great powers.[51]

As the Lodges continued their European tour, Roosevelt looked forward to a relaxing summer. Exhausted after years of intense work, the governor hoped time with friends and family would renew his energy. But rest was not in Roosevelt's character.[52]

In May the governor headed West for a series of speeches in Illinois and Michigan. The journey, originally intended as a reunion with the Rough Riders in Las Vegas, New Mexico, became a raucous whistle-stop tour with Roosevelt as the main attraction. As the colonel's train traveled the Santa Fe Railway from one state to the next, Roosevelt became overwhelmed by the reception he received. "At every station at which the train stopped . . . I was received by dense throngs exactly as if I had been a presidential candidate," Roosevelt wrote Lodge following the conclusion of his trip.[53]

The governor's tour generated much speculation about the possibility of a presidential campaign in 1900. Realizing the controversy that could develop, Roosevelt issued a statement declaring he had no interest in being a candidate. Arriving at Grand Central Station en route to Oyster Bay on June 28, 1899, a reporter inquired if the governor's comment meant he had simply "resigned his claims to the Presidency in favor" of the incumbent. According to the *New York Times*, Roosevelt, caught off guard by the question, grew silent. "I never used that word or any like it," T. R. replied tersely.[54]

Roosevelt was determined to end any presidential speculation. "My reception caused some talk," he wrote Lodge on July 1, "so I thought it better to come out in an interview stating that of course I was for President McKinley's nomination, and that everyone should be for it." T. R. did not want to do anything to alienate the president nor risk his own political future.[55]

Remaining committed to the president's renomination, the experience in the West fired Roosevelt's ambitions for national office. With no viable opportunities in the Senate, Lodge began pursuing a more dramatic strategy. Increasingly fearful that populism was gaining an upper hand throughout the nation, the senator began discussing the prospect of Roosevelt replacing the frail and unassuming Garret A. Hobart as McKinley's vice president.[56]

It is unknown when the senator first broached the idea. Initially intrigued by the proposal, Roosevelt believed the opportunity to serve as McKinley's No. 2 was preferable to his "unstable" role as governor of New York.[57]

T. R. also favored the VP option over concerns with the rapidly changing tastes of the American public. "I am not taken in by the crowds in the West or by anything else in the way of vociferous enthusiasms for the moment," he commented to Lodge in July 1899. While the governor may have found the idea of running with McKinley appealing, Edith Roosevelt did not.[58]

Having known her husband since childhood, New York's first lady was concerned the vice presidency gave Roosevelt little to do. In the past, idleness and inactivity had caused T. R. to become depressed, leading to conflict between the two. Beside concerns over her husband's psychological health Edith also had financial worries. Leaving the governorship and its annual salary of $10,000 for a government stipend that paid $2,000 less was not viewed by the first lady as a promotion.[59]

As Roosevelt approached the new legislative session questions remained about his future. The governor's unpopularity with Platt led Roosevelt to believe that once his term ended, he would return to political limbo. "I should like to be reelected Governor, but I do not expect it," Roosevelt wrote Lodge.[60]

Surveying the political landscape, the governor saw few opportunities. Initially, Roosevelt considered jumping from the governorship to the position of secretary of war. But the moment quickly vanished when McKinley chose to replace the ineffective Russell Alger with Roosevelt's old friend Elihu Root.[61]

With no other cabinet position available, Lodge believed the vice presidency remained the only option. However, Edith's strong objections caused Roosevelt to reconsider the idea. "As for the Vice Presidency, I do not think there is anything in that," Roosevelt wrote Lodge at the end of August.[62]

Roosevelt was happy being governor. The relationship with Platt was challenging but the work allowed T. R. to make an impact in people's daily lives. The vice presidency offered little room for any kind of mental stimulation. The governor had no interest in presiding over the Senate nor attending to matters requiring little experience or ability.[63]

On November 21, 1899, the senator's question about the vice presidency gained greater relevance following the sudden death of Garret Hobart. Lodge, who returned from Europe two days earlier, immediately began lobbying Roosevelt to consider filling the vacancy. "My own opinion has not changed. I can put it most tersely by saying if I were a candidate for the Presidency, I would take the Vice Presidency in a minute at this juncture," Lodge wrote on December 7.[64]

The senator understood it was up to Roosevelt to make the choice. It was difficult for Lodge to restrain his enthusiasm. In the past each position Lodge had recommended, from police commissioner to assistant secretary of the navy, had elevated Roosevelt's profile. With Hobart's death, Lodge believed the vice presidency was another credential to help his friend achieve the ultimate prize.[65]

Since Roosevelt and Lodge had emerged from the debacle of 1884, each had achieved prominence and power in public life. As President McKinley searched for a new vice president, he also faced a growing crisis in the Philippines. Lodge was determined to help the commander in chief solve both dilemmas while assuring that his vision of the United States achieving international prominence remained secure.

Despite Roosevelt's confident demeanor, the governor believed his career was on the verge of tumbling into the abyss. Preparing to begin the new legislative session in Albany, T. R. remained concerned with the nation's growing tensions over economic disparity and its ability to adapt to the expanding industrial age. Roosevelt believed he had the capacity to solve these enormous problems if he could remain politically viable. The events that occurred over the next two years would not only bring Roosevelt to the height of political leadership but would test his talents in ways he never could have imagined.

TEN
An Unhappy Choice

"Theodore, the way to break a precedent is to make one."[1]

—Henry Cabot Lodge

D espite Roosevelt's refusal to consider the vice presidency, Lodge had placed the bug in the governor's ear. Even as the senator promised to no longer discuss the issue, Roosevelt continued the conversation. "It seems to me that the chance of my being a presidential candidate is too small to warrant very serious consideration at present," T. R. informed Lodge on December 11, 1899.[2]

Roosevelt believed that even with the addition of the vice presidency and the momentum of his success as police commissioner, assistant secretary of the navy and governor of New York would not hold the public interest for an additional four years. The governor had other concerns with the office. Roosevelt wanted a position that possessed authority and allowed him to do serious work. The vice presidency contained neither of those options.[3]

As the months passed, T. R. appeared to dismiss the idea. Writing Bamie on December 17 he commented that "I have told Cabot that I did not want, and would not take, the Vice-Presidency." Since Platt appeared to favor Roosevelt's renomination little reason existed to consider serving as McKinley's running mate. As the Easy Boss encouraged Roosevelt to serve another term in Albany, New York's corporate interests did their utmost to convince Platt to send the troublesome Republican anywhere other than back to the Executive Mansion.[4]

Being a canny politician, Platt never mentioned his concerns about keeping Roosevelt off the 1900 gubernatorial ticket. However, during a meeting with Lodge, the New York senator presented an alternative view to his colleague by stating that that none of the candidates being considered for vice president were very formidable. "[Platt] agreed with me that you had merely to say the word to have the V.P.; so, you see I am no dreamer on that point," Lodge wrote T. R. on December 19.[5]

Almost immediately following the Easy Boss's conversation with Lodge, Senator Platt changed his mind, informing the governor that accepting the vice presidency would prove a mistake. The senator believed Roosevelt would grow frustrated in an office that gave him nothing to do. Platt believed the lack of activity could cause Roosevelt to clash with McKinley, a conflict that could cause significant problems for the administration.[6]

Lodge was taken aback when Roosevelt shared the news. The New Englander tried to explain Platt's thinking by contending that the New York politician did not want to give T. R. false hope following conflicting rumors that McKinley was considering the idea of offering the vice presidency to Elihu Root as well as several other politicians. Lodge believed Roosevelt could still benefit from the situation. If Root did agree to run with McKinley, a vacancy would then become available in the War Department, a position that the governor coveted.[7]

Days later Roosevelt heard from several political colleagues that Platt had again reversed his decision. The Easy Boss believed that due to the inevitable flow of events, Roosevelt had no choice but to accept the second spot on the ticket. The governor was at a loss for words. "I do not understand what was up, or . . . what is up now . . ." Roosevelt wrote Lodge December 30.[8]

It is difficult to know what drove Platt to make such conflicting statements. Viewing the retention of power as his top priority, Platt may have considered what was most beneficial to his party as well as his state. A year earlier, Roosevelt's popularity had saved the New York GOP from defeat. Platt may have wanted to keep Roosevelt in the governorship to prevent Republicans from losing the state in 1900. While T. R. was a popular and charismatic personality, he was a difficult and unpredictable person to work with, even among Republicans. These were the obstacles confronting Platt as he vacillated on whether to keep Roosevelt in Albany or send him back to Washington.[9]

As Platt considered pushing the governor out of New York, Lodge attempted to convince Roosevelt that the vice presidency was a chance worth taking. On January 10, 1900, the senator delivered a memorial speech in honor of the late vice president, Garret Hobart. Throughout the address Lodge not only discussed Hobart's previously unknown influence in the administration but used his historical knowledge to emphasize the importance of the office.[10]

The senator argued that the framers of the Constitution believed the vice presidency should stand "on a plane of absolute equality with the president." Lodge knew Roosevelt was concerned about accepting a position with so little responsibility. By articulating a strong argument, the senator demonstrated to his friend that the vice presidency was designed by Hamilton and Madison with an important purpose in mind.[11]

As Roosevelt and Lodge debated the issue the New Englander kept up a breakneck schedule. Busy in the Senate, Lodge continued renovating his home in Washington while focusing on his growing family. In 1894 Constance and her husband Gus Gardner had presented the Lodges with their first grandchild. There was also news to report in Bay's personal life. In January 1900, the senator and his wife announced the engagement of their eldest son to the beautiful Mathilda Elizabeth Frelinghuysen Davis.[12]

Davis was the daughter of Assistant Secretary of State John Davis and the ambitious socialite Sally Frelinghuysen. "Bessy," as Bay's fiancée was known, had met her future husband at a dinner given by Senator Lodge in 1895. Henry Adams could only smile when he heard the news. Recalling Davis's appearance as Cleopatra at a royal ball honoring Queen Victoria, the commentator thought Bay's future bride was so exquisite her beauty represented nothing less than Michelangelo's Madonna. Tall, with a luminous smile and a sophisticated bearing, Bay Lodge was immediately intrigued when he first encountered the glamorous eighteen-year-old.

Like Nannie Lodge, Bessy was more than a great beauty. An avid reader of history who studied with a private tutor at Versailles, the future Mrs. Lodge was fluent in French, German, and Latin. Believing no man would want to marry "a literary bore," Bessy's mother removed her daughter from school at age sixteen, a disappointment the young woman never forgot.[13]

Bay may have possessed impeccable social credentials, but Sally Davis was determined to have her daughter marry a man of means. Those who knew Mrs. Davis were not surprised by her agenda. Known for being surrounded by the most influential people in Washington, Bessy's mother was the longtime mistress of President Chester A. Arthur. When her husband, John Davis, was named assistant secretary of state, few who inhabited the nation's capital were surprised at the coincidence.[14]

Lodge's son understood his future mother-in-law disliked his choice of career and its meager financial rewards. Despite parental objections Bay continued to not only encounter Bessy around Washington, but also during his travels in Europe.[15]

As time went on Bay and Bessy found themselves growing increasingly attracted to one another. Spending time together at Maine's Bar Harbor, Bessy was clearly intrigued by Bay's lean good looks and romantic nature. The couple's courtship flourished throughout 1899 with their engagement occurring against Bessy's mother's wishes early the following year.[16]

Happy for his son, Lodge's life remained troubled by other issues. The senator's beloved mother Anna was in poor health. The other issue concerned strained relations with Nannie over her close relationship with John Hay.[17]

Unlike Hay's close friendship with Henry Adams, the senator's and the secretary's relationship was cordial at best. While it remains unknown if the senator was aware of his wife's liaison with Hay, the families nonetheless continued to encounter one another around Washington. Hay, however, found Lodge obnoxious, abrasive, and far too politically conservative to suit his taste.[18]

While both men were devoted Republicans, they shared little in common. Lodge remained passionate about the nation's expansionist foreign policy while Hay remained suspicious. However, disagreement over the direction of the nation's place in the world soon caused tensions to reach a breaking point. The issue concerned the construction of a canal across Central America. The subject, under discussion between the United States and Great Britain for the last half century, was important to Lodge in his objective to expand the country's international interests.[19]

The initial negotiation between Washington and London concerned the Clayton-Bulwer Treaty. The bilateral agreement signed by the two nations in 1850 stated each country's commitment to the construction of a Central American waterway. Following the conclusion of the Spanish-American War, Roosevelt and Lodge believed a canal represented the perfect symbol of their nation's industrial might. In lieu of a growing hubris following the victory against Spain, Congress demanded that any canal constructed with American resources should remain under the auspices of the United States.[20]

President McKinley called on Secretary of State Hay to address the canal issue with the British. That required amending the original Clayton-Bulwer Treaty, an idea the nation's chief diplomat resisted. Hay was dismissive of the canal. As one who believed the railroad remained the wave of the future (a conviction that also dictated the secretary's investment portfolio), Hay chose to allow Britain's ambassador, Lord Julian Pauncefote, to initiate the drafting of an addendum to the original agreement.[21]

In previous discussions, Lodge warned the secretary of state that the treaty would not survive a vote by the Foreign Relations Committee if the interests of the United States were not prioritized. Despite Lodge's warnings the diplomat did not take these concerns seriously.[22]

The new Hay-Pauncefote Treaty, completed on February 3, 1900, did give the United States the opportunity to construct the canal. However, under the confines of the new agreement Washington did not have sole access nor did it have the authority to add implementations to the new international waterway. The new draft agreement outraged Lodge. The senator and his allies refused to ratify the treaty unless language permitting the United States to fortify the canal was integrated into the agreement.[23]

Those who were familiar with Hay's attitudes were not surprised by the developments. The secretary had little respect for the political class. The author and journalist concurred with his close friend Henry Adams that Lodge and his colleagues were only concerned with the retention of political power and uninterested in the long-term priorities of the nation. The diplomat, however, did not understand the intensity of imperialist feeling in the country nor the hurt Lodge experienced about being left out of the full details of the negotiations.[24]

On another level the animosity between Hay and Lodge went much deeper. As the two men's angry exchanges over the treaty intensified, Henry Adams worried how the contentious relationship would affect Nannie Lodge. "I foresee the bitterest kind of breach between Hay and Cabot . . . but Sister Anne will feel a quarrel and if Hay is forced out of office by Cabot's act . . . you can judge better than I whether sister Anne will feel it," Adams wrote Lizzie Cameron.[25]

Watching the growing animosities smolder between the two men, Henry Adams found he despised his former pupil even more. The historian had once held Lodge in high regard. As he witnessed the senator's haughty attitude, drive for power, and dismissive attitude toward Nannie, Adams had come to loathe the New England politician. "It is quite useless for me to play pretend about Cabot. He knows by instinct my contempt; and Sister Anne and Bay know it still better," the historian wrote to Lizzie in February.[26]

Adams's analysis has merit. However, the commentator was also jealous of Lodge and the political prominence he had achieved. Much of Lodge's class had chosen traditional professions, such as law, business, or academia. The senator chose a life that allowed him to shape events rather than observe them from the confines of the Boston Atheneum or the Somerset Club.[27]

Adams was also "at odds with [his] time." He was disappointed in Lodge because he had initially believed the two men shared similar attitudes. Lodge considered himself an honorable and moral man; but he understood that one needed to possess a certain pragmatism to succeed in public life. Adams thought the opposite. The historian believed Lodge had compromised his virtues and values in the name of political power. It was a decision the author found reprehensible and unable to tolerate.[28]

The enmity Adams held toward Lodge was unrealistic. Henry Adams did not possess the skill or temperament to succeed within the political arena of the 19th century. The historian had hoped to mirror the career of his illustrious ancestors. Other than serving as an informal adviser to John Hay, Adams's outspoken and abrasive commentary was more successful in alienating those in positions of power than attracting them.[29]

Adams was also bitter about the rapid growth of the nation and the changes occurring around him. As the commentator sat in his home on Lafayette Square waiting for a call from the Executive Mansion he knew would never come, Adams grew ever more bitter about the state of the nation. "I detest it, and everything that belongs to it, and live only in the wish to see the end of it, with all its infernal Jewry," he commented in one of his many bitterly written correspondences.[30]

The senator did not feel the same way. Ironically, while Lodge was a partisan figure, he respected Adams's intellect and appreciated the help the historian had given him as a young man. Lodge also understood the adoration Adams had toward his wife and family. While finding Adams's tangents occasionally tedious, Lodge respected Adams's ability and the political reform he had tried to achieve.[31]

Busy in New York during the controversy over the canal treaty, Roosevelt remained in conversation with Platt and Lodge over the vice presidency. The Easy Boss gave the impression that without a formidable figure on the 1900 ticket, McKinley's return to the presidency was not guaranteed. "[Platt] fears now that unless I take it nobody will be made Vice President from New York," T. R. wrote Lodge in late January as he ruminated about the loss of the Empire state in the upcoming election.[32]

The New York boss had other reasons for wanting to rid the state of Roosevelt. Behaving as if his days in New York were numbered, the governor delivered a series of comments during his annual address on January 3, 1900 that suggested Albany impose oversight regulations to curtail the power of the state's corporations. Proposing the state's lawmakers be given the power to prevent monopolies, Roosevelt recommended all companies' earnings reports be made available to the public. Roosevelt also went on the attack against legislators in both parties who used their public positions to help wealthy constituents pass legislation tailored to benefit their interests.[33]

Platt was not happy with Roosevelt's remarks. "I want to get rid of the bastard. I don't want him raising hell in my state anymore. I want to bury him," the Easy Boss informed a colleague. Behind the scenes Lodge was trying to help Platt achieve his objective. In the latter part of January 1900, Lodge informed Roosevelt that he was going to approach the president about considering T. R. for governor general of the Philippines.[34]

The senator still urged Roosevelt to consider being on the ticket with McKinley. If Roosevelt preferred an opportunity abroad Lodge was happy to try to bring it to fruition. As Roosevelt contemplated other opportunities, he knew his chances of remaining as governor were fading. Following the controversial address the Easy Boss issued a brief statement, emphasizing that it was vital for the governor as a duty to his nation and his state to consider taking the vice presidency.[35]

With Platt making Roosevelt's renomination as governor unrealistic, T. R. began to ponder Lodge's suggestion of being governor general of the Philippines. But that opportunity failed to materialize. Over the next few days, the spot as McKinley's running mate appeared to represent Roosevelt's only political option. Following a meeting with the president on January 27, Lodge informed the governor that McKinley believed he would easily be nominated.[36]

Lodge emphasized that time was short. "I am clear in the opinion that the time has come when you should make up your mind . . . to refuse to be the candidate for Vice President . . . or let your name be brought forward for the second place on the national ticket." Regardless of the senator's advice, Roosevelt continued to vacillate.[37]

Even as the governor remained against the vice presidency, he expressed appreciation for all Lodge had done to keep his name in the public eye. Over the last sixteen years, the Massachusetts politician had lobbied and cajoled one person after another to help T. R. grind his way up the political ladder. "You are the only man whom, in my life, I have met who has repeatedly and in every way done for me what I could not do for myself, and what nobody else could do," T. R. wrote on January 30.[38]

Lodge still had work to do. The senator remained determined to convince Roosevelt to accept the vice presidential opportunity. When Lodge stated that the position was the "true stepping stone . . . either toward the Presidency or the Governor Generalship of the Philippines," Roosevelt believed it was not worth giving up another opportunity to serve as governor of New York.[39]

The one person who remained a hurdle to Roosevelt retaining the position was Senator Platt. To change the GOP boss's mind, Roosevelt explained to the Easy Boss that he had no interest in the vice presidency. In making his argument T. R. contended the governorship was a wonderful position, and one that he hoped would continue. Roosevelt's comments fell on deaf ears.[40]

In the coming days Platt continued to put pressure on Roosevelt to decide about the vice presidency. Shortly after their meeting, an article appeared in the February 1 edition of the *New York Sun* claiming that representatives of the Republican National Committee had approached Roosevelt concerning his interest in being McKinley's No. 2. An additional article published that same day discussed rumors that many in Washington believed T. R. was the ideal choice for the second spot on the ticket.[41]

Roosevelt was dismayed when he read the news. The governor suspected Platt had planted the story to force him to accept the vice presidential nomination. The paper was also accurate concerning certain members of Congress being favorable to a McKinley-Roosevelt alliance. Hoping to gain more influence over the management of the convention, Lodge asked McKinley to name him chairman of the proceedings. The president, always amenable to a favor, was happy to grant the senator's request.[42]

Roosevelt remained determined not to accept the position. Writing Lodge on February 2, the governor reiterated that it was not in his interest to take the vice presidency. Roosevelt argued that he neither wanted the position nor could afford it, believing that the governorship was where he belonged. "I am a comparatively young man and I like to work," T. R. wrote, dismissing Lodge's argument.[43]

Rejecting Lodge's advice was not easy. Despite his friend's insistence, the governor could not reconcile himself to the idea of accepting what he viewed as a ceremonial position. "There is ample work for me to do in another term—work that will need all my energy and capacity—in short, work well worth any man's doing," Roosevelt stated to Lodge.[44]

T. R. realized his renomination for governor remained unlikely. Following another meeting with Platt on February 10, T. R. again informed the senator that if offered the vice presidency he would refuse to accept. Roosevelt then went on the offensive. Visiting Chicago, the governor issued a statement that if offered the nomination he would decline the opportunity. Upon hearing of the announcement, Lodge, despite remaining positive that the VP position was ideal for Roosevelt, decided to no longer press the issue.[45]

In the second week of February 1900, while working diligently on the upcoming Republican convention and addressing the problems in the Philippines, Lodge received word that his mother had suffered a fatal heart attack. "A great blank has come, a great silence fallen," Lodge wrote in his journal.[46]

Roosevelt was heartbroken when reading of Anna Lodge's passing. "[Y]ou know we both loved her dearly, and she loved us because she knew next to herself and Nannie you had no people in the world who cared for you quite as we do." T. R. understood the depth of his friend's pain. Throughout Lodge's life, his mother had encouraged and fondly recorded every one of her son's accomplishments. With her death, one of the most important people in the senator's life was gone.[47]

As Lodge mourned the death of his mother events abroad and at home caused him to try to put Anna Lodge's passing behind him. On March 7, the senator delivered a three-hour address on the critical nature of the Philippines to the strategic interests of the United States. Democrats argued that Washington's occupation of the islands was nothing more than an excuse to exploit the country for its resources and doing nothing to serve the interests of its people.[48]

Lodge claimed that based on the opposition party's odious history with the African American community, their sudden sympathy for people of color in other nations carried little sincerity. The senator contended the United States was undertaking a mission of noble responsibility that embodied its duty as a great people. "I believe . . . this necessity for watching over the welfare of another people will . . . raise the tone of public life, and make broader and better all our politics," Lodge stated.[49]

The remarks were not only designed to express Lodge's approval of the nation's new expansionist agenda, but to illustrate his belief in the United States as an exceptional nation. "Men who have done great things are those who have never shrunk from trial or adventure,"

Lodge said in his high gravelly voice familiar to so many of his colleagues.[50]

The senator's statement was once again based on political calculation. The comments painted an optimistic future of a nation that was thriving domestically and internationally. With the upcoming presidential election, the senator implied in his remarks that the dramatic changes Bryan and his populist compatriots hoped to impose on the country were not only unnecessary but dangerous.[51]

Following his comments on the Philippines, Lodge again focused his attention on Roosevelt and the vice presidential nomination. Knowing he had promised to remain quiet on the issue, Lodge believed Roosevelt was wasting his potential by remaining in Albany. "I see so many possible dangers in New York that I should like more than ever to get you out of those troubled waters," the senator wrote in a letter on April 16.[52]

In discussing the matter with Secretary of War Elihu Root, T. R. commented to Lodge that Root had given him the impression that major figures in the administration had given up on the idea of a McKinley-Roosevelt ticket. Lodge disagreed, contending that the people who really had the president's ear believed T. R. was the only man who could help the party win in November.[53]

The senator also informed Roosevelt that if the governor remained uninterested in the vice presidential nomination, he should forgo attending the convention as a delegate. Lodge believed Roosevelt's presence in Philadelphia would lead to the delegates nominating him for the position. If that occurred and the governor declined the opportunity, his political future would be irreparably damaged.[54]

Roosevelt believed skipping the convention would lead to a public embarrassment. Convinced the governor was well regarded by Republican faithfuls, Lodge contended no one would view

Roosevelt's decision to skip the proceedings as anything but good intentions.[55]

The senator also believed the only way his friend could attend the convention was if the party found another individual to serve as vice president. Roosevelt thought the idea was more than possible. There were plenty of capable men willing to share the platform with the president. Lodge disagreed. The GOP contained many able candidates, but no one possessed the notoriety and charisma of his closest friend.[56]

Throughout Lodge's conversations with Roosevelt, the senator never stopped believing the governor was indispensable to Republican success. Not everyone agreed. President McKinley remained his usual convivial self, but Mark Hanna let it be known he was opposed to having the Rough Rider on the ticket. The Ohioan had never liked nor trusted the New York governor. He believed Roosevelt's reform agenda was divisive to the party and was convinced that Roosevelt aspired to use the vice presidency as a foundation for winning the presidential nomination in 1904.[57]

Roosevelt's belief that he was not favored by the administration made him question whether the vice presidency would present him with any opportunities for leadership. The governor was also frustrated that no matter how adamant his response Lodge refused to listen. "The qualities that make Cabot invaluable . . . as a public servant also make him quite unchangeable when he has determined that a certain course is right," T. R. commented to Bamie in the spring of 1900.[58]

Roosevelt's sister was all too familiar with the senator's persistent nature. In the last week of April, the two had clashed over her brother's political future. During a heated exchange at Bamie's home in Washington, Lodge had accused Roosevelt's sibling of being "wrongheaded" when she stated that returning to Albany was preferable to the vice presidency. Bamie believed that for T. R., being locked away in a ceremonial office was a fate worse than death.[59]

For all of Roosevelt's apparent resistance to the vice presidency, the governor remained uncertain what action to take. On April 23 T. R. appeared to reconsider his interest in the position. "By the way," Roosevelt commented, "I did *not* say that I would not under any circumstances accept the Vice-Presidency." The statement directly contradicted T. R.'s earlier statement in Chicago when he informed the press that he would not accept the nomination. As Roosevelt's most thorough biographer Edmund Morris observes, hearing T. R.'s odd statement must have turned Lodge's head.[60]

With Roosevelt's governorship coming to an end, he continued to irritate many of Senator Platt's wealthy donors. The situation involved the firing of the state superintendent of insurance, Louis F. Payn. A favorite of Platt's, the bureaucrat kept company with several wealthy insurance executives, a situation that made Roosevelt concerned about a potential conflict of interest. When the superintendent was terminated many believed his uncomfortable associations with corporate elites were responsible. However, Payn had also played a role in leaking the affidavit questioning T. R.'s New York residency during his fight for the gubernatorial nomination.[61]

In the first week of May, still uncertain about accepting the role as vice president, the governor made a visit to Washington. Arriving in the nation's capital Roosevelt asked the opinion of several prominent politicians about serving as McKinley's running mate. For all T. R.'s claims that he was a sought-after candidate, Secretary of State John Hay found it amusing that no one seemed the least bit interested in the New Yorker's political machinations.[62]

One of McKinley's biographers argues that the cool reception Roosevelt received should not have surprised him. Two months earlier, following a visit to the Executive Mansion, the Columbia academic

Nicholas Murray Butler had informed the governor of McKinley's indifference and Hanna's determination to keep T. R. off the ticket. Butler's unfavorable report caused Roosevelt to become so angry that he began to give serious consideration to accepting the idea of becoming the president's running mate.[63]

As the convention approached Roosevelt decided to attend the festivities. Taking the railroad to Philadelphia, T. R. made himself the center of attention as he chatted with passengers and joked with journalists. Wearing a gregarious expression and sporting his signature cowboy hat, the governor appeared like a man about to accept a nomination for high office.[64]

Edith Roosevelt's mood was just the opposite. Joining her husband at the Hotel Walton, New York's first lady begged him to decline the vice presidency. Roosevelt remained in a quandary.[65]

Following a lengthy meeting in Senator Platt's suite the governor informed the Easy Boss that he would only accept the nomination if he was selected by acclamation. Mark Hanna remained adamantly opposed to the idea of T. R. sharing the stage with the president. Following a question by Roosevelt's friend Henry Clay Payne about the issue, McKinley's adviser exploded with the ironic statement, "What is the matter with all of you?" He shouted, "Don't any of you realize that there's only one life between that madman and the presidency?"[66]

Determined to put an end to T. R.'s political rise, the Ohio politico used all his skill to convince the delegates to consider naval secretary John D. Long or several other possible choices. Hanna could do little. Roosevelt was too popular.[67]

Realizing little chance of his reelection as governor existed, Roosevelt decided to follow Lodge's advice. As he prepared to accept a position that just days earlier he had shown little interest in, Roosevelt hoped that his willingness to put the party above his own career would benefit him in four years' time. "It was the feeling of the great bulk of the Republicans that I would strengthen the National ticket," Roosevelt wrote Bamie following the conclusion of the convention.[68]

Roosevelt's decision to defer to the delegates was probably the result of T. R.'s irritation with McKinley and Hanna for not being supportive of his candidacy. Roosevelt had no interest in being second choice, but the prideful politician also wanted to prove his doubters wrong. "He wanted to be the corpse at every funeral and the bride at every wedding," said Theodore's daughter Alice Roosevelt Longworth. Despite Hanna's efforts to prevent Roosevelt's nomination the governor became the man of the hour.[69]

On June 20, 1900, delegates to the Republican National Convention nominated McKinley and Roosevelt respectively for president and vice president of the United States. Following the renomination of McKinley by the Ohio senator Joseph B. Foraker, Roosevelt rapidly moved to the platform to second the president's nomination. As the spectators displayed their approval Lodge turned to Roosevelt with an anxious expression. It was an emotional moment for the senator. The occasion proved so overwhelming that Lodge briefly bowed his head in the direction of the chairman's table before he could resume his remarks.[70]

Roosevelt, caught off guard by his friend's display, quickly collected himself. Addressing the crowd, T. R. embraced the significance of the moment. "We stand on the threshold of a new century big with the fate of mighty nations. It rests with us now to decide whether in the opening years of that century we shall march forward to fresh triumphs or whether at the outset we shall cripple ourselves for the contest." As Roosevelt basked in the ovation of the Republican faithful, those words proved prophetic.[71]

⚙

Standing on the stage in Philadelphia with Lodge at his side, Roosevelt could not help but reflect how each man's political career had nearly ended before it even began. "It certainly is odd to look back sixteen years, when you and I sat in the Blaine convention on the beaten side while the Mugwumps foretold our utter ruin, and then in this convention . . . to think how you recognized me to second McKinley's nomination and then afterward declared . . . myself nominated in the second place on the ticket," Roosevelt wrote from Albany on June 25.[72]

Following the nomination Roosevelt received a letter from Winthrop Chanler. A member of the Astor family and a proud Republican, Chanler thought it amusing that Lodge's powers of persuasion had convinced Theodore to accept the vice presidency. "The wily one has won the day, in spite of your titanic struggle to disappoint him. It is the first time you have been beat, old man," Chanler said as he congratulated Roosevelt on his new opportunity.[73]

As the 1900 campaign began, Lodge's prominence in New England stood second to none. The senator had not only set the United States on a course toward becoming a world power but had helped his friend become the vice president of the United States. With a position on the Senate Foreign Affairs Committee, Lodge believed that only through the good graces of the Republican Party could the nation remain prosperous and secure.

Roosevelt hoped his experience as vice president would be a productive one. Assuming the GOP was victorious in November, the governor wondered if McKinley would take advantage of his new vice president's unique capabilities. T. R. knew he had the experience and the knowledge to be of value to the administration. For all his talents, however, Roosevelt also knew that Hanna's disdain for his political attitudes and aggressive personality could result in being shut out of any meaningful political role.

Throughout Roosevelt's life his family's influence and financial good fortune had allowed him to be a master of his own fate. By accepting a position that President John Adams once referred to as the most insignificant office ever created, Roosevelt wondered if he had ceded his own political future for an opportunity that might never materialize. As the vice presidential nominee prepared for the 1900 presidential campaign, he wondered what the next four years would bring. Would his tenure be one of action and political reward or merely a ceremonial title that would leave him frustrated and unfulfilled?

ELEVEN
Rendezvous with Destiny

"I have very ugly feelings . . . that I am leading a life of
unwarranted idleness."

—Theodore Roosevelt

enator Lodge was delighted with Roosevelt's nomination.
Addressing a crowd following his return from Philadelphia the
senator made a joke about the poor condition of his voice. "But
I know very well what sort of voice I have got here. It resembles the
edge of a saw, and the sound it gives forth is something like that
which issues when the useful instrument is being filed." With his
goal of Roosevelt becoming vice president accomplished Lodge could
afford to relax.[1]

Following the Democrats again nominating William Jennings
Bryan, Roosevelt was anxious to go on the attack. The vice presidential nominee looked forward to barnstorming across the nation
while the stout McKinley once again cultivated his supporters from
his front porch in Canton, Ohio.[2]

Having served as convention chairman, Lodge scheduled a visit
with the president in July to notify McKinley of his renomination.
With T. R. still conflicted over his decision, Lodge remained adamant
he had made the right choice. "I do not pretend to say that the office

in itself is suited to you and your habits, but for the future it is, in my judgment, invaluable," Lodge wrote T. R. on June 29.[3]

Preparing for the 1900 campaign, Lodge raised a delicate subject. The senator understood that Roosevelt was a man of strong opinions who adored being at the center of attention. With McKinley at home in Canton, it was left to T. R. to highlight the successes of the administration. "We must not permit the President or any of his friends, who are, of course, in control of the campaign, to imagine that we want to absorb the leadership and the glory. I want you to appear everywhere as the champion of the party, and above all as the champion of the President . . . This is going to be of immense importance to us four years hence," Lodge wrote.[4]

The senator used the word *we* to emphasize that he and Roosevelt were viewed as a team. Any actions that sought to undermine the administration would not only undercut both men's relationship with the administration but jeopardize Roosevelt's future chances for president.

"No one can tell what will happen in four years," the senator wrote ominously on June 29.[5]

Lodge also took a moment to admit the emotion he experienced when Roosevelt accepted the vice presidential nomination. "I was so anxious that I bowed my head over the table when you began, and did not know that you saw it," Lodge admitted. The senator, however, was not embarrassed by his actions and praised Roosevelt for his inspiring performance and remarks.[6]

During the campaign the vice presidential nominee stretched himself to the very limits of his abilities. Still exhausted from the convention, Roosevelt crisscrossed the country, giving nearly seven hundred speeches in twenty-four states. During these visits the candidate hammered Bryan's populist rhetoric contending that a victory by the Democrats would wreck the nation's economy.[7]

Even with Lodge's advice Roosevelt didn't always follow the correct script. During several campaign stops the candidate promoted the progressive policies he had undertaken as governor. Touting his accomplishments in initiating factory inspections and creating the eight-hour workday, Roosevelt also called for the need of greater equality between the forces of labor and management.[8]

Lodge watched approvingly as Roosevelt and Bryan battled one another around the country. During that summer the senator was shocked to learn that Bay and his fiancée Bessy Davis had decided to elope. The development was no surprise to those like Henry Adams, who noted to Lizzie Cameron that the Davises "were not enchanted by the prospect of a poet-son-in-law." The observation extended to Lodge as well. Neither family was a fan of the other.[9]

While Sally Davis had hoped her daughter would marry the wealthy and eligible George Vanderbilt, the senator thought little of Bessy's parents, who he believed possessed questionable moral character. Sally Davis had a similar opinion of Bay's father, viewing the senator as a "boring, pompous, self-righteous puritan." With animosity among their respective parents neither Bay nor Bessy wanted to spend the happiest day of their lives surrounded by bickering relatives.[10]

Lodge found the couple's decision unappealing but understood their decision. In responding to a congratulatory note from Roosevelt in the latter part of August, the senator mentioned that Bay and Bessy "could not stand the ordinary fashionable wedding" and chose the alternative of a quiet ceremony.[11]

In the latter part of September, Roosevelt and the Lodges traveled to Colorado on a specially designed campaign train. Arriving in the town of Eaton, the vice presidential nominee along with the senator,

Nannie, and Colorado senator Edward Wolcott were welcomed by children waving American flags. Catching a glimpse of the stars and stripes Roosevelt remarked that he was proud to see so many young people holding the emblem of the United States.[12]

The theme of American exceptionalism was also the subject of many of Roosevelt's campaign appearances. As Bryan castigated the McKinley Administration's occupation of the Philippines, Roosevelt contended that nothing was further from the truth. Arguing that the conflict was "the most righteous foreign war . . . waged within the memory of the present generation," T. R. believed Bryan was hindering the United States from achieving its natural destiny. Regardless of Bryan's passionate efforts he remained unable to win the Presidency.[13]

Roosevelt and Lodge were delighted following the Republicans' overwhelming victory in the election of 1900. McKinley and T. R. won more than three quarters of a million votes while easily defeating Bryan in the Electoral College 292–155. Along with the positive economy, many viewed Roosevelt's fiery and engaging personality as responsible for the ticket's success. "I feel that I did as much as any one in bringing about the result," the new vice president wrote as he returned to New York to complete his tenure as governor.[14]

Lodge remained energized following his party's retention of the presidency. "No administration has ever been more cordially sustained than this one and no policies have ever been more thoroughly supported in an election than ours have been at this time," the senator declared during an address to the Middlesex Club on November 9. With another four years of Republican rule assured Lodge returned his attention to his dream of a canal connecting the Atlantic to the Pacific.[15]

The senator remained unhappy with the canal agreement. Believing changes to the treaty were required, Lodge expressed his concerns to McKinley as the two shared a train trip from Washington to Philadelphia on November 24. The president, aware of the realities of politics, agreed that revisions were necessary.[16]

On the surface, Secretary Hay appeared to concur with Lodge about alterations to the agreement. With the two men's relationship still filled with tension, Hay attempted to circumvent the senator's authority by contacting the membership of the Foreign Affairs Committee and encouraging them to approve the treaty without further changes. Hay's objective for that strategy was that he hoped to capitalize on the panel's state of disorganization following the death of its chairman, Senator Cushman K. Davis, on November 27.[17]

Following a series of Senate negotiations, the original Clayton-Bulwer Treaty was replaced by a new agreement containing three additional amendments. The central point gave the United States full autonomy in the building and fortification of the canal. Lodge was pleased with the results. With the British still required to concur, the senator believed the agreement represented a vital step in the nation's international growth. Lodge's opinion did little to convince the British, who rejected the agreement in March 1901.[18]

Having failed in his ability to obtain the treaty's ratification, Hay's resentment of Lodge increased. Following the agreement on the new treaty the secretary lashed out at the Bay State Republican. "The most exasperating thing about it is that a close analysis of the vote convinces me that the treaty could have been ratified without any amendment if our people had any pluck or if Lodge had acted squarely," Hay commented to Henry White.[19]

For Lodge, March was a month of mixed emotions. Disappointed with the results of the negotiations over the canal treaty, the senator nonetheless took delight in the inauguration of Roosevelt as vice president. Watching his friend take the oath of office from his seat on the reviewing stand, Lodge was thrilled at the reception T. R. received from spectators who filled the area around the United States Capitol.[20]

As Roosevelt prepared to embark on the next phase of his career, members of the press were speculating on who would lead the nation in 1904. Following the inauguration, the *Boston Globe*'s Washington correspondent attempted to anticipate who the Republican Party would nominate to replace President McKinley. With that fact in mind seven names were listed as favorites. Lodge and Roosevelt were both listed as under consideration.[21]

Roosevelt was not listed among the favorites. Despite the popularity of the new vice president, many within McKinley's circle cared little for the outspoken New Yorker. Lodge, content to remain in the Senate, was viewed more as a potential cabinet secretary than a Republican standard-bearer. With Roosevelt remaining popular throughout the West, T. R. had plenty of time to focus on his future presidential aspirations.[22]

Unsurprised, Roosevelt discovered the duties associated with his new office gave him little to do. Writing to Edith, who had returned to Oyster Bay, T. R. commented that he did not feel as though "I [am] justifying my existence." Following the adjournment of the Senate in the middle of March the vice president returned to his home at Sagamore Hill.[23]

Shortly before Roosevelt left Washington following the adjournment of the Senate, he expressed concern to journalist Arthur Dunn that "he was afraid he was going to find [the position] rather tame for a man of his temperament." That April Roosevelt confided to William Howard Taft, "I have very ugly feelings now and then that I am leading a life of unwarranted idleness." These emotions were what Roosevelt and his family had feared following Lodge's suggestion about seeking the second spot on the ticket.[24]

Enjoying the views and sounds of the ocean, Roosevelt spent his days supervising family activities and following global events. In a letter to Lodge at the end of March, T. R. contended the United States could not allow itself to lose sight of those nations looking for a foothold in the Western hemisphere. Believing it was essential to maintain a fortified navy, Roosevelt argued any complacency would give Germany and other European powers the belief they were free to make inroads in the West Indies or South America.[25]

The vice president also had concerns about the canal negotiations. T. R. believed the British needed to realize that the United States was determined to construct and fortify the canal on its own terms. Roosevelt admired the British but had little tolerance for those controlling the nation's foreign affairs. Lodge concurred. Remaining frustrated over the canal negotiations, the senator agreed, believing that the policy makers at Downing Street were highly problematic.[26]

Concerned that Hanna would use his influence with the president to keep him isolated, the vice president could do little to involve himself in administration affairs. "[McKinley] is perfectly cordial and friendly to me," Roosevelt wrote Bellamy Storer, "but he does not intend that I shall have any influence of any kind." With no outlet to allow his talents to flourish Roosevelt became consumed by melancholy. "He thought . . . that the vice presidency was the end of his career and he was very depressed about that," his daughter Alice Roosevelt Longworth recalled.[27]

Roosevelt's gloom momentarily lifted when on May 21 he and Lodge attended the opening of the Pan-American Exposition in Buffalo, New York. The upstate community represented the nation at its finest. Even with a booming economy symbolizing the nation's dynamic growth the senator had found the idea unappealing, following a visit by a delegation representing the city.[28]

Uncomfortable with the idea of mixing with the public, Lodge claimed his main reason for initially declining the opportunity was an uncertainty about how to commemorate the occasion. Despite the two men being at an initial loss for words their remarks were an enormous success. As the *Buffalo Review* commented, both speeches "were notable efforts and voiced a patriotism and a sturdy Americanism . . . peculiarly in keeping with the spirit of the times."[29]

The two addresses focused on themes of expansion. Lodge argued that the nation had an objective to fulfill its destiny by becoming a great international power. The senator voiced the country's determination to build a canal as well as the right to defend itself against any foreign adversary who dared encroach on the nation's borders.[30]

The men's remarks generated significant publicity. "Our speeches at Buffalo seemed to have made quite the sensation," Lodge wrote T. R. on June 17. Lodge particularly enjoyed the passionate media criticism as well as the strong reaction the addresses had received from the German press. "I think we have fully attained our object and have made Germany aware that we are watching her," Lodge commented to Roosevelt. While the trip generated several moments of joy, Roosevelt remained restless as he searched for a project to engage his time.[31]

Excluded from any meaningful work in the administration, T. R. focused on matters that fulfilled his own interests. These included the organization of a forum on the importance of public service. The event, "Applied Decency in Public Life," in cooperation with Harvard and Yale, was held at Sagamore Hill in the summer of 1901.[32]

One of the speakers at the conference was Roosevelt's future political adversary, Woodrow Wilson. A professor of government from Princeton University, the academic enjoyed the opportunity to exchange ideas with Roosevelt. Following the forum's conclusion,

Wilson commented that many of the ideas discussed were valuable and inspiring.[33]

The conference and other endeavors helped fill Roosevelt's time. But he still hungered for more to do. In August, the vice president traveled to Colorado to commemorate the twenty-fifth anniversary of its statehood. Roosevelt had accepted the invitation only after declining the opportunity to address Republican legislators. Knowing he had the tendency to be outspoken about party matters, T. R. remained wary of any actions that might cause unhappiness within the administration.[34]

The vice president's arrival in Colorado Springs resulted in an enormous ovation. "I have been greatly astonished at the feeling displayed for me, not only in Colorado and Kansas, but in Missouri and even in Illinois," T. R. wrote Lodge upon his return from the West on August 20. With little to look forward to in the immediate future, the vice president distracted himself by describing to Lodge how his popularity had generated a grassroots movement that could develop into support for a run for president in 1904. Aware of the fickleness of the American voter, Roosevelt refused to allow himself to become overconfident about an opportunity more than three years away.[35]

During these events Roosevelt was uncertain if that support would continue through his tenure as vice president. In addition, he was concerned about New York. Boss Platt had indicated that he would support Roosevelt for the nomination, but T. R. had his doubts. "[It] is of course very nearly out of the question that a man can be nominated with his own State against him, and it is practically certain that my State will be against me," he commented to Lodge.[36]

Following his enjoyable visit to the West, Roosevelt remained committed to a speaking schedule that included stops to Minnesota and Vermont. The vice president was then expected to join his family in the fall at a resort in the Adirondacks. Always delighted to return to the outdoors T. R. looked forward to taking extensive hikes and enjoying the tranquility of Upper New York State.[37]

On September 6, 1901, the vice president was in Vermont when he learned that a crazed anarchist, Leon Czolgosz, had shot President McKinley. The incident had occurred at the Pan-American Exposition in Buffalo, New York—the same event that Roosevelt and Lodge had attended months earlier.[38]

While Roosevelt related to Lodge that McKinley was expected to recover, the vice president related the "stunned amazement of the people over the attempted assassination of the President." "You and I have lived too long, and have seen human nature from too many different sides, to be astounded at ordinary folly or ordinary wickedness," Roosevelt wrote Lodge following the tragic events. The sudden and violent attack on the nation's chief executive had shaken Roosevelt to the core. "It was in the most naked way an assault not on power, not on wealth, but simply and solely on free government," Roosevelt commented from Buffalo.[39]

Even during the nation's darkest moment, Roosevelt could not help but mention to Lodge the ovations he received in his visit to Vermont. The vice president eagerly detailed members of the GOP who repeatedly informed Roosevelt they were anxious to nominate him for the presidency in 1904.[40]

The vice president's description of his popularity with members of the Republican Party in the same letter that described his reaction to McKinley's shooting can initially be viewed as insensitive. One could also view the shift in tone to mask the terror that Roosevelt experienced upon hearing about the attempt on the life of the president. With the incident occurring on the site where Roosevelt and Lodge had greeted the public three months earlier, either man could have had a similar experience.[41]

In Paris, Lodge was grateful to receive Roosevelt's detailed report from Buffalo. "It was almost impossible to get news here when we wanted it most. The miserable [*Paris Herald*] which will publish a yacht race bulletin every five minutes would give only one dispatch some 15 hours late in the day." Believing the event was "a hideous attempt at murder," the senator was glad to know that McKinley's condition had improved.[42]

Lodge understood how deeply Roosevelt wanted the presidency. These instincts might explain Cabot's lack of a response following T. R.'s descriptions of his popularity around the nation. The senator also must have realized the anxiety Roosevelt experienced knowing that no one was invulnerable from the violence that plagued the Gilded Age.

Roosevelt believed the person behind the attempted assassination of McKinley to be a victim of mental illness. Lodge did not agree. The senator was convinced that the anarchist who had pulled the trigger was a symbol of the undisciplined populism that plagued the nation. "These men are the enemies of government, society, and patriotism. We should fight them as we would any other enemy," Lodge wrote Roosevelt on September 19.[43]

Lodge was not wrong. The expansion of the economy had improved the lives of many. But not all Americans had benefited. As a result, random violence had shattered portions of the nation throughout the late nineteenth century.[44]

These attitudes of discontent were displayed by such acts of protest as the Great Railroad Strike of 1877 and the labor riots in Chicago's Haymarket Square in 1886. Many of these disputes were symbolic of the belief that the social contract between the public and its government had fallen into a state of dysfunction. Lodge contended legislation was necessary to aggressively respond to what he viewed as dangerous behavior.[45]

Believing McKinley was on the road to recovery the vice president headed to the Adirondacks. On September 13 Roosevelt and his family engaged in a leisurely climb up Mount Marcy. It was during their descent the following day when Roosevelt was informed that the president's condition was growing worse. A bullet lodged in McKinley's abdomen had resulted in a severe infection causing the president's condition to deteriorate. Late in the evening of September 14 the man known to his intimates as "the Major" passed away.[46]

Roosevelt immediately departed on a special train for the hundred-mile journey to Buffalo. Reaching the city at one-thirty in the afternoon, he immediately called on the president's widow. Shortly after gathering with members of McKinley's cabinet in the living room of the small house where the president had taken his last breath, Theodore Roosevelt became the twenty-sixth president of the United States. Lodge, still in Europe but aware of recent developments, was unable to advise his friend during the most critical moment of his career.[47]

Since becoming vice president, Roosevelt had believed that he had made a horrific mistake. McKinley and his associates had locked him away in a ceremonial office with no means of escape. Mark Hanna had warned those who wanted Roosevelt on the podium with the late president that they were placing a dangerous man one step away from the pinnacle of political power.

Roosevelt had indeed become president but not in the way he wanted. "It is a dreadful thing to come into the Presidency this way," he had written to Lodge. "Here is the task, and I have got to do it to the best of my ability; and that is all there is about it," T. R. wrote.[48]

From the moment Lodge had begun conversing with Roosevelt on a train ride to Washington in the spring of 1884, the Bostonian believed the young man had a rendezvous with destiny. The senator had pushed and prodded his friend to accept the secondary spot on the ticket with McKinley, never realizing what might occur.

In Roosevelt's address on "the strenuous life" in 1898, the former Rough Rider had encouraged his audience to test the limits of their abilities with the objective of seeking a life of "strenuous endeavor." Roosevelt had done his utmost to live by that credo. Preparing to embark on his new journey into the unknown, the new president instinctively understood one is rarely given the opportunity to make history. Realizing that moment had finally arrived, Theodore Roosevelt was not only determined to seize the opportunity but to do so with all deliberate speed.[49]

PART TWO
THE LIMITS OF FRIENDSHIP

TWELVE
The Changing of the Guard

"Instead of Lodge running me, I run Lodge."

—Theodore Roosevelt

T heodore Roosevelt's elevation to the presidency reverberated across Washington. Traveling in Europe, Henry Adams was unsurprised by the assassination of McKinley. "We have been fed so full of horrors that a mere political murder seems now a regular part of our lives," the author confided to John Hay on September 7, 1901.[1]

At the same time Adams's thoughts flashed to Roosevelt. "[I]n my mind, in all our minds, silent and awful like the Chicago express, flies the thought of Teddy's luck." Writing Hay on October 1, Adams believed that the nation's tradition demanded the American people support the new president. "We have got to rally around him," the historian declared.[2]

Preparing for his return to the nation's capital, Senator Lodge heard rumblings about being selected to replace Hay as secretary of state. Lodge was flattered but preferred to remain in the Senate. "I really think I can be of more use to him there than anywhere else," Lodge wrote Winthrop Chanler.[3]

Disappointed that he was unable to support Roosevelt during such dire circumstances, Lodge could do nothing more except empathize with the enormous challenge his friend was about to undertake. "Fate has brought you this burden & responsibility & glory of the greatest office Man can hold now on earth," Lodge wrote the new occupant of the Executive Mansion on September 15.[4]

As the senator returned from Europe, he remained confident that his friend was surrounded by experienced advisers. When Lodge learned that John Hay was to remain as secretary, the senator had nothing but praise for the nation's chief diplomat. Despite their disagreements, Lodge believed Hay a wise counselor who would continue to serve the nation well. While Hay was proud to remain within the administration, his opinion of Roosevelt's immature and boorish personality had not changed. "Well, he is here in the saddle again," Hay wrote in response to a note from Henry Adams describing Roosevelt's good fortune.[5]

Declaring the intention to represent T. R. in the Senate the Bostonian realized he was unable to do as much for his friend as he had in the past. Over the last decade and a half Lodge had enjoyed using his influence to help propel Roosevelt up the political ladder. As Roosevelt took his new position, the senator wondered if the new president would rely on his advice and counsel or turn to others in facilitating the business of the nation.[6]

For all of Lodge's concern, Roosevelt valued the senator's opinion. On October 11 T. R. requested his friend visit him at his earliest convenience. Lodge, still traveling abroad, was grateful to visit Roosevelt as soon as he returned.[7]

Arriving at the presidential residence recently renamed the White House, Lodge offered insightful comments about Roosevelt's first message to Congress. The president explained his positions on the economy would remain consistent with his comments during the campaign of 1900. In a discussion about filling federal appointments across the country, Roosevelt informed Lodge that he aspired "to appoint as good men in the South as in the North, and I want to take the best men, black or white." Both men shared the view that it was critical to retain people with the knowledge and expertise to elevate the quality of public service in all branches of the national government.[8]

Knowing that Roosevelt's rhetoric on economic matters was more liberal than his own, Lodge thought T. R.'s message was perfect in substance and in tone. The senator also praised Roosevelt's early administrative actions. "I cannot see that you have made a single mistake," the senator wrote following his visit.[9]

Returning to his role as Roosevelt's most ardent supporter, Lodge came to the president's defense during moments of controversy. Such was the case following T. R.'s controversial invitation to the prominent African American Booker T. Washington to dine at the White House.[10]

Roosevelt and Washington supported segregation, but both men also aspired to develop a strong African American presence within the Republican Party. In addition, the president believed people of color deserved an opportunity to vote without experiencing intimidation from white citizens.[11]

Washington's visit led to an uproar in the South. Media criticism of the president was scathing. T. R. was accused by the future governor of Mississippi, James K. Vardaman, of being "a coon-flavored miscegenationist" and Senator "Pitchfork" Ben Tillman of South Carolina believed that the president's actions could create a conflagration so severe it could result in the deaths of numerous Black people throughout the South.[12]

Throughout the controversy, Lodge remained upbeat. "Needless for me to say how utterly right I think you are," the senator commented on October 19. Regardless of his racial views Lodge had little love for those states that composed the old Confederacy. "I am always hoping that they will learn and broaden, and then comes a thing like this showing the narrow stolidity and imperiousness which are so disheartening," the senator commented following Washington's visit.[13]

The president concurred with Lodge's opinion that the spirit responsible for causing the Civil War was alive and well in that portion of the country. "If these creatures had any sense they would understand that they can't bluff me," T. R. angrily stated.[14]

Lodge also had a positive appraisal of Roosevelt's first address to Congress. Following the 20,000-word statement on December 3, the senator was pleased with the president's remarks and further stated that the reaction by the Republican caucus in both the House and the Senate was highly positive.[15]

Roosevelt had done his best to include complimentary language about the industrial benefits brought to the nation by American business. The president also stated his conviction that greater government oversight of the business community was necessary. "Corporations engaged in interstate commerce should be regulated if they are found to exercise a license working to the public injury," Roosevelt stated as part of his public comments.[16]

Whether the president was reassured to know that Lodge concurred with his remarks is debatable. For years T. R. was viewed around Washington as "the junior member of the firm of Lodge and Roosevelt." Admitting that Lodge's advice and support were invaluable, Roosevelt was miffed that many believed the senator had a metaphorical "latchkey" to the White House.[17]

The president's irritation over the issue was evident during a conversation with Washington correspondent Arthur Wallace Dunn. As Roosevelt adapted himself to the rigors of the office, Dunn asked if talk among senators about Roosevelt's overreliance on Lodge was problematic. "They don't understand it at all," Roosevelt responded dismissively, "Instead of Lodge running me, I run Lodge."[18]

The statement spoke volumes. Lodge occupied a prominent position in the Senate but that was the limit of his influence. Roosevelt was the nation's chief executive and didn't want anyone to forget it. Even as the president wrote in his autobiography that the relationship between the two men "remained unchanged" that statement was not entirely true. Lodge may have respected the shift in his and Roosevelt's roles, but the senator was not always successful in restraining himself from using access to the president to accomplish his own political objectives.[19]

T. R. found the gossip over Lodge's influence tedious. However, on occasion the president managed to turn the backroom talk into an enjoyable anecdote. One day young Quentin Roosevelt learned that a favorite police officer guarding the White House was shifting to another position. A precocious little boy, the Roosevelts' youngest child took action to reverse the decision. "I'm going to see Lodge; that's what Father tells everybody when he wants to have anything done." The newspaper item, preserved in Lodge's correspondence with Roosevelt is indicative that the senator found the story entertaining.[20]

Roosevelt's overwhelming responsibilities did not preclude him from maintaining the same frenetic social schedule he had enjoyed before taking office. "I am not going to be the slave of the tradition that forbids Presidents from seeing their friends," T. R. told John Hay. "I am going to dine with you and [Henry Adams] and [Cabot] whenever I like." The president did his best to keep his word. In January 1902, the Roosevelts invited the Hays, Lodges, and Henry Adams to an intimate evening in the Red Room of the White House.[21]

It was Adams's first formal dinner in the Executive Mansion since 1878. Then the historian had attended with his late wife, Clover, a moment he described to Lizzie Cameron as "the happiest time of my whole life." Entering the president's residence, Adams quickly regretted accepting the invitation.[22]

Referring to the White House as "the slaughter-house," Adams became increasingly depressed as he thought of his dearly departed wife. The historian's mood grew darker as his long strides took him into the first couple's red drawing room, a venue Adams could only describe to Lizzie Cameron as "hideous." Adams's tone grew surlier as he and other guests were forced to wait twenty minutes before the first couple finally arrived. "To say that I enjoyed it would be, to you a gratuitous piece of deceit," Adams wrote as he reflected on what he expected to be his final visit to 1600 Pennsylvania Avenue.[23]

For many attending, a White House dinner was a memorable event. Adams hated it. The president dominated the conversation. "Really, Theodore is exasperating even to me . . . and always was," Adams wrote disapprovingly.[24]

The historian enjoyed the Lodges' company, but believed it was just a matter of time before the senator's envy over Roosevelt's success ruptured their friendship. "But the most dangerous rock on Theodore's coast is Cabot. We all look for inevitable shipwreck there," Adams wrote ominously to Cameron on January 12.[25]

Lodge possessed no deep-seated jealousy over Roosevelt's good fortune. The senator adored T. R. and was grateful that he had helped place him in the position to gain the presidency. "I have shot my bolt . . . I go no higher," Lodge wrote Roosevelt in the summer of 1899.[26]

Roosevelt may have no longer depended on the senator for professional guidance, but he still enjoyed rides through the park, walks, and other gatherings with Lodge and his wife. "Would you and Cabot be willing to dine here entirely alone on Monday, Wednesday, Thursday, or Friday? I feel as though I should burst if I am not able to discuss at length and without my usual cautious reserve several questions . . ." the president wrote Nannie Lodge in an undated note from 1901.[27]

The invitations were plentiful and the activities enjoyable. However, T. R.'s correspondence with Lodge no longer possessed that air of emotional dependence as displayed so frequently in his exchanges with the senator during the 1880s and 1890s. Even as the Roosevelts kept Lodge informed about the progress of their children and other sensitive matters, the senator still desired to make his presence felt in the affairs of the nation. During the first months of 1902 Lodge decided he could begin fulfilling that objective by arranging for the appointment of his friend, Judge Oliver Wendell Holmes Jr., to the United States Supreme Court.[28]

In July 1902, Associate Justice Horace Gray retired from the bench, giving Roosevelt the opportunity to name a replacement. Gray, from Massachusetts, had suffered a stroke the previous February. By June the jurist realized he could no longer fulfill his obligations. Since the founding of the federal judiciary on March 4, 1789, a justice from the Bay State had always held a seat on the court. As discussion ensued about a replacement, many believed it was a foregone conclusion that a candidate from the Commonwealth would take Gray's place.[29]

Arriving at Nahant, Lodge wrote the president on June 5 to ascertain if the rumors of the justice's potential resignation were accurate. "I do not know whether it is true," the senator wrote, "but if it is I want of course to talk with you before you decide." In considering options, Lodge believed Holmes should receive the appointment.[30]

The men shared a longtime friendship. Holmes was one of the few members of the Boston aristocracy who came to Lodge's defense following his decision to support the Blaine nomination in 1884. With an opening on the court available, Lodge aspired to help his child-hood friend obtain the highest honor in the legal profession. Lodge, however, was wary in approaching the president about Holmes's promotion to the bench. "I have not bothered you because I thought [the resignation] would not come for some time but I have thought it over a great deal," the senator wrote in the first week of June.[31]

At the time of Holmes's appointment many in Massachusetts believed the jurist possessed an uncertain judicial ideology, making him an unpredictable personality for such an important position. Much of the criticism originated from Holmes's decisions during his tenure on the Massachusetts Supreme Court. In opinions involving disagreements between labor and management the jurist frequently sided with workers against their employers.[32]

Those members of Boston's corporate elite who disagreed with the judge on such decisions as protests not being a firing offense were unnerved by one of such progressive views sitting on the nation's highest court. Lodge and Roosevelt were unconcerned. The two were focused on finding a justice who would cement the court's decision on the status of Puerto Rico and other territories acquired during the Spanish-American War.[33]

On May 27, 1901, nearly two months before Justice Gray's resignation, the court ruled on *Downes v. Bidwell*. The matter involved the question of whether produce shipped from Puerto Rico to New York was considered interstate commerce. In a 5–4 decision the justices ruled that because these provinces were "inhabited by alien races," Puerto Rico, Guam, and the Philippines were international territories, falling under congressional not constitutional authority.[34]

Based on Lodge's and Roosevelt's belief in Anglo-Saxon superiority it is no surprise they viewed the inhabitants of these territories as alien. "I am absolutely for Holmes unless he should be adverse on Porto Rican cases, which I am informed he is not," the senator wrote the president on June 5. Knowing the spot on the court would soon be vacant, Lodge aggressively sought to uncover the reason for Holmes's unpopularity.[35]

Other than Massachusetts's senior senator George F. Hoar, and several members of the legal profession who resented Holmes because of several labor decisions, most of Lodge's conversations resulted in positive replies. "I have been talking quietly with lawyers here & there is no doubt that the great body of the bar would strongly approve," Lodge commented to T. R. following his unofficial survey.[36]

Following Roosevelt's friend William Howard Taft declining the opportunity, the president believed the jurist from Massachusetts possessed the qualities required of one who should serve on the bench. But Roosevelt remained uncertain if Holmes would represent the views as reflected by the nation's most prominent chief justice, John Marshall. Defining those qualities as one of "a constructive statesman, constantly keeping in mind his adherence to the principles and policies under which this nation has been built up . . ." T. R. wrote Lodge in describing his views of his ideal candidate for the court.[37]

As Roosevelt considered the Holmes appointment, Lodge attempted to use his personal relationship with the president to lobby for the jurist's selection. "It would I confess be a sore disappointment to me if you should decide . . . to pass Wendell over," the senator wrote Roosevelt on July 7. But Lodge knew all too well no one could pressure the president to act on any issue unless it was entirely his decision.[38]

Wanting to know more, the president asked Lodge to conduct an interview with the judge to get his views on the issues Roosevelt and the senator had previously discussed. "I can put it to Holmes with absolute frankness & shall for I would not appoint my best beloved on that bench unless he held the position you describe," Lodge wrote the president from Tuckernuck Island.[39]

Lodge's interview resulted in a conversation between Holmes and President Roosevelt in Oyster Bay on June 25, 1902. Following the interview, the president named the justice as his choice for Gray's seat. There is no doubt the senator was an important element in bringing Holmes to the attention of the president. However, the friendship between the two men was not the decisive factor in Roosevelt's choice to name the Bostonian to the bench.[40]

Holmes took positions that the president shared. T. R. also found the jurist a charming personality with a powerful intellect. Most important, with Massachusetts being a dependable Republican state, Roosevelt was able to keep a seat on the court in the hands of the GOP. Lodge was delighted at Holmes's appointment. "I have never known a nomination received in the Press with such a chorus of praise—here and everywhere," the senator wrote the president on August 17.[41]

Even while appreciating Lodge's insight on the Holmes appointment, the president remained wary of allowing his friend's requests from receiving too much public attention. Roosevelt understood more than most that in politics image frequently symbolized reality. Such was the case when in June 1902 an article appeared in the *Boston Sunday Post*, characterizing Lodge as the "boss of Washington."[42]

The publication had never viewed Lodge favorably and the commentary that weekend was no exception. Written under the pseudonym of "Norman," the piece described Roosevelt and Lodge as virtually inseparable. The senator was also referred to as "throned monarch of the national capital," "chaperone to the President," and "a dispenser of dull care when Theodore has an off day of that strenuous feeling. It's Lodge everywhere." As a final insult the newspaper illustrated Lodge's supposed control over the president by posting a caricature of a large telephone that read "direct to the president's ear."[43]

Within the newspaper's cartoon was a switchboard containing the words FOREIGN AFFAIRS, GREATER NAVY, and PHILIPPINES. In small print at the bottom of the drawing read the caption H.C. LODGE, OPERATOR. Such portrayals caused Roosevelt to be especially careful of displaying any kind of favoritism to his friend from Massachusetts. "I try to look at Lodge disinterestedly, and try not to let my personal friendship mislead me," Lodge wrote to *Outlook* editor Lyman Abbott.[44]

Even as Lodge submitted candidates for appointment with outstanding pedigrees in education and experience, the president remained cautious. Such was the case of Bostonian Cameron Forbes, whom the senator suggested for an administrative position in the Philippines. "I want you as a favor to me and in justice to him to read [the recommendations] over," Lodge asked Roosevelt on August 9, 1902.[45]

The diplomat was appointed but only after the president seriously considered an assortment of other candidates. "I guess I shall appoint Forbes, but I do not like even to express an opinion now, for I dare not make up my mind until I get the whole list before me," Roosevelt informed Lodge two days later.[46]

While the president remained cautious about appearing overly favorable to Lodge he had enormous respect for the senator, once telling an official that "there is no one who knows my mind better or whom I trust more." However, for all their conviviality the two men often differed when it came to certain matters relating to the stewardship of the country.[47]

Long before Roosevelt entered the world of politics, he had expressed concern about the unregulated growth of American business. The patrician believed the excess displayed by many corporate elites was responsible for the moral rot permeating society. Lodge, who viewed himself as a conservative, also disliked the garish displays and the dishonest manner that characterized many that dominated the nation's finances. "Money is no longer under a taboo," he had stated in 1913 regarding the decline of the nation's manners and morals.[48]

The senator had also exhibited frustration at those within the business sector who had opposed the nation's involvement in the war against Spain. Lodge not only resented Wall Street's dismissal of a policy he believed was in the national interest but criticized many businessmen's opposition to regulating the nation's immigration laws, fearing it would limit their access to cheap labor.[49]

The senator may have found many of the shifts occurring in society distressing, but being a historian, he realized that change was inevitable. "The modern tendency economically is toward consolidation. Nothing can stop it," Lodge told his personal physician. Believing that moderate regulation was a way to stem the many ills plaguing society, the senator and the president possessed similar views on enacting legislation to enforce their moralist sensibilities.[50]

Roosevelt hoped to employ the powers of his office to incrementally restrain those corporate executives not conducting themselves in a principled manner. By employing these actions, the president hoped to use his reformist sensibilities to instill within these individuals a responsibility to conduct their affairs with fairness and integrity.[51]

In that spirit of corporate restraint Roosevelt invoked the Sherman Antitrust Act to dissolve the Northern Securities Company in February 1902. The trust was a consolidation of several leading railroads controlled by industrialists J. P. Morgan, E. H. Harriman, and James J. Hill. Many believed the consortium was a monopoly, unfairly dictating the price businessmen were forced to pay to bring their product to market. While the case was not decided until 1904 the action gave the public the illusion of Roosevelt as a trustbuster, a label he happily exploited as the nation approached the off year elections.[52]

As the year continued, the president, energized by his confrontation with corporate America, set off on a late summer tour of New England. On the schedule was an August visit to Lodge's home at Nahant, where Roosevelt planned on delivering remarks at Lynn's city hall and Nahant's public library. T. R. had visited the Lodges' summer home on several occasions, but it was the first time the senator's family had hosted him as president.[53]

Arriving at the Lynn railroad station in the last week of August 1902, the president, wearing a top hat following a christening he had attended in Newport, Rhode Island, was greeted by a roaring crowd of 10,000 people. With bright sunshine and few clouds, Roosevelt and Lodge's wife were met by the family's personal coachman, Dennis Desmond. Attuned to the senator's tastes, Desmond had arranged for the open carriage to be drawn by two of the finest black bays in Lodges' stable.[54]

Preparing for the short trip to the Lodge compound, Nannie, seated next to the president and wearing a dark coat, silk scarf, and dark hat covering her tightly bobbed dark blond hair, was photographed glancing over her shoulder to check that everyone in the four-carriage procession was accounted for. Traveling four miles, the procession stopped at the Nahant border where it received a twenty-one-gun salute courtesy of a United States Navy Brigade.[55]

The senator had prepared for the visit in detail. With the objective of making Roosevelt's stay as private as possible, Lodge had enacted a series of security precautions that many believed were overly cautious. In addition to the presidential Secret Service detail, Lodge had arranged for ten members of the Lynn and Nahant police departments to stand guard around the family villa for the duration of the visit. Security was so stringent that one of Roosevelt's assistant secretaries was denied admittance until another official could verify the man's identity.[56]

Given a bedroom that overlooked the ocean, the president was the guest of honor at an intimate dinner of friends and family all scrupulously orchestrated by Nannie Lodge. Conversing until late in the evening the president nonetheless was up bright and early the next morning. Standing on the veranda that surrounded the upper portion of the house, Roosevelt waved to the assembled press while preparing for an address later that day at the Nahant Public Library.[57]

On August 25 with the American flag fluttering gently in the background, Roosevelt, standing on a makeshift platform in a vest and short jacket, addressed an animated crowd of 60,000 people. Throughout the speech, the president called on his audience to increase its moral fiber, rather than pursue material possessions. Lodge, listening intently, his head cocked to the left appeared to nod in agreement.[58]

Later that day during an address at Lynn's town hall, Roosevelt preached to his audience that the only way government institutions could achieve success was to have people in office who possessed credibility and skilled leadership. In highlighting the need for morality in public service the president emphasized his belief in a society where everyone received fair treatment under the law. As Roosevelt left Nahant to return to Washington, he was unaware that he would soon have to put those words into actions.[59]

In early 1900, following a coal strike across Pennsylvania, those in control of the mining industry fearing a victory by William Jennings Bryan had begrudgingly agreed to raise the wages of their employees by 10 percent. Two years later, with wages for a ten-hour day at an outrageous $1.87, the miners considered declaring another work stoppage. With the desire to limit the potential of any strike, employers had also capitalized on the era's increased immigration by taking advantage of those who had recently arrived on the nation's shores, paying them the cheapest wages possible.[60]

Unhappy with the treatment of the workers, John Mitchell, president of the United Mine Workers union, demanded an increase in wages and a shortening of the workday. When those conditions were refused in September 1902, 140,000 miners walked off their jobs. As winter approached, Roosevelt, wary of intervening in the strike, believed that the situation could bring the nation to a halt.[61]

By the late fall much of the public had grown concerned. With the price of coal rising from five dollars to twenty dollars a ton, many wondered if the strike would force the president's hand. Lodge believed the developing crisis could be disastrous for his party and his friend in the White House.[62]

Lodge and Roosevelt understood that the administration had no control over the price of coal. The senator stated that the public would think otherwise. "It hurts people and they say (this is literal) 'We don't care whether you are to blame or not. Coal is going up and the party in power must be punished.'" Lodge was concerned that the strike could lead to potential Republican losses in the eastern region of the country, and wondered if there was anything the president could do to bring the problem to an end.[63]

As the president considered his options, Lodge's concern about the situation grew more dire. "The worst is I cannot see what to do," the senator wrote three days later. "We are running straight on to what may become an overwhelming demand that the government take the mines—which would be an awful step." The senator believed the intransigence of the coal owners was responsible for the deadlock and urged T. R. to consult Attorney General Philander Knox about conducting private discussions with ownership.[64]

In addition to Lodge's concern about the state of the country he was concerned about the cost the strike could have on the Republican

Party. "If no settlement is reached it means political disaster in New England . . ." Lodge's son-in-law Gus Gardner was making a run for Congress and the senator believed that the turmoil of events could lead to Gardner's defeat. For all of Lodge's anxiety he refused to believe that a government takeover of the coal fields was the proper solution. "Why, sane, sensible conservative men are urging us to declare in our platform that the coal fields must be taken. We shall not do it of course but it is a bad sign," Lodge wrote the president as he recovered from a train accident following his tour of New England.[65]

Roosevelt understood Lodge's quandary. He had considered the idea of again employing the Sherman Anti-Trust Act against management of the mines. But Knox had vetoed the idea due to a lack of evidence. "The coal operators are not combined so as to enable us legally to call them a trust," the president informed Lodge on September 27. Used to employing his sizeable personality to shape the nature of events, Roosevelt experienced enormous frustration as he sought to solve the crisis. "There is literally nothing, so far as I have yet been able to find out, which the national government has any power to do in the matter," the president wrote.[66]

Knowing that some action was needed, Roosevelt recruited his secretary of war, Elihu Root, to discuss the coal impasse with his former client J. P. Morgan. The president's initial attempt at using a member of his cabinet to solve the crisis had met with failure, when Secretary of the Interior Carroll Wright was unable to reach an agreement with the two parties. As Root and Morgan met, Roosevelt inserted himself into the situation by arranging a meeting between labor and management.[67]

By the end of September 1902, rents were going up and riots were breaking out. Just a short walk from the White House, the Washington Monument had ceased operation due to lack of fuel to power the elevator. Roosevelt met with the representatives from the two sides on October 3 at Blair House. Still in recovery after a rail accident near Pittsfield, Massachusetts, the president remained confined to a wheelchair.[68]

Despite Roosevelt's urgent pleas including his suggestion of an independent commission to arbitrate the case, neither side would agree. Disappointed to learn of the president's failure, Lodge congratulated Roosevelt for his effort. "If I had let myself go I should have said some things about the operators which would have been pretty bitter." With no solution on the horizon, Lodge believed Pennsylvania governor William Stone should authorize the National Guard to protect those miners who wanted to return to work.[69]

While Stone did call out the guard as a means of restoring order, no miner took advantage by crossing the picket line. With negotiations at a standstill, the president was under pressure to take drastic action. "Most of my correspondence wish me to try something violent and impossible," Roosevelt wrote Lodge on October 7.[70]

The president understood his leadership was being tested. "My great concern is, of course, to break the famine; but I must not be drawn into any violent step which would bring reaction and disaster afterward." For all of Roosevelt's apprehension about the use of armed forces to end the strike, little else seemed possible.[71]

Lodge remained livid over the inability of the two sides to reach a compromise. "The Socialistic feeling is growing apace and the demand that the government take the mines—one of the greatest disasters that could befall us." The senator, concerned about the economy, also turned his eyes toward November. "If the strike continues until election no man can say how much it will hurt us," Lodge commented.[72]

Roosevelt's consideration about authorizing government control of the mines was contrary to his conservative instincts. The president also understood there were times when government action was necessary. As Roosevelt prepared to make the most pivotal decision of this presidency, Root continued to meet with J. P. Morgan.[73]

The banker had his own concerns about the crisis. Morgan worried that as prices rose the crisis could spread to other markets endangering the industrialist's other extensive investments. Attempting to work out a solution to the impasse, the former corporate lawyer met Morgan and continued their conversations on the banker's 302-foot yacht, *Corsair*. After some deliberation, it was agreed that the best solution was to return to T. R.'s idea of an independent commission to adjudicate the dispute.[74]

Roosevelt's persuasive talents proved successful. With ownership refusing to allow any representative of labor on the tribunal, the president convinced management to allow him to appoint what Roosevelt described as a "sociologist" to the committee. Though not possessing a PhD the new representative did have labor experience, having formally served in the position as chief of railway conductors. "The mighty brains of these captains of industry had formulated the theory that they would rather have anarchy than tweedledum, but that if I would use the word tweedledee they would hail it as meaning peace," the president wrote Lodge upon the conclusion of the crisis.

Following the workers' return to the coal fields, Roosevelt's commission soon released a report favoring the miner's call for an increase in wages. With the crisis solved, the owners agreed to another 10 percent salary increase as well as cutting the workday from ten hours to nine. Roosevelt had privately believed management was taking advantage of the mine workers. But the president's main concern was to prevent the strike from damaging the economy. "As for the multitude of creatures who want me to seize the coal barons by the throat . . . or stamp out the lawlessness of the trade unions by the instant display of force . . . why I couldn't begin to enumerate them," the president commented following the resolution of the crisis.[75]

Roosevelt biographer William Harbaugh also argues that Lodge's panic about a Democratic surge played a role in Roosevelt's decision-making. More important, by threatening to federalize the coal mines, the president was prepared to go beyond the confines of the Constitution to do what was necessary to preserve the nation's security and economic welfare.[76]

From the moment he was catapulted into the presidency, Theodore Roosevelt had shown himself as a man of formidable intelligence and skill. From his decision to use the arm of government to confront the titans of American business, the president had also stated his commitment to ensuring the nation's citizenry received a fair opportunity to achieve the American Dream. The president's settlement of the coal strike was viewed as a massive success. However, many within the corporate wing of the Republican Party remained concerned that Roosevelt was less interested in protecting the party's business interests and more concerned with embracing a reform agenda.[77]

Lodge, who viewed all events through a political eye, was not unfamiliar with Wall Street's concerns. The senator shared the president's view that some restraints on corporate America were necessary. But Lodge also believed that to keep the party's prospects positive Roosevelt needed to walk a delicate line in his relationship with the nation's moneymen. In that regard the senator realized he needed to apply as much of his persuasive powers as possible to keep his dearest friend on a winning path as the nation prepared for the 1904 election.

THIRTEEN
A Delicate Balance

"Excitement is impossible where there is no contest."
—Henry Cabot Lodge

I n November 1902, President Roosevelt's resolution of the coal strike resulted in the Republican Party maintaining its majorities in the House of Representatives and the Senate. In addition, Lodge's son-in-law Augustus Gardner successfully defeated his Democratic opponent to win a seat in the nation's lower chamber. In writing of Gardner's victory, Henry Adams commented to Lizzie Cameron that "Gussy's seat is said to have been the most expensive ever bought in the House." The historian's tart comment was no surprise. With Lodge being considered the political boss of Massachusetts Adams was convinced that Gardner had taken advantage of his father-in-law's influence to enter the political arena.[1]

Lodge had expressed confidence that Republicans would perform well. But the senator remained unhappy with the coal operators' inability to settle the strike independently. "It does seem to me that businessmen, with a few exceptions, are worse when they come to deal with politics than men of any other class," Lodge commented in a letter to Roosevelt following the settling of the dispute.[2]

The senator understood that Roosevelt's determination to restore a sense of moral order on Wall Street was not a popular initiative. The president's reform instincts had never ceased to irritate Republican regulars concerned about alienating the party's business wing critical to their success. Lodge employed his contacts within the investment community to reassure those like Lee Higginson's associate Gardiner Lane that T. R. was a moderate reformer concerned with furthering the party's goals of greater prosperity and moral authority in government. That task proved challenging as the president began promoting his economic themed policy platform known as the "Square Deal."[3]

On June 4, 1903, the president delivered an address near a memorial to Abraham Lincoln in Springfield, Illinois. Throughout Roosevelt's remarks he urged Americans to devote themselves to pursuing a spirit of good fellowship in their interactions with one another. Within his comments, T. R. also alluded to the dangers that could arise if his fellow citizens looked upon the pursuit of wealth as the only measure of success. "Mark what I said about the mob and plutocracy, and the crimes of greed on the one hand and of violence on the other," Roosevelt commented to Lodge.[4]

The senator expressed hope that Roosevelt's recent remarks could counter concerns he had heard over the president's recent economic rhetoric. Following appearances around the state Lodge stayed at the home of Massachusetts Supreme Court Judge Franklin G. Fessenden. In their conversations, the jurist had informed the senator he worried that the president was giving the appearance of siding with labor against the forces of big business. Lodge informed his constituent that the charges were untrue. Fessenden was grateful for Lodge's affirmation, however the New Englander remained concerned because the judge was an important member of the state GOP.[5]

The senator believed it was critical that the president be wary of adversely affecting the temperament of the party's business wing. "I have said before, these men are spreading the statement that you are taking sides with labor against them unduly and you would not enforce the law rigidly in both directions," the senator commented following his reading of Roosevelt's Springfield address.[6]

Roosevelt resented being lectured by those he characterized as the "dishonest rich." During a visit out West a month earlier, the president had commented to Lodge how those like J. P. Morgan and others were prepared to employ their resources to send Grover Cleveland back to the White House. The senator believed the former president was a weak candidate and concluded it was more likely that the Democrats would search for someone new to face the president in 1904.[7]

The senator's concern that Roosevelt's progressive policies might disrupt the GOP's delicate coalition did not prevent him from remaining committed to extending American power abroad. Throughout 1902 and 1903, controversies over the United States' occupation of the Philippines and a boundary dispute with Canada over the American territory of Alaska illustrated that not everyone had a positive impression of Washington's expansionist ambitions.[8]

In March 1902, the commanding general of the United States Army, Nelson A. Miles, angry over a reprimand he had received from the commander in chief, leaked information to members of Congress that US troops had committed torture, reckless destruction of property, and other atrocities in the Philippines.[9] Over the next six months the controversial military campaign was splashed across the nation's newspapers. When a classified report detailing the criminal behavior of American soldiers was released, the evidence was so damning that Lodge was forced to sit quietly as his Senate committee investigated the matter.[10]

The criticism Lodge and his colleagues endured over these brutalities was not confined to the media. Henry Adams informed Lizzie Cameron that not only was Lodge in a bad mood over the investigation, but Bay, always the contrarian, was having a delightful time berating his father about the events in the Pacific. As the senator endured media criticism he was also involved in a debate with a member of the British commonwealth over the borders of Alaska.[11]

When the United States had purchased the undeveloped territory from Russia in 1867, the borders that connected the southeastern part of the region to Canada was never properly defined. That issue, never of particular interest to either the United States or Canada, immediately changed when gold was discovered in the Klondike region in 1897 leading to 100,000 prospectors rushing to the territory. In studying the dimensions of the area agreed to by Russia and Britain in the 1825 Treaty of St. Petersburg, Lodge determined the boundaries were explicit and the Canadians had no claim to contest the issue.[12]

The president was in complete agreement. In 1902, when Secretary of State John Hay recommended negotiations between the United States and the British dominion, the president, at Lodge's suggestion, informed his chief diplomat that he was considering dispatching troops to the disputed area. Hoping to deter any violence between Canadians and Americans, the president was also determined to prevent any encroachment by the United Kingdom into American territory.[13]

A year later, the Senate ratified an agreement authorizing an international tribunal to mediate the Alaskan dispute between the two countries. The commission was composed of six members: three from the United States and three from the United Kingdom. Roosevelt selected Secretary of War Root, Senator Lodge, and former senator George Turner of Washington State. The British and Canadian side was composed of the royal chief justice of England Lord Richard Webster, Canadian lawyer A. B. Aylesworth, and former justice of the Quebec Supreme Court Sir Louis-Amable Jette.[14]

With Lodge's rigidity over the issue and a strong anti-Canadian presence in Turner's home state there was little left to the imagination about the president's motivation for naming his appointees. "In the principle involved there will be of course no compromise," Roosevelt noted in a memo to the delegation in late March.[15]

With the discussions slated for September in London Lodge became increasingly annoyed as the British found reasons to delay the talks. The senator's temperament was not helped by the effects of an intestinal virus that had nearly incapacitated him during spring 1903. Following the loss of ten pounds that left him physically exhausted Lodge returned to his senatorial duties after an extended convalesce on Tuckernuck Island.[16]

In July 1903, Lodge requested Roosevelt allow him and Nannie to travel to Britain ahead of Root and Turner. The senator hoped to employ his relationship with British politicians to settle the formal date for the hearings. "I am certain that I can do this and force an early meeting of the Tribunal," Lodge stated. Receiving permission from the White House the Lodges departed New York aboard the White Star Line's RMS *Cedric* for the voyage to England.[17]

Arriving in Liverpool on July 29, Lodge was happy to return to the United Kingdom. Over the years he and Nannie had developed a wide circle of acquaintances across the spectrum of politics and society. The senator adored English food and, fully recovered from his illness, probably gorged himself on frequent servings of kippers, steak and kidney pie, and Yorkshire pudding.[18]

With the challenge of creating a formal starting time for the talks, the senator remained doubtful of the commission achieving success. In discussions with several British politicians Lodge found the English amenable to reaching a solution on the boundary issue. Downing Street was not the problem. "We shall have trouble with the Canadians & I fear they will bring the whole thing to naught,"

Lodge wrote his daughter Constance Gardner. Roosevelt understood Lodge's apprehensions. However, the president believed the negotiations were the last best hope to solve the situation.[19]

When arguments formally began on September 15, Lodge regretted his participation. Over the next several weeks the senator was forced to endure countless hours of unspeakable boredom as he listened to one pointless argument after another. Enjoying occasional respites with Nannie in Paris, Lodge looked forward to returning to Washington where other matters required his attention.[20]

Roosevelt applauded Lodge and his colleagues' refusal to alter their position. After weeks of little progress each side achieved their objective. In exchange for the Canadian side concurring to the American boundary specifications, Roosevelt happily released two islands in the Portland Canal to the British protectorate. Lodge had created a strong relationship with Lord Aylseworth and while his diplomacy did not play a decisive role in the negotiations it may have contributed to the mediation's success. [21]

Several Roosevelt biographers believe the willingness on the part of the British to negotiate so freely was due to the pressure of Roosevelt's threat to send troops into the disputed territory. There were also other issues of contention between Washington and London. A growing dispute involving Venezuela had caused the British to conclude that creating greater acrimony with the United States was inadvisable.[22]

The president was elated with the decision. "You have rendered one of those great substantial benefits to the country," he wrote as Lodge was preparing to return home. With the controversies of the Philippines and the Canadian border negotiations behind them Roosevelt and Lodge were pleased to focus their attentions on the 1904 election.[23]

In the Senate, Lodge focused his energy on the issue of the construction of a canal connecting North and South America. From the beginning of their careers Roosevelt and Lodge had envisioned a waterway connecting the Atlantic and the Pacific. When Lodge was abroad, Colombia declined the Roosevelt Administration's offer of fifteen million dollars to build a canal across the Isthmus of Panama.[24]

Several reasons existed for the rejection. In addition to the country recovering from a recent civil war, Germany was attempting to use its influence with Bogotá to gain a presence in the region by trying to negotiate its own deal for an international waterway. While negotiations grew more contentious between Bogotá and Washington, discontent in the Colombian colony of Panama soon presented Roosevelt with an unexpected opportunity.[25]

In late October 1903, after receiving intelligence about a potential Panamanian uprising, the president dispatched US Marines and several naval vessels to the Panamanian coast. When the revolution occurred the American military's show of force successfully deterred Colombia and any other country from interfering in the Latin American nations' drive for independence. Following the successful coup Roosevelt immediately recognized the independent government. Over the next few months, a new treaty was initiated that permitted the United States to construct a waterway across Panamanian territory.

Roosevelt, Lodge, and other imperialists were delighted by recent events. There were those, however, within the president's own party who believed T. R. had circumvented congressional authority. The arguments included failing to consult the legislative branch in his decision to not only recognize the new Panamanian government but employing the military to enable the revolution.[26]

As the president fumed over his treatment by his fellow Republicans, Lodge stepped into the breach. On January 5, 1904, the senator delivered a meticulously researched two-hour address defending the administration's decision to validate the new Panamanian government. Throughout his lengthy presentation, the senator from Massachusetts quoted numerous legal precedents that stated President Roosevelt was entirely within his right to acknowledge the new state.[27]

Contending that the Panamanian revolution had occurred entirely at the initiative of the Latin American nation, Lodge stated that the United States had remained neutral throughout the process. In terms of the argument that Roosevelt was responsible for igniting the conflict between Panama City and Bogotá, the senator stated the opposite. In authorizing the US Navy into the area, Lodge contended that the president had prevented an escalation of violence from spreading throughout the region. Concluding that a new birth of freedom had occurred within the Western Hemisphere, Lodge called upon his colleagues to praise the president rather than condemn him.[28]

Following Lodge's speech, the president remained exuberant over his success in Latin America. That wild enthusiasm was witnessed in its entirety two nights later by Henry Adams at another dinner in the White House.[29]

Invited at the last minute as a substitute for Nannie Lodge, the historian gritted his teeth as the president prattled on endlessly about his achievement. "We were overwhelmed in a torrent of oratory, and at last I heard only the repetition of I-I-I attached to indiscretions greater one than another," Adams commented to Lizzie Cameron. Overwhelmed by the experience, Adams described the president's behavior as so outrageous that he belonged in an asylum. Days later, as Adams attempted to comprehend Roosevelt's behavior, he failed to understand how the president could become so physically animated despite not having consumed even a single drop of champagne.[30]

Roosevelt considered the building of the Panama Canal as the most significant contribution of his presidency. Despite the celebrations within the imperialist wing of the Republican Party, historian

H. W. Brands observes that the administration's agreement with Panama was not viewed with the same enthusiasm by the American people. More important, Roosevelt remained an anathema to much of Wall Street. The president's desire to regulate the aggressive attitudes of American business did little to endear him to the nation's moneymen.[31]

As Roosevelt prepared for his reelection campaign, many did not suspect that beneath the upbeat exterior was a man desperately worried that defeat, not victory, awaited him in November. Lodge did his utmost to dispel those moments of self-doubt. "I know that you . . . always have been a pessimist in regard to yourself and your prospects," the senator wrote from London while still negotiating the Alaskan boundary dispute.[32]

Attempting to empathize with Roosevelt's concerns, Lodge described himself as one who also possessed a dark view of human nature, thereby causing him to perceive the world in a cynical manner. Lodge's melancholy attitude was illustrated in his unhappiness over Roosevelt's burst of populist rhetoric. However, these apprehensions were calmed following the president's annual December address to Congress in 1903.[33]

On two separate occasions during his remarks Roosevelt calmly explained that the policies he had pursued in relation to American business were moderate to conservative in nature. The president argued that he had pursued the creation of certain regulatory measures with the goal of preventing criminality from flourishing. Praising the business community for enhancing the nation's growth, the president emphasized that the measures undertaken were conducted with only minimal reform in mind.[34]

Based on the senator's apprehension he was no doubt pleased with the address's conciliatory language. For all of Roosevelt's bluster, he was aware of the uncertainty that many in the financial world held toward his administration. Understanding the business flank of the party required constant reassurance, the president was grateful for Lodge's and Root's strong relationships within that section of the GOP.[35]

In the third week of June 1904, as Lodge traveled to Chicago's Colosseum for the party convention, the senator had little concern about Roosevelt's nomination. In addition to keeping the president up-to-date through letters and telegrams, Lodge and others used a private telephone line that went from the basement of the convention hall directly to the White House. Believing Roosevelt was using the communication device to manipulate the convention, some delegates chose not to attend.[36]

As the proceedings commenced, the party commemorated the recent passing of Senator Mark Hanna by hanging a large oil painting of the politician from the rafters of the convention hall. Observing the enormous portrait, Senator Lodge considered the memorial as representative of the last gasp of those who had controlled the party during the presidency of William McKinley.[37]

With the party under the control of Roosevelt's handpicked chairman George Cortelyou, Lodge expressed displeasure of no significant image of Roosevelt in the arena. Rapidly searching for a solution, convention organizers finally found a small painting of the president. When Cortelyou realized the image bore no resemblance to the commander in chief, the portrait vanished as quickly as it had appeared.[38]

In a lengthy letter describing the details of the convention, the senator wrote of the measures he and Elihu Root had taken in praise of Roosevelt's tenure in the White House. "[A]fter the way in which [Root] and I strained and racked our consciences in what we said of you in speech and platform it will be necessary for us to join some church which is able to give full absolution," Lodge wrote in a letter to the president on June 25.[39]

While praising Roosevelt's powerful hold on the party, the senator's political instincts told him the opposite. Hoping to have Illinois remain in the GOP column that November, Roosevelt had lobbied for Congressman Robert R. Hitt to serve as vice president.[40]

When it came time for the nomination the land of Lincoln showed little interest in nominating the Illinois politician. In addition, railroad tycoon E. H. Harriman aggressively lobbied delegates from New York, Pennsylvania, and other parts of the Northeast to select the business-friendly Senator Charles Fairbanks of Indiana. Believing the relationship with Harriman and his colleagues were a priority, neither Lodge nor Root challenged the Hoosier's selection.[41]

Addressing the delegates from the convention floor, Lodge measured his words carefully when discussing the Republican platform. Not wanting to alienate the business wing of the party, the senator remained neutral on subjects ranging from trusts to the tenuous relationship between labor and management. On other matters, some liberal Republicans had hoped for a resolution that resembled Lodge's 1890 Force Bill dealing with African American voting rights.[42]

The measure called for the penalization of Southern congressional districts that prevented African Americans from exercising their right to vote. Writing the president from the convention, Lodge believed while the concept was admirable, it called for the party to "do something that in all probability we shall not have the nerve to do." Not wanting to make race relations any worse than they were the president was in complete agreement in choosing to keep the proposal out of the platform.[43]

Even with Lodge's positive report, Roosevelt remained uncertain about his electoral prospects. Realizing he was someone who generated sharp debate within the country, the president concluded there was no guarantee that the voters would return him to office. Knowing there was little he could do to control the campaign T. R. appeared content with his legacy. "Whatever comes . . . I have as president done some things worth doing," Roosevelt wrote Nannie Lodge in the latter part of June.[44]

Henry Adams shared Roosevelt's belief that those who held the power in the Republican party had grown tired of the president. "Roosevelt has no friends. I doubt whether he has in all Washington, including his own cabinet." The historian was convinced that if the president was returned to office, he would make life difficult for those who controlled the business wing of the GOP. Adams believed Senator Lodge was no different. "Cabot can hardly be called a devoted follower of anyone, except as a kitten follows his own tail." When all was said and done Adams believed wealthy Republicans would flee the party, taking their money with them.[45]

As Roosevelt's opponent, the Democrats selected the bland New York judge Alton B. Parker. While T. R. believed his administration's economic policies would cause disgruntled party members to support Parker, Lodge disagreed. Scrupulously analyzing the terrain for November, the senator happily notified the president that Parker's support was limited and that his fiscal conservatism would cause many disillusioned voters to either support populist candidate Thomas Edward Watson or another choice on election day.[46]

Campaigning on the East Coast, Lodge continued to massage the egos of the party's conservative wing. Visiting Wall Street in New York and State Street in Boston, the senator believed there was little chance of those within the nation's boardrooms defecting to the Democrats. Realizing he could not take any Republican constituency for granted, the senator remained at the beck and call of the party's power brokers throughout the duration of the campaign.[47]

On election day, Lodge's prediction of Roosevelt's election victory came true. With thirty states and 7.6 million votes, the nation gave the president a broad mandate of approval. In Massachusetts the Lodges were elated as Roosevelt amassed more than 250,000 votes. "You have received the greatest honor which can come to an American, and no man ever deserved it better," Lodge wrote in an emotion-filled note following the election.[48]

As Roosevelt basked in the glow of being elected to the presidency in his own right, he declared he would not run for reelection in 1908. Hearing the statement for the first time Edith Roosevelt was noticeably shaken. Knowing that her husband found the presidency more fulfilling than any job he had ever had in public life the first lady was devastated that her husband had made such an inadvisable choice.[49]

The president's statement also caught Lodge by surprise. Aware that Roosevelt might not seek another term the senator was taken aback by the immediacy of the statement. In a note to Nannie Lodge, Roosevelt confessed he believed the moment was right to announce his decision to follow George Washington's precedent of not seeking a third term in office.[50]

As Roosevelt addressed the events that were to cross his desk in 1905, he remained determined to pursue his agenda of national reform. Lodge, always cautious, urged the president to contain his grand pronouncements due to the Republicans' narrow hold on Congress. With that thought in mind the senator suggested Roosevelt do nothing to shake the status quo. Lodge's counsel proved correct. By the time T. R. commenced his second term, the powerful Congressional "Old Guard" had decided that none of Roosevelt's policies for socioeconomic reform would see the light of day.[51]

Knowing he only had four years to implement his policy objectives, the president was determined to bend Congress to his will on issues of railroad rates and enhanced rights of labor. There was also the issue of the tariff to consider. The economic measure had once benefited the average citizen by placing a huge tax on foreign goods. As time progressed, Elihu Root and others believed what once had benefited a large segment of the American people did little other than serve the interests of large manufacturers.[52]

As Roosevelt's presidency continued, he remained wary about exerting his influence to help Lodge secure appointments beneficial to his constituents. In 1905 the senator asked that diplomat H. H. D. Peirce receive a position in the State Department. Roosevelt rejected the idea. "I do not have to tell you how careful I have to be . . . It is not that I have any candidate, but you know how some of your colleagues watch to see if I am giving improper preference to Massachusetts," the president commented.[53]

Lodge saw other requests to the president declined as well. As biographer Kathleen Dalton observes, these included "customs relief for picture frames for the [Boston] Museum of Fine Arts, extra [presidential] appearances in vulnerable congressional districts and battleships to defend Gloucester fishermen" against Newfoundland over the issue of international shipping. One matter that appeared to cause friction between the two men concerned Lodge's inquiring if Roosevelt would consider writing a congratulatory letter honoring the bicentennial of the city of Brookline. [54]

On September 23, 1905, the president responded to the senator's request with a gentle but firm reprimand. "Now, old man, you must not ask me to write such a letter . . . It is the kind of request I am receiving day by day, sometimes two or three a day. I simply cannot do it." Aware of Roosevelt's quick temper, the senator quickly apologized, describing the matter as a misunderstanding. "I was only joking about it," Lodge stated. "My request . . . was sheer thoughtlessness . . . I should have known that it was out of the question and should never have mentioned it to you." Lodge was taken aback. As one who rarely joked about anything, the senator may have realized he had overstepped his bounds.[55]

Lodge, however, understood Roosevelt's intentions of wanting to avoid any conflict of interest. The president viewed himself as a man who served at the pleasure of the people, whose decisions were dictated by neither fear nor favor. Any political scandal would cause the nation to view Roosevelt as just another politician using the presidency for his own ends.

The president's cautious attitude about his professional dealings with Lodge would have come as a surprise to those like Henry Adams and others who believed the senator had free reign over the White House. It is unlikely that Adams believed such a myth. While the commentator possessed refined elegance and literary talent, the historian often allowed the vitriol he felt for Lodge to cloud his normally astute judgment.[56]

Adams's hope that such rumors of Lodge's interference in Roosevelt's affairs would cripple the two men's relationship did not come to fruition. However, Lodge remained frustrated over the president's unwillingness to reconsider his decision about confronting the Republican Congress over a variety of regulatory matters. Roosevelt's determination to address these problems was summed up in a conversation he had with John Hay the night before his 1905 inauguration. "Tomorrow I shall come into my office in my own right. Then watch out for me," he declared triumphantly to his secretary of state.[57]

The statement illustrated Roosevelt's determination to enact his reform agenda as he began his final term in office. In considering his decision to regulate railroad rates, the president was not unaware of the great challenge that lay ahead. Roosevelt realized the railroad interests had many influential relationships in Congress, including Senator Nelson W. Aldrich, the father-in-law of John D. Rockefeller Jr., and Roosevelt critic, Ohio senator Joseph B. Foraker.[58]

In the years of the late nineteenth and early twentieth centuries large businesses like Rockefeller's Standard Oil and Andrew Carnegie's U.S. Steel had taken advantage of the proliferation of railroads by demanding ownership charge them lower rates for transporting their goods from one part of the country to the other. Depending on these large revenues, railroad executives had little choice but to comply. To compensate for their loss of profits, the railroads raised their rates on small business owners. Dependent on the rail system as the only way to bring their goods to market, these businessmen could do nothing but follow the rates the railroads set.[59]

In 1903, with the goal of creating a more equitable environment, President Roosevelt signed the Elkins Act. Under the new legislation, discrimination by either the railroad or business was ruled illegal. Roosevelt also ordered the Interstate Commerce Commission (ICC) to serve as an umpire by alerting both sides when a rate was unacceptable. The president's initial hope of using the ICC to regulate prices proved ineffective due to limitations on its power by several Supreme Court decisions. With the agency powerless to restrain either business or the railroads to do as they chose the situation remained unchanged.[60]

Despite the Elkins Act's lack of effectiveness, Lodge remained in favor of the present system. In January 1905 the senator expressed his opinion on the rates question during a dinner in his honor at the Brunswick Banquet Hall in Middlesex, Massachusetts. Referring to Roosevelt's management of the issue as "conservative," Lodge argued that employing the judiciary to solve disagreements over rate issues was preferable to inserting the powers of government into the workings of the railroad industry.[61]

In his attempt to find common ground on the issue, Lodge believed a solution was required to prevent those who favored government ownership of the railroads from having their way. "If we meet now . . . without either thoughtless conservatism or thoughtless radicalism, we shall settle it with great benefit to our country, to our race and to Western civilization," Lodge declared at the conclusion of his remarks.[62]

With the nation calling for action on the issue, two pieces of legislation were initiated in the House of Representatives. In February 1905, a bill named for congressmen John J. Esch of Wisconsin and Charles E. Townsend of Michigan authorized the ICC as the sole arbiter of railroad rates across the nation. In January 1906, Congressman William Hepburn introduced a bill that gave the ICC the authority to dictate rates. Hepburn's bill was somewhat broader, as it allowed for the establishment of a special court that gave businessmen the right to contest a rate if they believed the rate charge was too high.[63]

The president favored Hepburn's legislation, believing it represented a limited government response to the issue. With many members of the Senate Old Guard opposed to any regulation, Roosevelt believed that even the barest reform was better than giving the impression of the government taking over the railroad industry. These were some of the thoughts the president communicated to Lodge as T. R. attempted to confront the lack of cooperation by the nation's railroad executives.[64]

Following the Esch-Townsend bill being blocked in the Senate, many wondered if the president had the political will to convince Congress to pass the Hepburn Act. Lodge believed the use of a government agency to set railroad rates for the entire nation was extreme and ineffective. "I still think it a physical impossibility to have any board to establish specific rates for all our vast business," Lodge wrote the president while vacationing in Florence. The senator believed that with rates at their lowest in memory the essence of the problem related to creating a competitive situation that allowed fairness for all.[65]

Knowing Lodge was not supportive of Roosevelt's rate strategy did not prevent the president from sharing extensive details with his friend regarding the 1904–1905 conflict between Russia and Japan. In a battle to decide which nation would dominate Northeast Asia, Japan's limited resources forced them to ask Roosevelt to mediate the dispute between the two nations.[66]

Greatly satisfied over the opportunity to settle the conflict with the two warring parties, Roosevelt was also saddened by the July 1905 passing of Secretary of State John Hay. In his last days, the diplomat had journeyed to Nauheim, Germany, where his family hoped the town's regenerative waters would strengthen Hay's weakened heart. The therapy was ineffective, and Hay died a short time later while recovering in New Hampshire. Roosevelt thought Hay was an intelligent and articulate man. However, as one who was accustomed to having his own way, the president refused to give Hay credit for any accomplishments during his tenure in the administration. "But in actual work I had to do the big things myself," T. R. wrote Lodge shortly after the secretary's death.[67]

Lodge was shocked when he learned of Hay's passing. Respecting the late diplomat's abilities and devotion to Republican government, the senator nonetheless remained resentful of Hay's dismissive attitude toward those in political power.[68]

Viewing Hay's death as a great loss, the president chose to fill the void by appointing former secretary of war Elihu Root to lead the nation's foreign affairs. Lodge was elated with the selection, viewing the sixty-year-old lawyer as one of the nation's finest public servants. The president concurred that Root's experience and skills could result in him being the greatest secretary of state in US history.[69]

Root proved himself an astute diplomat. Unlike his predecessor, the former secretary of war understood the importance of keeping the Senate informed of any developments that would require its approval.

The fact that the corporate lawyer was one of Lodge's closest friends made for an ideal situation. With the nation's diplomacy in confident hands the president surged ahead in his negotiations with Russia and Japan while keeping his eyes on developments between France and Germany over the latter's growing presence in Morocco.[70]

There was no doubt the president enjoyed exercising power over international affairs. Roosevelt had also not forgotten his intentions of reforming portions of the nation's socioeconomic system. As the president's second term progressed Lodge and Roosevelt remained in disagreement over the relationship between labor and management and the level of government regulation to employ in restraining the power of the nation's corporations.[71]

Moving toward the 1906 congressional elections, Lodge grew increasingly apprehensive that Roosevelt's moralist passions could damage his party's electoral majority. Throughout the president's tenure in the White House, Lodge had instructed Roosevelt to remain wary of alienating the conservative wing of the GOP. But T. R. seemed absorbed in other matters more important than listening to the man who had played such a pivotal role in his rise to power.

Having won the presidency in his own right Roosevelt was free to run the nation as he saw fit. Throughout his long friendship with the president, Lodge had employed much of his energies in restraining Roosevelt's impulsiveness. With T. R. determined to fulfill his reformist agenda Lodge faced the dilemma of how to help Roosevelt succeed without damaging the Republican Party in the process.

Anna Cabot Mills Davis Lodge (1850–1915) in carriage with Theodore Roosevelt (1858–1919) in Lynn, Massachusetts, en route to Nahant. *Courtesy of the Massachusetts Historical Society.*

ABOVE: Henry Cabot Lodge (1850–1924) with Theodore Roosevelt and others at Northfield, Massachusetts, September 1, 1902. *Courtesy of the Massachusetts Historical Society.* BELOW: Henry Cabot Lodge full equestrian portrait by Barnett M. Clinedinst, 1905. *Courtesy of the Library of Congress.*

George Cabot Lodge (1873–1909), taken in 1899. *Courtesy of the Massachusetts Historical Society.*

John Hay, 1902. *Courtesy of the Library of Congress.*

Mrs. Elizabeth Cameron, taken between 1890 and 1910 *Courtesy of the Library of Congress.*

Henry Cabot Lodge, ca late 1800s. *Courtesy of the Massachusetts Historical Society.*

Theodore Roosevelt on horseback jumping over a split rail fence,
May 17, 1902. *Courtesy of the Library of Congress.*

Henry Cabot Lodge, January 1, 1905.
Courtesy of the Library of Congress.

Henry Cabot Lodge, 1916. *Courtesy of the Library of Congress.*

President Roosevelt, Nahant, Massachusetts, 1902. *Courtesy of the Library of Congress.*

Henry Cabot Lodge at funeral for Theodore Roosevelt, Oyster Bay New York, 1919. *Courtesy of the Library of Congress.*

Theodore Roosevelt, 1885. *Courtesy of the Library of Congress.*

Theodore Roosevelt, 1910. *Courtesy of the Library of Congress.*

Theodore Roosevelt, 1910. *Courtesy of the Library of Congress.*

Theodore Roosevelt's favorite portrait of Edith that he carried with him on his African safari trip. *Courtesy of the Sagamore Hill Historic Site.*

Theodore Roosevelt at Sagamore Hill, 1905. *Courtesy of the Sagamore Hill Historic Site.*

Archie, Quentin, Ethel, Theodore, Edith, and Belle Roosevelt (Kermit's wife) on a picnic, 1915. *Courtesy of the Sagamore Hill Historic Site.*

Quentin, Theodore, Archie, Edith, Ethel, Ted Jr, and Kermit at Sagamore Hill, 1907. *Courtesy of the Sagamore Hill Historic Site.*

RIGHT: Senator Henry Cabot Lodge making a speech, 1922. *Courtesy of the Library of Congress.* BELOW: Anna Cabot Mills Davis Lodge, in the Parlor of the Wadsworth family estate, Geneseo, N.Y., 1890. *Courtesy of Mrs. Curtis Guld Jr., Boston Atheneum.*

ABOVE: Elliott Bulloch Roosevelt (1860–1894),
Courtesy of the National Park Service. LEFT: Sir Cecil
Spring Rice, ca. 1910. *Courtesy of the Library of
Congress.*

FOURTEEN
The Gathering Storm

"He and I differ radically on certain propositions."
—Theodore Roosevelt

As the calendar progressed through 1905, President Roosevelt found himself unable to find common ground with Senator Lodge on several issues. Roosevelt was frustrated with his mentor in other ways, too. Initially favoring the elevation of Oliver Wendell Holmes to the Supreme Court, T. R. had become disillusioned with his new addition to the bench.[1]

In the spring of 1904, the Northern Securities case involving the holding company that controlled the railroad lines of the great Northwest finally reached the court. Having discussed labor issues with Holmes at the time of his appointment, Roosevelt expected the justice to support the arguments made by the administration. When the court voted 5–4 in favor of breaking up the trust, Holmes's vote was not among the majority.[2]

The president was stunned by the justice's dissent. Holmes contended that despite the railroad trust's enormous size it did not constitute a threat to interstate commerce. Roosevelt was disappointed. Once believing the jurist shared his sympathies, T. R. showed his displeasure by no longer inviting the Bostonian to dinner at the White House.[3]

The Holmes appointment was not the only tension that existed among Roosevelt and the senator. Throughout 1905, the relations between the president and the Republican Old Guard remained at odds over railroad regulation. In May, during a speech in the West, the president declared his intentions to make the Interstate Commerce Commission the lone arbiter of railroad rates across the nation. Lodge found the idea of a small group of men dictating the behavior of an entire industry troubling. "If the Government undertakes to fix all the specific rates everywhere it appears to me equivalent to taking the railroads," the senator wrote in the first week of October.[4]

Roosevelt's annual speech to Congress in December 1905 highlighted the disagreements between the two men. Reiterating concern about the overwhelming power of big business, the president not only called for the ICC to set universal rail rates but declared the commission audit the accounts of the entire railroad industry. The president believed "the fortunes of the large corporations had become so . . . powerful that effective public supervision . . . was a necessity." The senator believed the railroad shipping price system needed reform, but contended it was a matter of degree how much government should interfere in matters of the private sector.[5]

Lodge's opposition to the ICC being given control of railroad rates was illustrated by his comments on the floor of the Senate on February 12, 1906. "I have the gravest doubts . . . as to the wisdom of government rate-making even in the most limited form," the senator said of Roosevelt's agenda.[6]

With the issue coming to a head, Roosevelt did his best to separate his political disagreements with Lodge from their personal relationship. "I say deliberately during [Lodge's] twenty-years . . . in Washington he has been on the whole the best and most useful servant of the public to be found in either house of Congress," the president wrote *Outlook* editor Lyman Abbott in February 1906.[7]

While praising Lodge's commitment to public service, the president was not shy in admitting that the two men "differed radically on certain propositions." In their disagreement on the railroad question, Roosevelt described the senator as possessing "strong convictions" that at times were viewed as "narrow and obstinate." Knowing Lodge as well he did the president respected his friend's opinions. At the same time, Roosevelt could not help but admit that Lodge possessed a "certain aloofness and coldness of manner" causing those who were not accustomed to his temperament to view the New Englander negatively.[8]

Still, Roosevelt hoped Lodge would concur with his point of view. "I think he is entirely mistaken in being against us," the president said in another note to Abbott. Searching for an ally to help resolve the impasse between the two men, the president enlisted the support of Nannie Lodge. "I write to you because I feel more confidence in my ability to exert a favorable response from you than from Cabot," Roosevelt wrote the senator's wife on March 11.[9]

The president asked Nannie to organize an intimate evening and include members of Lodge's extended family. With good food and enjoyable company, Roosevelt believed he could soften the Boston Republican's disposition on the rate issue. "Can you have me to dinner either Wednesday or Friday. Would you be willing to have Bay and Bessy also?" Roosevelt asked. The evening was enjoyable. But Lodge refused to change his mind.[10]

On February 12, during a debate on the railroad issue in the Senate, Lodge argued that natural economic forces could settle the issue far better than any government body. In illustrating the lack of progress made by both parties on the subject, the scholar quoted a passage from Samuel Taylor Coleridge's 1836 work, *Table Talk*. "I have heard but two arguments of any weight," Lodge said on the Senate floor. "We will blow your brains out if you don't pass it; and we will drag you through a horse pond if you don't pass it; and there is a good deal of force in both." Concerned that the president had the votes to pass his proposal, the Republicans managed to limit the influence of the ICC by approving an amendment declaring that a court serve as the final arbiter to determine the equality of rates.[11]

It is unknown whether Lodge and Roosevelt had any additional conversations regarding the final railroad bill known as the Hepburn Act. Since the legislation allowed both men to achieve their mutual goals, perhaps neither believed the issue was worth further discussion. However, even with the rate issue resolved, Lodge remained concerned about other "progressive reforms" the president seemed determined to bring to fruition.[12]

For all of Lodge's comments criticizing the president's policies, the senator was no ideologue. Believing that government intervention was occasionally necessary, the senator contended that "wise and moderate regulation" was the most prudent way to proceed. At the same time Lodge realized that Roosevelt needed to tread delicately when invoking the powers of government to intervene in the affairs of American corporations.[13]

Even in their disagreements over policy, the president and the senator remained congenial as ever. That collegiality also extended to the relationship between their wives and children. Throughout 1906, Roosevelt encouraged Bay Lodge in the development of his poetry, while also assisting Cabot's younger son John E. Lodge in pursuing his love of Far Eastern art.[14]

Lodge did his best to use his resources to help Roosevelt's children as well. In the first week of October 1906, Theodore Roosevelt Jr. became indirectly involved in a friend's drunken altercation with the Cambridge, Massachusetts police. Left behind following the dispute as his classmate eluded capture, the junior Roosevelt endured a brutal beating at the hands of the outraged officers.[15]

THE ROUGH RIDER AND THE PROFESSOR

Refusing to reveal the name of the offending party to the authorities, a warrant was issued for Roosevelt's arrest. Immediately attending to the situation, Lodge managed to use his contacts with local law enforcement to get the matter resolved. Despite some bad publicity the incident had no impact on the younger Roosevelt's record.[16]

Even in the president's disagreements with Lodge, T. R. realized it was unwise to try to use government power to reform everything all at once. Such was the issue of the nation's tariff, which both Lodge and Roosevelt believed required revision. With the tariff central to Republican philosophy, the president and the senator were wary of causing any fiscal disruption, especially with continuing economic prosperity. "The fact that wages have been raised, for instance, throughout the great cotton and woolen industries has weakened the agitation against the Republicans in behalf of changing the tariff," Lodge wrote Roosevelt in August 1906, regarding the nation's positive economic conditions.[17]

While Roosevelt believed in supporting the status quo there were other moments when he and Lodge clashed over the direction of the country. That same year in the hope of easing the political divide between Democrats and Republicans, the president decided to consider the controversial proposal of appointing Judge Horace H. Lurton, a Democrat, to the Supreme Court.

Following another refusal by William Howard Taft to serve on the high court, the secretary of war suggested the alternative of appointing the Tennessee lawyer to the bench. Roosevelt also considered Attorney General William H. Moody, who, like Justice Oliver Wendell Holmes, came from Lodge's home state of Massachusetts.[18]

Taft and others did not consider Lurton's party affiliation problematic, believing the judge held the right positions on the issues that would come before the court. Lodge did not share Taft's view. The senator wrote that he was concerned by Lurton's potential appointment. The objection had little to do with the judge's experience or character, but involved Lurton's membership in the Democratic Party.[19]

The senator believed an appointment of a Republican was essential because "the Supreme bench . . . is necessarily called upon to decide questions of wide political bearing." Lodge understood that the president often displayed the sympathies of an idealist. Despite appreciating the inclination, Lodge believed Roosevelt's instincts were misplaced. "It is a rare thing to find a Democrat who is at heart a Federalist and an old Whig . . . and it is not a chance to be taken," the New Englander wrote on the first day of September.[20]

Lodge may have believed Roosevelt's reasoning was motivated by the frustration over the Holmes appointment. The senator, however, was more concerned about the effect the president's selection of Lurton could have on the attitude of the GOP. "From a party point of view . . . I think that all of our people who have supported you and your policies so strongly would feel very badly if this was done." Realizing the president no longer sought his advice as he once had, Lodge nonetheless remained passionate about the issue, saying, "I feel certain that I am right in my opinion." [21]

Roosevelt appreciated the advice, but vehemently disagreed. "[Lurton] is right on the Negro question; he is right on the power of the Federal government; he is right on the insular business; he is right about corporations; and he is right about labor." T. R.'s passionate response showed his attempt to convince Lodge that picking someone from the same party didn't assure the justice would make the expected ruling on a particular issue. "[T]he *nominal* politics of the man has nothing to do with his actions on the bench. His real politics are all important." But Lodge was determined to make his feelings known regardless of the arguments made by the president.[22]

Lodge understood the president remained bothered by the Holmes appointment. However, the senator believed that just because "there have been one or two Republican disappointments does not seem to me to militate against the proposition." In Lodge's view, placing a Democrat on the court was contrary to someone who viewed the Constitution from a conservative perspective. "What I want on the bench is a follower of Hamilton and Marshall and not a follower of Jefferson and Calhoun, whose disciples carried their doctrines into the practical form of secession." In making his argument Lodge had not lost his distrust or distaste for those men who had once sworn their loyalty to the Confederate States of America.[23]

Following a more detailed investigation of Lurton's record, Attorney General Moody reported that under decisions relating to Interstate Commerce legislation, the justice had sided with the plaintiff on every occasion except one. The information was enough for Roosevelt to reconsider the Southerner and appoint Moody to the court in December 1906.[24]

During the Lurton controversy, Lodge remained concerned with the president's rhetorical focus on the use of government as a restraint on corporate power. Following a speech in the fall of 1906, Roosevelt disputed Lodge's claim that he "had dwelt too strongly upon the necessity for curbing and controlling the great trusts, while not making any attack upon the demagogue and agitator." It is unclear what comments Lodge made to precipitate such a response.[25]

What the senator found specifically disconcerting was not so much the rhetoric, but Roosevelt's inability to focus his wrath on adversaries other than the malefactors of great wealth. "[I]t might be wise to emphasize a little more the dangers from the demagogue and agitator as well as the abuses of corporate capital," the senator wrote T. R. as the 1906 off year elections grew closer.[26]

The senator's reference to "demagogue and agitator" was primarily focused on two targets. In New York, the populist newspaper baron William Randolph Hearst was running for governor, while progressive district attorney John Moran was in contention for the Massachusetts statehouse. Lodge believed that Roosevelt was also neglecting the influence of labor unions, which the senator believed were as corrupt as the trust system. The New Englander had little faith in Roosevelt's attempt to cultivate the labor movement. The senator viewed many of these organizations as dominated by progressives who he believed were easily manipulated by the agents of socialism, whose solution to the nation's problems was greater control by the state.[27]

Lodge contended these factors were indicative of what he viewed as a growing crisis. A "contest is coming," the senator wrote in a lengthy letter to the president in October 1906. "I do not think it rests on the wrong-doing of corporate wealth, although that is an existing cause." What the senator believed was that the growing polarization over wealth disparity, workers' rights, and other issues could lead to class warfare.[28]

Politics remained at the heart of Lodge's concerns. Believing that Democratic rule symbolized instability and chaos, the senator remained apprehensive that Roosevelt's behavior as the Sheriff of Wall Street would alienate members of the corporate elite. "We do not want to run the risk of making the great body of well meaning, conservative American voters think that we are opposed only to the wrong doing of the unscrupulous capitalists," Lodge commented to the president.[29]

Without question, Roosevelt saw Hearst's growing popularity as a dangerous threat. T. R., however, was intelligent enough to realize that the political support for the newspaper baron was symbolic of "the great agitation and unrest which we have witnessed during the last eighteen months." The president contended that the populists were attempting to exploit the anger among those affected by the disparities of income and the corruption in the corporate class. Roosevelt believed for all the celebrity around Hearst's campaign, he would not win the election.[30]

As election day drew closer, Roosevelt grew more apprehensive. But the president understood that despite a booming economy most Americans possessed a sense of complacency by taking their good fortune for granted. "People are so prosperous that they feel at liberty to indulge themselves in experiments," Theodore commented to the senator.[31]

On November 7 narrow victories by Republicans Charles Evans Hughes and Curtis Guild Jr. in the New York and Massachusetts gubernatorial elections cheered the president and other Republicans. Despite these electoral successes Lodge remained unhappy that the victories by the two Republicans were not as large as anticipated. Concerned with the strong performance of the two losing candidates, Lodge viewed the growing Democratic popularity as "melancholy to the last degree."[32]

With the newspaper baron winning the votes of those across New York City and Republican support in the Bay State being lower than in the past, Lodge remained filled with anxiety. "We have got a terrible struggle before us to save the country from a movement which strikes at the very foundations of society and civilization," Lodge wrote regarding his concern over the growing populist wave.[33]

During an annual message to Congress on December 6, 1906 Roosevelt expressed Lodge's concern about those citizens who sought to incite class warfare against those across the nation who symbolized financial success. But to Lodge's dismay, T. R. also called for corporations to not only publish their earnings but allow government auditors to analyze those earnings in the name of greater transparency.

Throughout the rest of 1906 and 1907 Roosevelt was inundated with a series of challenges that pushed his abilities and temperament to the limit. In October 1906 the president ordered the deployment of American troops to quell a military insurgency in Cuba. Instability in the Philippines had increased as well. The development had prompted the president to send his old Rough Rider companion, Leonard Wood, out to the Pacific to subdue a resistance movement by members of an Islamic sect known as the Moro people.[34]

As one who enjoyed a display of power on the battlefield, Wood was determined to give the Moros "a good spank." The two-year battle to subdue the indigenous tribe culminated in an incident resulting in the deaths of more than six hundred women and children. Those moments of international turmoil all paled to the president's disgraceful treatment of African American troops following a disturbance in Brownsville, Texas, in the summer of 1906.[35]

Following a riot in the community that left one man dead, many of the town's white citizens placed responsibility for the disturbance on a regiment of Black soldiers stationed at Fort Brown. Despite a local investigation absolving the soldiers of blame, an air of suspicion remained over the African American troops. As inquiries continued, the situation grew more contentious following the refusal by members of the regiment to testify against their comrades.[36]

Roosevelt viewed the troops' refusal to name names as a blemish on the honor of the United States military. As punishment, the president demanded a dishonorable discharge of all 167 members of the regiment. The decision, which resulted in the expulsion of six winners of the Congressional Medal of Honor, polarized the nation.[37]

Ohio's Senator Joseph B. Foraker, a staunch opponent of the president's attacks on the nation's corporate class, demanded a congressional investigation. The Republican was considering a run for the presidency in 1908 and Roosevelt believed the Midwestern politico was using the incident to enhance his name recognition among African American voters. The situation between the two men grew worse during a fiery confrontation over the Brownsville affair at Washington's annual Gridiron Dinner in January 1907. During Roosevelt's comments, his remarks became so heated that the following day, editorialist Albert J. Taylor of the *Los Angeles Times* visually depicted T. R. chasing Foraker through the Senate door with a hot poker.[38]

Lodge worried that Foraker's investigation was causing great dissension within the Republican Party. "Is there no way in the world in which we can put a detective or a Secret Service man on these fellows?" the senator inquired in June 1907 as he considered how to discover what Foraker was planning to reveal in his report on the Brownsville issue. Always trying to temper any controversy before it became unmanageable, the senator hoped to shut down the investigation as soon as possible. Lodge's reasoning was not only political but also personal. With only a brief period left in Roosevelt's presidency, Lodge did not want his friend to lose focus on portions of his agenda that remained unfulfilled.[39]

Roosevelt wanted to rid himself of the Brownsville controversy as well. "If I send Secret Service men . . . would there not be a good chance of Foraker or his crowd making a drive at me for doing it?" As one option, Lodge had suggested placing Gilchrist Stewart, an attorney associated with the investigation, under surveillance.[40]

But the senator changed his mind, believing the attorney would have little success at finding credible witnesses to dispute Roosevelt's decision. Nonetheless, Lodge remained concerned about the impact the investigation could have on the image of the president. "It would have great effect unless we could break [the witnesses] down. It would mislead, probably, a good many people," Lodge commented to T. R.[41]

Roosevelt was uncertain about whether to speak out on the controversy before Foraker's report was issued. The president thought little of the Ohio Republican, whose slavish devotion to corporate interests was one of the worst examples of political corruption he had ever seen. The senator had received a consulting fee from Standard Oil for legal work but appeared no worse than those other members of the Old Guard who were strong supporters of corporate interests.[42]

Writing Lodge near the end of June, the president considered going on the offensive against the senator at an event in Ohio later that fall. Lodge thought the idea was a mistake and encouraged the president to wait for the publication of the committee's report at the end of the year. The senator also believed the issue was losing momentum with the public, based on the tepid response to a speech Foraker had recently delivered about the issue.[43]

Foraker's attempt to use the Brownsville crises as a platform for his presidential aspirations was also problematic for Roosevelt and Lodge. As the Republican Party began to consider who to nominate in 1908, many viewed another Ohioan, Secretary of War William Howard Taft, as Roosevelt's heir apparent.[44]

The legal scholar and the Rough Rider had known each other since the 1890's, when both worked for the Harrison Administration. The two had grown increasingly close, and in 1904 the president asked the former governor general of the Philippines to replace Elihu Root as secretary of war, leading to an even closer relationship between the charismatic New Yorker and the contemplative jurist from Ohio.[45]

Lunching with Roosevelt at the White House and dining with his family in the evenings, one had the impression Taft had become even closer to the president than Lodge. A man of conservative temperament as well as strong administrative capability, Taft increasingly impressed Roosevelt with his knowledge of legal questions, as well as those on public policy.[46]

In 1906, knowing of his friend's desire to serve on the Supreme Court, Roosevelt promised to name Taft as chief justice should the opportunity arise. A seat on the high court was the secretary's lifelong ambition. Taft's wife, the socially aggressive Nellie Taft, objected to the idea believing her husband capable of greater achievements.[47]

In the fall of that year following a luncheon with the president at the White House, Roosevelt informed Mrs. Taft that her husband was his first choice for president. While Secretary of State Elihu Root was T. R.'s ideal successor, Root was closer to Lodge politically than Roosevelt, which explained why the president and the secretary did not always agree on matters of policy.[48]

With these differences it is no surprise that Lodge preferred Root as well. The senator was well acquainted with Taft, having met the rotund lawyer at a dinner during his first week in Washington. Unlike the senator and the president, Taft was not a social animal, preferring to spend long hours in the capital or at his office in the Justice Department.[49]

For all of Taft's conviviality, the Ohio judge was not a dynamic thinker. He did not possess the president's intellectual creativity, his desire to implement progressive change, nor his passion for political battles. "Taft, thank Heaven, is up to the point of making an aggressive fight against Foraker," Roosevelt commented to Lodge regarding the secretary of war's decision to confront the Ohio legislator over the Brownsville affair.[50]

Unlike so many who surrounded the president, Taft had little interest in being Roosevelt's successor. Preferring a seat on the Supreme Court, the war secretary believed T. R. should seek a third term. At times the president felt the same way. "I should greatly have liked to . . . keep my hands on the levers of this mighty machine," T. R. commented as his tenure in the White House neared its conclusion.[51]

A figure of enormous popularity, Roosevelt believed if the 1908 convention chose to nominate him by acclamation, he had little choice but to accept. "For his own sake, for his future fame, his present happiness & health I hope that he will not have the nomination forced on him," Lodge wrote in his journal in the last month of 1907.[52]

Lodge's point also represented a view within the Republican Party. The dislike for the president among those in the business community was so severe rumors began circulating that he was not only addicted to morphine and alcohol but had gone "insane." Believing these comments were beyond the pale, Lodge concluded that these libelous accusations could have only come from T. R.'s bitter opponents on Wall Street.[53]

In August of 1907 that animosity towards Roosevelt's economic policies grew even more contentious when a brief economic crisis struck the nation. In detailing the oncoming crisis, Lodge used the example of where his own fortunes would stand if he had to rely purely on his investment portfolio. "If I were compelled to sell what I own I should get thirty percent less than what I should have got last January," Lodge wrote in an ominous letter to the president.[54]

In correspondence with Roosevelt, Lodge questioned the president's decision to prosecute large corporations as responsible for the market's plunging fortunes. As one of Roosevelt's biographers writes, the economic crisis, known as the Panic of 1907, had little to do with pursuing those companies who had violated the Sherman Anti-Trust Act and more to do with unregulated borrowing and rampant speculation on the part of the investment community.[55]

As Roosevelt worked with J. P. Morgan to stem the panic, Lodge—following a conversation with Boston investor Thomas Jefferson Coolidge—reviewed a speech Roosevelt was preparing to give on the nation's economic instability. Examining the text, the senator advised the president to desist in his attacks on corporations. In support of the administration, Lodge had prepared his own address with the objective of calming the nerves of the nation's financiers.[56]

Lodge did not disagree that the president's progressive attitudes were partially responsible for the animosity that existed towards his administration on Wall Street. At the same time, the senator contended that the populist venom around the country was a warning to those who believed a Democrat in the White House was preferable to another four years of Roosevelt progressivism. "[I]f our friends [on] Wall Street and State Street could only read the handwriting on the wall or anywhere else they would see in large bold letters that the only things that stands between them and the triumph of the wildest radicalism are your policies and principles," the senator commented to Roosevelt.[57]

In November 1907, following Republican victories in Massachusetts, Kentucky, and New Jersey, Lodge remained concerned about the state of the Republican majority. Anticipating the election of 1908, the senator warned those GOP critics like his financial adviser, Henry Higginson that if they did not stand behind Taft, Roosevelt would run for a third term. The threat caused Lodge's cousin to change his tune. "We should be very content if we could be sure of having Mr. Taft," the moneyman commented to the senator. What Lodge did not tell Higginson was that he remained less than confident that Taft could unite the party. The point was illustrated by Lodge's decision to withhold support until the secretary of war's nomination was virtually assured.[58]

Even as Lodge pressed those within the business wing of the party to support the mild-mannered judge, the senator believed that only the president possessed the intellectual talent and the political ability to hold the Republican Party together. "I wish most deeply you could be president again for the next four years," Lodge wrote during the latter part of September 1907. Always thinking three steps ahead of everyone else, Lodge remained uncertain if Taft, with his lack of political experience and sedate personality, could manage the growing wave of populist sentiment that Roosevelt had managed to keep at bay. As the president's final term neared its conclusion, he continued to launch verbal attacks on those Republican financiers who played such a significant role in keeping the party treasury solvent.[59]

Even as Lodge had warned the president about moderating his tone against corporate America, T. R. dismissed the senator's advice by delivering a passionate attack on the nation's monied interests. In a speech to Congress in January 1908, the president contended that those editorialists who criticized him were indirectly compromising the nation's youth by teaching them that success could only come through behaving dishonestly due to an obsession for financial gain. Finding Roosevelt's rhetoric disconcerting, Lodge could do little except comment that the president should restrain himself from making certain suggestions in the future.[60]

The lengthy address did little to endear Roosevelt to those like railroad titan E. H. Harriman. When asked if the railroad tycoon wanted to donate to T. R.'s postpresidential tour of Africa, the blunt-speaking industrialist stated that he would not contribute a penny.[61]

With little opposition from other Republican candidates, Taft easily won the party's nomination. During the convention in Chicago, Lodge served once again as chairman, and attempted to construct a moderate platform to appease both the liberal and conservative wings of the party. Writing to Roosevelt following the convention, Lodge contended that he had managed to adopt a platform that all the delegates could agree on.[62]

The observation was not entirely true. The major issue of contention was over the reform of the tariff. While the subject was mentioned in the platform to prevent a demonstration by either wing of the party, Lodge and his colleagues never clearly stated how the GOP should address the new terms.[63]

Serving as Roosevelt's spokesman, Lodge, in good spirits, vigorously addressed the convention. Highlighting the successes of the administration, the senator had to wait only a few moments before a huge roar of adulation reverberated throughout the arena. As the massive demonstration swept across the venue, Lodge, his face flushed with happiness, made only a minimal effort to quiet the crowd. Resigned to the outpouring of affection for Roosevelt, the senator could do nothing but slowly walk back and forth across the platform as a local band played the president's favorite tune, "There'll Be a Hot Time in the Old Town Tonight."[64]

As the convention took up the chant of "Four, Four, Four Years More!" Lodge felt a stirring of emotion. Reflecting on the love and admiration he and so many of his fellow citizens had for the president, the senator could not help but feel wistful knowing that the end of Roosevelt's final term in office was approaching. After forty-five minutes of jubilation Lodge, with the help of a band that played a particularly loud and snappy version of the 1860s tune "Garryowen" restored the delegates to order. While the chairman knew that preventing a unanimous call for Roosevelt's renomination was what the president wanted, the senator found himself deeply conflicted. "The hardest thing I ever had to do in public life was . . . to shut you out of the White House," Cabot wrote following his return from Chicago.[65]

Roosevelt was gratified by Lodge's praise, along with his ability to manage the passions of the delegates. "In point of judgment, taste, and power it would be literally impossible to better either his words or his actions," the president wrote to Nannie of her husband's performance.[66]

But Roosevelt believed the senator had done much more. "He was in a peculiar sense the guardian not only of the national interests but of my own personal honor, and to do his full duty as guardian . . . it was absolutely necessary that any stampede for me should be prevented." Roosevelt believed that if he allowed vanity to seduce him into accepting the nomination, his supporters would perceive him as a figure whose "actions did not really square with the highest and finest code of ethics." As a man who believed virtue was the foundation of character, the president was grateful to Lodge for preventing him from making a costly mistake.[67]

In the same letter to Nannie, Roosevelt reflected on his time as president. "I do not believe anyone else has ever enjoyed the White House as we have enjoyed it and now we are ready to leave it without a pang, with plenty of interest and pleasure ahead of us." Following the convention, the Roosevelts decamped to Oyster Bay for the remainder of the summer while the Lodges prepared to visit England and France. Lodge had lost his elder sister months earlier and following events in Chicago was looking forward to filling his stomach with English food and his mind with European art on the other side of the Atlantic.[68]

In November Taft easily defeated William Jennings Bryan's third and final attempt to win the presidency. With Taft's election, Roosevelt prepared for his departure from the White House. Thankful his friend could enjoy some much-needed rest and relaxation, Lodge worried about the unity of the Republican Party. The new president was not a fighter, nor was he a man of great popularity. Lodge understood that change was inevitable, but the senator remained concerned about growing tensions between conservatives and progressives over the issue of government to restrain the power of the nation's corporate interests.[69]

As Roosevelt prepared to depart on an African safari, neither man could imagine that over the next few years Theodore Roosevelt would embark on a series of political decisions that Henry Cabot Lodge could neither condone nor support. That disagreement would not only test the Lodge-Roosevelt friendship of more than a quarter-century but be responsible for changing the Republican Party for decades to come.

FIFTEEN
Return to the Arena

"There is a consistently growing thought of you and your return to the Presidency."

—Henry Cabot Lodge

A s Roosevelt prepared to depart from Washington after nearly eight years in the White House, tensions were beginning to develop between him and president-elect Taft. Determined to exercise his autonomy the former secretary of war replaced several officials who had occupied positions in the former president's cabinet, including secretary of the interior and Roosevelt confidant James R. Garfield. Initially believing the incoming president would maintain the same personnel, Roosevelt was troubled by Taft's decision. "After the election Taft changed his mind," Roosevelt wrote to Lodge's friend, the historian Charles Washburn in January 1915.[1]

Following a lunch with Taft on December 9, 1908, Lodge was offered the opportunity to replace the retiring Elihu Root as secretary of state. Roosevelt had told Taft that Lodge would never leave the Senate. After waiting two days to meet with the incoming president, Lodge was "flattered" by the offer to run the State Department but preferred to remain in the Capitol.[2]

Following the selection of Philander Knox as the nation's chief diplomat, Roosevelt remained disturbed at the changes that Taft had made in the composition of his staff. The senator took the opposite attitude. "Taft will do what he thinks best for his own purposes," Lodge stated in a note to Senator Murray Crane. While Lodge believed Taft had every right to make changes to his cabinet, the senator realized that life in Washington would lose a bit of its sparkle with Roosevelt no longer occupying the Executive Mansion.[3]

On March 24, 1909, at 11:00 in the morning, Colonel Roosevelt departed on the SS *Hamburg* from Hoboken, New Jersey, to begin what he described to Nannie Lodge as "the great adventure." Arriving at the dock to say farewell, Senator Lodge was not only overwhelmed by the 3,000 people who had come to cheer the ex-president, but also by the aura of adulation permeating the atmosphere. "I can see you now, as the ship moved slowly down the river, waving your hand to us from the bridge," Lodge wrote following the event. [4]

In addition, Taft's secretary Archie Butt presented Roosevelt with a letter from the new president thanking the former president for all he had done to help Taft obtain the White House. In Taft's appreciation he had also included his brother Charlie Taft, whom he believed had played a significant role in his success. Always temperamental, Roosevelt was insulted by Taft's familial reference. It was the beginning of a breach between the two old friends that soon became irreparable.[5]

Following Roosevelt's departure, the senator spent his days immersed in the debate over the revision of the nation's tariff law. Writing to Roosevelt during his African adventure, Lodge believed that if Congress reached a resolution "then prosperity will obliterate the feeling of disappointment and will save the party. If prosperity fails to come we shall find ourselves, I fear, in deep water." Even with Lodge's attentions consumed by the tariff debate, the senator studiously watched as Taft adapted to his new office. What Lodge saw was disconcerting.[6]

In a detailed letter to Roosevelt, Lodge contended that Taft appeared to lack certain abilities critical for presidential success. "The one thing which surprises me about Taft is that he does not know more about politics," the senator wrote. Understanding that a president had the capacity to use the office as a platform for legislative and electoral success, Lodge questioned whether Taft had the personality to succeed at such a task."[7]

The New Englander was also disappointed with Taft's performance on tariff legislation. The new president had aspired to develop tariff regulation in the hopes of benefiting most Americans. But the former solicitor general knew little about the subject and was forced to leave the legislation in the hands of Congress. Initially, the reform process started smoothly. In April 1909, the House of Representatives submitted a bill to the Senate lowering rates on such products as iron, sugar, and lumber. Other imports such as coal and animal hides were not taxed at all.[8]

When the bill reached the Senate, the debate became contentious. Believing low rates on certain goods would alienate their constituents, senators from the Great Plains added numerous amendments to the bill, thus raising prices on the same products the House had originally reduced. With only a small number of conservatives under the control of Senator Nelson Aldrich, the man from Rhode Island had no choice but to bow to his colleagues from the West.[9]

Refusing to allow legislators to add an income tax and concerned with retaining the unity of his conservative base, the president had no choice but to sign the bill. While many progressives within the GOP raged about the disparities, Taft further alienated the liberal wing of the party by boasting the legislation was the best tariff ever produced.[10]

It was the latter part of the summer of 1909 before the tariff issue was resolved. Lodge, physically depleted from the long days of negotiation, looked forward to a relaxing month away from Washington. The senator had arranged to spend time with Bay on Tuckernuck Island, located at the Western end of Nantucket, Massachusetts. During the late 1800s the island, known for its many herds of sheep, became a popular destination for elite members of New England society. Lodge's childhood friend William Sturgis Bigelow, known as "Dokko," treasured the summers on the quiet and sparsely populated oasis. Indulging in his library of more than 3,000 books, Bigelow frequently filled his home with the laughter and conversation of friends like the Roosevelts, Lodges, and Henry Adams.[11]

Bay and his father held a mutual love for the island as well. Both loved the sea, the serenity, and the natural beauty. Swimming in the rocky surf and taking leisurely walks on the beach allowed Lodge to experience a sense of renewal while the atmosphere fueled Bay's creativity and imagination.[12]

Over the last two years, Lodge's eldest son had devoted his efforts to writing a lengthy poetic tale titled *Herakles*, a Greek drama that featured his parents as the play's two prominent characters. Bay was also enjoying his growing family. By 1909 he and Bessy were the parents of three children. Henry Cabot Lodge Jr., John Davis Lodge, and Helena Constance Lodge all joined the young couple between 1902 and 1905.[13]

While Bay's plays and poetry received praise from friends and family, they generated little public notoriety or monetary success. At age thirty-five, struggling professionally and insecure about his place in the world, Bay remained dependent on his family for financial support. "I am almost crazed with the desire to be independent," he wrote Nannie as he grew steadily frustrated over his lack of accomplishment.[14]

For the moment, as the senator and his son relished the sun, the sea, and the gentle breeze coming off the Atlantic, Bay tried to forget his struggles and enjoy time with his father.

On August 18 the two men welcomed the lecturer and literary critic Alfred Hodgdon Brown. A good friend, the academic praised Bay's recent work and encouraged him to enhance his literary repertoire.[15]

The conversation raised Bay's spirits, and between the island's sunsets and delightful seafood father and son considered the trip a success. Following a rich dinner of clams, the Lodges each returned to their rooms where Bay wrote his wife a poetic letter celebrating their ninth anniversary.[16]

Later that evening Bay experienced sharp abdominal pains. Unable to sleep, he wandered along the seashore until early the following morning. Returning to the house, Bay told his father the discomfort he had experienced was growing worse.[17]

As the morning progressed the pain intensified. With Lodge watching helplessly, Bay was plagued by painful cramps, vomiting, and diarrhea. The senator, who concluded his son had contracted food poisoning, did his best to raise Bay's spirits by sitting at his bedside and reading aloud from the large selection of books at his disposal.[18]

That evening, believing the worst had passed, Bay and his father enjoyed a light dinner. Later that evening Bay's pain returned with even greater intensity. With no doctor on the island, Lodge learned that a physician from Nantucket could only reach the island the following morning. With Bay's illness increasing in severity, Lodge was advised to try remedies such as chloroform and mustard powder. Nothing worked.[19]

Arriving from the mainland early the following morning the doctor immediately administered morphine. Learning from Lodge that Bay suffered from a weak heart, the physician employed digitalis and nitroglycerin all in an attempt to stabilize the senator's son's condition. Having had little sleep or food and wracked with worry, Lodge found himself terrified over the young man's prospects. "I had death in my heart," he wrote Bigelow in a detailed description of events. In the hopes that Bay's illness would resolve, Lodge wrote Nannie a telegram informing her that Bay was experiencing indigestion and that the doctor was optimistic about his recovery.[20]

Convinced by the physician to rest, Lodge lay in his bedroom on the second floor and attempted to calm his nerves. Moments later he was jolted by the doctor's voice. Hearing the words "There is a sudden failure," Lodge raced down the stairs to Bay's bedroom. Knowing that his second child's spirit was drifting away, Lodge could do nothing but cradle his beloved son's head in his hands. "So he died in my arms," the senator wrote Bigelow, describing the unspeakable agony of the moment when Bay's pain and struggle for validation mercifully ended.[21]

Following any great loss, Lodge's indomitable will forced him to remain engaged with the world. While his devotion to friends, family, and civic duty never wavered, Bay's loss haunted the senator and his wife for the rest of their lives. "Cabot is shrunk and shriveled like me," Adams wrote to Lizzie Cameron during one encounter with the senator. While Lodge never lost his fondness for William Bigelow, the senator never returned to Tuckernuck again.[22]

The death of Bay Lodge, on August 21, 1909, brought the senator's world to a halt. Nannie and Bessy Lodge, who had captivated so many with their wit and beauty, were devastated to learn of the young poet's death. "Poor Cabot had to telegraph everywhere to get undertakers, steamers, and special trains, and stop Nannie somewhere on her way down, and everybody helped," Adams wrote Lizzie Cameron in describing the events that followed Bay's passing.[23]

Days later, clothed in black, their faces obscured by dark tulles, the two women quietly arrived at William Bigelow's Beacon Hill townhouse to await the arrival of Bay's body. During a brief ceremony in what Adams referred to as a "queer Bay-an," those in attendance read selections from Bay's poetry as well as those of his literary hero, Walt Whitman. Other prominent literary figures including the novelists Henry James and Edith Wharton wrote condolence notes to members of the Lodge family of how deeply they were affected by the young man's loss.[24]

A great admirer of Bay's and one who had encouraged his passions for literature, Theodore Roosevelt, deep in the African jungle, was deeply saddened by Bay Lodge's passing. "I loved him dearly," he wrote Nannie. "He was the truest and staunchest of friends, the most interesting of companions. He was the only man I have ever met whom I felt was a genius," T. R. commented in the middle of October.[25]

As one who understood the toll familial loss could have on the human spirit, Roosevelt encouraged Nannie not to allow Bay's death to prevent her from cherishing the simple pleasures of life that remained to her. "There is nothing in the world I can say to help you. Nannie, you are the daughter, the sister, the mother of fighting men; you have a valiant and gallant soul; you must let nothing, no sorrow beat you down." Roosevelt's words were heartfelt, but they were not enough to heal the mortal wound Bay's mother had suffered.[26]

Henry Adams worried about Nannie as well. In writing of the shattering effect Bay's death had on the family, the historian foresaw nothing but overwhelming heartbreak. "What we shall have to wait to know is the limits of the ruin this bomb will cause," Adams noted to Lizzie Cameron. The commentator believed Bay's widow would become reduced "to the mental stupor of an animal," while Nannie would silently endure the unspeakable trauma.[27]

Adams, who had endured his own tragedy in the loss of his wife Clover, also tried to encourage Nannie not to allow Bay's death to limit her passion for life and family. "You have so much left you, and so much to do for them! You are not alone . . . You have lived and will continue to live, in him." In a letter to Theodore Roosevelt's sister, Corinne, Nannie wrote of the unique position Bay had occupied in her world. "He was the center of us all, the one who made things worthwhile—whom we all wanted and longed to be with." For all the bravery Nannie displayed in communicating her deep sorrow, the loss left her inconsolable. Even as she tried to return to her daily activities as wife, mother, and hostess, friends noticed a physical and psychological deterioration, robbing Nannie of the sparkle and joy that once made her the center of social activity within the Federal City.[28]

As Roosevelt experienced the euphoria of pursuing big game on the continent of Africa, the former president attempted to remain engaged in public affairs. Writing Roosevelt, Lodge had proposed the idea of a potential United States Senate run. Upon deeper consideration, the senator believed the former president needed an opportunity equivalent to the special position he occupied in society.[29]

Even as the senator advised Roosevelt about his future, Lodge expressed concern about the nation's present circumstances. A growing concern over inflation was seen by the increased Democratic vote during the Massachusetts governor's race, a symptom Lodge believed had the potential to impact the Republican majority in Congress. President Taft was of little help. With prices rising and unhappiness with the tariff growing, one didn't need to possess a deep grasp of American politics to understand why the former judge was floundering. "All these things make me anxious about next year," Lodge wrote forebodingly about the upcoming 1910 elections.[30]

As Roosevelt reached Uganda, Lodge alerted him of his increasing doubt about Taft's ability to engage the nation. The senator was most concerned about the potential loss of the Republican majority in the House of Representatives. In an eight-page letter at the end of December 1909, Lodge contended that "this Administration, without doing anything wrong, is not strong in the country and is losing its hold." With Roosevelt's dynamic personality no longer present, political conflict between conservatives and progressives had become unmanageable.[31]

Barraging the former president with letters critical of the current president's actions, the senator believed Taft's White House tenure had become destructive to the Republican Party. One note concerned the firing of Roosevelt's favorite official, chief forester of the United States, Gifford Pinchot. A major symbol of Roosevelt's presidency, the dismissal of the progressive conservationist caused many liberals and independents to believe Taft was dismantling Roosevelt's legacy. That image was not helped by the president's preference of allowing "special interests" to increase their foothold within Congress and the White House.[32]

Monitoring developments from Washington, Senator Lodge believed circumstances were aligning for Roosevelt to seek a third term as president. "There is a consistently growing thought of you and your return to the Presidency," Lodge wrote as the former president headed toward the African capital of Khartoum. Knowing that the media was eager to discover Roosevelt's thoughts about the current administration, the senator advised his friend to avoid any comments about the state of the country. "I do not want any plotting or planning about the future by anyone, but I do want to keep your position such that no future can find you unprepared or open to criticism for anything that has been done." With the 1910 midterm elections six months away, the senator did not want Roosevelt to do or say anything that could jeopardize an already narrow Republican majority.[33]

Taft's firing of Pinchot may have increased Roosevelt's dissatisfaction with Taft, but the former president remained fully invested in his friend's success. "I wish, in my own mind, and to you, to give Taft the benefit of every doubt, and to think and say the very utmost that can be said and thought in his favor," T. R. wrote on April 11, 1909. But the removal of Pinchot had disturbed Roosevelt more than he was willing to admit. "I cannot believe it. I do not know any man in public life who has rendered quite the service you have rendered," Roosevelt wrote the environmentalist from Africa's Lado Enclave.[34]

As Roosevelt was met by one Lodge letter after another encouraging him to return to public life, T. R. believed he had little chance of being effective. While Roosevelt admitted that conservatives in Congress appeared to have lost their focus in the running of the country, he also expressed ambivalence about involving himself further in national affairs. "I have played my part, and I have the very strongest objections to having to play any further part," Roosevelt wrote Lodge as he enjoyed the tranquility of Porto Maurizio, an Italian suburb three hundred miles from Rome.[35]

As the Roosevelt's travels continued, Lodge's letters detailing the dire circumstances of the Republican Party plagued T. R. at every turn. "We are going to be defeated this year, so far as I can see," Lodge wrote ominously. As Roosevelt and his son Kermit traveled on the Orient Express bound for Paris, the senator attempted to enlist Roosevelt's support on enhancing the public's confidence in the GOP.

"The one positive feeling among the great masses of the American people today is the feeling for you," the senator wrote on April 25.[36]

Appreciating Lodge's appeals, Roosevelt was determined to remain in retirement. Resentful of those conservatives in Congress who had blocked his legislation from seeing the light of day, T. R. had no interest in saving the careers of a group of men whose interests were contrary to his own. "The instant the [1904] election was over they turned round with the utmost hilarity . . . saying that now I was dead and it was of no consequence what I did one way or the other." The experience had left Roosevelt bitter, with no interest in coming to the rescue of those who had done little to help his administration succeed.[37]

Even with Roosevelt's unwillingness about making any kind of public display to strengthen the GOP, the senator remained persistent. "They [the American people] are looking for you as the Moses to lead them out of the wilderness of doubt and discontent in which they find themselves," Lodge wrote, hoping to find a way of reengaging his friend's political interests. The senator was also a candidate for reelection in 1910, and while Lodge appeared confident of victory, Henry Adams was not so sure. "Cabot is even scared about himself," the historian wrote to a friend.[38]

Adams as usual was allowing his resentment for Lodge to cloud his judgment. Knowing the strength of the Massachusetts Republican Party, Lodge believed "There is no reasonable doubt that I shall be returned." While the senator also understood Roosevelt's anger at those in the party leadership, he also believed that Democratic control of the nation's agenda would result in nothing but economic and social disaster. "I do not want the Republican Party destroyed or disintegrated. It is the best instrument with all its defects, that we have to carry out what we both want to have done," Lodge wrote.[39]

After some consideration, Roosevelt responded that he was amenable to making a minimal effort to help prevent the party from fracturing. The former president admitted while he and Lodge had differences, the objectives they hoped to accomplish were the same. "There are points where you and I differ, not about objects, but about methods," T. R. wrote from the American Embassy in Paris at the end of April.[40]

From the French capital, the Roosevelts visited Norway to celebrate T. R.'s acceptance of the Nobel Peace Prize. As the former president prepared to receive the award honoring his service for negotiating a conclusion to the Russo-Japanese conflict five years earlier, he confided to Lodge that selecting Taft as his successor was a mistake. "I finally had to admit that he had gone wrong on certain points; and I then also had to admit to myself that deep down underneath I had all along known he was wrong," Roosevelt wrote the senator from the Norwegian community of Christiania during the first week of May.[41]

Even with his commitment to Lodge, Roosevelt remained ambivalent about returning to the center of GOP turmoil. "Ugh! I do dread getting back to America and having to plunge into this cauldron of politics," he wrote Lodge on May 5. Edith Roosevelt agreed. Many of the couple's friends had suggested that the former first lady keep her husband abroad for another year. "Why not for life," Henry Adams wrote in one of his countless letters criticizing his former dinner companion.[42]

On June 18, 1910, the Roosevelts returned to New York Harbor aboard the SS *Kaiserin Auguste Victoria* to an uproarious Manhattan welcome. Anchoring in the Hudson, the former president was met by a launch containing a welcoming party of Lodge and several members of Taft's administration. As the group boarded the ocean liner, Roosevelt was seen waving his hat in greeting to the many boats that celebrated his return to the city of his birth.[43]

Following two weeks in Oyster Bay, Lodge arranged a meeting between Roosevelt and the president. Scheduled to attend the 1910 Harvard commencement, Taft's summer home in Beverly, Massachusetts, was just a short ride from the Lodges' Nahant compound. Taft's secretary Archie Butt commented that the greeting between the two men appeared awkward, yet the occasion seemed happy.[44]

Standing near Roosevelt on that blustery afternoon, the senator watched as the two presidents engaged in polite conversation on the state of politics in New York. A discussion about the Empire State was not an ideal topic. With a low opinion of Taft, liberals and independents viewed the Republican Party as responsible for the problems that plagued the country.[45]

Lodge expressed a sense of relief when the tone of the conversation shifted following the arrival of Taft's wife and family. "I am sure that Senator Lodge advised the ex-president to pay this visit," Taft's gossipy secretary wrote. "I don't think it was all that altruistic on the part of Lodge either, for he wants the aid of both in the fight he is making in his state for reelection." Butt, whose life would meet a horrible end in 1912 as a passenger on the doomed RMS *Titanic*, believed Lodge was nothing more than a self-interested politician focused on doing what he could to retain political power.[46]

Returning home, T. R. spent the next few weeks meeting with members of the Republican Party. Aspiring to do his utmost to keep the GOP together in the face of populist momentum, Lodge encouraged T. R. to remain "aloof from all factions and speak for the party as a whole." Roosevelt remained amenable to the senator's strategy but remained unenthusiastic about going on a long speaking tour.[47]

Focused on reviving his party's declining fortunes, Roosevelt eventually agreed to embark on a three-week campaign swing from New York to Kansas. Before returning from his world travels the former president had arranged to serve as a contributor to the

Outlook. Expecting to receive occasional contributions during the trip, the publication's editor and T. R.'s old friend Lyman Abbott had provided the former president with a private railroad car for the entirety of the trip.[48]

T. R. viewed the journey with little enthusiasm. No longer privileged to have the protection of the Secret Service, Roosevelt believed he would spend most of the time being besieged with annoying questions by low-level government officials. Lodge tried to calm Roosevelt's temper. Praising T. R.'s strategy of meeting with all different factions of the party, the senator believed it was ideal that the former president serve as the party's elder statesman.[49]

But Roosevelt was also concerned about the growing insurgency in the West. Those like Senator Robert La Follette in Wisconsin and others were in the process of promoting democracy in its purest form. Throughout the region residents were exercising their rights in selecting candidates through an open primary system, voting on issues by referenda, and using ballot initiatives to recall officials they believed were not serving the public interest.[50]

Departing from Grand Central Terminal on August 23, 1910, the former president was joined on his travels by journalists from across the nation. Senator Lodge had emphasized that Roosevelt's objective was to revive the spirit of party unity. However, T. R. was concerned that Taft's policies had alienated voters so severely that they had given up on supporting the GOP regardless of who served as leader. While Lodge advised T. R. to focus on broad principles that tied all Republicans together, the senator knew that Roosevelt rarely followed instruction.[51]

To the journalists' delight, the former president was outspoken as soon as the trip began. In an interview with the *New York Times* during a stop in Utica, New York, Roosevelt unleashed a barrage of criticism on his successor. The Republican Party "was in for a licking,"

T. R. said, and President Taft "could do nothing to prevent it." Roosevelt also again admitted he had made an error in selecting Taft to succeed him. The former secretary of war was not an independent thinker and Roosevelt had become disappointed in his old friend's stewardship of the country.[52]

On August 29 the campaign tour continued to make news as Roosevelt addressed the Colorado legislature. In remarks that sent terror through the conservative wing of the party, T. R. condemned two Supreme Court decisions he believed had disregarded the public interest. Roosevelt believed that the 1895 decision *United States v. E. C. Knight Co.* and 1905's *Lochner v. New York* were rulings that had not only increased the power of big businesses but had limited individual equality.[53]

In the case of Knight, the court faulted the government for employing The Sherman Anti-Trust Act to prevent the American Sugar Refining Company from monopolizing its markets. The Lochner case concerned the justices' decision to overturn a New York state law that regulated working hours for employees. While Republicans had celebrated both rulings, claiming they set a barrier against the encroaching power of government, Roosevelt believed it was an attack on the American people and a violation of their natural rights.[54]

Lodge was surprised to read about Roosevelt's assault on the court. "I do not believe it is helpful to criticize specific decisions," the senator wrote. A devoted institutionalist, the senator was concerned that Roosevelt's commentary would cause public opinion to question the high court's credibility. "The courts are charged with the duty of saying what the law is . . . I think that to encourage resistance to the decisions of the courts tends to lead to a disregard of the law," Lodge commented upon reading Roosevelt's speech.[55]

T. R. was surprised at the tempest his comments had created. Little did he realize as he headed to his next stop to dedicate a memorial to abolitionist John Brown at Osawatomie, Kansas, on August 31, the controversy over his progressive rhetoric was just beginning.

Addressing a crowd of 10,000 people just southwest of Kansas City, the former president articulated an agenda the *Boston Evening Transcript* described as "a creed of progressive Republicanism." The address, titled "The New Nationalism," set T. R. on a collision course with Old Guard Republicans as he lamented the crisis of income inequality while criticizing those members of the special interests he believed were responsible for taking advantage of the nation's citizens.[56]

Standing on a makeshift platform during a speech lasting more than an hour, Roosevelt called for the establishment of a series of policies that advocated for those forgotten Americans unable to speak for themselves. These initiatives included such ideas as campaign finance reform, increased government oversight of corporations, revision of the tariff legislation, workman's compensation, and the creation of a national income and inheritance tax.[57]

Addressing these progressive concerns, the former president stated, "I think we have got to face the fact that such an increase in governmental control is now necessary." While many progressives were enthusiastic over the phrase "New Nationalism," the title was not new, but one used by author Herbert Croly in his progressive work, *The Promise of American Life*. The groundbreaking analysis, published in 1909, had caused a stir in liberal circles and caught the eye of Henry Cabot Lodge, who had recommended the work to Roosevelt.[58]

Reading the details of T. R.'s remarks Lodge was little concerned with the substance of the address. The two men had discussed many of the ideas before. While Lodge was no fan of many of these proposals, he believed the media had done his friend a disservice by making his views seem more extreme than they were.[59]

The one subject that caught Lodge by surprise was Roosevelt's commentary about property. Arguing that since one of the objectives of the United States was to promote the general welfare of its citizens, Roosevelt contended that one's "property [was] subject to the general right of the community to regulate its use to whatever degree the public welfare may require it." That passage, while also familiar to Lodge, caused the senator to inform Roosevelt that the subject could potentially have a negative perception throughout the entire spectrum of the Republican Party. "The small property owner is the backbone of this country. He is not easily frightened but when he is . . . he becomes more terrified than the man of many millions because he feels that his little all is at stake," Cabot wrote during the first week of September.[60]

Roosevelt was puzzled about the public uproar over his Kansas comments as well. Many of these ideas were subjects included in speeches he had delivered to Congress as president. While the ideas may have had a higher degree of precision in their recent delivery the principles remained the same. Lodge understood T. R.'s point. Always concerned with public perception, the senator believed the rhetoric "had startled" much of the country.[61]

Even with the excitement of Roosevelt's trip to the West garnering headlines, T. R.'s dynamism did little to smother the anger growing among Republican voters. While Lodge successfully won his nomination for reelection to the Senate, many in his party were not so fortunate. The coming Democratic wave that November was perfectly characterized by Elihu Root, who said, "The country was like a man in bed. He wants to roll over. He doesn't know why he wants to roll over, but he just does; and he'll do it."[62]

As Lodge, Root, and Roosevelt all predicted, the congressional results were nothing less than a resounding defeat for the GOP. With the loss of fifty-eight seats, Republicans became the minority in the House of Representatives for the first time since 1894. The Democratic wave even swept over the wall of the reliably Republican Senate. Lodge and his colleagues managed to maintain their majority, but the gap between the two parties in the nation's upper house narrowed from twenty-nine to ten.[63]

Lodge and Roosevelt were unsurprised by the poor Republican results. "[T]he tide was sweeping all over the country and nothing could stem it anywhere," the senator wrote a week after the elections. From Roosevelt's perspective he believed that with the public's low opinion of the GOP there was little possibility of him being nominated in 1912. "I am not really responsible for the present situation, and I don't want to have to take the responsibility," he wrote defiantly.[64]

For all his talk about not wanting to return to the White House, Roosevelt, encouraged by Lodge's belief that he was the only man who could deliver a party restoration, remained unwilling to dismiss the possibility. The former first lady had no such illusions. After hearing T. R. discussing the idea of returning to the presidency with New York politician Henry Stimson, Edith Roosevelt bluntly informed her husband, "Theodore, you will never be president of the United States again." Between that comment and Taft's failing presidency, Roosevelt could do nothing but grow increasingly depressed.[65]

In January 1911, Lodge was narrowly returned for a fourth term in the US Senate. It was one of the senator's most arduous campaigns. With a newly elected Democratic governor, Eugene N. Foss, doing his utmost to end the senator's career, the three-term Massachusetts Republican successfully defended his political legacy to a sold-out crowd of 6,000 at Symphony Hall. "Boston has seen some great political gatherings but never one like that," the *Boston Evening Transcript* commented.[66]

Upon reelection, the veteran legislator found himself back in the news with his opposition to a progressive campaign to create an amendment to directly elect candidates to the United States Senate. The movement had grown in popularity beginning in the 1880s, as many across the West expressed their concern over the corruption among state senators and the excessive power of Democratic and Republican bosses. With the progressive tide sweeping the country, the idea of popular elections further energized those who favored principles of direct democracy.[67]

A student of America's founding documents, Lodge was adamantly opposed to altering any portion of the Constitution. In an address delivered in 1911, the senator argued that those progressives who advocated that the people have the final say in the election of those to the legislature's upper house were creating a dilemma the founders had specifically tried to prevent. Lodge believed that while those who had assembled at Philadelphia in 1789 were focused on fulfilling the wishes of their fellow citizens, they were wary of voters being ruled by the passions of the moment.

In a letter to Roosevelt in the first week of February, the senator believed that if the amendment came to fruition, it would create an influx of money into the political process that was beyond imagination. "There may be a great advantage of having Senators elected, but keeping corruption out of the body politic is not one of them," he said. In addition, Lodge believed the movement to allow the recall of judges that was sweeping Arizona was one of the more treacherous ideas he had heard in some time. The senator saw both proposals as advocating mob rule, allowing the whims of the people to dictate the direction and the laws of the nation.[68]

While Lodge battled against the forces of progressive political change, Roosevelt embraced them. That spring, the colonel returned to the West where he received a hearty welcome from liberal

Republicans. As with all his encounters with the public, Roosevelt returned home revived and even more convinced that his progressive ideas were the wave of the future. To enhance his arguments, the colonel produced a variety of articles for the *Outlook*. Within these editorials, Roosevelt continued his attacks on the malefactors of great wealth, while praising the policies of Wisconsin's La Follette and taking policy positions like the platform he had advocated at Osawatomie, Kansas.[69]

Lodge remained unenthusiastic to many of Roosevelt's proposals. The senator believed T. R.'s potential return to the White House was preferable to the radicals in both parties, committed to running the nation into the ground. During a public appearance at the end of his senatorial campaign, Lodge had urged voters in Massachusetts to remain supportive of President Taft.[70]

Privately, however Lodge shared Roosevelt's disappointment with the former secretary of war. When Taft lowered tariffs on Canadian agricultural products and allowed the Justice Department to relitigate a case involving U.S. Steel's acquisition of a competitor during the economic downturn of 1907, Lodge commented that the president had "alienated both the radicals and the conservatives, which seems at first sight difficult to do." Even as Roosevelt remained uncertain about contesting Taft for the 1912 nomination, Lodge aggressively lobbied the former president to seize the opportunity.[71]

Over the last two years Henry Cabot Lodge had endured moments of personal tragedy and professional disappointment. Forced to battle for his political life against a wave of political radicalism, Lodge believed a return of Theodore Roosevelt to the White House was the only solution that stood between societal chaos and the reestablishment of Republican control.

Roosevelt, unhappy with the tenure of William Howard Taft, remained uncertain about his own political viability following a failure to prevent the Democratic takeover of the House of Representatives. As both men sought a solution to a potential Republican presidential defeat, neither realized that Roosevelt's growing progressivism and Lodge's staunch conservatism would culminate in a disagreement unlike any they had experienced before.

SIXTEEN
A Chorus of Disapproval

"I knew of course that you and I differed on some of these
points but I had not realized that the difference was so wide."

—Henry Cabot Lodge

I n the winter of 1912, Henry Cabot Lodge remained hopeful that
former president Roosevelt would consider challenging President
Taft for the Republican presidential nomination. Remaining
focused on serving his constituents in Massachusetts, the senator
needed to remain on good terms with the Taft Administration. Following a brief meeting at the White House with the president in the
second week of February, Lodge was confronted by Taft operative
Herbert Parsons.[1]

Knowing Lodge's devotion to Roosevelt, the New York politician
attempted to corner the Bay Stater to discover where he stood in a
potential Taft-Roosevelt battle. "I hope Massachusetts will follow the
example of New York," Parsons said. Lodge, temporarily caught off
guard, was uncertain what his fellow Republican meant. Moments
later the senator understood that Parsons was trying to pressure him
to support the president at the upcoming Chicago convention.[2]

With Taft standing a few feet away Lodge informed Parsons
that the president had a significant following in his state. But Parsons would not back down. "What we want is to have you declare

yourself," the Empire State Republican said. Knowing Taft was well acquainted with both him and the former president, Lodge informed Parsons that turning his back on Roosevelt would cause much of the country to view him "as the veriest dog that ever walked the earth." Taft soon came to Lodge's rescue by saying he understood what a difficult quandary the senator had before him.[3]

Parsons had also raised the issue about T. R.'s promise in 1904 not to seek another term. Lodge found the argument unconvincing, stating that in his opinion a president serving multiple terms held no danger to the Republic. In relating the anecdote to Roosevelt, the senator was unable to restrain himself from also informing T. R. that Henry Adams viewed his potential return to office as "inevitable." While Adams understood that Roosevelt had little interest in another term in the White House, he believed the ex-president could not decline the will of the people.[4]

Considering the idea of another term, Roosevelt concurred with Adams's advice. A presidential draft allowed T. R. to offer himself as a candidate while avoiding a vicious campaign that would rattle the party to its foundations. The news that Roosevelt was amenable to being recruited for another White House run ignited a large portion of the progressive movement. With no other candidate possessing the dynamism of the former president, a wave of support began to build urging T. R. to take up the challenge.[5]

With local Roosevelt clubs appearing around the country and T. R.'s popularity soaring, the former president announced his candidacy on February 21, 1912, during an address to the Ohio Constitutional Convention in Columbus. The speech written by Gifford Pinchot, titled "The Charter of Democracy," resembled T. R.'s Kansas address two years earlier.[6]

In calling for many of the same initiatives, Roosevelt also included ideas embraced by Senator La Follette and others. In the most

shocking part of the speech, the candidate called for the use of referenda to overturn judicial decisions if voters believed the justices did
not have the best interests of the public in mind.[7]

Roosevelt's speech reverberated across the conservative bow of the
Republican Party. Strongly disagreeing with the idea of judicial recall,
Lodge issued a terse statement in which he dissociated himself from
his friend's comments. "I am opposed to the constitutional changes
advocated by Colonel Roosevelt," the senator declared three days after
T. R.'s Columbus appearance.[8]

Throughout their decades of friendship, the senator had spent
countless periods advising Roosevelt what he believed was in the New
Yorker's best interests. Much of the time the former president had
listened, altering his positions in ways that Lodge believed benefited
his career and the fortunes of the Republican Party. However, in
the last few years T. R. had given his time to progressive voices like
Garfield and Pinchot, whose positions were often counter to Lodge's
recommendations.[9]

The disagreement between Lodge and Roosevelt demonstrated
how much their views had diverged. In 1884 both men viewed themselves as reformers unhappy with the Republican status quo. Over
time Lodge had reconciled himself to the conservative views of the
party but attempted to work within the political system to forge incremental change as a barrier against the growing threat of populism.
Roosevelt, who possessed a zeal for reform, was never comfortable
within the conservative confines of the Republican Party, constantly
taking positions that forced Republicans to address policy stances
they found disagreeable.

Throughout Roosevelt's career, he had sought to use political
power to create greater equity in American life. With a desire to
achieve a more balanced relationship between labor and management, limiting the power of corporations, and improving the living

and working conditions for men, women, and children, Roosevelt sought to fulfill Abraham Lincoln's vision, "with malice toward none with charity for all." Increasingly frustrated with the ideological rigidity of the party's conservative wing, the former president's burst of progressive fervor was of little surprise to those who had watched Roosevelt since he first came on the political scene more than two decades earlier.

Lodge, however, was visibly shaken by Roosevelt's progressive declaration. "I have had my share of mishaps in politics, but I never thought that any situation could arise which would have made me so miserably unhappy," the senator wrote Roosevelt on February 28. Having monitored Roosevelt's career more closely than almost anyone else, the senator was mystified in his inability to understand why he had so misread T. R.'s progressive attitudes. "That I failed to do so was very likely my fault, owing probably to my unwillingness to admit that there could be any serious difference of opinion between us on constitutional questions, which seemed to me vital." For Lodge these disagreements with his dearest friend over the fundamental role of American government represented a situation not easily reconcilable.[10]

Lodge had deep objections to the direct election of senators, contending that it would weaken the power of state legislators. The senator also believed the idea of referendums on complex issues were a disastrous idea. Believing that Republican government was fundamentally about elected officials applying their best judgement to address the needs of the people, the senator contended that certain pieces of legislation were far too complex for the average voter to decipher.

On the recall of judges, the senator concluded that if members of the third branch of government believed their decisions were under constant scrutiny it was unlikely the best legal minds would choose to seek the position. "The most vital . . . of all the great principles embodied in the Constitution is that of securing the independence of the judiciary," Lodge said during a speech at Princeton University. "No man fit to be a judge would . . . take office under the recall. In the end the bench would be filled by the weak and the unscrupulous." That address was the last public comment Lodge made until the end of the 1912 Republican convention.[11]

One of the senator's biographers argues that it was unfortunate that Lodge and Roosevelt should have such a severe disagreement over issues of little significance. The dispute was more than an argument over the two men's view of government. Over the last eleven years Roosevelt's growing progressivism had caused him to drift away from Lodge's conservative influence.

More important, Roosevelt's self-centered and reckless move to embrace an activist agenda when the Republican Party was in such a precarious state was a decision Lodge refused to condone. "I could not abandon my convictions," Lodge commented on the issue of Roosevelt's Columbus speech.[12]

Even in Lodge's fury he would not allow his political divergence from Roosevelt to jeopardize their nearly thirty-year relationship. "If I should fight him personally . . . I should be guilty of a disloyalty in friendship which in my opinion, ought to forfeit for me the respect of all decent men. I simply cannot do it." While many understood and respected the senator's neutrality during the 1912 campaign, the turmoil created in the Republican Party by Roosevelt's liberal turn led to gossip among friends and acquaintances of the two men.[13]

Henry Adams also resented the former president's selfish ambitions for driving a wedge within the Republican Party. "[Roosevelt's] mind has gone to pieces, and has disintegrated like the mind of society, till it has become quite incoherent and spasmodic," the commentator wrote his brother Brooks. Adams's views were also based on renewed rumors circulating around the capital that Roosevelt's temperament had become unhinged due to excessive consumption of alcohol.[14]

Even as Roosevelt admitted that the two men's political differences had grown over the last few years, T. R. also refused to allow such disagreement to affect their friendship: "My dear fellow you could not do anything that would make me lose my warm personal affection for you." Roosevelt wrote Lodge following the senator's expression of disappointment. The reply did little to heal the differences that separated the two Republicans. Nannie Lodge believed T. R.'s note to her husband symbolized "fond and amused contempt." While she understood the political disagreements between the two men were serious, Lodge's wife contended the ideological conflict would not affect their personal relationship.[15]

During the flurry of the GOP campaign, the Roosevelts and the Lodges continued to see one another. "Apparently the meeting was as though nothing had happened," Henry Adams wrote Lizzie Cameron in describing a gathering between the two couples. Lodge had informed Roosevelt that he would make no comment about the campaign and at least in the presence of Henry Adams he kept his promise. "Not a word passed about politics," Adams noted following a recent dinner the Lodges attended at his home in Washington.[16]

While Lodge displayed a polite front, beneath the surface he was troubled. In Roosevelt's decision to cast the conservative wing of the party aside Lodge believed he had not only weakened the GOP but endangered those like Lodge's son-in-law Gus Gardner, who was engaged in a difficult campaign for reelection to Congress in Massachusetts.[17]

While the senator spoke little about his disagreement with Roosevelt, Henry Adams, always trying to do his utmost to look beneath the public veneer of those in power, described both the former president and the senator as "pitiable wrecks." Adams was not wrong. Lodge was badly hurt by his disagreement with T. R. Believing his position to privately oppose Roosevelt's presidential ambitions was right, the senator wondered if he had responded too harshly following Roosevelt's address in Columbus.[18]

Admitting that T. R.'s political choices had caused him great pain, Lodge wrote on March 1, 1912, that he had overreacted to Roosevelt's progressive platform. "It was my fault no doubt that I had not read your views about submitting certain judicial decisions to popular revision. . . . For that reason, the declaration of the Columbus speech came to me as entirely new." There is no record of Roosevelt's reply to Lodge's letter.[19]

The sudden silence in what was once a prolific correspondence illustrated the strong disagreement that now consumed the relationship. While the two communicated intermittently, their conversation focused primarily on issues like immigration, American history, and the improvement of the navy. At one point, Roosevelt asked Lodge if he could convince Taft to run a civil campaign and not consider disclosing letters between the two men containing their private views.[20]

While Lodge made the effort to assist Roosevelt in that regard, the former president thought little of the senator during the 1912 campaign. As the colonel, President Taft, and Senator Robert La Follette fervently battled for delegates in primaries across the country, Lodge quietly watched the proceedings from his home on Massachusetts Avenue. Taft was successful in states that remained under the control of the party bosses, while Roosevelt won victories in communities where voters had championed open primaries.[21]

Knowing that Taft was gaining momentum and had also put the political mechanism in place to control the convention, did not stop Lodge from employing his network to tilt the Massachusetts primary in the president's favor. Whether T. R. knew that Lodge had assisted Taft is unknown. But Edith Roosevelt remained bitterly disappointed that neither the senator nor Elihu Root had chosen to support her husband's third bid for the presidency.[22]

Roosevelt arrived in Chicago in the second week of June needing seventy delegates of the two hundred and fifty that remained available to achieve the nomination. Unfortunately, the progressive had little control over who the delegates would support. With a committee that decided the contested delegates stacked in Taft's favor, the result was a foregone conclusion.[23]

Roosevelt was beside himself when he learned of what the president had done. Refusing to participate in a corrupt convention, the former president bolted the Republican Party to run an independent campaign to return to the White House. With Roosevelt gone, the party effectively split between progressives and conservatives.[24]

Lodge was happy with the convention's outcome. Shortly after Taft's renomination the senator joined his party colleagues in issuing a statement from Nahant supporting the president. Most important, Lodge announced that he fully supported the party standing "firmly for the Constitution and the independence of the courts."[25]

Not mentioning Roosevelt's name, the senator stated that he refused to criticize any of the other candidates who had stood for the nomination. As Lodge declared his loyalty to the Republican Party, his friend of twenty-eight years stood in Chicago's Orchestra Hall and declared himself the nominee of what became known as the "Bull Moose Party."[26]

While the Republicans were in turmoil, the Democratic Party nominated the governor of New Jersey, Woodrow Wilson, to stand against the incumbent president in the November election. Watching events carefully, Lodge had little confidence a divided party and a poor campaigner like Taft had much of a chance of success. "It looks simply like an overwhelming victory for Wilson," the senator wrote a friend that July.[27]

As Roosevelt, Wilson, Taft, and the socialist Eugene V. Debs campaigned across the nation, the Lodges briefly focused their attention on the health of Henry Adams. On April 24 Adams suffered what seemed a minor stroke. As the days passed the historian experienced a raging fever, hallucinations, and a delirium culminating in two attempts to leap to his death from a bedroom window.[28]

As Adams recovered, Lodge, monitoring the campaign closely, became resigned to Republican defeat. While many of his friends believed Armageddon was approaching, the senator calmly accepted the situation. "Revolutions come pretty slowly," Lodge wrote in a comment to William Sturgis Bigelow as he prepared for the unfortunate results.[29]

During the campaign the senator and the former president criticized one another as each made appearances in respective states. On August 17, a month after securing the progressive nomination, Roosevelt made an indirect reference to Lodge during a speech at "Point of Pines Park," in Revere, Massachusetts. Referring to both parties as "hopelessly corrupt and incompetent," the candidate then whipped up the crowd when he accused "certain of your New England Senators, who I regret to say took the lead . . . in putting through the steal of the Republican nomination in Chicago." Lodge punched back a month later following a campaign tour of Taft's home state of Ohio. In extensive comments published in the *Boston Globe*, Lodge contended that many in the West had grown tired of the colonel's complaining and were rapidly losing interest in his candidacy.[30]

Finding the entire campaign unpleasant, Roosevelt's wife remained relatively silent. In private the acrimony between Roosevelt and Lodge caused her deep aggravation. Throughout the election of 1912 Edith admitted that she had nightmares about Root and the treachery he had undertaken against her husband. When Lodge campaigned in Boston, the former first lady was gratified to learn that more than a thousand Republicans had instead chosen to attend a Bull Moose event featuring one of T. R.'s relatives.[31]

Despite Lodge's somewhat apologetic letter months earlier, the former president's sense of betrayal by his old friend had not abated. When Lodge's name came up in conversation, Roosevelt described him as "highly cultivated but entirely sterile," the same characteristics that composed a New England farm. As Roosevelt continued his tour of the country arriving in Milwaukee, Wisconsin on October 14, the former Rough Rider found the campaign so enjoyable the idea of defeat remained on the outskirts of his mind.[32]

Shortly before departing from the Gilpatrick Hotel to deliver a speech at the city's auditorium the progressive candidate was shot by a deranged saloonkeeper who opposed Roosevelt running for a third term. Firing at close range the bullet was miraculously slowed by a bulk of paper contained in the breast pocket of Roosevelt's jacket. Suffering a flesh wound, Roosevelt refused to seek medical attention. Stating that he cared "not a rap" at being shot, the candidate headed to the venue where he spoke for the next ninety minutes before finally consenting to go to the hospital.[33]

Along with the nation, Henry Cabot Lodge was stunned to hear of the attempt on the former president's life. "Distressed and very anxious," Lodge telegraphed Edith from Worcester, Massachusetts, two days following the incident. As Roosevelt's family raced to the candidate's side, the Lodges continued to offer their support to their friend in his time of trouble. "Our thoughts have been unceasingly with you," the senator wrote the following day. "Our distress and anxiety only equaled by our admiration for your wonderful and wholly characteristic nerve and courage." Recovering in a Chicago hospital, Roosevelt was grateful for the couple's heartfelt support. "It was fine to hear from you," T. R. wrote near the end of the month following his return to New York.[34]

While many voters sympathized with the former president, Roosevelt was unable to reclaim the presidency. When the totals were announced on November 5 T. R. finished ahead of President Taft but behind the victorious Democratic nominee, Governor Woodrow Wilson of New Jersey. Following the election, Roosevelt's and Lodge's old friend Cecil Spring Rice was appointed by London as ambassador to Washington. "But now I feel horribly at not being president," Roosevelt wrote in a congratulatory note to the diplomat who had served as his best man decades earlier.[35]

The deep emotion displayed in Lodge's telegrams following Roosevelt's assassination attempt proved significant in healing the breach between the two men. Following the election, the two renewed their correspondence while working on their respective memoirs. Published in 1913, Lodge's *Early Memories* had no discussion about his political experiences. However, Roosevelt's autobiography, released the same year, made nothing but flattering comments about Lodge's character and the devoted nature of their friendship.[36]

In April 1913 Roosevelt and Lodge celebrated the marriage of T. R.'s daughter Ethel. Gathering at Christ Church in Oyster Bay, the senator and his wife were among the few Republican friends in attendance who Roosevelt had associated with before the GOP schism of 1912. Lodge was grateful for the invitation as he thoroughly delighted in the youthful energy that surrounded him.[37]

The senator also appreciated the fact that the guests the Roosevelts had invited were invested in the event. The remark may also have referred to those T. R. had chosen to exclude from his daughter's nuptials. Neither President Taft nor Elihu Root received invitations. "I feel very strongly against Root," Theodore commented to Winthrop Chanler. "Root took part in as downright a bit of theft as ever was perpetrated by any Tammany ballot box stuffer."[38]

The former president was less harsh in his opinion about Lodge and several other friends in attendance. "But with Cabot . . . it was wholly different. [He] had the absolute right to do . . . exactly as he did and I never expected . . . [him] to follow me." With hostilities behind them, Lodge and Roosevelt remained uncertain about the new administration, as the Democrats gained control of the White House and both houses of Congress for only the second time since the Civil War.[39]

As the two men reunited following a disagreement that nearly destroyed their friendship, the two internationalists each cast their eye on the nation's affairs abroad. With William Jennings Bryan as Wilson's secretary of state, the colonel and the senator were increasingly apprehensive over the two men's complacent view regarding the military preparedness required to protect the interests of the United States. Years earlier, Roosevelt's friend Cecil Spring Rice had stated that the colonel was never happy unless he was in a battle. As an international cataclysm appeared on the horizon in Europe, Lodge's and Roosevelt's relationship became renewed as they battled Wilson, Bryan, and others who they believed were attempting to weaken the presence of the United States on the global stage.

SEVENTEEN

A Common Enemy

"I regard Wilson with contemptuous dislike."

—Theodore Roosevelt

I n the winter of 1913, Henry Cabot Lodge remained suspicious of Woodrow Wilson as he prepared to assume the presidency. Throughout Wilson's tenure as governor of New Jersey the former academic had occupied a position described by his biographer Arthur S. Link as "conservative to the core."[1]

Wilson's conservatism on many issues was not that different from Lodge's. In 1909, Wilson had contended that Roosevelt's progressive restraint on corporations "would enslave and demoralize the nation." When Roosevelt had sought to equalize the relationship between management and labor, Wilson believed the president's efforts did a disservice to American workers "by holding standards down to the lowest common denominator."[2]

Upon his decision to run for the presidency, Wilson reversed many of his positions. The Southerner called for an end to monopolies and attempted to attract labor interests by engaging in rhetoric more amenable to unions. Lodge, who believed that intellectual integrity was essential to the human condition, criticized Wilson for lacking the character indispensable to a president. "I think he would sacrifice any opinion at any moment for his own benefit," Lodge wrote the historian John T. Morse Jr.[3]

Lodge may have thought the new president lacked sincerity, but he was not ashamed to initially admit Wilson was a highly intelligent man. That belief had resonated with Lodge when, during his brief tenure as an editor at *The International Review* in 1879, he had accepted an article from the future president while a student at Princeton University.[4]

Early in the new administration Wilson ignited T. R.'s rage by removing all African Americans from the federal bureaucracy. Roosevelt also found reasons to criticize the administration's tariff legislation. While rates were cut to 25 percent (a goal the GOP was unable to accomplish), Roosevelt still viewed the bill as one Taft might have initiated.[5]

Lodge was no admirer of Wilson's policies either. Opposing the administration's tariff reduction with the comment that the bill was "the most grotesque thing I ever saw," the senator was unsurprised that Wilson's idea of improving the state of the country was "to take money from some people and give it to others." Lodge, however, understood that elections had consequences. The senator realized that he was obligated not only to contend that Wilson's agenda was not in the nation's best interest, but to offer alternatives that revived Republican popularity in preparation for the midterm elections of 1914.[6]

Neither Lodge nor Roosevelt was engaged with politics for the latter part of 1913. In September, the senator was forced to undergo surgery due to the development of "gastric ulcers." While the procedure was a success, it involved a lengthy recovery process. Roosevelt, at age fifty-four and believing the GOP nomination was stolen from him, decided to embark on an extensive trip to South America, culminating in an exploration of the Amazon's "River of Doubt."[7]

As Lodge recovered from his operation and Roosevelt prepared for his voyage both remained critical of the initial stages of Wilson's tenure in the White House. The two Republicans were dismayed following the president's selection of Bryan as his secretary of state. Always viewing the Midwesterner with suspicion, Lodge and Roosevelt both believed the former three-time presidential candidate was a poor choice to manage the nation's diplomatic affairs. "You can have no conception of Bryan's ignorance, and he has reached a point where he cannot learn," Lodge wrote T. R. that fall. With instability on the Balkan peninsula and revolution in Mexico, Lodge and Roosevelt believed American diplomacy required a steadier hand than the former boy orator from the Plains.[8]

In May 1911 General Victoriano Huerta took advantage of Mexican instability to appoint himself president. While the military man was no humanitarian, American businessmen with interests in the country asked Wilson to recognize the new government. Knowing that Huerta had obtained the presidency through a fraudulent election, Wilson refused to do so. No fan of American intervention, the president believed Mexico an independent nation with its citizens being responsible for their own affairs.[9]

With violence and factionalism growing, the Wilson administration decided to take the initiative. Attempting to assist the country in stabilizing its political situation, the White House called on the former governor of Minnesota, John Lind, to offer a series of proposals in exchange for United States recognition. When Huerta heard that one of Wilson's conditions called for his resignation, the Mexican president immediately dismissed any further discussions.[10]

While Lodge believed in the idea of bipartisan support in foreign policy, the senator found the president's strategy for solving the crisis laughable. "To open negotiations with the head of a government and put to him . . . that he should abdicate, is something new in diplomacy," Lodge wrote in a tart note to Roosevelt. Concerned that the crisis could spread to other nations in the region, and with little confidence in the Mexican people's ability to manage their own affairs, Lodge believed that Huerta's "strongman" tactics were the only way to pacify an unworkable situation.[11]

Watching Wilson's disorganized Mexican policy, Lodge had little positive to say. In comments to Roosevelt, the senator referred to the president as "overrated," "obstinate," and one who "lacked courage." Rarely taking his eyes off the condition of the nation's maritime fleet, the senator also expressed concern about the nation's defenses in the Atlantic and the Pacific. "The American Navy is at a standstill," Lodge wrote as he lamented the president's lack of urgency in the development of battleships.[12]

Roosevelt, frustrated that he was no longer commander in chief, joined in Lodge's assault by referring to Bryan as "the most contemptible figure we have ever had as Secretary of State." As T. R. watched the president reduce the nation to a laughingstock internationally, he referred to the Democrat as "a ridiculous creature in international matters," who was "ignorant," and "bitterly partisan."[13]

Preparing to depart for South America in September 1913, Roosevelt received a note from Lodge expressing concern about T. R.'s decision to explore the wilderness of the Amazon. Knowing that Roosevelt was addicted to testing the limits of his physical abilities, the senator worried the arduous journey was ill-advised. "I dread the trip through the heart of the continent because I believe it to be much worse than anything in Africa," Lodge wrote on the natural dangers of the region.[14]

Despite the senator's concerns, Roosevelt assured his friend that he intended on having a safe and rewarding journey. The colonel understood he was entering a part of the world where "living is something of an effort," and "where men cannot live without mosquito net."

Lodge's warnings however would prove prescient. The excursion was Roosevelt's "darkest journey" and one that caused him to come closer to death than any moment in his lifetime.[15]

As Lodge stayed informed about Roosevelt's travails in the rainforests of Brazil, the senator tried to refocus his attention on the toll the Democrats' fiscal policies were taking on the nation's economy. "I feel greatly alarmed about the outlook, for I fear we are on the edge of a condition which will cause great suffering in all directions," he wrote T. R. Discouraged with Wilson's economic decisions, Lodge could do nothing but watch as Wilson used the power of the Interstate Commerce Commission and the Justice Department to bring corporations and railroads to their knees.[16]

As the ICC had forced railroad executives to raise salaries, punitive regulations prevented these companies from raising their shipping rates. Unable to gain additional revenue, executives were forced to cut employment at a rapid rate. The senator found the event even more disturbing because it affected the rail system in Massachusetts. "Our New England system is being torn to pieces and both roads are on the edge of bankruptcy," Lodge angrily wrote.[17]

The senator also worried the government's wide-ranging prosecution of businesses great and small would negatively impact the economic confidence of the country. "[B]ut this indiscriminate assault on everything of course produces nothing but fear, and fear is more deadly to business than anything else," he wrote to T. R. in April 1914.[18]

In May, as Roosevelt began his return to the United States to recover from an illness he contracted during his trip abroad, Lodge wrote him outraged over the administration's decision to minimize the greatness of the Panama Canal. Preparing for the grand opening of the international waterway in August, Wilson and Secretary of State Bryan had decided to sign a treaty with

Colombia effectively apologizing for the United States' treatment of the South American nation during the Panamanian Revolution of 1903.[19]

In addition, Bryan offered to pay Bogotá $25 million as compensation for shifting the canal from its original property in Colombia. "I do not know anything this Administration has done which has angered me more than this Colombian treaty," Lodge wrote T. R. during the first week of May 1914. The senator believed the agreement's passage was unlikely. The canal was popular with both parties, and many members of Congress were offended at those colleagues ridiculing such an extraordinary industrial accomplishment. Refusing to have the greatest legacy of Roosevelt's presidency tarnished, Republicans managed to block the apologetic rhetoric from the treaty and tabled it until well after Roosevelt's death.[20]

The former president, who departed for his son Kermit's wedding in Europe almost immediately following his return from South America, had not communicated with Lodge about his views on either Mexico or the Colombian treaty. Following Huerta's refusal to resign his office, Wilson arranged for the lifting of an arms embargo, hoping it would not only increase pressure on the Mexican leader but encourage European nations to use their resources to oust the general from power.[21]

The subsequent arrest of several American sailors in the Mexican province of Tampico in April 1914 gave Wilson the excuse to authorize the navy to converge on Mexican shores. Without waiting for a miliary resolution from Congress, the president also ordered the marines to occupy the city of Veracruz to intercept a shipment of weapons from Germany to aid allies of Huerta. The attack led to nineteen deaths and international condemnation. Wilson was grateful when Argentina, Brazil, and Chile offered to intervene, but it did little to settle the situation.[22]

Roosevelt eventually issued his own attack on the administration's Mexico policy. On December 7 the *New York Times* and other publications published "Our Responsibility in Mexico." Throughout the lengthy article, T. R. accused the administration of engaging in a conflict that had resulted in nothing other than loss of life. Sharing Roosevelt's anger at Wilson's management of the nation's international affairs, Lodge applauded Roosevelt's insights with the only suggestion that, "like Oliver Twist I want some more."[23]

Referring to the president and Bryan as "the very worst men we have ever had in their positions," Roosevelt was saddened that so many of his friends and admirers seemed gratified with Wilson's peace policy. T. R. could not understand the rationale for such praise. The president's Mexican initiative was a disorganized catastrophe and lives were lost. In addition, the United States, which Lodge and Roosevelt had seen rise to greatness on the international stage in 1898, was being viewed as an indecisive embarrassment by those abroad.[24]

While Roosevelt and Lodge were focused on the nation's involvement in Mexico, an armed conflict was consuming Europe. Six months earlier, on June 28, 1914, the heirs to the throne of Austria-Hungary, Archduke Franz Ferdinand and his bride the Duchess of Hohenberg, were assassinated in Sarajevo. The culprit was a Serbian gunman outraged over Austria's growing encroachment on the Balkans. Following the murder of the royal couple, a war began that would consume the world for the next five years.[25]

Lodge and his family were traveling in Europe in early August when Germany declared war on France and moved its troops into neighboring Belgium. Bay Lodge's widow Bessy and Cabot's grandchildren were vacationing in Dieppe, a small community overlooking the Normandy coast. Lodge, who had developed diphtheria during the trip, arranged for his son-in-law Gus Gardner to retrieve Bessy and her children and ferry them to England.[26]

At Sagamore Hill, Roosevelt could only watch the war unfold in silence. T. R. was overcome by malaria, which brought a high fever. The former president was also suffering from a severe sore throat, leaving him unable to pontificate on the many issues in which he remained absorbed. "The situation in Europe is really dreadful," Roosevelt wrote his son Quentin, shortly after the war began.[27]

As the United States took a position of neutrality, the senator was disheartened that the Administration refused to allow Congress to undertake a detailed examination of the country's military defenses. Ambassador Cecil Spring Rice shared Lodge's concerns about the lack of American fortification. Writing to one of his many correspondents in the United States the British ambassador commented, "[Y]ou will want a big army one of these days and when you want it you'll want it damn bad and won't have it."

During the first weeks of 1915, Lodge derided Wilson's actions as "pro-German." Frustrated with Wilson's silence as Germany violated one nation's sovereignty after the other, the senator lambasted the president for his decision to prevent American banks from aiding the French as well as disallowing Bethlehem Steel's Charles Schwab from exporting hardware for submarines to the allies.[28]

Compensating for a lack of American shipping, Wilson proposed legislation to purchase merchant ships from American citizens as well as other nations including—Germany. Lodge believed that Wilson's plan to purchase German ships drydocked in American harbors was an odious proposition. "If this is done and the allies refuse to recognize the transfer of the flag . . . we shall find ourselves with government-owned ships afloat . . . which are likely to be fired on and sunk." The senator believed that the results of the potential transaction could lead to the United States going from a neutral nation to one at war.[29]

Working with Lodge to block Wilson's shipping bill, T. R. grew increasingly upset over the unspeakable brutality being conducted by the Germans in their invasion of Belgium. In January 1915, the colonel released a book containing a series of articles he had published on the growing war. The collection, titled *America and the World War*, advocated the United States employ defensive measures to protect the American people from the violence that was pulverizing Europe.[30]

T. R.'s tirade against Wilson was so vitriolic many of his friends thought he was doing a disservice to the country. While Roosevelt remained frustrated watching events unfold, he was also happy that he no longer was forced to restrain his opinions for the sake of GOP unity. "Thank Heaven, I no longer have to consider the effect of my actions upon any party," he wrote Lodge in February 1915.[31]

That declaration of intellectual freedom included Roosevelt attacking the German American community that sought to employ propaganda as an instrument in the interest of the Fatherland. T. R.'s belief that the nation was at risk of internal subversion by supporters of the German Empire was not far from the truth. Months later, the Secret Service uncovered a cabal of German agents coordinated by Berlin to undermine citizens and institutions who sought to support those nations allied against the Central Powers.[32]

These operations included Berlin's attempt to gain financial control of such publications as the *Washington Post* and the *New York Sun*. Other operations included attempts to sabotage munitions factories as well as other businesses across the country that sought to aid the allied forces. Despite having knowledge that Germany was attempting to undermine the industrial workings of the United States, Wilson concealed the information from the public.[33]

As the winter of 1915 progressed, Lodge and his Republican colleagues did their utmost to kill the president's bill to purchase foreign and domestic shipping. "The more I think of it the more positively criminal it seems to me for the president to have tried to jam that bill through," Lodge commented to Roosevelt about the large opposition to the legislation. Concerned that a disaster involving Americans could occur on the high seas, the senator concurred with Roosevelt's opinion of Wilson being "the most dangerous man that has ever sat in the White House," with the exception of James Buchanan.[34]

Following the passage of the shipping legislation in the House of Representatives, Lodge and his colleagues launched a filibuster against the bill in the Senate. Numerous speeches, some lasting thirteen hours, kept the capital abuzz until early the following morning. Still weak from his stomach surgery Lodge was unable to fully participate in the debate. To compensate, the senator oversaw the strategy for the Republican caucus. With seven Democrats contending that the purchasing of foreign ships could put the United States in jeopardy, the bill's opponents forced the administration to revise the legislation.[35]

The battle over the shipping issue caused Lodge to grow even more disdainful of Wilson. "[T]his man is dangerous from his determination to have his own way, no matter what it costs the country," the senator wrote in describing the president's stubborn temperament. While Lodge found the whole shipping bill debate disagreeable, his major issue was the government purchasing German ships for use in the Atlantic. As biographer John Garraty observes, if Wilson had discarded that portion of the bill, resistance would have ended. Either way the senator was happy with the outcome. "If we have won it is a victory well worth winning," Lodge wrote Roosevelt at the end of February.[36]

Roosevelt was delighted to hear about the senator's success. "Lord, I am feeling warlike with this administration," T. R. wrote as he described his upcoming attacks on Wilson's foreign policy on Germany and Mexico in the pages of *Metropolitan* magazine. Lodge was unsurprised by Roosevelt's reply. Writing several days later he commented, "I do not wonder that you feel warlike with this

Administration. I never expected to hate anyone in politics with the hatred I feel toward Wilson."[37]

Even as Lodge criticized Wilson's attitude toward the allies, the senator made sure that nothing occurred to place the United States at risk. During a March 1915 meeting with Herbert Hoover, who was focusing his energy and financial resources on a relief effort in Belgium, the senator threatened the future president of the United States with the Logan Act for his activities in supporting the victims displaced by the German war machine. Later, as Hoover shared the story with Roosevelt, T. R. made light of Lodge's obsession over US neutrality.[38]

With other nations advancing in the development of their military capability, the senator remained concerned about the preparedness of the American navy. Since its last refitting during the Spanish-American War in 1898, the fleet had become severely outdated. Initially informed in 1913 by navy secretary Josephus Daniels that the administration was preparing to construct new battleships, Lodge grew frustrated as little progress was made. "Wilson and Bryan are pushing us to a position which may bring war or humiliation and yet insist we shall remain defenseless," Lodge wrote Roosevelt.[39]

Following the May 7, 1915, torpedoing of the Cunard Line's RMS *Lusitania* by a German submarine, Lodge and Roosevelt grew more concerned about the country's lack of preparedness. Of the 1,200 lives lost, 128 were from the United States. Following a statement from the secretary of state that refused to harshly condemn Germany, Roosevelt informed Nannie Lodge in June 1915 that like her husband he believed communications should cease between Washington and Berlin.[40]

With an administration unwilling to listen to those who believed the country needed to undertake a more aggressive foreign policy, and with a public dismissive of the carnage occurring abroad, Roosevelt was doubtful that a shift in the status quo was possible. "I believe the pacifist propaganda of the last five years . . . has represented . . . a more permanent and degrading harm to the American people than corruption in politics or crookedness in business." Viewing "cowardice as a fundamental sin," T. R. chastised the Republican Party for its inability to stand united against the president's poor leadership because of its fear of becoming involved in the war.[41]

Lodge held a similar view as T. R. to the sinking of the British liner. On the evening the public learned of the enormous loss of life, Corrine Roosevelt and her husband Douglas Robinson saw Lodge standing on the stoop of his home waving the latest edition of a newspaper. The couple inquired what steps the president was going to take in response to Germany's actions. Lodge could do nothing but give a dour look and say, "Words, words, words."[42]

The senator reflected his feelings of discouragement in a letter to Roosevelt on June 4. Believing that the administration had no ability to stand up to German aggression, Lodge found the behavior of the president and his chief diplomat "sickening." The senator believed that the administration was employing polite admonishments in the hopes that other events would cause the loss of the ocean liner to drift from the public's memory. "I do not think the people are going to forget the *Lusitania*," Lodge wrote.[43]

Lodge's wishes for William Jennings Bryan's removal from office came quicker than anticipated. Following a disagreement with the president over his rhetoric following the sinking of the luxury liner, Bryan resigned his position as secretary of state. Roosevelt was pleased by Bryan's resignation, but concurred with Lodge that due to the pacifist mood consuming the nation the public had become uninterested with the suffering that was occurring across the Atlantic.[44]

The senator based his conclusion on the updates being received from his son-in-law, Massachusetts congressman Augustus Gardner. A staunch Republican, Gardner was campaigning around the nation

trying to ignite the American people's fervor for increased preparedness. Despite a strong effort, Gardner informed the senator that his
efforts were frustrated over the pacifism that permeated the nation.[45]

Gardner had begun voicing his concerns over an outdated navy
and an underdefended nation as early as 1914. In October 1915,
the congressman called for a committee to investigate the state
of American defenses. Lodge supported his son-in-law's proposal
only to see the Wilson Administration argue the War and Navy
departments were capable of policing themselves. After an internal
review the administration concluded that no additional improvements were necessary.[46]

The pervasiveness of the pacifist atmosphere also extended to a large
portion of those enrolled at elite institutions like Princeton, Columbia,
and Harvard. Lodge was angered that the young Americans who had
chosen to enlist in the armed forces were being harshly criticized by
their contemporaries. As one who valued military service as the finest
contribution one could make to their country, the senator was depressed
that so many young men sought to avoid the opportunity.[47]

Disgusted with those T. R. referred to as "college sissies and men
with mean souls," the colonel believed that Gardner and Lodge were
right about the public's lack of will for war. Viewing the "iniquitous
peace propaganda of the last fifteen years," as responsible, Roosevelt foresaw no solution to change the public mood unless disaster
occurred.[48]

As Roosevelt's and others' calls for preparedness started to slowly
take hold among the nation's populace, T. R.'s children began
preparing themselves for war. With Roosevelt's old friend Leonard
Wood opening a miliary camp in Plattsburgh, New York, the former
president's sons Archie and Quentin eagerly joined. During speeches
around Massachusetts, Lodge also noticed the resistance dissipating
among the public over the nation becoming involved in war. "There

is one thing which . . . meets with the utmost approval . . . and that is the demand for preparedness," Lodge wrote in September 1915.[49]

Still, most of the nation wanted nothing to do with war, and Lodge's constituents were no different. "[S]o long as he keeps us out of war, without any reference to the methods by which he does it," the public would continue to give him their support, Lodge wrote Roosevelt. As the senator traveled around Massachusetts calling for the enhancement of the nation's military capabilities, Lodge's endless capacity for work allowed him little time to focus on matters involving his wife.[50]

Since the death of her son six years earlier, Nannie Lodge had begun a physical and mental decay. "I am steepled in a very anguish of grief & nothing grows better or easier—only harder & more & more & more of a struggle," she confided to T. R.'s sister Corinne in one of their many correspondences. Despite the overwhelming sadness, Nannie attempted to follow the advice of Roosevelt and Henry Adams by remaining engaged with friends and family.[51]

Following dinner on the evening of September 27 the Lodges were preparing for bed. Gathering some papers for the following day, the senator heard Nannie briefly call for him from her dressing room. Opening the door, he found his bride of more than forty years on the floor, her body slumped and lifeless against the wall. "I raised her up in my arms, her head fell back on my shoulder. She was dead," Lodge wrote as he described the moment to Corinne Roosevelt Robinson.[52]

Nannie Lodge's cause of death was determined as a heart attack. The senator found that unusual. While his wife did have a heart ailment, her condition had not changed since 1909 when the condition was first diagnosed. Those close to Nannie Lodge believed her death was not due to any medical condition but overwhelming grief. "She never got over father's death," author Emily Lodge recalled hearing from her great aunt Helena Lodge.[53]

Reflecting on Nannie's loss, the senator noted that he had seen little to no decline in his wife physically or temperamentally. "That evening she looked handsome and well and full of charm and talk," Lodge recalled of the couple's last moments together. Lodge's wife did not hide her sorrow over Bay's loss from her husband, but image remained a priority. While Nannie may have tried to simply focus on the well-being of her husband and family, the independent-minded eighteen-year-old that Lodge had met decades earlier remained unable to endure the agony of a loss that had never subsided.[54]

Knowing Nannie's loss was irreplaceable, Roosevelt realized there was little he could do to console his friend during a time of such overwhelming grief. "It would be folly for me to try to say a word of comfort. There is none to be said," T. R. wrote on October 2. "We loved Nannie with all our hearts, and we love you." In considering ways to lift his friend's spirits, Roosevelt encouraged Lodge to focus his energies on the great tasks ahead.[55]

But even with the United States growing closer to war and an upcoming presidential campaign, Lodge appeared lost. "I wonder . . . what I am doing here in this particular world where I have no business to be, for my world went with her," the Bostonian wrote in a sorrowful letter to Corinne Roosevelt Robinson. Others like Cecil Spring Rice worried about how Lodge would weather such tragedy. "Poor Cabot it is dreadful to think of it," the British ambassador wrote Theodore Roosevelt several days after Nannie's death.[56]

Lodge knew that action was the solution. During trying moments, it was the work, the battle for the greater good that had always sustained him. Even with great determination, Lodge was unable to focus his attention on the job at hand. "But I am human, I suffer humanly, darkly, intensely," he told Corrine. With the world involved in one of the great conflicts in recent history, Lodge realized he had little choice, his leadership was required more than ever to sound the alarm about the dangers that lay ahead. "I can work and must work, I would not have it otherwise," he wrote T. R.'s sister.[57]

As Lodge regained his bearings at the end of 1915, his mind began considering the presidential election of 1916. The senator imagined that with Wilson's poor leadership an opportunity existed for the Republicans to return to power. "They have a very good chance to win the next time and they are bent on turning Wilson out," Lodge wrote as he began considering the next presidential campaign. Both Roosevelt and the senator believed that to achieve success, conservatives and progressives needed to settle their differences. "I think the Republican Party must be more amenable to reason," T. R. wrote commenting about the intellectual rigidity of the party's Old Guard.[58]

Since the progressive failure of 1912, the Bull Moose faction of the GOP had made little progress. During the 1914 congressional elections, Republican regulars had trained their fire on Wilson's vacillating foreign policy. When the votes were tallied, Republicans had won sixty-nine seats in the House of Representatives. Even with these victories the party leadership viewed the day as a lost opportunity. While many progressive Republican voters chose to return to the GOP fold, the few votes won by progressive candidates were not enough for the GOP to regain the majority in the nation's lower house.[59]

As the campaign for the 1916 Republican nomination began, many wondered who the Republicans would select to challenge the incumbent president. There were rumors that former president Taft was considering a run for a second term, a proposal Roosevelt thought was detrimental to GOP fortunes. "Personally, it does not seem to me . . . to be wise to put him up, with the certainty that the progressives as a whole will either come out for Wilson or run a third ticket." Believing the rumor was being spread by Taft's friends in the press,

Lodge viewed the idea as unrealistic. "I cannot believe that there is the slightest possibility of Taft receiving the Republican nomination."[60]

Even with the uncertainty over the nomination process and the problematic nature of the progressives, Lodge believed that a Wilson defeat remained possible. Despite much of the public remaining supportive of the president for keeping the nation out of war, Lodge believed that Wilson's domestic agenda had resulted in many voters believing that a replacement in the White House was warranted.[61]

Lodge viewed nominating former president Taft or Senator La Follette as "political suicide." The senator also admitted he "was so anxious to defeat Wilson," he believed almost any good Republican would do. While many thought Roosevelt was again the candidate of the hour, T. R. realistically did not believe he could win. The colonel thought his fiery war rhetoric had alienated "the German-Americans, the professional hyphenated-Americans . . . and the whole flapdoodle pacifists and mollycoddle outfit." Those groups as well as others would gladly take revenge by preventing him from obtaining the nomination.[62]

Despite their disagreements over 1912, Roosevelt remained Lodge's ideal candidate for president. However, the New Englander, always the pragmatist, believed that another term for T. R. in the White House was not possible. "I have always wished that, but I doubt if under existing circumstances, you would be nominated by the Republicans, and you could only be elected as the Republican nominee," Lodge wrote Roosevelt. Both men understood that the only way to turn the Virginian out of the Executive Mansion was for both conservatives and progressives to dismiss their differences and reunite under the GOP banner.[63]

While Lodge believed the former president might have a strong chance at reuniting the GOP, Roosevelt's temperament regarding the Republican Party remained unpredictable. Refusing to forget the injustice done to him by the political establishment four years earlier, the senator believed that "Theodore is bent on the destruction of the Republican Party." While Lodge's point was a relevant concern, T. R. seemed to dislike Wilson more than those Republicans he blamed for his defeat in 1912. "I hope that the Republicans will take action as to render it possible for the progressives to go in with them," he wrote Lodge. Roosevelt, for all his anger at his party colleagues, hoped that the GOP could leave its internal squabbles behind and focus on changing the direction of the country.[64]

As both men assessed potential candidates for the nomination, former governor of New York and associate justice of the Supreme Court Charles Evans Hughes seemed most amenable to all factions of the Republican Party. Neither Lodge nor Roosevelt found the justice a compelling potential nominee. But the issue was not the candidate's charisma; it was about his potential to win in November.[65]

As the end of the year approached, Lodge and T. R. remained critical of Wilson's foreign policy. Unable to calm the Mexican Revolution following the departure of President Huerta in July 1914, Wilson had eventually supported the Constitutionalist government presided over by Venustiano Carranza. The new president's rival, Francisco "Pancho" Villa, unhappy with Wilson's interference in his nation's affairs, raided the town of Columbus, New Mexico, in March 1916, killing seventeen residents. After Villa was pursued across Mexico by General John J. Pershing, Wilson positioned troops in the northern part of the country.[66]

With the issue of Mexico gaining public attention, Wilson finally decided to act on the issue of American defense. In a speech on November 5 before a partisan Democratic crowd at New York's Biltmore Hotel, Wilson announced a 400,000-man increase in the army over the next three years. To satisfy those who believed the navy was outdated, the president also declared he would improve the nation's maritime service to make it one of the most formidable fleets in the world.[67]

Lodge thought little of the speech. But the senator's personal opinions did not prevent him during an appearance at Washington's National Security League at the beginning of 1916 from declaring that he thought Wilson was moving in the right direction. Roosevelt did not believe Lodge's remarks were hawkish enough and chided him for supporting the administration's new defense measures. "The impression produced upon one staunch Republican . . . a great friend of yours who was present . . . was that you had upheld [Secretary of War] Garrison's plan."[68]

Roosevelt's criticism caused the senator to lash out at his old friend. Frustrated with an inability to have an impact on policy as he had for so many years, Lodge resented the fact that T. R. believed the senator was among a group of Republicans happily siding with the president. "If you will take the trouble to read what I said you will find that my speech was largely devoted to showing that [the administration] had lied about the number of ships, that their whole course was one of deceit," Lodge wrote Roosevelt at the beginning of February.[69]

Lodge also made it clear that whether or not he liked Wilson's speech, the president was gradually moving forward on home defense. "I have repeatedly said that this Administration has wasted one year in providing for the defense of the country and I want to prevent them if I can from wholly wasting another year." Even in his relationship with the opposition, Lodge took a gradualist approach, believing that getting 10 percent of what he wanted was better than nothing at all. But the senator remained determined to do all he could to enhance the nation's land and sea defenses.[70]

Preparing for the 1916 presidential election, Lodge and Roosevelt hoped that a united Republican Party would bring the hated Wilson

Administration to an end. The consummate politician, Lodge understood that working successfully within the political system required that he remain amenable to any measures the president took that remotely matched his own. Giving no quarter to those who believed the United States should remain disengaged from military conflict, Roosevelt continued to do all he could to prepare the nation for battle.[71]

On a personal level, the mutual anger and distrust of Lodge and Roosevelt toward Woodrow Wilson revived their dormant relationship. During the president's first term the two had not only restarted their rigorous correspondence but had finally begun visiting one another. Over the next few years both men sought to return their party to power as well as support the United States in turning the tide of the war in Europe. But Roosevelt's blatant hatred for Wilson and his rash, self-destructive statements against those who questioned America's military resolve would not only lead his friends to question the former president's sanity, but also result in extinguishing any hope Theodore Roosevelt had of returning to the White House.

EIGHTEEN
The Final Battle

"He is yellow all through in the presence of danger."
—Theodore Roosevelt

A s Roosevelt and Lodge continued to call for greater vigilance on preparedness, the issue had little popularity among those in Congress. Democrats, believing that the president's agenda would necessitate raising taxes, avoided addressing Wilson's proposal on defense. The controversy over the issue caused significant opposition from many within the House of Representatives and the Senate.

Believing that Wilson's initiative to expand the US Army placed the United States on a war footing, progressives in the House chose the path of least resistance by calling for the expansion of the National Guard. Using political skill, Wilson managed to convince his party to pass what became known as the National Defense Act. Under the new legislation, passed in June 1916, the army was expanded to over 200,000, while also placing the guard under federal control. Even as a portion of the public became more engaged with the idea of greater preparedness, much of the nation remained concerned about the prospect of young American men dying on the fields of France for interests that were not their own.[1]

As Wilson began to focus on those voters who believed he had not done enough to defend the nation, Lodge concluded that Republicans could regain command by focusing on the president's dovish attitude. But the senator believed the complacency of the American people remained problematic. Over the years Lodge and Roosevelt had expressed criticism that the public remained uninterested in personal improvement, moral uplift, or uniting to solve the great crises of the day. The senator and T. R. understood that the European war was a pivotal moment in history, yet it seemed to resonate little with the nation's voters.[2]

As the 1916 convention approached, Lodge informed the former president that the opportunity to become the standard-bearer for the GOP remained a distant possibility. "The only nomination that would be worth having . . . because the party, including both Republicans and progressives, felt that you were the only man to put up under present conditions." In an ideal world, Lodge believed Roosevelt was the best candidate.[3]

As the idea of returning to the presidency remained on T. R.'s mind, he and Edith departed on a cruise around the Caribbean. "If I were you I should not only do nothing but say nothing about my position," Lodge wrote in the first week of February, as many political analysts contended that Roosevelt was a leading figure for the Republican nomination.[4]

At the end of April, Roosevelt attended a luncheon at the Park Avenue home of his friend Robert Bacon. Also invited were Lodge, General Leonard Wood, and surprisingly, T. R.'s once close friend Elihu Root. The former president and his secretary of state had not spoken since their disagreement over Roosevelt's candidacy for president four years earlier. Following the luncheon, the announcement that Root and Roosevelt had reconciled gave many the impression that the GOP was aligning behind T. R. as a fusion candidate. But Roosevelt had returned from his Caribbean cruise uncertain whether to toss his hat back into the political ring.[5]

Based on their poor showing during the 1914 elections progressives had little influence among members of the GOP. Despite Roosevelt's criticism of Wilson over preparedness there was too much animosity toward T. R.'s actions in 1912 to make him a viable candidate. However, Roosevelt was unprepared to publicly dismiss a return to the White House. When the press wrote that the meeting between Root and Roosevelt was about the former secretary of state supporting his old boss for the nomination Root was outraged.[6]

The leak to the media probably also disturbed Lodge. While pleased that Roosevelt had returned to the warm arms of the GOP, one of T. R.'s biographers indicates the senator had already decided to support Charles Evans Hughes. That decision possibly explains the senator's rationale in encouraging Roosevelt to remain quiet about his interests in the presidency despite his name rising among the public. "The real thing that is standing in his way more than anything else is the fact that men are saying that he is not a Republican," Lodge told William Bigelow in late May.[7]

Even as Roosevelt and Lodge were focusing their attentions on the unity of the Republican Party, they remained frustrated with Wilson's poor leadership of the European war. Three weeks before the Root-Roosevelt summit, the French steamer *Sussex* was attacked by German torpedoes. Despite advice of Secretary of State Robert Lansing to terminate relations between Berlin and Washington, the president refused to follow the advice of his chief diplomat.[8]

Wilson's impassioned speech to Congress on April 18, in which he threatened to terminate the two nations' relationship unless Germany ceased submarine attacks, did nothing to enhance his credibility with Lodge and Roosevelt. But for all the senator's belief that the address was a "sham," Wilson's strong rhetoric caused Germany to promise to curb submarine activity on the part of neutral nations. The moment was not lost on Roosevelt. Between isolationist

Republicans in Congress and those Democrats impressed that Wilson was finally showing his spine in dealing with Germany, T. R. found the enthusiasm for his nomination beginning to decline.[9]

Refusing to give in and with his hatred of Wilson at a visceral level, T. R. continued to implore audiences around the country to press the administration to improve its policy on rearmament. During a tour of the Midwest, Roosevelt encountered a wall of isolationism and pacifism as he brought his message of military engagement to Kansas City and St. Louis. Addressing a gathering of the German American society, the colonel accused his audience of betrayal for their attempts to undermine the United States in favor of Germany. Those remarks in a region that was a hotbed of Republican support effectively ended T. R.'s quest for the 1916 Republican nomination.[10]

As Roosevelt attempted to engage Republicans around the nation, Lodge remained focused on uniting progressives and conservatives during the June convention in Chicago. In an example of the drama roiling the Republican Party, the two factions had coincidentally decided to hold their respective conventions in the Windy City. As the senator worked to heal the rift, neither the progressives nor the conservatives were able to coalesce around a nominee.[11]

Roosevelt still had the support of the progressives. But the large German American contingent, isolationists in the West, and those conservatives with 1912 fresh in their memories refused to support him. While Hughes remained the favorite, T. R. believed the former New York governor was not only a pawn of the Republican machine but potentially pro-German based on his poor enthusiasm toward greater preparedness.[12]

Hughes's low-key personality was also not popular among the delegates. But Lodge believed that he was the most electable of any candidate. The senator viewed Roosevelt as the favorite with the progressives, but unless the GOP moved to nominate him there was little chance of the colonel succeeding as the party's candidate.[13]

Following the dismissal of one candidate after another by the progressive convention, Roosevelt suddenly suggested in the early morning of June 10 that the delegates select the senior senator from Massachusetts. "I know Lodge's record like a book," Roosevelt told banker and progressive politician George Perkins. Roosevelt also believed that since Lodge had voted for him on the second ballot, that would make the senator acceptable to the progressive delegates.[14]

As Perkins listened to Roosevelt's suggestion on a phone line between his room in Chicago's Blackstone Hotel and the colonel's home in Oyster Bay, the progressive leader thought the Lodge choice was ridiculous. Roosevelt disagreed with Perkins's opinion. "I do not ask them to accept any man who isn't of the highest character and who does not stand absolutely square on the issues of today," T. R. declared. Many political experts agreed. In writing about the idea of Lodge as a potential solution to the party schism, the *Boston Globe*'s John D. Merrill contended the senator's selection was a strong possibility. Popular with Roosevelt as well as the party establishment, the publication believed that if Hughes was not selected, Lodge was the next best choice.[15]

When Roosevelt submitted a letter to both conventions formally nominating Lodge, the progressives were stunned. The senator had the intellectual capabilities to serve as president. But his lack of ability to engage the masses, a strong conservatism, and a lack of liberal sentiment made him a poor choice for the White House.[16]

While the Lodge suggestion went nowhere with either group, Roosevelt's decision to place his friend's name in nomination was twofold. With T. R.'s intense dislike of Hughes, the former president hoped that nominating Lodge would serve as a tactic to delay what many believed was a foregone conclusion. Finally, even as Roosevelt may have realized the conservative senator's name was a nonstarter, the gesture represented Roosevelt's deep gratitude for all that Lodge had done in the pursuit of the former president's career.[17]

Knowing there was little chance of defeating Wilson if the party was divided, T. R. declined the progressive nomination and begrudgingly supported Hughes. Writing Roosevelt following the proceedings in Chicago, Lodge was sorry about the way events had transpired. "I was anxious to have you nominated . . . and did all I was able to do in that direction; but it could not be affected in the Republican convention," Lodge wrote on June 14.[18]

While the senator was honored that Roosevelt had considered him as a solution to resolve the divide between liberals and conservatives, he knew the idea was unrealistic. "I am not fit to run a campaign, and I not only have no desire for the Presidency, but I should dread the mere thought of it, for reasons which you understand," Lodge told T. R.[19]

Even as Lodge realized Hughes was not the ideal candidate, defeating Wilson remained the senator's primary goal. "I feel that what is at stake far transcends all party considerations. The Wilson administration has debauched public sentiment . . . disintegrated the American spirit; and I shudder to think what four years more of that crowd would mean." The senator understood that Roosevelt was no fan of the justice, but Lodge was determined to do all he could to help Hughes win the election.[20]

Roosevelt was disappointed that he had not obtained the nomination. Visiting T. R. at his home after the convention, Lodge found the former president despondent. When someone suggested that Roosevelt should consider running for president in 1920, Roosevelt simply responded "This was my year—1916—my high twelve. In four years I will be out of it," the colonel commented dismissively.[21]

Roosevelt was happy to do what he could to help push the president out of office. Hughes's poor ability on the stump and the public satisfaction that Wilson had kept the nation out of the conflict in Europe made the campaign an uphill battle for the Republicans. The former governor was also no fan of Progressivism. With little sympathy for liberal causes, Roosevelt realized convincing those from the left wing of the party to support the GOP candidate was an unattainable goal.[22]

Despite Lodge and Roosevelt barnstorming portions of the country on Hughes's behalf, the prospects for a positive outcome did not improve. Besides campaigning for the GOP nominee, Lodge was also running to retain his Senate seat. Following a decision to amend the Constitution three years earlier, 1916 was the first time Lodge would have to depend on voters outside the smoke-filled room of the state legislature. Lodge had spent thirty years in Congress and between his stance on preparedness and his pragmatic positions on certain policies that favored the president, another six years seemed likely.[23]

In November Lodge defeated Democratic candidate John Fitzgerald—the grandfather of the future president John F. Kennedy—for his fourth term in the Senate. The Republicans were not so fortunate. Despite a close election, Wilson won with over nine million votes while Hughes totaled eight and half million. With Hughes carrying most of the Northeast and Midwest, he was unable to defeat the incumbent president, who won the South and portions of the Far West. Happy with another election victory, Lodge was again disappointed as Republicans were unable to take control of the Senate or the House of Representatives.[24]

On January 22, 1917, with the hopes of fulfilling the goal of keeping the United States out of war, Wilson announced to the Senate his intention to mediate an end to the conflict. The strategy, which the president referred to "as peace without victory," also contained diplomatic proposals including the idea of a League of Nations, freedom of the seas, and a policy for the limitation of armaments. Lodge found the whole speech contrary to the purpose of war. "I do not see how there can be any peace worth having in Europe unless the Allies win a decisive victory," Lodge wrote Roosevelt following the president's address.[25]

Viewing Wilson's strategy as simply a means of postponing the inevitable, Lodge lashed out at those GOP stalwarts like Elihu Root who seemed favorable to Wilson's proposals. "I am utterly at a loss to know what Root means by saying he sympathizes with [Wilson's] declaration . . . peace without victory," he commented in a January 26 letter to Roosevelt. Three days later Germany announced a resumption of unrestricted submarine bombardment. On February 3, following the sinking of the SS *Housatonic*, President Wilson severed relations between Germany and the United States.[26]

Lodge and Roosevelt believed Wilson's decision to cut ties with Berlin had little to do with some new policy of firmness. "[The President] would not have done it if he possibly could have helped it," the senator wrote following Wilson's decision. "His one desire is to avoid war at any cost, simply because he is afraid. He can bully Congressmen, but he flinches in the presence of danger, physical and moral." On Wilson's lack of courage Roosevelt was in thorough agreement, labeling the president "yellow all through in the presence of danger." These comments and more were indicative of T. R.'s view that Wilson was a coward who possessed no respect for the character of the United States.[27]

In late February Lodge speculated that Wilson was preparing to ask the Congress for permission to arm merchant shipping. The senator believed that the sooner Wilson moved to prepare the nation for military hostilities, the better. "I am ready to give him all the war authority and all the money he can possibly need," Lodge wrote, believing it was his duty to push the president as far as he could on enhancing national defense.[28]

Even as Wilson moved the nation closer to war, Roosevelt and Lodge believed the president was leading from a position of weakness. Watching Wilson placate the pacifists within his party caused Roosevelt to shake his fists with rage. "[H]is extreme adroitness in appealing to all that is basest in the hearts of our people has made him able for the time being to drug the soul of the nation into a coma," the colonel commented to the senator on February 28.[29]

At the end of February the atmosphere between Germany and the United States grew even more tense following the leak of the infamous Zimmermann Telegram. On March 1, 1917, the White House released a document revealing that following the commencement of war with the United States, Berlin's foreign secretary, Arthur Von Zimmermann, had requested his representative in Mexico City to encourage the government to ally itself with Germany. Zimmermann stated if Mexico could convince Japan to also ally with Berlin, the Mexicans would receive a financial remuneration, as well as a promise that Germany would assist them in reclaiming the former territories of Texas, New Mexico, and Arizona.[30]

When Lodge read the contents of the telegram, he became convinced that war was inevitable. "We have discovered the Germans actually parceling out our country and offering our territory to Mexico as a reward for coming in." While the senator believed Wilson remained ambivalent about war, Lodge realized the flow of events had gone beyond the president's control.[31]

In the latter part of March, as German submarines targeted US shipping, Roosevelt informed Lodge that he was going to make his opinion known in a statement about the conduct of the nation's foreign policy. The former president was a believer in rallying around the flag when the nation was under attack. However, when the man leading the country appeared to have no ability to make the right decision, action was required. "Taft, Hughes, and even Root take part in the general idiot cry which aligns us behind the President right or wrong—and he is 99 percent wrong," Roosevelt commented to the senator.[32]

On the evening of March 20 T. R. stood before six hundred guests at New York's Union League Club and declared that the United States had no choice but to declare war against Germany. With the audience waving American flags and a local band playing "The Star-Spangled Banner," Roosevelt, along with Charles Evans Hughes and Elihu Root, challenged the Wilson Administration to respond aggressively to the threat that faced the nation. In Roosevelt's opinion, there was only one way to fight a war, and that was to use the power of overwhelming force.[33]

Roosevelt was anxious to hit the enemy literally as hard as he could. With the desire to form a regiment to fight in Europe, the veteran of the Spanish-American War was receiving no encouragement from the War Department. In a letter, Secretary of War Newton D. Baker informed Roosevelt that authorization could only occur through an act of Congress. Refusing to give in, T. R. was determined to employ whatever means were available to achieve his objective.[34]

Lodge understood Roosevelt's desire for one last military campaign. "Of course . . . you have been Commander in Chief and besides that you are you," Lodge wrote supportively on March 23, 1917. Determined to help Roosevelt achieve his goal, the senator arranged a conversation with Secretary of State Lansing. Hearing that Wilson was on the verge of declaring war on Germany, the senator pushed the nation's chief diplomat to convince the War Department to grant Roosevelt's proposal.[35]

Departing for Punta Gorda, Florida, for a holiday of big game fishing, Roosevelt asked Lodge to please include him in any legislation that involved authorizing American soldiers to serve abroad. Caring little if Baker agreed to his request, Roosevelt stated he was content to develop a militia based entirely on his own resources. "I think that when the stress comes they will find some difficulty in refusing me, and if they do refuse me I believe I can raise the division by myself for service in France under the American flag but under the command of the French Generals," the colonel wrote Lodge in the last week of March.[36]

Roosevelt had scheduled his return to New York from Florida for April 3, 1917. Twenty-four hours earlier, as American ships were assaulted by German torpedoes, Wilson called on Congress to declare war. Arriving at Washington's Union Station on his way to New York, Roosevelt informed those who welcomed him that Wilson's statement was "a great state paper which will rank in history."[37]

Lodge was also gratified by the president's message. Following the address, the senator emotionally grasped Wilson's hand in congratulations. According to the *Boston Globe*, the senator's praise of Wilson's remarks was the first time they had spoken since the early days of the administration.[38]

Lodge's gesture of goodwill toward Wilson was not the only surprising event that occurred that day. Shortly before the president's announcement, the senator was confronted by a hostile antiwar crowd as he walked toward his office in the Capitol. As the group drew closer, Lodge attempted to quietly back away from the unruly assembly. "I regret that I cannot agree with your position, but I must do my duty as I see it," the senator said as he attempted to elude the group of irate constituents.[39]

As the senator tried to escape into the confines of his office, he was confronted by thirty-five-year-old former minor league baseball player Alexander Bannwart. A real estate professional of German descent and an admirer of Woodrow Wilson, Bannwart had graduated from Princeton University and Harvard Law School.[40]

Believing that Lodge had the power to influence the president's mindset, Bannwart shouted at Lodge in frustration that he was a "dammed coward." A man who prided himself on the strength of his character and convictions, the sixty-seven-year-old Lodge refused to allow the remark to pass.[41]

Standing toe to toe with the former second baseman, Lodge called Bannwart a "dammed liar." Following a verbal exchange that resulted in some pushing and shoving, Lodge promptly punched the younger man in the face. Bannwart struck back. Losing his balance, the senator crashed against the heavy doors of his office. Before the scuffle could continue, Lodge's aides attacked Bannwart, beating the man severely.[42]

Choosing not to press charges, Lodge, who was unhurt, found the moment exhilarating. "At my age there is a certain aspect of folly about the whole thing and yet I am glad that I hit him," he wrote Roosevelt following the altercation. "[I]f you had knocked down that pacifist last May my message to the Republican Convention would have borne fruit in your nomination," Theodore quipped following his friend's confrontation. Hearing from one of his dinner guests of "Cabot having a free fight with a belligerent pacifist in his committee room," Henry Adams may have wondered what would happen next.[43]

Along with Roosevelt's congratulations, Lodge was probably tickled to read a small item days later in the *Boston Globe*. Describing the senator as having taken lessons from an accomplished Boston boxing coach in his youth, the author known only as "sportsman" characterized "the senior senator from Massachusetts" as "a pretty good man with the gloves."[44]

Roosevelt joined Lodge in Washington the following week as a former president attempted to convince the current president that he was ready to take to the battlefield once again. The meeting was positive, and Wilson appeared to enjoy T. R.'s company. "Yes, he is a great big boy. I was as formally charmed by his personality," Wilson told an aide. For all the apparent conviviality between the two men, the president had no intention of allowing Roosevelt to regain the national spotlight.[45]

Refusing to delay his crusade, Roosevelt continued to badger Secretary of War Baker. Along with letters and telegrams, Roosevelt sent a fourteen page document detailing all aspects of his military record during the 1898 Spanish-American War. Baker was not impressed.[46]

Lodge believed Wilson was deliberately excluding Roosevelt from military service for political reasons. "Wilson is trying to make this a party war and shut out all persons of eminence who are Republicans from any share in it." The senator was also attempting to pass an amendment authorizing Roosevelt to raise a militia but was uncertain whether the effort would succeed.[47]

With the help of Ohio senator Warren G. Harding, the Republicans sponsored a bill to authorize four volunteer divisions. "He is known in Europe as is no other American . . . His presence there would be a help and an encouragement to the soldiers of the allied nations," Lodge said of Roosevelt in a speech on the Senate floor. But Wilson remained adamant that those who represented the United States in the European theater would remain composed of an army raised through the military draft process. Despite the colonel's continued requests Wilson's decision was final. "I really think the best way to treat Mr. Roosevelt is take no notice of him," the president told his private secretary.[48]

When Lodge learned of Wilson's rejection of the amendment in the middle of May, he was furious. The senator was amazed that Roosevelt kept his temper upon learning of Wilson's decision. As always following moments when Roosevelt experienced disapointment, Lodge tried to raise the former president's spirits. The senator expressed that even with Wilson's decision, the passage of the amendment was an indication of the high regard in which Roosevelt was held by so many in Congress.[49]

Wilson's decision to declare war on Germany brought Lodge and Roosevelt closer than they had ever been. The former president, denied his opportunity to again display his courage under fire, devoted his waning energies to encouraging the nation's young men to volunteer for what he viewed as a great crusade. As the two friends prepared for members of their respective families to enter the battle to save democracy, Roosevelt and Lodge would each suffer a loss resulting in unspeakable pain that only one of them could endure.

NINETEEN
Twilight

"I hope you continue to improve. You cannot think what
a joy it was to me to have those two talks with you."

—Henry Cabot Lodge

F ollowing Wilson's refusal to allow Roosevelt to fight abroad,
the senator and T. R. continued their critique of the president's
management of the war. "Congress has done excellently; the
fault is exclusively with the administration," Roosevelt wrote in
the late summer of 1917. Wilson's mistreatment of Roosevelt as well
as the president's attempt to blame Congress for the nation's poor war
preparation caused Lodge unmanageable frustration.[1]

The senator's anger was compounded by Wilson's decision to
place stifling economic regulations on American corporations. "The
primary object of the administration appears to be to cut all the
industries down to the barest living profit . . . We cannot carry on
a war against American business and a war against Germany at the
same time," Lodge lamented to T. R.[2]

From Lodge's perspective, Wilson was an isolated, frightened
man unwilling to meet with members of his military staff for fear of
what they might tell him. Disorganization ran rampant. Men were
idle. Rifles and other weapons of war were nowhere to be found and
the secretary of war was the most "incompetent" man to ever hold

the position. The "men of the conscript army . . . will be drilled with broomsticks and wooden guns," Lodge wrote, irate over the inadequate preparation of the nation's troops.[3]

While Roosevelt remained disappointed that he could not display his heroism on the Western Front, his four sons were eager to experience the thrill of military glory. In the summer of 1917, each of Roosevelt's boys departed to fight the war in Europe. With the assistance of his father Quentin, the youngest, despite having poor eyesight joined the army air corps. Theodore Jr. and Archie enlisted as army privates and were among the first group of troops to arrive in France under the command of General Pershing.[4]

In addition, Kermit, also with his father's assistance, chose to join the British army to fight in Mesopotamia. Lodge, whose late son Bay and son-in-law Gus Gardner had served during the Spanish-American War, saw his grandson-in-law Grafton Minot head off to Europe while Gus Gardner took a commission in the National Guard.[5]

Roosevelt could do little but offer his children love and moral support. Lodge did his best to encourage the war effort as well. As American troops prepared to engage the enemy, he sought to end his feud with the president. "I have cast no party vote and made no party speech in the Senate since the war began," the senator wrote a friend.[6]

Lodge was also devoted to the welfare of his country. That commitment to his nation made him duty bound to criticize the administration if he deemed it necessary. The senator believed it was his responsibility "to oppose what his patriotism and his conscience tell him is wrong or dangerous to the country's quick success," he wrote Roosevelt.[7]

Despite trying to find common ground with Wilson, Lodge's dislike of the former academic never remained dormant for long. When Gus Gardner was recalled to active service, Lodge believed Wilson was personally responsible. Gardner was not a well man. The senator was terrified that any combat experience could kill his son-in-law. As a congressman, Gardner had the option to decline military service. With a desire to return to the field of battle, the ambitious legislator chose not to inform his father-in-law that he had decided to take a demotion, guaranteeing another opportunity to test his courage under fire.[8]

With his sons abroad, Roosevelt sought to fill his time by writing commentary on the war for the *Kansas City Star*. In the fall of 1917, he and Edith also toured the West trying to convince more Americans to enlist. Even with an active schedule Roosevelt was unable to contain his overwhelming anxiety. As he wrote and traveled, his comments about Wilson growing ever more severe, the former president's nervous energy and voracious appetite resulted in the development of hypertension.[9]

In February 1918 Roosevelt's growing health problems resulted in hospitalization to treat several abscesses in his ears and buttock. The surgeries left him in a weakened condition, forcing him to remain bedridden until released from the hospital a month later.[10]

Riddled with pain from rheumatism, blind in one eye as the result of a boxing incident in 1904, and hard of hearing following his recent hospitalization, Roosevelt soldiered on. Speaking at a gathering of the Maine Republican Party in March, T. R. called for the GOP to return to the days when it served as a representative for those regardless of class or income. Arguing for positions that were the foundations of his philosophy, the former president spoke of government serving as a moderating influence between citizens of great wealth and those who sought to limit economic opportunity.[11]

Lodge thought the speech commendable, but believed Roosevelt needed to emphasize his remarks more on the present than the future. "My only doubt is whether it is wise . . . to give so much more space to what is to be done after the war," the senator commented in the first week of March.[12]

As the war raged in Europe, Woodrow Wilson's "Fourteen Points" address to Congress (delivered two months earlier on January 8, 1918) presented a vision of a new world order. These proposals included an end to secret treaties, freedom of the seas for all whether in peace or war, a call for global free trade, and a path to arms limitations by all members of the global community. Other issues addressed included Wilson's conviction that nations who held colonies were required to give those under their charge greater autonomy in how their affairs were conducted.[13]

The president also proposed equitable territorial agreements among the nations of Europe and the Ottoman Empire. The final point was a proposal calling for the creation of a League of Nations. Wilson envisioned an international organization that not only stimulated geopolitical harmony but guaranteed each nation mutual independence and "territorial integrity."[14]

Lodge favored the reconfiguration of Europe based on "nationalistic lines." However, he believed many of the president's other proposals were premature and overly idealistic. The allies were still enduring heavy losses at the hands of the Germans and the most important objective remained winning the war. "We were very far from being on the eve of victory," the senator wrote in his memoir, *The Senate and the League of Nations.*[15]

From Lodge's perspective, Wilson had not changed. Regardless of the indignities and losses suffered by the United States, fear had dictated his decision to keep the country out of war for as long as possible. As the Germans appeared to gain the upper hand, uncertain if the allies had the ability or the will to win, the president appeared to search for a strategy to pull his nation out of the conflict.[16]

As with so many affected by the numerous casualties of the conflict, Lodge was not immune. During the first week of January 1918, Gus Gardner died of pneumonia while at a training camp in Georgia.

Due to the brutally cold winter, the nation's textile companies were unable to produce enough wool, placing American servicemen in a precarious position.[17]

There were other tragedies as well. The following month brought the sad news that the ebullient Cecil Spring Rice had died following his unceremonious recall as the British ambassador to the United States.[18]

In March Lodge and Roosevelt were saddened by the death of Henry Adams. In poor health, the historian had suffered a fatal stroke. Lodge lamented the death of his mentor. "[H]e is a terrible loss to me, for he has been one of the most intimate friends I had for 40 years," the senator wrote the historian Worthington Chauncey Ford.[19]

Despite the passing of those close to him, Lodge continued to follow the war's progress. During the spring of 1918, as the Germans battled the allies, the senator remained determined that no peace terms other than Germany's unconditional surrender would be acceptable. Roosevelt also believed that nothing was sufficient except total victory.[20]

The former president, still disappointed that Wilson had not permitted him to lead a militia in battle, could only live vicariously through the progress his sons were making in their respective military campaigns. For all the former Rough Rider's dreams of glory, the harsh reality of war visited him on July 18. Four days earlier the Roosevelts' youngest son, twenty-year-old Quentin, the mischievous young man the public had come to know during his years in the White House, was killed when his fighter plane was shot out of the air while patrolling a sector in Northern France.[21]

When the colonel was informed, he was uncertain what to do. "But—Mrs. Roosevelt? How am I going to break it to her," he asked an aide. Half an hour later the Roosevelts issued a brief statement. The former president and his wife stoically praised their son's bravery in the preservation of democracy.[22]

Having lost a son, as well as knowing Quentin since he was a small child, Lodge expressed his grief in a condolence letter to Roosevelt. Describing T. R.'s youngest son's death as emblematic of the courage he had displayed in service to his nation, the senator could do nothing more but offer his sympathies during a heartbreaking moment. While the letter was excluded from Lodge's papers, the senator had preserved a small item from the *Washington Post*, detailing an entertaining anecdote from Roosevelt's youngest son's childhood.[23]

It was the story of the youngster visiting Lodge, hopeful the senator could use his influence to prevent Quentin's favorite White House policeman from being assigned to another post. Lodge did not retain the piece for the benefit of ego, but merely as a reminder that Quentin Roosevelt was once a very special little boy.[24]

Quentin's death was a blow from which Roosevelt never recovered. Despite all the physical pain and grief T. R. had endured throughout his life, his great will refused to allow him to rest. In the same manner that Lodge had persevered following Bay's death, and then Nannie's, Roosevelt pressed on. There were still tasks ahead and duties to perform.

Roosevelt and Lodge attempted to return their focus to the war. As the conflict began to shift in favor of the allies, the senator remained adamant about communicating any terms of surrender. On August 23, 1918, Lodge's conviction was displayed for all to see during his premier speech as minority leader of the Senate.[25]

Addressing a packed chamber, Lodge spoke of the nations of Europe being restored to their former borders. The senator emphasized that to prevent Germany from expanding in the East, the states of Czechoslovakia, Yugoslavia, and Poland required independence. Lodge also called for the breakup of the Ottoman and Austro-Hungarian empires, all in the name of greater international stability.[26]

As the senator had expressed to Roosevelt, Lodge's entire proposal was based on the idea of preventing Germany from ever tormenting the world again. "No peace that satisfies Germany can ever satisfy us," Lodge declared, reemphasizing his call for unconditional surrender. The address received massive press coverage and positive remarks in the United States, France, and Britain. Roosevelt thought the speech fantastic, a comment that left Lodge deeply gratified. "I am rejoiced to have your commendation," the senator replied on the last day of August. Like his friend, T. R. viewed Wilson's call for a League of Nations and the reduction of armaments as utopian and naïve. Since treaties had not worked to prevent the present conflict, the colonel believed national defense remained vital. Without an ability for the nations of the world to protect themselves Wilson was inviting another world war. [27]

The only way to prevent such a disaster was to support an international organization that possessed an international peacekeeping force. Roosevelt further worried that under Wilson's plan the United States would be committed to address one international squabble after another.[28]

In September 1918, after initially rejecting an invitation to negotiate an end to the conflict from Austria-Hungary, Wilson chose to discuss peace terms with Germany. "I am living in constant anxiety now of a sudden plunge of the Administration for a negotiated peace," Lodge wrote T. R. during the first week of October. "At this point, if we make an armistice we have lost the war and we shall leave Germany about where she started." Lodge believed that the president was not following the American people's wishes for an unconditional surrender. The senator contended that the nation had lost blood and treasure during the conflict and the only way it could achieve justice was a victory on German soil.[29]

During that same month, Roosevelt also continued his onslaught against Wilson's Fourteen Points. In a lengthy telegram addressed to Lodge, Roosevelt stated that the conditions highlighted by the president's international agenda was "entirely satisfactory to every . . . pacifist and socialist and anti-American who breathed air." The colonel also launched his attacks on Wilson not only in his newspaper column but on the stump.[30]

During a two-hour address at New York's Carnegie Hall on the eve of the 1918 congressional elections, Roosevelt accused Wilson of using the context of the war to manipulate the country into handing complete power over to the Democratic Party. During the campaign Wilson portrayed the GOP as obstructionist and isolationist. The president contended that if the Republicans regained control of Congress, they would divide the nation, leaving Wilson unable to conduct international affairs. "I am glad that Mr. Wilson has now cast off the mask," Roosevelt said to the delight of a jam-packed audience.[31]

As Lodge also campaigned, he criticized Wilson's divisive rhetoric, arguing that the nation needed to come together to defeat a common foe. Lodge's bipartisan message helped the Republicans regain the Congressional majority in both Houses of Congress with many viewing the GOP victory as a defense of the party's patriotism. However, historian Lewis Gould writes that the shift was also a normal public reaction to a president who had held power for half a dozen years.[32]

Several days after the elections the Germans agreed to an unconditional surrender. Lodge remained concerned that Wilson did not have the courage to lay down restrictions strong enough to prevent Berlin from starting another war. "We must not fail in the council," Lodge wrote, thinking of the hurdles that awaited American negotiators.[33]

On November 11, 1918, the day the Armistice was signed, officially ending World War I, Roosevelt was back in a New York hospital. The rheumatism had become overwhelming to the point where the colonel was unable to tie his shoes. "I cannot bear to think . . .

of your suffering so much pain," Lodge wrote in the middle of November.[34]

Even in unbearable discomfort, Roosevelt tried to focus his thoughts on the development of the postwar world. As Wilson prepared to meet with the allies in Paris at the beginning of 1919, T. R. remained more favorable to an international organization that allowed the nations of the world to defend themselves.[35]

Lodge also remained ambivalent about Wilson's peace agenda. "I do not believe the United States . . . ought to consent to join any international body which would arrange our immigration laws or our tariff laws, or control the Monroe Doctrine or our actions in our own hemisphere," the senator commented. Lodge believed Wilson's league represented an attempt to take international decisions out of the hands of elected officials, an idea he did not believe the American people would support.[36]

Throughout the fall Roosevelt remained in poor health. Despite regaining a portion of his mobility, walking and sitting caused him great pain. It was the fifth week of his illness and other than dictating the occasional letter to his many acquaintances there was little he could do to impact the upcoming peace negotiations.[37]

In the middle of December, Corinne Roosevelt Robinson, one of Nannie Lodge's closest friends, wired the senator asking if he could visit the ailing Roosevelt in New York. Lodge had known about T. R.'s poor health but was unable to escape his work in Washington. Arriving in the weeks before Christmas, Lodge spent two mornings at the former president's bedside discussing the League of Nations.[38]

Despite physical discomfort, Roosevelt and Lodge engaged in a spirited conversation. While there is no record of the discussion, the two old friends probably reflected on subjects such as presidential history, the latest books, updates on friends and family, or a discussion of one another's recent literary efforts. Sitting in a hospital room named for Roosevelt's family, both men, despite showing signs of age, displayed evidence of a spirit that reflected the passion and drive that had defined their lives.[39]

In Corrine Robinson's memoir of T. R.'s life, his sister wrote of Lodge that she knew of no one "whose stimulating mentality my brother took keener pleasure." The senator and the former president severely disagreed on many issues. Each could frequently get irritated with the other and during the election of 1912 those disagreements nearly cost them their friendship.[40]

But Roosevelt's sister also contended that one of the reasons the two men's relationship flourished was that each possessed a devotion to the fundamental ideas responsible for the founding of the United States. Those qualities allowed each not only to fight for positions that allowed the nation to flourish but resulted in the two statesmen standing "invariably as one man."[41]

Returning to Washington, Lodge was filled with emotion. "[W]hat a joy it was to have those two talks with you," he wrote T. R. two days before Christmas. The senator looked forward to visiting with Roosevelt again. They still had much to discuss and there was no time to waste. Despite Roosevelt being in a poor condition, his doctors allowed him to return to his beloved Sagamore Hill. Lodge had stayed there many times. Though noisy and chaotic the home was filled with constant visitors and warm memories of family and friends.[42]

Lodge never had that opportunity to visit with Roosevelt again. On the afternoon of January 6, 1919, he received a telegram from Corinne. "Edith telephoned me. Theo died last night in his sleep with no suffering." Roosevelt was just sixty. Throughout his full and exuberant life, the countless falls from horses, illnesses, and other mishaps had slowly taken a toll on his health. But as with Nannie Lodge, many believed that the loss of his youngest child was a blow that Roosevelt was unable to endure. "Words fail me. I am overwhelmed," Lodge wrote in a telegram to Edith as he prepared to travel to Oyster Bay for a final farewell.[43]

Despite remaining trim and in good physical condition, Lodge had aged as well. Years of professional and familial anxiety had caused his once lush brown hair to turn white. The chiseled features remained strong, but the lines in his forehead and under his eyes were indictive of a man who had never stopped striving to make a difference in the nation he so loved. When Lodge arrived at Oyster Bay's Christ Church on January 7 the day was cold, and the falling snow had begun to fade. At a service reserved for less than 500 people, several of those with whom Roosevelt had clashed on the battlefield of ideas were in attendance. These included former president William Howard Taft and the 1916 Republican presidential nominee Charles Evans Hughes. While no eulogies were delivered, Edith had arranged for the playing of her husband's favorite hymn, John Rippon's 1787's "How Firm a Foundation."[44]

A month later, on February 9, at just after three o'clock in the afternoon, as Roosevelt was honored throughout the world, Henry Cabot Lodge delivered a eulogy commemorating the life and legacy of his closest friend. In what the *Washington Post* described as "the most distinguished" gathering "the capital has ever witnessed," dignitaries from each of the three branches of government filled the House of Representatives to honor one of the country's most prominent citizens. Among the 2,000 attendees were members of the Supreme Court, Vice President Thomas Marshall, and former president Taft. Lodge, appearing noticeably exhausted, spoke for nearly two hours, devoting his address to the contributions Roosevelt had made to the nation during his celebrated career.[45]

Throughout his comments, the senator remained calm and dignified. Standing in front of the Speaker's platform, the senator spoke in "clear, even tones," illuminating the former president's journey in rich historical detail. As he commented about his friend's final moments, Lodge's "voice broke, and he had to steady himself" before he could conclude his remarks. Sinking back into his chair in a moment of obvious relief, the senator received a standing ovation from the large audience.[46]

With Roosevelt no longer by his side it was difficult for Henry Cabot Lodge to carry on. There was little choice. With Nannie, Bay, Cecil Spring Rice, Henry Adams, and so many others gone, the fight to preserve the international autonomy of the United States was all that remained.[47]

As the senator reiterated his vision for the postwar world, he remained wary of President Wilson's idea of a League of Nations. "I will not put my hand to a treaty that promises to do things which we know we would not do," the senator had written Roosevelt years earlier, in the context of his disagreement regarding several treaties negotiated by the Taft Administration.[48]

Throughout Lodge's decades-long career in politics, he had always thought of the primary interests of the United States. In the senator's mind such an organization as Wilson proposed would diminish the nation's influence as well as force its people to sacrifice their independence. Lodge had always believed in "America First." Any action that caused his country to compromise that perspective was one that he would not support. Lodge also believed that Wilson had created the initiative motivated by the megalomaniacal desire to achieve a third term as president.[49]

Lodge was not opposed to peace but refused to abide by the idea of peace at any price. The senator believed the League put the United States in a position that forfeited its autonomy in international decision-making. In a different world the League was a wonderful idea. Lodge, however, did not believe the organization that Wilson described was possible without the United States being allowed to exercise greater autonomy over its destiny.[50]

On February 28, 1919, Lodge's opposition to the League of Nations culminated in a speech delivered on the Senate floor. The senator reemphasized his point that by becoming a part of the international organization the United States would lose its ability to decide its own fate. "We are asked also to give up in part our sovereignty and our independence and subject our own to the will of other nations if there is a majority against our desires," Lodge stated.[51]

That point included the issue of immigration, one that Lodge believed required limitation if the United States was to remain a socially and economically stable nation. "Are we ready to give to other nations the power to say who shall come into the United States and become citizens of the Republic?" he asked. "If we do this," he cautioned, "we are prepared to part with the most precious of sovereign rights, that which guards our existence and our character as a nation." As always Lodge delivered his arguments with great elegance and precision. While his comments were partisan they were as always thoughtful and thoroughly researched.[52]

Knowing Lodge's opposition, President Wilson, returning from the Paris peace negotiations, immediately went on the attack for national approval of his international peace plan. Attending a rally in Boston, the president never mentioned Lodge's name. Those within the audience understood who Wilson was addressing when he made the following remarks: "Any man who resists the present tides that run in the world, will find himself thrown upon a shore so high and barren that it will seem as if he had been separated from his human kind forever." The senator did not respond to the president's comments. Instead, he chose to use his power to pass a resolution that blocked the ratification of any agreement that broached the idea of an international organization.[53]

Following the signing of the Treaty of Versailles in Paris on June 28, Wilson returned to Washington with the hopes of receiving approval of the agreement by the nation's upper house. When the president presented the treaty to the Senate in July, Lodge politely asked if he could carry the treaty. "Not on your life," Wilson said. Following the president's speech on behalf of ratification, Lodge decided to kill the agreement using every procedure he had at his disposal. Taking his time, the senator spent two weeks reading the entire treaty aloud.[54]

As head of the Foreign Relations Committee, Lodge also decided to hold hearings examining every aspect of the agreement no matter how minor. During his extensive questioning of witnesses the senator added a countless number of amendments, some of which were valid while others were simply meant to deliberately delay the approval process. By September, Wilson realized the only way to break Lodge's strategy in the Senate was a nationwide campaign to marshal the nation to help him pass the agreement.[55]

October 2, 1919, as Wilson toured the country in support of the treaty, the Virginian suffered a debilitating stroke. Following the president's return to Washington, the Senate and the White House remained unable to come to terms on the many concerns that Lodge had expressed regarding the League charter. When the vote was finally taken in the Senate on November 19, the treaty fell short of ratification by eight votes. While many viewed the conflict as a victory for Lodge, the senator may have preferred to interpret his legislative accomplishment as one that preserved the individual greatness of the United States.[56]

Following the defeat of the League of Nations, Lodge remained in the Senate. As he grew older, he spent more time on historical scholarship and nurturing his grandchildren. Never losing his love of Shakespeare, the senator continued to enjoy the bard's work.[57]

Sitting in bed wearing blue-and-white striped pajamas, Lodge also delighted in the tales of Charles Dickens and Arthur Conan Doyle's Sherlock Holmes. There was also his own writing that included a memoir of his actions regarding the League of Nations and the record of his thirty-five-year correspondence with Theodore Roosevelt.[58]

In reviewing the letters between the senator and his old friend, Lodge reminisced about the odyssey the two men had experienced. While the senator did his best to maintain his health it soon began to fail. During the summer of 1924, Lodge was forced to leave Nahant to undergo two surgeries for a condition related to his prostate. Following the first procedure, Lodge recovered at Charlesgate Hospital in Cambridge, Massachusetts. The senator had a pleasant room allowing him to gaze out at Boston's Back Bay, giving him the opportunity to dream of the waters that crashed off the cliffs near his Eastpoint home.[59]

Lodge was happy to briefly enjoy the pleasures of the New England shoreline before returning to Cambridge for his second surgery. "The Doctors promise prompt recovery," Lodge wrote to President Calvin Coolidge on October 29. But on November 9, 1924, Lodge experienced a fatal heart attack. The senator was seventy-four years old.[60]

While Lodge was not buried on Nahant, being interred in Boston was just as fitting.

In 1884 Lodge and Roosevelt were both viewed as unscrupulous politicians more focused on their ambitions than loyalty to their class. Despite personal and political disappointments, both men persevered to play a significant role in the growth of their nation and its role in the world. When each finally succumbed to age and infirmity the announcements of their passings were noted on the front pages of newspapers throughout the nation and around the globe.

Theodore Roosevelt and Henry Cabot Lodge never lost their faith in the greatness of the United States. They believed the nation deserved to occupy a special position in the world and were prepared to do whatever was necessary to defeat those who sought to do it harm. They were proud, patriotic, and passionate men who believed in taking a position and defending it, while doing their utmost to help the United States of America achieve the greatness they believed it deserved. Each man possessed many imperfections. They could be shortsighted, arrogant, and highly partisan. However, both possessed a devotion to service, love of country, and aspired to do their utmost to leave their nation more prosperous, more secure, and more successful than they found it.

Acknowledgments

A book, like any creative endeavor is a team effort and *The Rough Rider and the Professor* is no exception. First and foremost, I would like to express my love and gratitude to my wife, Jorie Waterman, and our son, Elliot Jurdem. I want to thank my agent, Suzy Evans, and everyone at the Sandra Dijkstra Literary Agency for allowing me to achieve my dream of publishing a work of popular nonfiction. I have always viewed myself as a storyteller and I am grateful to Suzy for finding my narrative a fantastic home with Pegasus Books. At Pegasus I want to thank Claiborne Hancock, Jessica Case, Maria Fernandez, Meghan Jusczak, and their entire team for being such a pleasure to work with and for creating such a wonderful book.

I also want to thank my fabulous research assistant, Stevie Martin of Fordham University. Stevie was a delightful person to work with and proved diligent and resourceful in digging up documents that played a vital role in the completion of the manuscript.

The narrative was researched and written at the height of the Pandemic. During much of the research the Massachusetts Historical Society, where the Lodge-Roosevelt Correspondence are housed, was closed. I was fortunate that the library had a duplicate set of microfilm that I was able to borrow and view with the assistance of Tina Boothe, Colleen Wood, and their fabulous team at the Darien Public Library. The project could never have been completed on time without their help. At the MHS I want to thank the society's incredible chief historian, Peter Drummey, for helping me understand Henry Cabot Lodge and his world. I would also like to thank Hannah Elder for being so helpful in finding certain photographs of Henry Cabot Lodge and his family that were critical to the production of this book.

On the archive side I would also like to thank Erik Johnson and his team at the Theodore Roosevelt Center at Dickinson State University. Henry Cabot Lodge's handwriting is highly challenging, and I am grateful to Erik for supplying me with printed transcripts which were pivotal in helping me complete my work. Thanks as well to curator Victoria Cacchione of the Sagamore Hill Historic site for supplying me with several great photographs and for hosting a terrific tour of Theodore Roosevelt's home.

I also want to express my appreciation to everyone who was kind enough to read sections of the manuscript. My thanks to Vincent Cannato, Andrea, and Dan Elish, Alvin Felzenberg, Steve Gillon, Edward Kohn, Thomas Mackey, Donald A. Ritchie, Amity Shlaes, T. J. Stiles, and Stephanie Bridges Waterfield.

Finally, I would like to send a special thanks to Douglas Brinkley and H. W. Brands for encouraging me to pursue this enormously rewarding and fun project.

Sources

A nyone who writes a book on any aspect of the life of Theodore Roosevelt is fortunate to stand on the shoulders of many great scholars who have come before. Such is the case of my experience in writing a narrative on the friendship between President Roosevelt and Senator Henry Cabot Lodge.

As one of the nation's most interesting and important presidents, Roosevelt is the subject of some wonderful biographies and analysis. I would like to express my gratitude to John Blum, H. W. Brands, Kathleen Dalton, Paul Grondahl, William Harbaugh, Edmund Morris, David McCullough, Patricia O'Toole, and many others for their great storytelling and scholarship.

On Henry Cabot Lodge, my narrative was not possible without the great work of John A. Garraty. Although *Henry Cabot Lodge: A Biography* was produced in the 1950s, it is the most comprehensive volume on the senator's life. Karl Schriftgiesser's *The Gentleman from Massachusetts* contains some valuable information about Lodge's years. However, it is a highly partisan volume, and is lacking in reliability due to the author having no access to any of Lodge's papers.

There are several other biographies of Lodge by authors Charles Washburn, William Lawrence, and several others. However, they are dated and do not include any of Lodge's personal documents. William C. Widenor's *Henry Cabot Lodge and the Search for an American Foreign Policy* is an analysis of impeccable scholarship primarily focusing on Lodge's views and vision of international affairs. Emily

Lodge's memoir, *The Lodge Women*, is a highly valuable book filled with interesting letters and intimate reminiscences about the Lodge family and their times.

The most detailed information about the relationship between Lodge and Roosevelt comes from their thirty-five-year correspondence contained in 2,500 letters located at the Massachusetts Historical Society. Roosevelt had encouraged Lodge to edit and publish their exchanges in full, contending that the book "would be the most interesting ever published in the United States." Following Roosevelt's passing, Lodge worked very closely with his widow, Edith Roosevelt on the two-volume collection that was published a year after Lodge's death in 1925.[1]

As a historian, one would have expected Lodge to produce a collection with all the words and phrases intact. He chose not to do so. As John Garraty has written, Lodge was heavily involved in the events of his times and was unable to look at the people and situations he and Roosevelt encountered with any objectivity.[2]

Roosevelt was as uninhibited in his words as he was in his actions. In Lodge's address commemorating Roosevelt's career, the senator highlighted the fact that "[Roosevelt] had no secrets in his life—he kept nothing from the people because he had nothing to hide." Ironically that sense of spontaneity that so defined Roosevelt's spirit was one that Lodge hoped to conceal from the public. "There are words resembling invectives, let us say, such as he did not print in his autobiography and which were not printed during his life . . . which ought to be left out because they were so extreme," the senator wrote to T. R.'s sister Bamie.[3]

Lodge also believed he himself had made comments about certain people in a manner not becoming of a United States senator. "I know there are things in these which might cause pain to people of whom I am fond. I have never allowed anybody to see them," he commented to Edith Roosevelt. In addition to removing some of President Roosevelt's more candid comments, Lodge edited his own statements as well. "I think I know now very well just how you want them to appear," Lodge wrote Roosevelt's widow in May 1924.[4]

While I have used the two-volume published collection, I have done my best to compare the edited versions with the originals as well as using a large portion of the letters not included in the published edition.

As with all public figures, Lodge attempted to use the correspondence with Roosevelt to paint a portrait that would present both men in a favorable light. The senator was also a professional historian who had the opportunity to create a work that if done transparently would have emerged as one of the foundational works on the life and career of Theodore Roosevelt. The fact that he was unable to do that resulted in *The Selected Correspondence Between Theodore Roosevelt and Henry Cabot Lodge* being problematic and unreliable.

On a larger scale Lodge's volumes fail to convey the authentic manner in which Roosevelt lived his life. As one who prided himself as a historian of the United States, Lodge did a disservice to the profession by not employing the intellectual integrity necessary to give his relationship with Roosevelt the respect it warranted.

Bibliography

Abbott, Lyman. "More Rooseveltiana." *The Outlook*, April 29, 1925. Fordham University Database.

"Abraham Lincoln and St. John's Episcopal Church." Abraham Lincoln Online—Your Source for Lincoln News and Information, n.d. http://www .abrahamlincolnonline.org/.

Abrams, Roger I. *The First World Series*. Boston: Northeastern University Press, 2003.

Adams, Henry, and Worthington Chauncey Ford. *Letters of Henry Adams (1892–1918)*. Boston: Houghton Mifflin Co., 1938.

Adams, Henry, Jacob Clavner Levenson, and Jayne Newcomer Samuels. *The Letters of Henry Adams, 1899–1905*. Vol. V. Cambridge, Mass.: Harvard University Press, 1988.

Adams, Henry. *The Education of Henry Adams*. Boston: Massachusetts Historical Society, 1917.

Adams, Henry. *The Letters of Henry Adams, 1868–1885*. Vol. II. Edited by J. C. Levenson, Ernest Samuels, Charles Vandersee, and Viola Hopkins Winner. Cambridge, Mass.: Harvard University Press, 1982.

Adams, Henry. *The Letters of Henry Adams, 1886–1892*. Vol. III. Edited by J. C. Levinson, Henry Samuels, Charles Vandersee, and Viola Hopkins Winner. Cambridge, Mass.: Harvard University Press, 1982.

Adams, Henry. *The Letters of Henry Adams, 1892-1899*. Vol. IV. Edited by J. C. Levinson, Ernest Samuels, Charles Vandersee, and Viola Hopkins Winner. Cambridge, Mass.: Harvard University Press, 1988.

"Alert Republicans." *Brooklyn Union*, Oct. 18, 1885. Newspapers.com.

Amory, Cleveland. *The Proper Bostonians*. Orleans, Mass.: Parnassus Imprints, 1947.

"Andrew Johnson Suite." US Department of the Treasury, March 31, 2021. https://home.treasury.gov/about/history/the-treasury-building/andrew -johnson-suite.

"At Chicago." *Boston Evening Transcript*, June 4, 1884. Newspapers.com.

Bacon, Kate. "The Dark Side of the Gilded Age." *The Atlantic*, June 2007. www .atlantic.com.

Beatty, Jack. *Age of Betrayal: The Triumph of Money in America 1865–1900*. New York: Vantage Books, 2007.

Benson, Godfrey. *Theodore Roosevelt*. Boston, Mass.: Atlantic Monthly Press, 1923.

Beran, Michael Knox. *Wasps: The Splendors and Miseries of an American Aristocracy*. New York: Pegasus Books, 2021.

Berfield, Susan. "The Coal Strike That Defined Theodore Roosevelt's Presidency." July 15, 2020. http://www.smithsonianmag.org/.

Beschloss, Michael. "When T.R. Saw Lincoln." *New York Times*, May 21, 2014. www.nytimes.com.

"Biography of James W. and Elisha S. Converse." Access Genealogy, Nov. 12, 2012. https://accessgenealogy.com/connecticut/biography-of-james-w-and -elisha-s-converse.htm.

Bishop, Joseph Bucklin. *Theodore Roosevelt and His Time: Shown in His Own Letters Vol. I*. New York: Charles Scribner's Sons, 1920.

Blakemore, Erin. "How American 'Dollar Princesses' Invaded British High Society." A&E Television Networks, n.d. http://www.history.com/.

Blodgett, Geoffrey T. "The Mind of the Boston Mugwump." *Mississippi Valley Historical Review* 48, no. 4 (1962): 614. https://doi.org/10.2307/1893145.

Blum, John Morton. *The Republican Roosevelt*. New York: Atheneum, 1972.

Brands, H. W. *Woodrow Wilson*. New York: Times Books, 2003.

Brands, H. W. *T.R.: The Last Romantic*. New York: Basic Books, 1997.

A Brief History of the Somerset Club of Boston, with a List of Past and Present Members, 1852–1913. Cambridge, Mass.: Riverside Press, 1914.

Brown, David S. *The Last American Aristocrat: The Brilliant Life and Improbable Education of Henry Adams*. New York: Scribner, 2020.

Bryan, William Jennings, and John Burns. *The Commoner Condensed*. Lincoln, Neb.: Jacob North & Co., 1903.

Burrows, Edwin G., and Mike Wallace. *Gotham: A History of New York to 1898*. New York: Oxford University Press, 1999.

Burton, David Henry. *Cecil Spring Rice: A Diplomat's Life*. Cranbury, N.J.: Associated University Press, 1990.

Butt, Archibald Willingham, and Lawrence F. Abbott. *The Letters of Archie Butt, Personal Aide to President Roosevelt*. Garden City, N.Y.: Doubleday, Page & Company, 1924.

Butt, Archibald, William Howard Taft, and Theodore Roosevelt. *The Intimate Letters of Archie Butt: Military Aide. Vol. I*. New York: Doubleday, Doran & Company, 1930.

Chalfant, Edward. *Better in Darkness: A Biography of Henry Adams, His Second Life, 1862–1891*. New York: Archon Books, 1994.

Chalfant, Edward. *Improvement of the World: A Biography of Henry Adams, His Last Life, 1891–1918*. Hamden, Conn.: Archon Books, 2001.

Chanler, Margaret. *Roman Spring: Memoirs*. Boston: Little, Brown and Company, 1934.

Chanler, Winthrop. *Winthrop Chanler's Letters*. New York: privately printed, 1951.

Cherny, Robert W. *American Politics in the Gilded Age: 1868–1900*. Malden, Mass.: Harlan-Davidson Inc., 1997.

Chessman, G. Wallace. "Theodore Roosevelt's Campaign Against the Vice-Presidency." *The Historian* 14, no. 2 (1952): 173–90. https://doi.org /10.1111/j.1540-6563.1952.tb00132.x.

"Civil Service Reform." *Indianapolis Journal*, June 21, 1889.

Cleveland, Grover. "President Cleveland Vetoes a Law Restricting Immigration." Miller Center, n.d. http://www.millercenter.org/.

"Constitution of The League of Nations." United States Senate, Classic Senate Speeches, Feb. 28, 1919. https://www.senate.gov/artandhistory/history /common/generic/Speeches_Lodge1919.htm.

"Convention Clears the Way for Nominations." *San Francisco Call*, June 21, 1900. Newspapers.com.

"Convention Proceedings." *New York Times*, June 21, 1900. Newspapers.com.

"The Convention." *Chicago Tribune*, June 1, 1884. Newspapers.com.

"The Conventions First Work." *New York Times*, June 4, 1884. Fordham University database.

Cooper, John Milton. "The Last Time America Turned Away from the World." *New York Times*, Nov. 21, 2019.

Cooper, John Milton. *The Warrior and the Priest: Woodrow Wilson and Theodore Roosevelt*. Cambridge, Mass.: Harvard University Press, 1983.

Crapol, Edward P. *James G. Blaine: Architect of Empire*. Wilmington, Del.: Scholarly Resources Inc., 2000.

Crocker, H. W. "The Roosevelt Sons in World War I." History on the Net, n.d. www.historyonthenet.com.

Crowley, John W. "'Dear Bay,' Theodore Roosevelt's Letters to George Cabot Lodge." *Journal of New York History* 53, no. 2 (April 1972).

Cummins, Genevieve. "The Wearing of Watches." Antique Clocks, Watches and Barometers. (Antike Uhren, Antieke klokken, Horlogerie Ancienne), n.d. http://www.antique-horology.org/.

Dalton, Kathleen M. *Theodore Roosevelt: A Strenuous Life*. New York: Vintage Books, 2004.

Dalton, Kathleen M. "Theodore Roosevelt: Knickerbocker Aristocrat." *New York History* 67, no. 1 (Jan. 1986).

BIBLIOGRAPHY

"Davis 1: Torpedo Boat #12, 'Naval History and Heritage Command'." *Naval History and Heritage Command*, n.d. http://www.history.navy.mil/.

Davis, Oscar King. *Released for Publication: Some Inside History of Theodore Roosevelt and His Times*. Boston: Houghton-Mifflin, 1925.

"Day's Work at the Convention." *Boston Globe*, June 18, 1908. Newspapers.com.

"Decisions, Decisions." *The New Yorker*, July 3, 2005. http://www.thenewyorker.com/.

Dorsey, Leroy G. "Theodore Roosevelt and Corporate America 1901–1909: A Reexamination." *Presidential Studies Quarterly* 25, no. 4 (1995).

Dorwart, Bonnie Brice. "Disease in the Civil War." Essential Civil War Curriculum, n.d. https://www.essentialcivilwarcurriculum.com/.

Dotson, David Wendell. "Henry Cabot Lodge: A Political Biography, 1887–1901," dissertation, University of Oklahoma, 1981.

"Downes v. Bidwell—182 U.S. 244, 21S. Ct. 770 (1901), Law School Case Brief."

Dunn, Arthur Wallace. *From Harrison to Harding: A Personal Narrative, Covering a Third of a Century, 1888–1921*. New York: G.P. Putnam, 1922.

Dyer, Thomas G. *Theodore Roosevelt and the Idea of Race*. Baton Rouge.: Louisiana State University Press, 1980.

Evers, Donna. "Historical Landscapes: Two Families One Roof." *Washington Life Magazine*, 2006.

"Ex-Governor Black Dies at His Troy Home." *New York Times*, March 13, 1913. Fordham University database.

Fall River Daily News, June 4, 1884. Newspapers.com.

"The Financial Panic of 1873." US Department of the Treasury, n.d. http://www .treasury.gov/.

Foraker, Joseph Benson. *Notes of a Busy Life. Vol. 1*. Cincinnati: Stewart & Kidd Company, 1916.

Foraker, Joseph Benson. *Notes of a Busy Life. Vol. II*. Cincinnati: Stewart & Kidd Company, 1916.

Fredrickson, George M. *The Inner Civil War*. New York: Harper and Row, 1965.

Freeman, Castle. "John Jay Chapman: Brief Life of a Neglected Critic." *Harvard Magazine*, Jan. 1, 2001.

"From Mr. Roosevelt." *Saint Paul Globe*, June 13, 1884. Newspapers.com.

"The Gardner House." *The Landowner*, March 1872, n.d. www.Chicagology.com.

Garraty, John A. *Henry Cabot Lodge: A Biography*. New York: Alfred A. Knopf, 1953.

Garraty, John A. "Holmes Appointment to the U.S. Supreme Court." *New England Quarterly* 22, no. 3 (Sept. 1949).

Garraty, John A., and Henry Cabot Lodge. "Henry Cabot Lodge and the Alaskan Boundary Tribunal." *New England Quarterly* 24, no. 4 (Dec. 1951): 469. https://doi.org/10.2307/361339.

Garraty, John. "Spoiled Child of American Politics." *American Heritage* 6, no. 5 (Aug. 1955). https://www.americanheritage.com/spoiled-child-american -politics.

"Gave Life to Service." *Washington Post*, Feb. 10, 1919.

"Going Slow at Chicago." *The Sun*, June 4, 1884.

Goodwin, Doris Kearns. *The Bully Pulpit: Theodore Roosevelt, William Howard Taft and the Golden Age of Journalism*. New York: Simon & Schuster, 2013.

Gosnell, Harold F. "Thomas C. Platt—Political Manager." *Political Science Quarterly* 38, no. 3 (September 1923): 443. https://doi.org /10.2307/2142366.

Gould, Lewis L. *Grand Old Party: A History of the Republicans*. New York: Random House, 2003.

"Gov. Roosevelt in 1900 Will Not Be a Candidate for President." *New York Times*, June 30, 1899. Fordham University database.

"Governor Powell Clayton." National Governors Association, n.d. http://www .nga.org/.

"Governor Roosevelt in Denver." *New York Times*, Sept. 26, 1900. Fordham University database.

Graff, Henry F. "The Campaign and Election of 1892." The Miller Center, n.d. www.millercenter.org.

"The Grand Pacific Hotel." Chicagology, n.d. http://www.chicagology.com/.

Gratton, Brian. "Race or Politics: Henry Cabot Lodge and the Origins of the Immigration Restriction Movement in the United States." *Journal of Policy History* 30, no. 1 (Jan. 19, 2018): 128–57. https://doi.org/10.1017 /s0898030617000410.

Grondahl, Paul. *I Rose Like a Rocket: The Political Education of Theodore Roosevelt*. New York: Free Press, 2004.

Gwynn, Stephen. *The Letters and Friendships of Sir Cecil Spring Rice: A Record, Vol. II*. Boston: Houghton Mifflin, 1929.

Gwynn, Stephen. *The Letters and Friendships of Sir Cecil Spring Rice: A Record, Vol. 1*. Boston: Houghton Mifflin, 1929.

Hagedorn, Hermann. *Roosevelt in the Badlands*. Boston: Houghton-Mifflin, 1921.

Hagedorn, Hermann. *The Boys Life of Theodore Roosevelt*. New York: Harper Brothers, 1919.

Halford, E. W. "Roosevelt's Introduction to Washington." *Frank Leslie's Weekly*, March 1, 1919.

Harbaugh, William Henry. *Power and Responsibility: The Life and Times of Theodore Roosevelt*. New York: Farrar Strauss & Giroux, 1961.

Hazelgrove, William. *Forging a President: How the Wild West Created Teddy Roosevelt*. New York: Regnery, 2017.

"Henry Cabot Lodge Imports His Young Friend Roosevelt." *Boston Daily Globe*, Oct. 21, 1884.

"Henry Cabot Lodge Park." Roadtrippers, n.d. https://maps.roadtrippers.com /us/nahant-ma/points-of-interest/henry-cabot-lodge-park-nahant.

Hess, Stephen. *America's Political Dynasties*. Washington: Brookings Institution, 2015.

"The Historian and the Hostess." *Washington Post*, Dec. 25, 1983. www .washingtonpost.com.

Hofstadter, Richard. *The Age of Reform: From Bryan to FDR*. New York: Vintage Books, 1955.

"Home of Henry Cabot Lodge, 31 Beacon Street, City Walking Guide." City Walking Guide, n.d. http://www.citywalkingguide.com/.

Howell, Kenneth. "The Doom of Reconstruction: The Liberal Republicans in the Civil War Era." H-Civil War, February 2008. https://networks.h-net.org /networks.

"Hughes Is Elected." *Brooklyn Citizen*, Nov. 7, 1906. Newspapers.com.

Hunt, H. Draper. "The Plumed Knight at Home: An Intimate Sketch of James G. Blaine." *Maine History* 1 (1988).

Hurd, D. Hamilton. *History of Essex County, Massachusetts: With Biographical Sketches of Many of Its Pioneers and Prominent Men*. Vol. II. Philadelphia: J. W. Lewis and Co., 1888.

"In Honor of Mr. Blaine." *Boston Daily Globe*, Nov. 4, 1884. Newspapers.com.

Jaffa, Harry V., Thomas B. Silver, Peter W. Schramm, and Patrick J. Garrity. "Young Men in a Hurry: Roosevelt, Lodge and the Foundations of the Twentieth Century Republican." In *Natural Right and Political Right: Essays in Honor of Harry V. Jaffa*, 225–235. Durham, N.C.: Carolina Academic Press, 1984.

Jeffers, Harry Paul. *Commissioner Roosevelt: The Story of Theodore Roosevelt and The New York City Police 1895–1897*. New York: J. Wiley & Sons, 1994.

Jessup, Philip C. *Elihu Root, 1905–1937*. Vol. II. Hamden, N.J.: Archon Books, 1964.

"John R. Lynch, 1847–1939." U.S. House of Representatives: History, Art & Archives, n.d. https://history.house.gov/Home/.

Johnson, Ben. "Bright Young Things." Historic UK, n.d. http://www.historicuk.com/.

"Joseph B. Foraker." Ohio History Central, n.d. http://www.ohiohistorycentral.org/.

Josephson, Matthew. *The President Makers: The Culture of Politics and Leadership in an Age of Enlightenment, 1896–1919*. New York: Putnam, 1979.

"The Journalists: Horace White, 1834–1916." Mr. Lincoln and Friends, n.d. https://www.mrlincolnandfriends.org/.

Klein, Christopher. "How Teddy Roosevelt's Views on Race Shaped His Politics." History Stories, August 20, 2020. www.history.com.

Klein, Christopher. "Theodore Roosevelt Shot in Milwaukee." This Day in History, May 6, 2022. www.history.com.

Klein, Christopher. "When Teddy Roosevelt Was Shot in 1912, a Speech May Have Saved His Life," Oct. 12, 2012. www.history.com.

Knokey, Jon A. *Theodore Roosevelt and the Making of American Leadership*. New York: Skyhorse, 2015.

Kohlsaat, Herman Henry. *From McKinley to Harding: Personal Recollections of Our Presidents*. New York: Charles Scribner's Sons, 1923.

Kohn, Edward P. "A Necessary Defeat: Theodore Roosevelt and the New York Mayoralty Election of 1886." *New York History* 87, no. 2 (2006).

Kohn, Edward P. *Heir to the Empire City: New York and the Making of Theodore Roosevelt*. New York: Basic Books, 2014.

Kohn, Edward. "Crossing the Rubicon: Theodore Roosevelt, Henry Cabot Lodge and the 1884 Republican Convention." *The Journal of the Gilded Age and Progressive Era* 5, no. 1 (Jan. 2006): 19–45. https://doi.org/10.1017/s1537781400002851.

Lamb, Bill. "Alexander Bannwart." Society for American Baseball Research, n.d. www.sabr.org.

Landrigan, Dan, and Leslie Landrigan. *Bar Harbor Babylon: Murder, Misfortune, and Scandal on Mount Desert Island*. Camden, Me.: Down East Books, 2019.

Lansford, Tom. *Theodore Roosevelt in Perspective*. New York: Novinka Books, 2005.

"The Last Marks of Respect to Our Late President." *New York Times*, April 14, 1865. Fordham University database.

"Last Speeches on President's List." *New York Times*, June 4, 1903. Fordham University database.

"Launching the Corsair." *New York Times*, Dec. 13, 1898. Fordham University database.

Lawrence, William. *Henry Cabot Lodge: A Biographical Sketch*. Boston: Houghton Mifflin Company, 1925.

Lawrence, William. *Roger Wolcott*. Boston: William Lawrence, 1902.

Leech, Margaret. *In the Days of McKinley*. New York: Harper Brothers, 1999.

Leland Hotel. n.d. *Chicago, Passage of Time, 1880s*. www.chicagophotographs.com.

Lewis, R. W. B. "The Second Mrs. Roosevelt." *Washington Post*, June 29, 1980.

"Lodge and Congress Honor Roosevelt." *New York Times*, Feb. 10, 1919. Fordham University database.

"Lodge and Wilson Make Up." *Boston Globe*, April 3, 1917. Newspapers.com.

"Lodge Calls for Action." *Boston Evening Transcript*, Jan. 10, 1905. Newspapers.com.

"Lodge Comes Out for Taft." *Boston Globe*, June 24, 1912. Newspapers.com.

"Lodge Demands a Dictated Peace Won by Victory." *New York Times*, Aug. 24, 1918. Fordham University database.

"Lodge For a Rate Court." *New York Times*, Jan. 21, 1905. www.nytimes.com.

"Lodge Memo." *Lodge-Roosevelt Correspondence, MHS*, Jan. 24, 1908.

"Lodge on Campaign Issues." *New York Times*, Oct. 25, 1898. Fordham University database.

"Lodge Reviews His Public Record." *Boston Evening Transcript*, Jan. 4, 1911. Newspapers.com.

Lodge, Emily. *The Lodge Women, Their Men and Their Times*. New York: Emily Lodge, 2014.

Lodge, Henry Cabot, and Theodore Roosevelt. *Hero Tales from American History*. Louisville, Ky.: The McConnell Center, 2011.

Lodge, Henry Cabot, *Selections from the Correspondence of Theodore Roosevelt, and Henry Cabot Lodge, 1884–1918. Vol. II.* New York: Charles Scribner's Sons, 1925.

Lodge, Henry Cabot, *Selections from the Correspondence of Theodore Roosevelt, and Henry Cabot Lodge, 1884–1918. Vol. I.* New York: Charles Scribner's Sons, 1925.

Lodge, Henry Cabot. *Early Memories*. New York: Charles Scribner's Sons, 1913.

Lodge-Roosevelt Correspondence, Massachusetts Historical Society.

Lodge, Henry Cabot. Papers, Massachusetts Historical Society.

Lodge, Henry Cabot. "Senator Lodge's Speech." *Brooklyn Eagle*, June 6, 1904. Newspapers.com.

Lodge, Henry Cabot. *The Senate and the League of Nations*. New York: Charles Scribner's Sons, 1925.

"Lodge's Seaside Home." *Boston Post*, June 21, 1896.

"Long Has the Most Senators." *Boston Daily Globe*, October 24, 1886. Newspapers.com.

Long, John D., and Lawrence Shaw Mayo. *The Diary of John D. Long*. Boston: Atlantic Monthly Press, 1923.

"Looking Ahead—Republicans Planning for 1904." *Boston Globe*, March 3, 1901. Newspapers.com.

Lynch, John R. *Reminiscences of An Active Life: The Autobiography of John Roy Lynch*. Oxford: University Press of Mississippi, 2008.

Mack, Doug. "The Strange Case of Puerto Rico." *Slate*, Oct. 9, 2017. www.slate.com.

"Makes Appeal to Idealists." *Boston Globe*, Aug. 17, 1912. Newspapers.com.

Manners, William. *T.R. and Will: A Friendship That Split the Republican Party*. New York: Harcourt, Brace & World, 1969.

Martelle, Scott. "Opinion: Like Teddy Roosevelt Trump Wants to Be the Bride at Every Wedding." *Los Angeles Times*, June 2, 2017.

Matthews, Mimi. "A Century of Sartorial Style: A Visual Guide to Nineteenth Century Men's Wear." Historical nonfiction and Victorian romance, Feb. 21, 2022. http://www.mimimatthews.com/.

Mayer, George H. *The Republican Party, 1854–1966*. New York: Oxford
    University Press, 1967.

"Mayor Shepard Sees the President and Mrs. Henry Cabot Lodge Off from Lynn for
    the Lodge Villa at Nahant." *Boston Globe*, Aug. 25, 1902. Newspapers.com.

McCullough, David G. *Mornings on Horseback*. New York: Touchstone, 1981.

Measuringwealth.com, n.d. http://www.measuringwealth.com/.

"Memorandum on Recollections of Geoge H. Lyman." *Lodge-Roosevelt
    Correspondence*, MHS, n.d.

Merrill, John D. "Lodge Talked of as Possible Compromise." *Boston Globe*, June 9,
    1916. Newspapers.com.

Merry, Robert W. *President McKinley: Architect of the American Century*. New
    York: Simon & Schuster, 2018.

Miller, Nathan. *Theodore Roosevelt: A Life*. New York: William Morrow, 1992.

"A Miner's Story." eHISTORY, Ohio State University, n.d. http://www.ehistory
    .osu.edu/.

"Miscellaneous." *Boston Evening Transcript*, Oct. 11, 1884. Newspapers.com.

"Miscellaneous." *Boston Evening Transcript*, Oct. 19, 1886. Newspapers.com.

Moen, John R., and Ellis W. Tallman. "The Panic of 1907." Federal Reserve
    History, n.d. http://www.federalreservehistory.org/.

"Montgomery Ward Issues the First Mail Order Catalog for the General Public."
    Historyinformation.com, n.d. http://www.historyinformation.com/.

Morris, Edmund. *Colonel Roosevelt*. New York: Random House, 2010.

Morris, Edmund. *The Rise of Theodore Roosevelt*. New York: Modern Library,
    2001.

Morris, Edmund. *Theodore Rex*. New York: Random House, 2002.

Morris, Sylvia Jukes. *Edith Kermit Roosevelt: Portrait of a First Lady*. New York:
    Modern Library, 1980.

Morrison, Elting E. *The Letters of Theodore Roosevelt: Vol. I: The Years of
    Preparation, 1868–1898*. Cambridge, Mass.: Harvard University Press,
    1954.

Morse, John T. "Henry Cabot Lodge." *Harvard Graduates Magazine* 33, 1925.

Mowry, George E. *The Era of Theodore Roosevelt 1900–1912*. Cambridge, Mass.:
    Harper & Row, 1981.

"Mr. Blaine's Man Is Beaten." *The Sun*. June 4, 1884. Newspapers.com.

"Mr. Lodge Reviews His Party's Record." *New York Times*, June 21, 1900.
    Fordham University database.

"Mr. Lodge's Prediction." *Boston Daily Globe*, June 6, 1884. Newspapers.com.

"Mrs. Lodge Sponsor." *Boston Globe*, August 22, 1902. Newspapers.com.

Muccigrosso, Robert, and David R. Contosta, eds. *Henry Adams and His World*.
    Philadelphia: American Philosophical Society, 1994.

"Municipal Administration: The New York Police Force." *The Atlantic.* 1897.

Nichter, Luke A. *The Last Brahmin: Henry Cabot Lodge Jr. and the Making of the Cold War.* New Haven, Conn.: Yale University Press, 2020.

"No Inspiration in Beer Says Mr. Roosevelt." *Indianapolis Journal,* July 9, 1889. Newspapers.com.

"Nomination Put Off." *Washington Post,* June 21, 1900. Fordham University database.

"Norman on Henry Cabot Lodge as the Boss of Washington." *Boston Sunday Post,* June 8, 1902. Newspapers.com.

"The Northern Securities Case." Theodore Roosevelt Center, Dickinson State University, n.d. www.theodorerooseveltcenter.org.

O'Neill, Johnathan. "Constitutional Conservatives in the Progressive Era: Elihu Root, William Howard Taft and Henry Cabot Lodge, Sr." *First Principles, Heritage Foundation,* Feb. 15, 2013.

O'Toole, Patricia. *The Five of Hearts: An Intimate Portrait of Henry Adams and His Friends, 1880–1918.* New York: Simon & Schuster, 1990.

O'Toole, Patricia. *When Trumpets Call: Theodore Roosevelt After the White House.* New York: Simon & Schuster, 2005.

"Our Course in Panama." *Washington Post,* Jan. 6, 1903. Fordham University database.

"Our New Senator." *Boston Post,* Jan. 18, 1893. Newspapers.com.

"Panama as an Issue Pleases Mr. Lodge." *Cincinnati Inquirer,* Jan. 6, 1904. Newspapers.com.

"Panic of 1893." Ohio History Central, n.d. http://www.ohiohistorycentral.org/.

"Patry's Duty." *Boston Sunday Globe,* Nov. 11, 1900. Newspapers.com.

"The Philippine-American War 1899–1902." U.S. Department of State. Office of the Historian, n.d. http://www.history.state.gov/.

Photographs and Clippings of President Roosevelt's Visit, Nahant & Lynn. 1902. Photograph. Essex National Heritage Area.

Pietrusza, David. *TR's Last War: Theodore Roosevelt, the Great War, and a Journey of Triumph and Tragedy.* Guilford, N.H.: Lyons Press, 2020.

Platt, Thomas Collier. *The Autobiography of Thomas Collier Platt.* New York: B. W. Dodge & Co., 1910.

Porcellian Club Centennial, 1791–1891. Cambridge, Mass.: Riverside Press, 1891.

"The Private and Family Life of Theodore Roosevelt." Google Arts & Culture. n.d. https://artsandculture.google.com/.

Putnam, Carleton. *Theodore Roosevelt: The Formative Years, 1858–1886.* New York: Charles Scribner's Sons, 1958.

"Quietly Married at the Advent." *Bostonian Evening Transcript,* Aug. 20, 1900.

"Republican National Convention." *Boston Evening Transcript*, June 9, 1990. Newspapers.com.

Residence of J. T. Wilson, Nahant, Massachusetts, n.d. www.digitalcommons .salesmate.edu.

Ricard, A. Serge. *A Companion to Theodore Roosevelt*. Hoboken, N.J.: Wiley-Blackwell, 2012.

Richardson, Heather Cox. *To Make Men Free: A History of the Republican Party*. New York: Basic Books, 2014.

Riis, Jacob A. *Theodore Roosevelt: The Citizen*. New York: MacMillan, 1912.

Risen, Clay. *The Crowded Hour: Theodore Roosevelt, the Rough Riders and the Dawn of The American Century*. New York: Scribner, 2019.

Risen, Clay. "Who Owns Theodore Roosevelt." *New York Times*, July 27, 2019. www.nytimes.com.

Robinson, Corinne Roosevelt. *My Brother Theodore Roosevelt*. New York: Charles Scribner's Sons, 1921.

Roosevelt Detail Silver Hunting Knife. n.d. *Library of Congress*. http://www.loc .gov/pictures/item/2002723991/.

"Roosevelt Extolled Throughout World Eulogy at Solomon Services." *New York Herald*, Feb. 10, 1919. Newspapers.com.

"Roosevelt in Lynn." *Boston Evening Transcript*, Aug. 25, 1902. Newspapers.com.

"Roosevelt Plan Would Increase Rates." *New York Times*, Feb. 10, 1905. www .nytimes.

"Roosevelt States His Creed." *Boston Evening Transcript*, Sept. 1, 1910. Newspapers.com.

Roosevelt, Theodore, and Anna Roosevelt Cowles. *Letters from Theodore Roosevelt to Anna Roosevelt Cowles, 1870–1918*. New York: Charles Scribner's Sons, 1924.

Roosevelt, Theodore, and H. W. Brands. *The Selected Letters of Theodore Roosevelt*. New York: Cooper Square Press, 2001.

Roosevelt, Theodore. "The Strenuous Life." Voices of Democracy: A U.S. Oratory Project. admin /wp-content/uploads/2014/07/vod-logo.png, April 10, 1899. https://voicesofdemocracy.umd.edu/.

Roosevelt, Theodore. "Theodore Roosevelt on Lincoln." Teddy Roosevelt, May 31, 2019. http://www.teddyrooseveltlive.com/.

Roosevelt, Theodore. *Theodore Roosevelt: An Autobiography*. New York: Charles Scribner's Sons, 1913.

Roosevelt, Theodore. Papers, Library of Congress.

"Roosevelt's Rough Ride Led to Montauk." *New York Times*, May 17, 1998. www.nytimes.com.

Rothman, David J. *Politics and Power: The United States Senate 1869–1901*. New York: Harvard University Press, 1966.

"The Rough Riders Land at Montauk." *New York Times*, Aug. 16, 1898. Fordham University database.

"Rough Riders Landed." *Washington Post*, Aug. 16, 1898. Fordham University database.

Ruddy, Daniel. *Theodore the Great: Conservative Crusader*. Washington: Regnery Publishing, 2016.

Safire, William. *Safire's Political Dictionary*. Oxford, UK and New York: Oxford University Press, 2008.

Samuels, Ernest. *Henry Adams: The Middle Years*. Cambridge, Mass.: Harvard University Press, 1958.

"Say Brownsville Men Were Rioters." *New York Times*, July 26, 1907. Newspapers.com.

Schriftgiesser, Karl. *The Gentleman from Massachusetts: Henry Cabot Lodge*. Boston: Little, Brown and Company, 1944.

Seale, William. *The Imperial Season: America's Capital in the Time of the First Ambassadors, 1893–1918*. Washington: Smithsonian Books, 2013.

"Senator Attacks Constituent." U.S. Senate, June 2, 2021. https://www.senate .gov/artandhistory/history/minute/Senator_Attacks_Constituent.htm.

"Senator Lodge's Speech." *Buffalo Review*, May 21, 1901. Newspapers.com.

"Simple Funeral of Colonel Roosevelt." *Boston Globe*, January 8, 1919. Newspapers.com.

Simpson, Brooks D. "Henry Adams in the Age of Grant." *Hayes Historical Journal* 13, no. 3, 1989.

Simpson. "Henry Adams in the Age of Grant." *Hayes Historical Journal* 8, no. 3, 1989.

Singley, Carol J. "Wharton, Edith, 1832–1937." Walt Whitman Archive, n.d. www.whitmanarchive.org.

Smith-Brownstein, Elizabeth. "The Willard Hotel—The White House Historical Association." n.d. http://www.whitehousehistory.org/.

Spinzia, Raymond E. "Elliott Roosevelt Sr.—A Spiral into Darkness: The Influences." *The Freeholder* 12, no. 4, 2007.

Stahl, Jonathan. "The Controversy Over the Direct Elections of Senators." National Constitution Center. April 8, 2016. https://constitutioncenter.org/.

"Stalwarts, Half Breeds, and Political Assassination." National Parks Service, James A. Garfield National Historic Site. U.S. Department of the Interior, n.d. http://www.nps.gov/.

"Statesmen Dined: The Most Magnificent Banquet on Record." *Washington Post*, May 1, 1889. Fordham University database.

Stealey, Orlando Oscar. *Twenty Years in the Press Gallery: A Concise History of Important Legislation from the 48th to the 58th Congress*. New York: Publishers Printing Company, 1906.

"A Successful Celebration." *Buffalo Review*, May 21, 1901. Newspapers.com.

Sullivan, Mark. *Our Times: The United States, 1900–1925, Pre War America.* *Vol. III.* New York: Charles Scribner's Sons, 1930.

Sullivan, Mark. *Our Times; The United States, 1900–1925, The Turn of the Century. Vol. I.* New York: Charles Scribner's Sons, 1926.

Summers, Mark Wahlgren. *Rum, Romanism, and Rebellion: The Making of a President 1884.* Chapel Hill: University of North Carolina Press, 2000.

Summers, Mark. "Grover Cleveland's 1884 Election." C-SPAN, Oct. 7, 2020. https://www.c-span.org/.

Sweetser, M. F., and Simeon Ford. *How to Know New York City, A Serviceable Guide.* New York: Kessinger Publishing, 1887.

"Table Gossip." *Boston Daily Globe*, Nov. 2, 1884. Newspapers.com.

"Taft Gaining, Says Lodge." *Boston Globe*, Sept. 26, 1912. Newspapers.com.

Tager, Jack, and John W. Ifkovic. "Massachusetts and the Age of Economic Revolution." In *Massachusetts in the Gilded Age: Selected Essays.* Amherst: University of Massachusetts Press, 1985.

Taliaferro, John. *All The Great Prizes: The Life of John Hay, from Lincoln to Roosevelt.* New York: Simon & Schuster, 2013.

"A Talk with Theodore." *New York Herald*, June 10, 1884. Newspapers.com.

Tehan, Arline Boucher. *Henry Adams in Love: The Pursuit of Elizabeth Sherman Cameron.* New York: Universe Books, 1983.

"Theodore Roosevelt Birthplace Virtual Tour." National Parks Service. US Department of the Interior, n.d. http://www.nps.gov/.

"Theodore Roosevelt Papers, Series I, Letters and Related Material 1759–1919." Library of Congress, n.d. https://www.loc.gov/.

"Theodore Roosevelt." *Indianapolis Journal*, June 29, 1889. Newspapers.com.

Thomas, Evan. *The War Lovers: Roosevelt, Lodge, Hearst, and the Rush to Empire, 1898.* Boston: Little, Brown, 2010.

Tinsley, James A. "Roosevelt, Foraker, and the Brownsville Affray." *Journal of Negro History* 41, no. 1, Jan. 1956: 43–65. https://doi.org /10.2307/2715720.

Trickey, Eric. "Why Teddy Roosevelt Tried to Bully His Way on to the World War I Battlefield." *Smithsonian*, April 10, 2017. www .smithsonianmag.org.

Tucker, David M. "Justice Horace Harmon Lurton: The Shaping of a National Progressive." *American Journal of Legal History* 13, no. 3, July 1969: 223. https://doi.org/10.2307/844528.

Tucker, David M. *Mugwumps: Public Moralists of the Gilded Age.* Columbia: University Press of Missouri, 1999.

"Ulysses Still Leading in The Fight." *Boston Evening Globe*, June 2, 1880. Newspapers.com.

"United States v. E. C. Knight (1895)." Supreme Court: Landmark Cases, n.d. www.pbs.org.

"W. M. Laffan Dead of Appendicitis." *New York Times*, Nov. 20, 1909. Fordham University database.

"Walker Blaine Dead." *New York Times*, Jan. 15, 1887. Fordham University database.

Waring, Yasmin Elaine. "Dining at Delmonico's in 1881." Yasmin Waring, n.d. www.yasminwaring.com.

"When the President Comes." *Boston Evening Transcript*, Aug. 15, 1902. Newspapers.com.

White, Richard D. *Roosevelt the Reformer: Theodore Roosevelt as Civil Service Commissioner 1889–1895*. Tuscaloosa: University of Alabama Press, 2013.

White, Richard D. "Theodore Roosevelt as Civil Service Commissioner: Linking the Influence and Development of a Modern Administrative President." *Administrative Theory & Praxis* 22, no. 4, Dec. 2000: 696–713. https://doi.org/10.1080/10841806.2000.11643484.

White, Richard. *The Republic for Which It Stands: United States in Reconstruction and The Gilded Age 1865–1896*. New York: Oxford University Press, 2017.

"Who Made America? | Innovators | John Wanamaker." Public Broadcasting Service, n.d. https://www.pbs.org/wgbh/theymadeamerica/whomade/wanamaker_hi.html.

Widenor, William C. *Henry Cabot Lodge and the Search for an American Foreign Policy*. Berkeley: University of California Press, 1980.

"Wilson Outlines Nation's Defenses." *New York Times*, Nov. 5, 1915.

Wood, Gordon S. "The Massachusetts Mugwumps." *New England Quarterly* 33, no. 4, Nov. 1960: 435. https://doi.org/10.2307/362673.

Zimmermann, Warren. *First Great Triumph: How Five Americans Made Their Country a World Power*. New York: Farrar, Straus and Giroux, 2002.

"'Theodore Roosevelt's Receipt from the Metropolitan Club Restaurant,' Library of Congress Manuscript Division." T. R. Center—Theodore Roosevelt Center Home, n.d. http://www.theodorerooseveltcenter.org/.

Endnotes

Prologue: Fire and Ice

1   "Extracts from memorandum of Theodore Roosevelt, February 10, 1908,"
    Henry Cabot Lodge, "Selections from the Correspondece of Theodore
    Roosevelt and Henry Cabot Lodge (New York: Charles Scribner's Sons,
    1925), 25.

2   "Convention Proceedings," *New York Times*, June 21, 1900, 2;
    "Convention Clears the Way for Nominations," *San Francisco Call*, June 21,
    1900, 2, Newspapers.com.

3   "Convention Proceedings, *New York Times*, June 21, 1900, 2.

4   "Convention Proceedings," *New York Times*, June 21, 1900, 2.

5   William Hazelgrove, *Forging a President: How the Wild West Created
    Teddy Roosevelt* (New York: Regnery History, 2017); David McCullough,
    Mornings on Horseback (New York: Simon & Schuster, 1981), 367;
    Edmund Morris, *The Rise of Theodore Roosevelt* (New York: Modern
    Library, 2001), xx–xxxiii.

6   In a letter to an unknown recipient from June 13, 1906, Roosevelt wrote
    "I do not have to tell you that my great hero is Abraham Lincoln, and I
    have wanted while President to be the representative of the 'plain people'
    in the sense that he was—not, of course, with the genius and power that
    he was, but according to my lights, along the same lines." "Theodore
    Roosevelt on Lincoln," www.teddyrooseveltlive.com; Heather Cox
    Richardson, *To Make Men Free: A History of the Republican Party* (New
    York: Basic Books, 2014), 154, 178; As historian Lewis Gould writes of
    the GOP during the late nineteenth century: "The impression that the
    Republicans were the party of big business was solidifying. Their senators
    were identified with corporate affairs, and the party's early emphasis on
    the unity of capital and labor was giving way to a sympathy with business
    at the expense of other segments of society." Lewis L. Gould, *Grand Old
    Party: A History of the Republicans* (New York: Random House, 2003),
    132; Kathleen Dalton, *Theodore Roosevelt: A Strenuous Life* (New York:
    Vintage Books, 2004), 121.

7   Richard Hofstadter, *The Age of Reform: From Bryan to FDR* (New York:
    Vintage Books, 1955), 5.

8   Richardson, *To Make Men Free*, 178. As one of Roosevelt's biographers,
    Kathleen Dalton, writes of Roosevelt during the 1900 campaign: "T. R. . . .

had begun to see that modern industrial society was incapable of deep change without expert knowledge and without the intervention of the federal government in the economy." Dalton, *Theodore Roosevelt*, 162; In 1923, the historian Lord Charnwood wrote about the new influx of wealth into the United States, "That wealth compelled attention by its sudden growth, its disproportion to the ordinary rewards of good service and the difficulty of its scarcely fortunate possessors in enjoying it. It excited disgust through the knowledge that it was often ill gotten." Lord Charnwood, *Theodore Roosevelt* (Boston: Atlantic Monthly Press, 1923), 71.

9   Patricia O'Toole accurately characterizes the differences in personality between Roosevelt and Lodge when she writes, "To grasp the differences between the two, one only had to ride with them in Rock Creek Park. Both were excellent horsemen, but Lodge moved with the grace of an English country squire while Roosevelt favored the thundering style he had acquired among the buffalo herds and cowboys of the Wild West." Patricia O'Toole, *The Five of Hearts: An Intimate Portrait of Henry Adams and his Friends 1880-1918* (New York: Simon & Schuster, 1990), 209; "Nomination Put Off," *Washington Post*, June 21, 1900, 3.

10   "Senator Attacks Constituent," April 2, 1917, United States Senate, www.US Senate.gov; https://www.senate.gov/artandhistory/history/minute/Senator _Attacks_Constituent.htm; John Garraty, "Spoiled Child of American Politics" *American Heritage*, August 1955, Vol. 6, No. 5. https://www .americanheritage.com/spoiled-child-american-politics (May 7, 2021).

11   "Senator Attacks Constituent," April 2, 1917, United States Senate. https://www.senate.gov/artandhistory/history/minute/Senator_Attacks _Constituent.htm; Garraty, "Spoiled Child of American Politics" *American Heritage*, August 1955, Vol. 6, No. 5. https://www.americanheritage.com /spoiled-child-american-politics (May 7, 2021). In a profile in the *Saturday Evening Post*, the senator was described as one "who considers himself so far superior to the ordinary run of people that the mere addition of another enemy to his long string means nothing to him one way or the other."; John Taliaferro, *All the Great Prizes: The Life of John Hay from Lincoln to Roosevelt* (New York: Simon & Schuster, 2013), 260.

12   Garraty, "Spoiled Child of American Politics" *American Heritage*, August 1955, Vol. 6, No. 5. https://www.americanheritage.com/spoiled-child -american-politics (May 7, 2021).

13   Richardson, *To Make Men Free*, 166; John M. Blum, *The Republican Roosevelt* (Cambridge, Mass.: Harvard University Press, 1977), viii.

14   Garraty, "Spoiled Child of American Politics," *American Heritage*, August 1955, Vol. 6. No. 5. https://www.americanheritage.com/spoiled-child -american-politics (May 7, 2021); Carleton Putnam, *Theodore Roosevelt: The Formative Years, 1858–1886* (New York: Charles Scribner's Sons), 1958, 426; Evan Thomas, *The War Lovers: Roosevelt, Lodge, Hearst, and*

the Rush to Empire, 1898 (Boston: Little Brown, 2010), 37; Warren
Zimmermann, *First Great Triumph: How Five Americans Made Their
Country A World Power* (New York: Farrar Straus and Giroux, 2002),
187; Henry Cabot Lodge, *Early Memories* (New York: Charles Scribner's
Sons, 1913), 113; In comments about Lodge's tedious speaking style,
Massachusetts senator George Hoar referred to Cabot as "the worst
stump speaker on this planet." Thomas, *The War Lovers*, 35.

15   Orlando Stealey further describes Wolcott's gambling habits. "Mr. Wolcott
was also a dead game sport and would stack up the blue chips on a faro layout
as high as the ceiling, if the dealer would permit." During one of Wolcott's
senatorial campaigns, it was rumored that the former schoolteacher had lost
twenty-two thousand dollars at faro. In response to charges of recklessness,
the senator boldly declared "Whose business is it but mine? I am an
unmarried man and there is no one but myself upon whom any disgrace can
fall. While it is true that I lost a large sum of money at faro, it is also true that
I had won the money the previous afternoon on the races." Orlando Oscar
Stealey, *Twenty Years in the Press Gallery* (New York: Publishers Printing
Company Printers, 1906), 472–473.

16   "Nomination Put Off," *Washington Post*, June 21, 1900, 3. No one knows
exactly when Lodge raised the idea of Roosevelt seeking the 1900 vice
presidential nomination. However, the first record of the issue being
discussed is in a letter from Roosevelt to Lodge on July 1, 1899; Morris,
The Rise of Theodore Roosevelt, 741.

17   Morris, *The Rise of Theodore Roosevelt*, 741; "Convention's Proceedings,"
New York Times, June 21, 1900, 2; "Mr. Lodge Reviews His Party's
Record," *New York Times*, June 21, 1900, 3.

18   Patrick J. Garrity, "Young Men in a Hurry: Roosevelt, Lodge and the
Foundations of the Twentieth Century Republican," *Natural Right
and Political Right Essays in Honor of Harry V. Jaffa*; Thomas B. Silver,
ed. (Durham: Carolina Academic Press, 1984), 225–235; Blum, *The
Republican Roosevelt*, 2.

19   H. W. Brands, *T.R: The Last Romantic* (New York: Basic Books, 1997), 546.

20   Jonathan O'Neil, "Constitutional Conservatives in the Progressive Era:
Elihu Root, William Howard Taft and Henry Cabot Lodge, Sr." *First
Principles*, Heritage Foundation, February 15, 2013, 1.

21   Roosevelt further elaborated: "For the past twenty-four years I have
discussed almost every move I have made in politics with him . . ."
Theodore Roosevelt, "Extracts from Memorandum of Theodore
Roosevelt, February 10, 1908." Lodge, *Selections from the Correspondence
of Theodore Roosevelt and Henry Cabot Lodge, Volume I* (New York:
Charles Scribner's Sons, 1925), 25; John A. Garraty, *Henry Cabot
Lodge: A Biography* (New York: Alfred A. Knopf, 1953), 86–87; Email
correspondence with Edward P. Kohn, unknown date, 2020. Lodge was

a serious man, who rarely displayed any kind of humor. On one occasion following an unflattering portrait in one of the newspapers, Cabot asked Roosevelt why journalists constantly characterized him as "cold and removed." Without hesitating, T. R. replied "I can tell you Cabot—it's because you are." Thomas, *The War Lovers*, 36.

22 Thomas, *The War Lovers*, 31–32.

23 Ibid., 32.

24 Brands, *T. R.*, 595; Carlton Putnam, *Theodore Roosevelt: Volume I: The Formative Years 1858–1886* (New York: Charles Scribner's Sons, 1958), 428; Thomas, *The War Lovers*, 32.

25 While Matthew Josephson's 1940 *The President Makers* discusses Lodge's counsel as being critical in Roosevelt's rapid political rise, little scholarship has been devoted to the Lodge-Roosevelt relationship. The last study of Lodge, published in 1980 states "Lodge guided Roosevelt's career from the start."; William C. Widenor, *Henry Cabot Lodge and The Search for an American Foreign Policy* (Berkeley: University of California Press, 1980), 127; Karl Schriftgiesser, *The Gentleman from Massachusetts: Henry Cabot Lodge* (Boston: Little, Brown and Company, 1944), 200; Morris, *The Rise of Theodore Roosevelt*, 241; Thomas, *The War Lovers*, 42; Widenor, *Henry Cabot Lodge and the Search for an American Foreign Policy*, 127.

26 Clay Risen, "Who Owns Theodore Roosevelt," *New York Times*, July 27, 2019, www.nytimes.com.

27 Lodge disliked "the immorality and vulgarity of the new rich. He complained that the society pages were filled with accounts of their excesses of all kinds, their parties, lavish to the point of criminal waste, their divorces, their scandals." Garraty, *Henry Cabot Lodge*, 226; Roosevelt shared a similar perspective and the societal erosion driven by the excessive wealth during the late nineteenth century. As biographer Kathleen Dalton writes, Roosevelt and many of his contemporaries ". . . . felt their lives diminished and their social world cheapened by the change. Roosevelt, along with his contemporary, the novelist Edith Wharton, viewed these developments "as a class usurpation and a personal disruption." Kathleen Dalton, "Theodore Roosevelt: Knickerbocker Aristocrat," *New York History*, (January 1986), Vol. 67 No. 1., 50.

28 Blum, *The Republican Roosevelt*, 5–6.

29 "To Henry Cabot Lodge the success of the Republican Party was of paramount importance." Garraty, *Henry Cabot Lodge*, 356. Blum, *The Republican Roosevelt*, 5–6.

Chapter One: A Common Code

1 "The Last Marks of Respect to Our Late President," *New York Times*, April 14, 1865, 1.

2   "The Last Marks of Respect to Our Late President," *New York Times*, April 19, 1865, 1.

3   "The Last Marks of Respect to Our Late President," *New York Times*, April 19, 1865, 1; Genevieve Cummins, "The Wearing of Watches," www .antiquehorology.org; Mimi Matthews, "A Century of Sartorial Style: A Visual Guide to 19th Century Men's Wear," www.mimimatthews.com; "The Private and Family Life of Theodore Roosevelt," www.artsandculutre .google.com; "Andrew Johnson Suite," https://home.treasury.gov/about /history/the-treasury-building/andrew-johnson-suite.

4   McCullough, *Mornings on Horseback*, 32; Morris, *The Rise of Theodore Roosevelt*, 4–5 10.

5   Morris, *The Rise of Theodore Roosevelt*, 8–10.

6   Dalton, *Theodore Roosevelt*, 27. Nathan Miller, *Theodore Roosevelt: A Life* (New York: William Morrow, 1992), 34; Dr. Bonnie Brice Dorwart, "Disease in the Civil War," www.essentialcivilwarcurriculum.com.

7   Morris, *The Rise of Theodore Roosevelt*, 8–10. McCullough, *Mornings on Horseback*, 28–29. Dalton, *Theodore Roosevelt*, 49.

8   Dalton, *Theodore Roosevelt*, 40. "Abraham Lincoln and St. John's Episcopal Church," www.abrahamlincolnonline.org; McCullough, *Mornings on Horseback*, 59–60; Elizabeth Smith-Brownstein, "The Willard Hotel," The White House Historical Association, www .whitehousehistory.org.

9   Dalton, *Theodore Roosevelt*, 40. "Abraham Lincoln and St. John's Episcopal Church." www.abrahamlincolnonline.org; McCullough, *Mornings on Horseback*, 59–60. Smith-Brownstein, "The Willard Hotel," The White House Historical Association, www.whitehousehistory.org; Roosevelt worshiped President Abraham Lincoln. Roosevelt once said that "Lincoln was my great hero and that he meant more to me than any other of our public men." There is a famous photo of Roosevelt and his future wife Edith Carow watching Lincoln's casket being led down Broadway from Roosevelt's grandfather's townhouse on Union Square in April 1865. Michael Beschloss, "When T. R. Saw Lincoln," May 21, 2014, *New York Times*, www.nytimes.com.

10   Lodge, *Early Memories*, 23, 31; Garraty, *Henry Cabot Lodge*, 4; D. Hamilton Hurd, *History of Essex County, Massachusetts: With Biographical Sketches of Many of Its Pioneers and Prominent Men*, Vol. II (Philadelphia: J. W. Lewis and Co., 1888), 1425; Emily Lodge, *The Lodge Women* (New York: Emily Lodge, 2013), 53.

11   Karl Schriftgiesser, *The Gentleman from Massachusetts: Henry Cabot Lodge* (Boston: Little, Brown and Co., 1944), 22; McCullough, *Mornings on Horseback*, 38; Garraty, *Henry Cabot Lodge*, 12.

12   Schriftgiesser, *The Gentleman from Massachusetts*, 22; McCullough, *Mornings on Horseback*, 38; Garraty, *Henry Cabot Lodge*, 12.

13   Lodge, *Early Memories*, 27; *Theodore Roosevelt, An Autobiography* (New
      York: Charles Scribner's Sons, 1913), 7; Home of Henry Cabot Lodge,
      31 Beacon Street, City Walking Guide www.citywalkingguide.com;
      "Theodore Roosevelt Birthplace virtual tour," www.nps.gov; Thomas,
      The War Lovers, 15.

14   Lodge, *Early Memories*, 22–23.

15   Dalton, *Theodore Roosevelt*, 28. McCullough, *Mornings on Horseback*, 31.

16   Blum, *The Republican Roosevelt*, viii–xi.

17   Lodge, *Early Memories*, 26–28; Garraty, *Henry Cabot Lodge*, 4; Luke
      Nichter, *The Last Brahmin: Henry Cabot Lodge Jr. and the Making of the
      Cold War*, (New Haven, Conn.: Yale University Press, 2020), 11; Lodge,
      The Lodge Women, 53; Evan Thomas further characterizes the influence
      John Lodge and T. R. Sr. had on their two sons. "Roosevelt and Lodge
      believed they had a duty to face the coming storm, which is one reason
      why they venerated courage, why they placed such unrelenting emphasis
      on the duty to sally forth against danger. Life was a contest, a constant
      battle to be fought, no matter the odds. Such was the duty seared into
      both men by the example of their fathers—worshipped men, seemingly
      so strong yet defeated by the forces of life." Thomas, *The War Lovers*, 38.

18   Thomas, *The War Lovers*, 38.

19   McCullough, *Mornings on Horseback*, 36, 112; Lodge, *Early Memories*,
      84, 87; Miller, *Theodore Roosevelt*, 33.

20   Lodge also enjoyed skinny-dipping, a common hobby among those
      who vacationed in the area. There is an undated photograph of a young,
      naked Lodge diving into the surf from a cliff near his home. Lodge, *Early
      Memories*, 29, 35–36, 85; Garraty, *Henry Cabot Lodge*, 5–7. "Lodge's
      Seaside Home," *Boston Post*, June 21, 1896, 24. "Henry Cabot Lodge
      Park." https://maps.roadtrippers.com/us/nahant-ma/points-of-interest
      /henry-cabot-lodge-park-nahant.

21   Dalton, *Theodore Roosevelt*, 181; Morris, *The Rise of Theodore Roosevelt*,
      15–6. Encountering these stories gave Roosevelt the first instincts of the
      kind of person he would like to be. "I was nervous and timid," he wrote
      in his autobiography. "Yet from reading of the people I admired—ranging
      from Valley Forge and Morgan's Riflemen to the heroes of my favorite
      stories . . . and from knowing my father, I felt a great admiration for men
      who were fearless and could hold their own in the world, and I had a
      great desire to be like them." Morris, *The Rise of Theodore Roosevelt*, 16;
      "Constitution of The League of Nations," February 28, 1919, *Classic Senate
      Speeches*, United States Senate, www.ussenate.gov.

22   Dalton, *Theodore Roosevelt*, 181; Morris, *The Rise of Theodore Roosevelt*,
      15–16. Encountering these stories gave Roosevelt the first instincts
      of the kind of person he would like to be. "I was nervous and timid,"
      he wrote in his autobiography. "Yet from reading of the people I

admired—ranging from the soldiers of Valley Forge, and Morgan's Riflemen, to the heroes of my favorite stories . . . and from knowing my father, I felt a great admiration for men who were fearless and could hold their own in the world." Morris, *The Rise of Theodore Roosevelt*, 16; "Constitution of The League of Nations," February 28, 1919, *Classic Senate Speeches*, United States Senate, https://www.senate.gov /artandhistory/history/common/generic/Speeches_Lodge1919.htm.

23   Lodge, *Early Memories*, 123; Widenor, *Henry Cabot Lodge and The Search for an American Foreign Policy*, 18.

24   George M. Fredrickson, *The Inner Civil War* (New York: Harper and Row, 1965), 224–225. McCullough, *Mornings on Horseback*, 54.

25   Brands, *T. R.*, 17; Roosevelt, *Autobiography*, 11; Brands, *T. R.*, 19; Fredrickson, *The Inner Civil War*, 224–225; Miller, *Theodore Roosevelt*, 35; Roosevelt, *Autobiography*, 11.

26   Ibid.

27   Ibid.

28   Lodge, *Early Memories*, 123–124.

29   Ibid.

30   Lodge, *Early Memories*, 106; William Lawrence, *Roger Wolcott* (Boston: William Lawrence, 1902), 235.

31   Morris, *The Rise of Theodore Roosevelt*, 56–57; Garraty, *Henry Cabot Lodge*, 22–23.

32   Garraty, *Henry Cabot Lodge*, 24, 30; Lodge, *Early Memories*, 180; William Lawrence, *Henry Cabot Lodge: A Biographical Sketch* (Boston: Houghton Mifflin Company, 1925), 15; Cleveland Amory, *The Proper Bostonians* (Orleans: Parnassus Imprints, 1947), 303; Hofstadter, *The Age of Reform*, 11.

33   William Roscoe Thayer, *Theodore Roosevelt: An Intimate Biography*, (Boston: Houghton Mifflin, 1919), 18; Roosevelt, *Autobiography*, 22.

34   Paul Grohdahl, *I Rose Like a Rocket: The Political Education of Theodore Roosevelt* (New York: Free Press, 2004), 33–36.

35   Grohdahl, *I Rose Like a Rocket*, 33–36.

36   Morris, *The Rise of Theodore Roosevelt*, 70–72.

37   McCullough, *Mornings on Horseback*, 204–207, 215; Morris, *The Rise of Theodore Roosevelt*, 62; Dalton, *Theodore Roosevelt*, 89; *The Porcellian Club Centennial 1791–1891* (Cambridge, Mass.: Riverside Press, 1891); Thomas, *The War Lovers*, 31.

Chapter Two: Irreversible Change

1   Garraty, *Henry Cabot Lodge*, 30; Lodge, *The Lodge Women*, 71.

2   Ibid.

3   Lodge, *The Lodge Women*, 66–67; Davis 1: Torpedo Boat #12, "Naval History and Heritage Command" www.history.navy.mil.

4   Lodge, *The Lodge Women*, 21, 66–67.

5   Ibid.

6   Garraty, *Henry Cabot Lodge*, 30–32.

7   Ibid.

8   Garraty, *Henry Cabot Lodge*, 32.

9   Lodge, *The Lodge Women*, 72; Garraty, *Henry Cabot Lodge*, 33.

10   Lodge, *The Lodge Women*, 73; Garraty, *Henry Cabot Lodge*, 35.

11   Ibid.

12   McCullough, *Mornings on Horseback*, 218; Morris, *The Rise of Theodore Roosevelt*, 80.

13   McCullough, *Mornings on Horseback*, 219.

14   Ibid., 220.; Morris, *The Rise of Theodore Roosevelt*, 86.

15   McCullough, *Mornings on Horseback*, 222, 230; Morris, *The Rise of Theodore Roosevelt*, 102, 115.

16   Ibid.

17   Brands, *T. R.*, 64–65.

18   Lodge, *Early Memories*, 232–233; Garraty, *Henry Cabot Lodge*, 33.

19   Garraty, *Henry Cabot Lodge*, 34.

20   Lodge, *Early Memories*, 235–236; Garraty, *Henry Cabot Lodge*, 34.

21   Ibid.

22   Garraty, *Henry Cabot Lodge*, 34; O'Toole, *The Five of Hearts*, 8–9.

23   Garraty, *Henry Cabot Lodge*, 34; O'Toole, *The Five of Hearts*, 8–9; David S. Brown, *The Last American Aristocrat: The Brilliant Life and Improbable Education of Henry Adams* (New York: Scribner, 2020), 6–7; Roger I. Abrams, *The First World Series* (Boston: Northeastern University Press, 2003), 89; Ernest Samuels, *Henry Adams: The Middle Years* (Cambridge, Mass.: Belknap, 1958), 174.

24   Garraty, *Henry Cabot Lodge*, 34; O'Toole, *The Five of Hearts*, 8–9; Brown, *The Last American Aristocrat*, 6–7; Abrams, *The First World Series*, 89; Samuels, *Henry Adams: The Middle Years*, 174.

25   Garraty, *Henry Cabot Lodge*, 37–38; Henry Adams, *The Letters of Henry Adams*, Vol. II 1868–1885; J. C. Levinson, Ernest Samuels, Charles Vandersee, Viola Hopkins Winner, eds. (Cambridge, Mass.: Harvard University Press, 1982), 138.

26   Lodge, *Early Memories*, 240; Brown, *The Last American Aristocrat*, 149; Schriftgiesser, *The Gentleman from Massachusetts*, 35.

27   The Lodge and Adams families were extremely close. According to Lodge's great, great granddaughter, Henry Adams was a lifelong friend of Nannie Lodge. His brother Brooks Adams was her brother-in-law as well as also being a close friend of Henry Cabot Lodge. They were so close in fact, that Nannie frequently called Henry "brother" and she was referred to as "sister" by him. Adams was known as "Uncle Henry" to the Lodge children and "Dordy" to their grandchildren. Lodge, *The Lodge Women*, 69.

28 Gould, *Grand Old Party*, 84–85; Mark Summers, "Grover Cleveland's 1884 election," C-SPAN, October 7, 2020, www.cspan.org.

29 Gould, *Grand Old Party*, 84–85.

30 Robert W. Cherny, *American Politics in the Gilded Age: 1868–1900* (Wheeling, Ill.: Harlan Davidson Inc., 1997), 23–24.

31 Cherny, *American Politics in the Gilded Age*, 5, 7.

32 Kenneth Howell, "The Doom of Reconstruction: The Liberal Republicans in the Civil War Era." H-Civil War, February 2008, networks.HNet.org; Cherny, *American Politics in the Gilded Age*, 53–54.

33 David R. Contosta and Robert Muccigrosso, eds., *Henry Adams and His World*, (Philadelphia: American Philosophical Society, 1993), 38; Brooks D. Simpson, "Henry Adams in the Age of Grant," *Hayes Historical Journal*, Vol .13, No. 3, Spring, 1989, www.rbhayes.org.

34 Cherny, *American Politics in the Gilded Age*, 54.

35 Ibid.

36 Gould, *Grand Old Party*, 82–83; Richard White, *The Republic for Which it Stands: United States in Reconstruction and The Gilded Age 1865–1896,* (New York: Oxford University Press, 2017), 273; Richardson, *To Make Men Free*, 196–197; Cherny, *American Politics in the Gilded Age*, 22–23. "The Financial Panic of 1873," US Department of the Treasury, www .treasury.gov.

37 Gould, *Grand Old Party*, 82–83; White, *The Republic for Which it Stands*, 273; Richardson, *To Make Men Free*, 196–197.

38 Gould, *Grand Old Party*, 62; Garraty, *Henry Cabot Lodge*, 40–42; Brown, *The Last American Aristocrat*, 133–134; Edward C. Chalfant, *Better in Darkness: A Biography of Henry Adams 1862–1891*, (New York: Archon Books, 1994), 296; Bay Lodge's nickname came from the childhood nickname "Bay Bee."; Arline Boucher Tehan, *Henry Adams in Love*, (New York: Universe Books, 1983), 159.

39 Gordon S. Wood, "The Massachusetts Mugwumps," *New England Quarterly*, Vol. 33, No. 4, Nov. 1960, 436; Cherny, *American Politics in the Gilded Age*, 32.

40 Garraty, *Henry Cabot Lodge*, 42.

41 Ibid.

42 David M. Tucker, *Mugwumps: Public Moralists of the Gilded Age*, (Columbia: University Press of Missouri, 1999), 74.

43 Richardson, *To Make Men Free*, 196–197; Mark Wahlgren Summers, *Rum, Romanism and Rebellion: The Making of a President, 1884,* (Charlotte: University of North Carolina Press, 2000), 27–28.

44 Garraty, *Henry Cabot Lodge*, 48–50.

45 Chalfant, *Better in Darkness*, 773.

46 Richardson, *To Make Men Free*, 196–197; Summers, *Rum, Romanism and Rebellion*, 27–28.

47 Richardson, *To Make Men Free*, 196–197.

48 Ibid.

49 Ibid., 202–204.

50 "Stalwarts, Half Breeds and Political Assassination," James A. Garfield National Historic Site, www.nps.gov.

51 Richardson, *To Make Men Free*, 204–205; Gould, *Grand Old Party*, 95–96.

52 Morris, *The Rise of Theodore Roosevelt*, 117–120; Putnam, *Theodore Roosevelt: The Formative Years*, 222.

53 Ibid.

54 Morris, *The Rise of Theodore Roosevelt*, 122; Putnam, *Theodore Roosevelt: The Formative Years*, 215; Kathleen M. Dalton, "Theodore Roosevelt, Knickerbocker Aristocrat," *Journal of New York History*, Jan. 1986, Vol. 67, No. 1, 48–49; Yasmine Elaine Waring, "Dining at Delmonico's in 1881," www.yasminewaring.com.

55 Putnam, *Theodore Roosevelt: The Formative Years*, 219–220; Roosevelt, *Autobiography*, 54, 56; Brands, *T. R.*, 126, 129.

56 Ibid.

57 Morris, *The Rise of Theodore Roosevelt*, 123, 125; Brands, *T. R.*, 126, 129; Hermann Hagedorn, *The Boys Life of Theodore Roosevelt*, (New York: Harper Brothers, 1919), 66.

58 Grondahl, *I Rose Like a Rocket*, 61, 66–67; Morris, *The Rise of Theodore Roosevelt*, 126, 128; Dalton, *Theodore Roosevelt*, 166; Brands, *T. R.*, 126, 129.

59 Ibid.

60 Ibid.

61 Garraty, *Henry Cabot Lodge*, 51, 53; Zimmermann, *First Great Triumph*, 156.

62 Ibid.

63 Garraty, *Henry Cabot Lodge*, 55–56.

64 Widenor, *Henry Cabot Lodge and the Search for an American Foreign Policy*, 2, 29.

65 Jack Tager, "Massachusetts and the Age of Economic Revolution," *Massachusetts in the Gilded Age: Selected Essays*, Jack Tager and John W. Ifkovic, eds. (Amherst: University of Massachusetts Press, 1985), 6–8.

66 Jack Tager, "Massachusetts and the Age of Economic Revolution," Tager and Ifkovic, *Massachusetts in the Gilded Age*, 6–8. "Montgomery Ward Issues the First Mail Order Catalog for the General Public." www .historyinformation.com; Hofstadter, *The Age of Reform*, 8–9.

67 Widenor, *Henry Cabot Lodge and the Search for an American Foreign Policy*, 2, 29; Lodge, *Early Memories*, 208.

68 Zimmermann, *First Great Triumph*, 161; Widenor, *Henry Cabot Lodge and the Search for an American Foreign Policy*, 2, 29; Lodge, *Early Memories*, 208.

69   Lodge, *Early Memories*, 211; Erin Blakemore, "How American 'Dollar Princesses' Invaded British High Society," www.history.com.

70   Widenor, *Henry Cabot Lodge and the Search for an American Foreign Policy*, 8; Lodge, *Early Memories*, 211; Blakemore, "How American 'Dollar Princesses' Invaded British High Society," www.history.com.

71   Widenor, *Henry Cabot Lodge and the Search for an American Foreign Policy*, 45–46.

72   Lodge, *Early Memories*, 13; Widenor, *Henry Cabot Lodge and the Search for an American Foreign Policy*, 45–46.

73   Tager, *Massachusetts in the Gilded Age*, 24–25; Lodge, *Early Memories*, 13; Widenor, *Henry Cabot Lodge and the Search for an American Foreign Policy*, 45-46. Widenor further writes of Lodge's growing ambivalence about the state of change that "everywhere he looked things were no longer ordered as they once had been. He wanted to turn the clock back to the emotional security of his childhood, to the time when the preeminent position of his kind of people . . . and the Anglo-Saxon way of doing things were taken for granted . . . He wanted to preserve as much of that society as possible and to that end was willing to make his accommodation with change and yet never quite sure how to proceed."

74   Garraty, *Henry Cabot Lodge*, 60–63.

75   McCullough, *Mornings on Horseback*, 258–263; Brands, *T. R.*, 137; Morris, *The Rise of Theodore Roosevelt*, 147; Lewis L. Gould, *Theodore Roosevelt*, (Oxford, UK: Oxford University Press, 2012), 10.

76   Dalton, "Theodore Roosevelt, Knickerbocker Aristocrat," 45–46, 48–49, 50–51.

77   Dalton, "Theodore Roosevelt, Knickerbocker Aristocrat," 45–46, 48–49, 50–51. Edwin G. Burrows and Mike Wallace, *Gotham: A History of New York to 1898*, (New York: Oxford University Press, 1999), 1076.

78   Grondahl, *I Rose Like a Rocket*, 99, 102; Brands, *T. R.*, 150.

79   Brands, *T. R.*, 145–146; Grondahl, *I Rose Like a Rocket*, 103.

80   Dalton, *Theodore Roosevelt*, 180; Grondahl, *I Rose Like a Rocket*, 106–107, 117.

81   Dalton, *Theodore Roosevelt*, 180.

82   Brands, *T. R.*, 165; Morris, *The Rise of Theodore Roosevelt*, 230–231.

83   Garraty, *Henry Cabot Lodge*, 63.

84   Garraty, *Henry Cabot Lodge*, 64; "Residence of J. T. Wilson, Nahant, Massachusetts," www.digitalcommons.salesmate.edu.

85   Garraty, *Henry Cabot Lodge*, 65–66.

86   Garraty, *Henry Cabot Lodge*, 65–66; "The Gardner House," *The Landowner*, March 1872, www.Chicagology.com.

87   Garraty, *Henry Cabot Lodge*, 65–66; "The Gardner House," *The Landowner*, March 1872, www.Chicagology.com; "Ulysses Still Leading in the Fight," June 2, 1880, *Boston Evening Globe*, Newspapers.com, 1; "Republican National Convention," June 9, 1880, *Boston Evening Transcript*, 1.

88 Garraty, *Henry Cabot Lodge*, 68; "Biography of James W. and Elisha S. Converse," www.accessgeneoglogy.com.

89 Garraty, *Henry Cabot Lodge*, 68.

90 Garraty, *Henry Cabot Lodge*, 68; "Biography of James W. and Elisha S. Converse," www.accessgeneoglogy.com.

91 Garraty, *Henry Cabot Lodge*, 68–69.

92 Ibid.

93 Gould, *Grand Old Party*, 99; Richardson, *To Make Men Free*, 206–207.

94 Summers, *Rum, Romanism and Rebellion*, 61; Gould, *Grand Old Party*, 99.

Chapter Three: Valley of Decision

1 Morris, *The Rise of Theodore Roosevelt*, 238–239; Brands, *T. R.*, 165.

2 Morris, *The Rise of Theodore Roosevelt*, 240–244, 248; Summers, *Rum, Romanism and Rebellion*, 127.

3 Morris, *The Rise of Theodore Roosevelt*, 240–244, 248.

4 Ibid.

5 Ibid., 248.

6 Garraty, *Henry Cabot Lodge*, 75; T. R. to HCL, May 5, 1884, Lodge, Lodge-Roosevelt Selected Correspondence, Vol. I, 1.

7 Gould, *Theodore Roosevelt*, xi.

8 Theodore Roosevelt to Henry Cabot Lodge, May 5, 1884, Lodge, Roosevelt, and Lodge, Vol. I, 1; Summers, *Rum, Romanism and Rebellion*, 127; Gould, *Grand Old Party*, 99.

9 "The Convention," *Chicago Tribune*, June 1, 1884, 9.

10 Summers, *Rum, Romanism and Rebellion*, 61; Dan Landrigan and Leslie Landrigan, *Bar Harbor Babylon* (Lanham, Md.: Down East Books, 2019), 78; H. Draper Hunt, "The Plumed Knight at Home: An Intimate Sketch of James G. Blaine." *Maine History* 28 (1), 1988, 2, 8; John R. Lynch, *Reminiscences of An Active Life: The Autobiography of John Roy Lynch*, (Oxford: University Press of Mississippi, 2008).

11 Mark Summers, "Grover Cleveland's 1884 election" C-SPAN, October 7, 2020; Landrigan, *Bar Harbor Babylon*, 78; Edward Kohn, "Crossing the Rubicon: Theodore Roosevelt, Henry Cabot Lodge and the 1884 Republican Convention," *Journal of the Gilded Age and Progressive Era*, Jan. 2006, Vol. 5 #1, 23; Mrs. Winthrop Chanler, *Roman Spring: Memoirs* (Boston: Little Brown and Company, 1934), 193; Edward P. Krapol, *James G. Blaine, Architect of Empire*, (Wilmington, Del.: Scholarly Resources, Inc., 2000), 44. Blaine; Future president James A. Garfield, and several other Republican congressmen became ensnared in the 1892–1893 Credit Mobilier scandal. The complex affair involved kickbacks of stock by shareholders of the Union Pacific Railroad. While Garfield managed to escape the scandal relatively unscathed, Blaine became further involved in scandal when he was accused of stealing

letters from James Mulligan that contained evidence that Blaine was guilty of corruption. Krapol, *James G. Blaine*, 44; Taliaferro, *All the Great Prizes*, 154–155, 193.

12   Mark Summers, "Grover Cleveland's 1884 Election," C-SPAN, October 7, 2020, www.cspan.org; Summers, *Rum, Romanism and Rebellion*, 4, 68.

13   Morris, *The Rise of Theodore Roosevelt*, 250; McCullough, *Mornings on Horseback*, 311–312.

14   Morris, *The Rise of Theodore Roosevelt*, 250; Putnam, *Theodore Roosevelt: The Formative Years*, 428–429; Blodgett, "The Mind of the Boston Mugwump," 615.

15   Lodge, Lodge-Roosevelt Correspondence, Vol. I, see note 2.

16   Garraty, *Henry Cabot Lodge*, 76–77. There is no clear evidence as to when the decision to support the convention choice took place. The conversation between Roosevelt and Lodge that is quoted by John Garraty was mentioned in Lodge's journal on March 20,1885, nearly a year after the convention took place. Lodge by this time had essentially dismissed his independent status and was fully committed to making his fight "inside the party," an intention he made clear two years earlier in a letter to his mother. Garraty, *Henry Cabot Lodge*, 76.

17   T. R. to HCL, May 26, 1884, Lodge, Lodge-Roosevelt Correspondence, Vol. I, 2. T. R. to HCL, May 5, 1884, Lodge-Roosevelt Correspondence, Vol. I, 1. Brands, *T. R.*, 168.

18   Ibid.; Garraty, *Henry Cabot Lodge*, 77; McCullough, *Mornings on Horseback*, 294.

19   McCullough, *Mornings on Horseback*, 294; Morris, *The Rise of Theodore Roosevelt*, 251; "The Grand Pacific Hotel," www.chicagology.com.

20   McCullough, *Mornings on Horseback*, 289; Garraty, *Henry Cabot Lodge*, 77; Morris, *The Rise of Theodore Roosevelt*, 251; "Leland Hotel," Chicago, Passage of Time, 1880s, www.chicagophotographs.com.

21   Morris, *The Rise of Theodore Roosevelt*, 251.

22   McCullough, *Mornings on Horseback*, 296–297.

23   "The Conventions First Work," *New York Times*, June 4, 1884, 1; "Going Slow at Chicago," *Sun*, June 4, 1884, 1; "At Chicago," *Boston Evening Transcript*, June 4, 1884, 8; Morris, *The Rise of Theodore Roosevelt*, 254; Putnam, *Theodore Roosevelt, The Formative Years*, 433.

24   "Going Slow at Chicago," *Sun*, June 4, 1884, 1; "At Chicago," *Boston Evening Transcript*, June 4, 1884, 8; Morris, *The Rise of Theodore Roosevelt*, 254; Garraty, *Henry Cabot Lodge*, 78; "Mr. Blaine's Man Is Beaten," *Sun*, June 4, 1884,1; Putnam, *Theodore Roosevelt, The Formative Years*, 433.

25   Garraty, *Henry Cabot Lodge*, 78; "Governor Powell Clayton," National Governors Association, www.nga.org; "Going Slow at Chicago, *Sun*, June 4, 1884, 1; Summers, *Rum, Romanism and Rebellion*, 137; Kohn, "Crossing the Rubicon," 32.

26   Garraty, *Henry Cabot Lodge*, 78; "Governor Powell Clayton," National
      Governors Association, www.nga.org; "Going Slow at Chicago, *Sun*,
      June 5, 1884, 1; Summers, *Rum, Romanism and Rebellion*, 137; Kohn,
      "Crossing the Rubicon," 32.
27   "The Conventions First Work," *New York Times*, June 4, 1884, 1; "Lynch
      John R. 1847–1939," www.historyhouse.gov; Joseph Henry Foraker,
      Notes from a Busy Life, Volume 1, (Cincinnati: Jonson and Hardix, 1916),
      158; Putnam, *Theodore Roosevelt The Formative Years*, 431–432.
28   Thomas G. Dyer, *Theodore Roosevelt and the Idea of Race*, (Baton Rouge:
      Louisiana State University Press, 1980), 96–97. As Dyer argues while
      "Roosevelt may have been a moderating force in an age of high racism,
      he nevertheless harbored strong feelings about the inferiority of blacks,
      feelings which suggested the pervasiveness of racism and the harsh
      character of racial moderation in turn-of-the-century America." Dyer,
      Theodore Roosevelt and the Idea of Race, 92.
29   Christopher Klein, "How Teddy Roosevelt's Views on Race Shaped His
      Politics," *History Stories*, August 11, 2020, www.history.com.
30   Thomas, *The War Lovers*, 45; Dyer, *Theodore Roosevelt and the Idea of
      Race*, 96–97; Zimmermann, *First Great Triumph*, 459.
31   "The Conventions First Work," *New York Times*, June 4, 1884, 1; Putnam,
      Theodore Roosevelt: The Formative Years, 433; "Mr. Blaine's Man is Beaten,"
      Sun, June 4, 1884, 1; Morris, *The Rise of Theodore Roosevelt*, 255.
32   "Mr. Blaine's Man is Beaten," *Sun*, June 4, 1884, 1; Morris, *The Rise of
      Theodore Roosevelt*, 255; Kohn, "Crossing the Rubicon," 32.
33   Ibid.
34   "Mr. Blaine's Man is Beaten," *Sun*, June 4, 1884, 1; Morris, *The Rise of Theodore
      Roosevelt*, 255; Summers, *Rum, Romanism and Rebellion*, 138; Kohn, "Crossing
      the Rubicon," 32; McCullough, *Mornings on Horseback*, 297.
35   Ibid.
36   Morris, *The Rise of Theodore Roosevelt*, 255–256.
37   Summers, *Rum, Romanism and Rebellion*, 140; "Mr. Lodge's Prediction,"
      Boston Daily Globe, June 6, 1884, 2.
38   Summers, *Rum, Romanism and Rebellion*, 141; Morris, *The Rise of
      Theodore Roosevelt*, 258.
39   Ibid.
40   Morris, *The Rise of Theodore Roosevelt*, 258.
41   Putnam, *Theodore Roosevelt: The Formative Years*, 445.
42   Morris, *The Rise of Theodore Roosevelt*, 258; Putnam, *Theodore Roosevelt:
      The Formative Years*, 445.
43   *Fall River Daily News*, June 4, 1884, 2; Schriftgiesser, *The Gentleman
      from Massachusetts*, 82.
44   Putnam, *Theodore Roosevelt: The Formative Years*, 446; "The Journalists:
      Horace White, 1834–1916," www.mrlincolnandfriends.org.

45   Putnam, *Theodore Roosevelt: The Formative Years*, 446; Kohn, "Crossing the Rubicon," 35.
46   Putnam, *Theodore Roosevelt: The Formative Years*, 447–448; Kohn, "Crossing the Rubicon," 35.
47   Putnam, *Theodore Roosevelt: The Formative Years*, 447–448.
48   Ibid.
49   Elting E. Morrison, *The Letters of Theodore Roosevelt: Vol. I: The Years of Preparation,1868–1898*, (Cambridge, Mass.: Harvard University Press, 1954), 71; Roosevelt, *Autobiography*, 94.
50   Morris, *The Rise of Theodore Roosevelt*, 259; Hermann Hagedorn, *Roosevelt in the Badlands* (Boston: Houghton Mifflin, 1921), 3; "A Talk with Theodore Roosevelt," *New York Herald*, June 10, 1884, 1; Brands, *T. R.*, 172.
51   Garraty, *Henry Cabot Lodge*, 78–79.
52   Kohn, "Crossing the Rubicon," 37–38.
53   Ibid.
54   Garraty, *Henry Cabot Lodge*, 78–79; Schriftgiesser, *The Gentleman from Massachusetts*, 84.

Chapter Four: Guiding the Rocket

1   Roosevelt, *Autobiography*, 94; Hagedorn, *Roosevelt in the Badlands*, 3–4.
2   Brands, *T. R.*, 173.
3   McCullough, *Mornings on Horseback*, 308; "From Mr. Roosevelt," *Saint Paul Globe*, June 13, 1884, 5.
4   Putnam, *Theodore Roosevelt: The Formative Years*, 449; McCullough, *Mornings on Horseback*, 310; Morrison, *The Letters of Theodore Roosevelt: Vol. I, The Years of Preparation*, 72; Kohn, "Crossing the Rubicon," 36; Morris, *The Rise of Theodore Roosevelt*, 262. Roosevelt detail silver hunting knife, http://www.loc.gov/pictures/item/2002723991/.
5   Wood, "The Mind of the Massachusetts Mugwump," *New England Quarterly*, Vol. 33, No. 4, November 1960, 436; In a memo of events from 1884 Lodge described the reaction to the Blaine nomination among his Beacon Hill contemporaries. "As I was then somewhat conspicuous among the Republicans of the State, being Chairman of the state committee and being the candidate of my party for Congress, the hostility of these persons in Boston and Massachusetts who had bolted from the Republican Party concentrated itself in large numbers upon my devoted head." Lodge Memo, January 24, 1908, Reel 5, Lodge-Roosevelt Correspondence, MHS.
6   Garraty, *Henry Cabot Lodge*, 79; *A Brief History of the Somerset Club of Boston*, (Boston: The Somerset Club, 1914), 53.
7   Chalfant, *Better in Darkness*, 562; Adams believed it was important to remain in the know. The only way to do that was to maintain relationships with people who were involved in public life. Adams may not have always

liked the people he socialized with, but if he wanted to continue to gather important information those relationships needed to be maintained. Adams wrote some of the most valuable descriptions and commentary of the 19th century. The historian, however, could be a guttersnipe. He disliked Jews and his letters are filled with nasty and underhanded comments about his friends and acquaintances. When the spirit moved him, Adams could also display great charm and a keen wit. Garraty, *Henry Cabot Lodge*, 100; Lodge, Memorandum on recollections of George H. Lyman, January 24, 1908, Reel 5, Lodge-Roosevelt Correspondence, MHS.

8   Garraty, *Henry Cabot Lodge*, 79–80; Kohn, "Crossing the Rubicon," 36; Stephen Hess, *America's Political Dynasties* (Washington: Brookings Institution, 2015), 452; Morris, *The Rise of Theodore Roosevelt*, 271.

9   Garraty, *Henry Cabot Lodge*, 79–80, 82; Kohn, "Crossing the Rubicon," 36.

10   Ibid.; Hess, *America's Political Dynasties*, 452; Those who welcomed his friendship in Boston were not the only ones who thought highly of him. In her 1932 memoir, Margaret Chanler describes Lodge as "a very real man whom one could not but like, respect and grow to love. He was a true scholar and a true friend . . ." Chanler, *Roman Spring*, 194.

11   Lawrence, *Henry Cabot Lodge*, 39.

12   Garraty, *Henry Cabot Lodge*, 82–83.

13   Ibid.

14   Widenor, *Henry Cabot Lodge and the Search for an American Foreign Policy*, 3; Garraty, *Henry Cabot Lodge*, 83.

15   Widenor, *Henry Cabot Lodge and the Search for an American Foreign Policy*, 3; Garraty, *Henry Cabot Lodge*, 83; Chanler, *Roman Spring*, 193.

16   Garraty, *Henry Cabot Lodge*, 84. In the years following the Civil War, many of these elite Harvard men had "a desire to escape the status fitted for them by indulgent families, an eagerness to break loose from their role as passive heirs." Blodgett, "The Mind of the Boston Mugwump," *Mississippi Valley Historical Review*, Vol. 48, No. 4, March 1962, 615.

17   Putnam, *Theodore Roosevelt: The Formative Years*, 462.

18   T. R. to HCL, June 18, 1884, Lodge, Lodge-Roosevelt Correspondence, Vol. I, 4.

19   T. R. to HCL, June 18, 1884, Reel 1, Lodge-Roosevelt correspondence, Massachusetts Historical Society (hereafter T. R. to HCL and MHS).

20   Putnam, *Theodore Roosevelt: The Formative Years*, 465–466; Morris, *The Rise of Theodore Roosevelt*, 271; Schriftgiesser, *The Gentleman from Massachusetts*, 89.

21   Putnam, *Theodore Roosevelt: The Formative Years*, 467.

22   Ibid., 466.

23   T. R. to Nannie Lodge, July 20, 1884, Reel 1, Lodge-Roosevelt correspondence, MHS.

24   Roosevelt also described a confrontation with one of the major mugwumps. "He told me with great austerity that he could not

understand my conduct: to which I pleasantly responded that I doubted if he was capable of understanding anything." T. R. to Nannie Lodge, July 20, 1884, Reel 1, Lodge-Roosevelt correspondence, MHS; Brands, *T. R.* 177; T. R. to HCL, July 28, 1884, Lodge, Lodge-Roosevelt Correspondence, Vol. I, 5, 11.

25   Putnam, *Theodore Roosevelt: The Formative Years*, 466, 491–492; McCullough, *Mornings on Horseback*, 315; Roosevelt clearly enjoyed the belief on the part of many in New York that he was under the sway of "the morally unscrupulous machine manipulator of Nahant." T. R. to HCL, August 12, 1884, Lodge, Lodge-Roosevelt Correspondence, Vol. I, 5–6.

26   McCullough, *Mornings on Horseback*, 355.

27   Ibid.

28   Morris, *The Rise of Theodore Roosevelt*, 282.

29   Morris, *The Rise of Theodore Roosevelt*, 282, 284; "Henry Cabot Lodge Imports His Young Friend Roosevelt," *Boston Daily Globe*, October 21, 1884, 4; "Miscellaneous," *Boston Evening Transcript*, October 11, 1884, 2; "Table Gossip," *Boston Daily Globe*, November 2, 1884, 12.

30   Garraty, *Henry Cabot Lodge*, 85.

31   "In Honor of Mr. Blaine," *Boston Daily Globe*, November 4, 1884, 5.

32   Garraty, *Henry Cabot Lodge*, 85; "In Honor of Mr. Blaine," *Boston Daily Globe*, November 4, 1884, 5.

33   Ibid.

34   Gould, *Grand Old Party*, 102; White, *The Republic for Which It Stands*, 471–472.

35   White, *The Republic for Which It Stands*, 470–471; Garraty, *Henry Cabot Lodge*, 85; John T. Morse, Jr., "Henry Cabot Lodge," *Harvard Graduates Magazine*, Vol. 33, 1925, 433.

36   Garraty, *Henry Cabot Lodge*, 86; T. R. to HCL, November 7, 1884, Lodge, Lodge-Roosevelt Correspondence, Vol. I, 10.

37   Morris, *The Rise of Theodore Roosevelt*, 284–285; T. R. to Lodge, November 7, 1884, Lodge, Lodge-Roosevelt Correspondence, Vol. I, 10; Putnam, *Theodore Roosevelt: The Formative Years*, 506.

38   T. R. to HCL, November 11, 1884, Lodge, Lodge-Roosevelt Correspondence, Vol. I, 26.

39   Ibid.

40   Morris, *The Rise of Theodore Roosevelt*, 285; Kohn, "Crossing the Rubicon," 36.

41   Brands, *T. R.*, 190; While biographer Morris believes Blaine would have offered T. R. a position in the administration, Edward P. Kohn disagrees. Roosevelt never fully embraced Blaine's candidacy, and at times during the campaign was quite critical of it. Kohn, "Crossing the Rubicon," 42.

42   Morris, *The Rise of Theodore Roosevelt*, 291–292; Brands, *T. R.*, 190.

43   Garraty, *Henry Cabot Lodge*, 88–89.

ENDNOTES

Chapter Five: From Outsiders to Insiders

1   T. R. to Nannie Lodge, August 10, 1885, Reel 1, Lodge-Roosevelt Correspondence, MHS.

2   Brands, *T. R.*, 189.

3   Garraty, *Henry Cabot Lodge*, 123. Putnam, *Theodore Roosevelt: The Formative Years*, 549.

4   "Alert Republicans," *Brooklyn Union*, October 18, 1885, 2; Putnam, *Theodore Roosevelt: The Formative Years*, 549; Garraty, *Henry Cabot Lodge*, 123.

5   Putnam, *Theodore Roosevelt: The Formative Years*, 549.

6   Morris, *The Rise of Theodore Roosevelt*, 309–310.

7   Putnam, *Theodore Roosevelt: The Formative Years*, 549; Edward P. Kohn, *Heir to the Empire City: New York and the Making of Theodore Roosevelt*, (New York: Basic Books, 2013), 103.

8   Kohn, *Heir to the Empire City*, 103; Thomas, *The War Lovers*, 46.

9   R. W. B. Lewis, "The Second Mrs. Roosevelt," *Washington Post*, June 29, 1980, www.washingtonpost.com.

10   Kohn, *Heir to the Empire City*, 103. Thomas, *The War Lovers*, 46.

11   Ibid.

12   Ibid.

13   T. R. to HCL, February 7, 1886, Reel 1, Lodge-Roosevelt Correspondence, MHS. Morris, *The Rise of Theodore Roosevelt*, 309.

14   Morris, *The Rise of Theodore Roosevelt*, 309; Garraty, *Henry Cabot Lodge*, 90.

15   Garraty, *Henry Cabot Lodge*, 90.

16   T. R. to HCL, February 7, 1886, Reel 1, Lodge-Roosevelt Correspondence, MHS; Morris, *The Rise of Theodore Roosevelt*, 309; Garraty, *Henry Cabot Lodge*, 90.

17   Sylvia Jukes Morris, *Edith Kermit Roosevelt: Portrait of a First Lady* (New York: Modern Library, 1980), 83; T. R. to HCL, March 27, 1886, Lodge, Lodge-Roosevelt Correspondence, Vol. I, 38; T. R. to HCL, April 16, 1886, Lodge-Roosevelt Correspondence, Vol. I, 39.

18   Morris, *The Rise of Theodore Roosevelt*, 328.

19   T. R. to HCL, August 10, 1886, Lodge, Lodge-Roosevelt Correspondence, Vol. I, 45. Morris, *The Rise of Theodore Roosevelt*, 334.

20   Ibid.

21   T. R. to HCL, August 10, 1886, Lodge, Lodge-Roosevelt Correspondence, Vol. I, 44; Morrison, *Letters of Theodore Roosevelt*, Vol. I, 107.

22   Garraty, *Henry Cabot Lodge*, 91.

23   Edward P. Kohn, "A Necessary Defeat: Theodore Roosevelt and the New York Mayoralty Election of 1886," *New York History*, Spring 2006, Vol. 87, No. 2, 216.

24   T. R. to HCL, October 17, 1886, Lodge, Lodge-Roosevelt Correspondence, Vol. I, 48; Kohn, "A Necessary Defeat: Theodore

Roosevelt and the New York Mayoralty Election of 1886," *New York History*, Spring 2006, Vol. 87, No. 2, 216.

25   Morris, *The Rise of Theodore Roosevelt*, 341; Brands, *T. R.*, 191; T. R. to HCL, October 28, 1886, Reel 1, Roosevelt–Lodge Correspondence, MHS.

26   Kohn, "A Necessary Defeat," 217–218; Dalton, *Theodore Roosevelt*, 220.

27   Kohn, "A Necessary Defeat," 207–208, 215. T. R. to HCL, October 17, 1886, Lodge, Lodge-Roosevelt Correspondence, Vol. I, 47.

28   Garraty, *Henry Cabot Lodge*, 91; "Long Has the Most Senators," *Boston Daily Globe*, October 24, 1886, 4; "Miscellaneous," *Boston Evening Transcript*, October 19, 1886, 2.

29   Ibid.

30   Grondahl, *I Rose Like a Rocket*, 169–170; Morrison, *Letters of Theodore Roosevelt, Vol. I*, 107.

31   Grondahl, *I Rose Like a Rocket*, 169–170; Kohn, "A Necessary Defeat," 222–223.

32   Dalton, *Theodore Roosevelt*, 223; T. R. to HCL, November 2, 1886, Lodge, Lodge Roosevelt Correspondence, Vol. I, 49–50; Morris, *The Rise of Theodore Roosevelt*, 356.

33   On September 18, 1886, an item appeared in the society section of the *New York Times* announcing Edith and Theodore's engagement. A week later the paper printed a retraction, "probably inserted by Bamie or Corinne." Morris, *Edith Kermit Roosevelt*, 89; Kohn, "A Necessary Defeat," 224.

34   T. R. to Nannie Lodge, November 1, 1886, Reel 1, Lodge-Roosevelt Correspondence, MHS.

35   Morris, *The Rise of Theodore Roosevelt*, 309; T. R. to Nannie Lodge, November 1, 1886, Reel 1, Lodge-Roosevelt Correspondence, MHS.

36   T. R. to Nannie Lodge, November 1, 1886, Reel 1, Lodge-Roosevelt Correspondence, MHS; Putnam, *Theodore Roosevelt: The Formative Years*, 559.

37   T. R. to Nannie Lodge, November 1, 1886, Reel 1, Lodge-Roosevelt Correspondence, MHS; Putnam, *Theodore Roosevelt: The Formative Years*, 559. Roosevelt had also written a similar note to HCL, expressing the closeness he felt toward him and how he viewed the couple like a member of his own family. T. R. to Nannie Lodge, November 1, 1886, Reel 1, Lodge-Roosevelt Correspondence, MHS; O'Toole, *The Five of Hearts*, 217.

38   Morris, *The Rise of Theodore Roosevelt*, 356–357.

39   Morris, *The Rise of Theodore Roosevelt*, 357; Stephen Gwynn, *The Letters and Friendships of Sir Cecil Spring Rice: A Record, Vol. I*, (Boston: Houghton Mifflin, 1929), 2. According to his friend Margaret Chanler, Spring Rice had a wonderfully creative mind and enjoyed telling Chanler's children Japanese fairy tales. A lover of literature, the British

diplomat "made himself write" [a fourteen line] "sonnet on every book
that had interested him." Chanler, *Roman Spring*, 205.

40   Morris, *Edith Kermit Roosevelt*, 98; Daniel Ruddy, *Theodore the Great: Conservative Crusader*, (Washington: Regnery, 2016). T. R. to HCL, November 22, 1886, Lodge, Lodge-Roosevelt Correspondence, Vol. I, 50.

41   T. R. to HCL, November 22, 1886, Lodge, Lodge-Roosevelt Correspondence, Vol. I, 50; Morris, *The Rise of Theodore Roosevelt*, 358; Gwynn, *The Letters and Friendships of Sir Cecil Spring Rice: A Record, Vol. I*, 50.

42   Morris, *The Rise of Theodore Roosevelt*, 359; Morris, *Edith Kermit Roosevelt*, 100.

43   Morris, *Edith Kermit Roosevelt*, 106; Gwynn, *The Letters and Friendships of Sir Cecil Spring Rice: A Record, Vol. I*, 48; Garraty, *Henry Cabot Lodge*, 98–99; Spring Rice also enjoyed the company of an intelligent and attractive woman. The British diplomat liked and appreciated Edith Roosevelt, but he loved Nannie Lodge. "I adore you as you know," Spring Rice in one of his many letters to Lodge's wife. The Englishman's biographer writes that Spring Rice "was at times mesmerized by Nannie Lodge." David H. Burton, *Cecil Spring Rice: A Diplomat's Life*, (Plainsboro Township, N.J.: Associated University Press, 1990), 58.

44   Morris, *Edith Kermit Roosevelt*, 106; Roosevelt was pleased that Lodge and Edith got along so well. "Cabot has been a real comfort to her," Theodore wrote Bamie. "He is one of the few men I know who is as well read as she is in English literature, and she delights to talk with him." Doris Kearns Goodwin, *The Bully Pulpit: Theodore Roosevelt, William Howard Taft and the Golden Age of Journalism* (New York: Simon & Schuster, 2013), 141.

45   Garraty, *Henry Cabot Lodge*, 94; Henry Adams, *The Letters of Henry Adams, Volume III 1886–1892*, J. C. Levinson and Henry Samuels, Charles Vandersee, Viola Hopkins Winner, eds. (Cambridge, Mass.: Harvard University Press, 1982), 87.

46   Garraty, *Henry Cabot Lodge*, 95.

47   Ibid.

48   Garraty, *Henry Cabot Lodge*, 97; Morris, *Edith Kermit Roosevelt*, 126.

49   Ibid.

50   Garraty, *Henry Cabot Lodge*, 98.

51   O'Toole, *The Five of Hearts*, 90–91. Sylvia Jukes Morris, "The Historian and the Hostess," *Washington Post*, December 25, 1983, www .washingtonpost.com; Taliaferro, *All the Great Prizes*, 333.

52   Taliaferro, *All the Great Prizes*, 188–189.

53   O'Toole, *The Five of Hearts*, 50, 59–60, 120–122, 126–127, 217; Taliaferro, *All the Great Prizes*, 10; William Seale, *The Imperial Season: America's Capital in the Time of the First Ambassadors 1893–1918*, (Washington: Smithsonian Books, 2013), 22.

54   In a privately published series of reminiscences, Lodge wrote of his wife, "These rare intellectual qualities . . . for nearly half a century inspired my admiration and taught me what it was best and most worthy to know, to love and to reverence . . . If I have been of any use in the world, if I have attained any small measure of success, to her I owe it." Garraty, *Henry Cabot Lodge*, 102; Lodge, *The Lodge Women*, 289.

55   Tehan, *Henry Adams in Love*, 142; The marriage was difficult. Lodge for all his warmth and generosity was often vain and self-centered. During one heated exchange, Nannie Lodge got so upset she said, "I realize you are upset, Cabot, but you don't have to kick me downstairs." Lodge, *The Lodge Women*, 81.

56   Morris, *The Rise of Theodore Roosevelt*, 390–391.

57   "John Wanamaker, Department Store," Who Made America, www.pbs.org.

58   White, *The Republic for Which it Stands*, 621–622.

59   Morris, *The Rise of Theodore Roosevelt*, 396.

60   Morris, *The Rise of Theodore Roosevelt*, 396; T. R. to HCL, October 19, 1888, Lodge, Lodge-Roosevelt Correspondence, Vol. I, 72.

61   Garraty, *Henry Cabot Lodge*, 103.

62   Garraty, *Henry Cabot Lodge*, 103–104; Lodge, *The Lodge Women*, 83. The information relating to Blaine's letter was included in a letter from Lodge to his mother. Cabot seemed quite flattered that Blaine was paying so much attention to Nannie and was proud that the new secretary was consulting her on national affairs.

63   Garraty, *Henry Cabot Lodge*, 103–104; Lodge, *The Lodge Women*, 83.

64   Garraty, *Henry Cabot Lodge*, 104; Schriftgiesser, *The Gentleman from Massachusetts*, 101–102.

65   Ibid.

66   William Henry Harbaugh, *Power and Responsibility: The Life and Times of Theodore Roosevelt* (New York: Farrar Strauss & Giroux, 1961), 74–75; T. R. to HCL, March 25, 1889, Lodge, Selections from the Lodge-Roosevelt Correspondence, Vol. I, 74.

67   Harbaugh, *Power and Responsibility*, 74–75; T. R. to HCL, March 25, 1889, Lodge, Lodge-Roosevelt Correspondence, Vol. I, 74.

68   Garraty, *Henry Cabot Lodge*, 104, 108; Schriftgiesser, *The Gentleman from Massachusetts*, 101–103.

69   Brands, *T. R.*, 229–230.

70   HCL to T. R., March 30, 1889, Lodge, Lodge-Roosevelt Correspondence, Vol. I, 76; Garraty, *Henry Cabot Lodge*, 104, 108; Schriftgiesser, *The Gentleman from Massachusetts*, 101–103; "Walker Blaine Dead," *New York Times*, January 15, 1890, 1; Richard D. White, *Roosevelt the Reformer: Theodore Roosevelt as Civil Service Commissioner 1889–1895* (Tuscaloosa: University of Alabama Press, 2003), 12–14; White makes clear that Lodge was responsible for T. R. obtaining the position in the Harrison

Administration. However, there appears to be two versions of how Roosevelt was formally offered the opportunity. Morris states that Lodge informed Roosevelt of the opportunity at the centennial celebration of the US government in New York. In a published reminiscence written in 1919, Harrison's secretary, Elijah W. Halford, writes that Roosevelt was offered the position by President Harrison following an interview at the White House. Col. E. W. Halford, "Roosevelt's Introduction to Washington," *Frank Leslie's Weekly*, March 1, 1919, Accessible Archives, Fordham University.

71   "Statesmen Dined: The Most Magnificent Banquet on Record," *Washington Post*, May 1, 1889, 1.

72   Morris, *The Rise of Theodore Roosevelt*, 398; HCL to T. R., April 4, 1889, Lodge, Lodge-Roosevelt Correspondence, Vol. I, 77.

Chapter Six: Climbing the Greasy Pole

1   White, *Roosevelt the Reformer*, 8–9; Joseph Bucklin Bishop, *Theodore Roosevelt and His Time, Shown in His Own Letters: Vol. I*, (New York: Charles Scribner's Sons, 1920), 45.

2   White, *Roosevelt the Reformer*, 23–24.

3   T. R. to HCL, June 29, 1889, Lodge, Lodge-Roosevelt Correspondence, Vol. I, 79; Adams, *The Letters of Henry Adams III 1886–1918*, 175; Morris, *The Rise of Theodore Roosevelt*, 425. Tehan, *Henry Adams in Love*, 78.

4   T. R. to HCL, June 29, 1889, Lodge, Lodge-Roosevelt Correspondence, Vol. I, 79.

5   Morris, *The Rise of Theodore Roosevelt*, 404, 407; White, *Roosevelt the Reformer*, 23–24; Dalton, *Theodore Roosevelt*, 129.

6   Ibid.

7   T. R. to HCL, June 29, 1889, Lodge, Lodge-Roosevelt Correspondence, Vol. I, 80.

8   Roosevelt was covered constantly during his tenure as civil service commissioner. An interview he gave about the role of the Civil Service was carried throughout the country, while notices of his arrival and activities in certain states were carried by the local papers as well. "No Inspiration in Beer Says Mr. Roosevelt," *Indianapolis Journal*, July 9, 1889, 4; "Theodore Roosevelt," *Indianapolis Journal*, July 29, 1889, 4; "Civil Service Reform," *Indianapolis Journal*, June 21, 1889, 4; White, *Roosevelt the Reformer*, 24–25; Dalton, *Theodore Roosevelt*, 129.

9   "No Inspiration in Beer Says Mr. Roosevelt," *Indianapolis Journal*, July 9, 1889, 4; "Theodore Roosevelt," *Indianapolis Journal*, July 29, 1889, 4; "Civil Service Reform," *Indianapolis Journal*, June 21, 1889, 4; White, *Roosevelt the Reformer*, 24–25; Dalton, *Theodore Roosevelt*, 129.

10   T. R. to HCL, July 1, 1889, Lodge, Lodge-Roosevelt Correspondence, Vol. I, 81; Dalton, *Theodore Roosevelt*, 129; White, "Theodore Roosevelt

as Civil Service Commissioner: Linking the Influence and Development of a Modern Administrative President," *Journal of Administrative Theory and Praxis*, Vol. 22, No. 4, Dec. 2000, 703.

11   Dalton, *Theodore Roosevelt*, 136.

12   T. R. to HCL July 1, 1889, Lodge, Lodge-Roosevelt Correspondence, Vol. I, 81; Roosevelt understood his tendency to be frequently outspoken. In that respect he was always grateful to have Edith and Lodge close by. "His tendency to orate," T. R. said "was only held in check by the memory of the jeers of my wife and intimate friend." Dalton, *Theodore Roosevelt*, 136.

13   Garraty, *Henry Cabot Lodge*, 105.

14   Ibid.

15   Garraty, *Henry Cabot Lodge*, 117; Schriftgiesser, *The Gentleman from Massachusetts*, 105, 111.

16   White, *The Republic for Which It Stands*, 628.

17   Garraty, *Henry Cabot Lodge*, 118–119, 123.

18   Ibid.; O'Toole, *The Five of Hearts*, 208. John Singer Sargent, *Henry Cabot Lodge*, 1890, National Portrait Gallery, Smithsonian Institution, nag.si.edu.

19   White, *The Republic for Which It Stands*, 629; Serge Ricard, *A Companion to Theodore Roosevelt*, (Hoboken, N.J.: Wiley-Blackwell, 2011).

20   Garraty, *Henry Cabot Lodge*, 119–120.

21   Ibid.

22   Ibid., 12.

23   White, *Roosevelt the Reformer*, 25.

24   Ibid., 30–31.

25   White, *Roosevelt the Reformer*, 30–31; HCL to T. R., August 15, 1889, Theodore Roosevelt Center, Dickinson State University, Dickinson, N.D.

26   T. R. to HCL, August 1, 1889, Lodge, Lodge-Roosevelt Correspondence, Vol. I, 87–88; Roosevelt continued to complain to Lodge about Harrison's lack of support. "I do wish the President would give me a little active, even if only verbal encouragement; it is a dead weight to stagger under, without a particle of sympathy from any one of our leaders here . . ." T. R. to HCL, July 28, 1889, Lodge, Lodge-Roosevelt Correspondence, Vol. I, 86. Morris, *The Rise of Theodore Roosevelt*, 413.

27   T. R. to HCL, July 28, 1889, Lodge, Lodge-Roosevelt Correspondence, Vol. I, 86; Morris, *The Rise of Theodore Roosevelt*, 413.

28   Morris, *Edith Kermit Roosevelt*, 126.

29   White, *Roosevelt the Reformer*, 41–43; Morris, *The Rise of Theodore Roosevelt*, 421.

30   Morris, *Edith Kermit Roosevelt*, 126; Lodge, *The Lodge Women*, 85; Donna Evers, "Historical Landscapes: Two Families One Roof," *Washington Life Magazine*, Spring 2006, eversco.com; While Edith

and Theodore spent frequent periods enjoying the hospitality of Henry Adams, they were with the Lodges frequently as well. During Roosevelt's tenure with the Civil Service Commission, Theodore and Edith dined at the Lodge's without fail every Christmas night. Zimmermann, *First Great Triumph*, 173.

31   Dalton, *Theodore Roosevelt*, 136–137. Roosevelt fondly recalled the first time he met his future secretary of state. As a child, T. R.'s father had invited Hay to visit their house in Oyster Bay. One day it had rained so heavily that Hay's umbrella had blown inside out. Zimmermann, *First Great Triumph*, 213.

32   Dalton, *Theodore Roosevelt*, 136–137. Morris, "The Historian and the Hostess," *Washington Post*, December 25, 1983, www.washingtonpost.com.

33   T. R. to HCL, July 13, 1889, Reel 1, Lodge-Roosevelt Correspondence, MHS.

34   Grondahl, *I Rose Like a Rocket*, 198; Morris, *The Rise of Theodore Roosevelt*, 434–436, 451. On one occasion in the spring of 1890, Roosevelt invited Cecil Spring Rice to accompany him on a visit with President Harrison and his wife. The Englishman was not impressed. "They are both small and fat," Spring Rice commented in a note to his brother, Stephen. Gwynn, *The Letters and Friendships of Cecil Spring Rice: A Record, Vol. I*, 104.

35   Garraty, *Henry Cabot Lodge*, 191–193. While Bay had matured into a young man with rugged good looks and an outgoing personality, he had not always displayed those qualities. The Lodges' good friend, Mrs. Winthrop Chanler, had described the young man as "a rather unkept and uncouth boy who had suddenly emerged into an immensely attractive and accomplished youth." Tehan, *Henry Adams in Love*, 160.

36   Garraty, *Henry Cabot Lodge*, 191–193; Morris, *Edith Kermit Roosevelt*, 127–131.

37   Garraty, *Henry Cabot Lodge*, 191–193; Morris, *Edith Kermit Roosevelt*, 127–131; T. R. to HCL, September 7, 1890, Reel 1, Roosevelt-Lodge Correspondence, MHS; John W. Crowley, "Dear Bay: Theodore Roosevelt's Letters to George Cabot Lodge," *Journal of New York History*, Vol. 53, No. 2, April 1972, 179; Brands, *T. R.*, 243.

38   "Theodore Roosevelt's Letters to George Cabot Lodge," *Journal of New York History*, Vol. 53, No. 2, April 1972, 179.

39   Crowley, "Dear Bay: Theodore Roosevelt's Letters to George Cabot Lodge," *Journal of New York History*, Vol. 53, No. 2, April 1972, 180.

40   Crowley, "Theodore Roosevelt's Letters to George Cabot Lodge," *Journal of New York History*, Vol. 53, No. 2, April 1972, 180; Garraty, *Henry Cabot Lodge*, 192; In addition, Lodge wrote Adams that Bay "seems to have no interest or ambitions & to love more stupid idling beyond anything. What can one do?" Garraty, *Henry Cabot Lodge*, 192.

ENDNOTES

41 Crowley, "Dear Bay: Theodore Roosevelt's Letters to George Cabot Lodge," *Journal of New York History*, April 1972, Vol. 53, No. 2. 177, 181, 183.

42 One of Bay Lodge's contemporaries, the novelist Edith Wharton described him as "one of the most complete examples I have ever known of a young genius before whom an adoring family unites in smoothing the way." In commenting on the work, itself, the literary critic Edmund Wilson wrote, "One cannot say he was a bad poet: he was hardly a poet at all . . ." Hess, *America's Political Dynasties*; Garraty, *Henry Cabot Lodge*, 193.

43 Garraty, *Henry Cabot Lodge*, 122; White, *The Republic for Which It Stands*, 318–319.

44 Morris, *The Rise of Theodore Roosevelt*, 436; Garraty, *Henry Cabot Lodge*, 122; White, *The Republic for Which It Stands*, 318–319.

45 O'Toole, *The Five of Hearts*, 217; Lodge, *The Lodge Women*, 70; Taliaferro, *All the Great Prizes*, 263–264; "Remarks by Jon Meacham at the State Funeral of President George Herbert Walker Bush," Washington National Cathedral, December 5, 2018, President George Herbert Walker Bush, Eulogy and Media Tribute Collection, December 2018, 6–10, www.cdn.bush41.org.

46 Taliaferro, *All the Great Prizes*, 263–265. Seale, *The Imperial Season*, 23.

47 Taliaferro, *All the Great Prizes*, 23, 244, 263-265; Seale, *The Imperial Season*, 23.

48 O'Toole, *The Five of Hearts*, 222.

49 Taliaferro, *All the Great Prizes*, 264–265.

50 O'Toole, *The Five of Hearts*, 218.

51 O'Toole, *The Five of Hearts*, 219; Taliaferro, *All the Great Prizes*, 265.

52 Ibid. The visit to New York was not the first time the two had managed to stay in the same city. A year earlier when Hay gave a dinner at the Knickerbocker Club, Nannie had managed to be in town as well. O'Toole, *The Five of Hearts*, 219; Taliaferro, *All the Great Prizes*, 268.

53 Taliaferro, *All the Great Prizes*, 267.

54 Taliaferro, *All the Great Prizes*, 267; Dalton, *Theodore Roosevelt*, 137; Lodge, *The Lodge Women*, 110–111.

55 Taliaferro, *All the Great Prizes*, 394.

56 It is difficult to know how intimate the relationship became. According to Lizzie Cameron, "Nannie destroyed all her letters in a panic of terror . . . in order that she could truly say she possessed no letters at all. Taliaferro, *All the Great Prizes*, 268; Ben Johnson, "Bright Young Things," Historic UK, www.historicuk.com.

57 T. R. to HCL, July 22, 1891, Reel 1, Lodge-Roosevelt Correspondence, MHS; T. R. to HCL, August 28, 1891, Reel 1, Lodge-Roosevelt Correspondence, MHS; Brands, *T. R.*, 244–249.

58 Matters remained tense as T. R. commented to Lodge that following a brief summer respite he returned to find people chatting about "rumors of my own removal." Morris, *The Rise of Theodore Roosevelt*, 454; During that summer, T. R. had continued to rant to Lodge over his frustrations with Harrison. "He is genial little runt, isn't he?" Roosevelt wrote of Harrison on July 1, 1891. Morris, *The Rise of Theodore Roosevelt*, 451.

59 Raymond E. Spinzia, "Elliott Roosevelt Sr.—A Spiral into Darkness: The Influences," *The Freeholder*, Vol. 12, No. 4, (Fall, 2007) 2, 4–5.

60 T. R. to HCL, August 28, 1891, Reel 1, Lodge-Roosevelt Correspondence, MHS; Brands, *T. R.*, 244–249; Raymond E. Spinzia, "Elliott Roosevelt Sr.—A Spiral into Darkness: The Influences," *The Freeholder*, Vol. 12, No. 4, (Fall, 2007) 2, 4–5.

61 T. R. to HCL, August 28, 1891, Reel 1, Lodge-Roosevelt Correspondence, MHS; Brands, *T. R.*, 244–249.

62 Brands, *T. R.*, 249; T. R. to HCL, October 10, 1891, Reel 1, Lodge-Roosevelt Correspondence, MHS; Henry Adams had learned they did not approve of the marriage. The reasons for their opposition remain unknown. The disapproval of the union was illustrated by the look on the face of Nannie Lodge, described by Lizzie Cameron as one of "grim determination and suffering." Tehan, *Henry Adams in Love*, 135; Cecil Spring Rice, however, wrote a congratulatory letter indicating Lodge had a positive impression of Gardner. "Do you remember talking to me on the subject and the young man at Newport, and saying how you liked him." Gwynn, *The Letters and Friendships of Cecil Spring Rice: A Record, Vol. I*, 115; Schriftgiesser, *The Gentleman from Massachusetts*, 130.

63 Garraty, *Henry Cabot Lodge*, 129.

64 Ibid., 129–131; T. R. to HCL, September 25, 1892, Lodge, Lodge-Roosevelt Correspondence, Vol. I, 123–124; Lodge turned down the role to run for governor. However, he played a key role in selecting his childhood friend, Roger Wolcott as an alternative. David Wendell Dotson, "Henry Cabot Lodge: A Political Biography," Doctoral Dissertation, University of Oklahoma, 157.

65 T. R. to HCL, September 25, 1892, Lodge, Lodge-Roosevelt Correspondence, Vol. I, 124.

66 "The Campaign and Election of 1892," The Miller Center, www .millercenter.org.

67 Ibid.

68 Brands, *T. R.*, 251. T. R. to HCL, September 25, 1892, Lodge, Lodge-Roosevelt Correspondence, Vol. I, 124.

69 Garraty, *Henry Cabot Lodge*, 132; Dotson, "Henry Cabot Lodge: A Political Biography," 151; Monitoring the election from Lafayette Square, Henry Adams wryly commented to John Hay on Lodge's victory. "Dear Cabot seems to be the only man who has the people with him. True heart! Pure

people's Patriot! He and Cleveland. Two stuffed prophets! How I love the people; they are always right." Henry Adams, *The Letters of Henry Adams, Vol. IV: 1892–1899*, J. C. Levinson, Ernest Samuels, Charles Vandersee, Viola Hopkins-Winner, eds., (Cambridge, Mass.: Harvard University Press, 1988), 78. "Our New Senator," *Boston Post*, January 18, 1893, 1.

70   T. R. to HCL, January 10, 1892, Reel 1, Lodge-Roosevelt Correspondence, MHS; Morris, *The Rise of Theodore Roosevelt*, 467.

71   Morris, *Edith Kermit Roosevelt*, 145; Brands, *T. R.*, 253–254; Grondahl, *I Rose Like a Rocket*, 202.

72   Dalton, *Theodore Roosevelt*, 141.

73 ·   Ibid. T. R. to HCL, August 18, 1893, Reel 1, Lodge-Roosevelt Correspondence, MHS. Elliott Roosevelt died on August 14, 1894; The fact that T. R. dated his note to Lodge as 1893 illustrates the devastation he was experiencing as related to his brother's death. Miller, *Theodore Roosevelt: A Life*, 224–225. In a note to Bamie, T. R. described in detail what caused Elliott's death. "It was his fall, aggravated by frightful drinking, that was the immediate cause; he had been drinking whole bottles of anisette and green mint, besides whole bottles of raw brandy and of champagne, sometimes half a dozen a morning." Morris, *Edith Kermit Roosevelt*, 143.

74   White, *The Republic for Which It Stands*, 767–768, 771; "Panic of 1893," Ohio History Central, www.ohiohistorycentral.org.

75   Morris, *The Rise of Theodore Roosevelt*, 485; Zimmermann, *First Great Triumph*, 173, www.measuringwealth.com.

76   Morris, *The Rise of Theodore Roosevelt*, 485; Zimmermann, *First Great Triumph*, 173.

77   Garraty, *Henry Cabot Lodge*, 133–134; Thomas, *The War Lovers*, 57; Lodge, *The Lodge Women*, 105.

78   Adams, *The Letters of Henry Adams, Volume IV: 1892–1899*, 115.

79   O'Toole, *The Five of Hearts*, 266.

80   Miller, *Theodore Roosevelt*, 224–225; Morris, *The Rise of Theodore Roosevelt*, 487.

81   T. R. to HCL, October 11, 1894, Reel 1, Lodge-Roosevelt Correspondence, MHS; Miller, *Theodore Roosevelt*, 225–226. Roosevelt believed by turning down the opportunity to run for mayor of New York he had done himself an enormous disservice. "I had no illusions about ever having another opportunity; I knew it meant the definite abandonment of any hope of going on in the work and life for which I care for more than any other . . . At the time with Edith feeling as intensely as she did, I did not see how I could well go in . . . I have grown to feel more and more that in this instance I should have gone counter to her wishes . . . the fault was mine, not Edith's . . ." Morris, *The Rise of Theodore Roosevelt*, 489.

82   Dalton, *Theodore Roosevelt*, 148; Anna Roosevelt Cowles, *Letters from Theodore Roosevelt to Anna Roosevelt Cowles 1870–1918*, (New York: Charles Scribner's Sons, 1924), 149.
83   Theodore Roosevelt and Henry Cabot Lodge, *Hero Tales from American History*, (Louisville, Ky.: The McConnell Center, 2011); In the spring of 1895, Roosevelt wrote Lodge that a bibliography should be assembled for each chapter to give those interested greater context of the individuals and events discussed in the book. "For Washington we could refer to your Life and for Lincoln to Morse's Life, for Clark and Boone to my 'Winning of the West' and for the 'Armstrong Privateer,' 'The Cruise of the Wasp,' and the 'Battle of New Orleans,' to my 'War of 1812,' etc." T. R. to HCL, May 21, 1895, Lodge-Roosevelt Correspondence, Vol. I, 144–145.
84   Morris, *The Rise of Theodore Roosevelt*, 491.
85   During the first week of April 1895, the *New York Times* published an article that discussed the possibility of Roosevelt being appointed one of the police commissioners in the new administration. "IF NOT MR. ROOSEVELT, WHO?" blared the headline. H. Paul Jeffers, *Commissioner Roosevelt: The Story of Theodore Roosevelt and The New York City Police 1895–1897*, (New York, J. Wiley & Sons, 1994), 60; Dalton, *Theodore Roosevelt*, 149, 561.
86   Morrison, *The Letters of Theodore Roosevelt, Vol. I, The Years of Preparation, 1868–1898*, 437; Morris, The *Rise of Theodore Roosevelt*, 491.
87   T. R. to HCL, April 3, 1895, Lodge, Lodge-Roosevelt Correspondence, Vol. I, 141–142. Morris, *The Rise of Theodore Roosevelt*, 492.

Chapter Seven: Forging an Agenda
1   Garraty, *Henry Cabot Lodge*, 134; David J. Rothman, *Politics and Power: The United States Senate 1869–1901*, (Cambridge, Mass.: Harvard University Press, 1966), 139.
2   Schriftgiesser, *The Gentleman from Massachusetts*, 131.
3   Joseph Benson Foraker, *Notes of a Busy Life, Vol. II*, (Cincinnati: Stewart & Kidd Company, 1916), 9.
4   Ibid.
5   Garraty, *Henry Cabot Lodge*, 134; White, *The Republic for Which It Stands*, 634; Jack Beatty, *Age of Betrayal: The Triumph of Money in America 1865–1900*, (New York: Vantage Books, 2007), 337.
6   Ibid.
7   Ibid.
8   Garraty, *Henry Cabot Lodge*, 111–112; Following the vote to repeal the Sherman Act, Lodge, Senator Donald Cameron, and several others representing the anti-Sherman coalition held a celebratory dinner at Henry Adams's home on Lafayette Square. Henry Adams, *The Education of Henry Adams*, (Boston: Massachusetts Historical Society, 1917), 343.

9   Widenor, *Henry Cabot Lodge and the Search for an American Foreign Policy*, 59–60; Schriftgiesser, *The Gentleman from Massachusetts*, 114–115. Henry Cabot Lodge, *Congressional Record*, February 19, 1891, 2956; Brian Gratton, "Race or Politics: Henry Cabot Lodge and the Origins of the Immigration Restriction Movement in the United States," *Journal of Policy History*, Vol. 30, No. 1 (January 2018), 133–134.

10   Widenor, *Henry Cabot Lodge and the Search for an American Foreign Policy*, 60; Gratton, "Race or Politics: Henry Cabot Lodge and the Origins of the Immigration Restriction Movement in the United States," *Journal of Policy History*, Vol. 30, No. 1 (January 2018), 133–134.

11   Gratton, "Race or Politics," *Journal of Policy History*, Vol. 30, No. 1 (January 2018), 134.

12   Garraty, *Henry Cabot Lodge*, 141; Gratton, "Race or Politics," *Journal of Policy History*, Vol. 30, No. 1 (January 2018), 141; Unlike Lodge, Roosevelt did not immerse himself in the debate over immigration restrictions. However, T. R. shared the New Englander's concerns over the flood of the uneducated and impoverished masses from abroad. The future president did share Lodge's view that many of those from Southern Europe as well as "Irish," "Slavs," and other ethnicities did not have the ability to adapt to a life in the United States nor possessed the moral character to assimilate into the American fabric. Harbaugh, *Power and Responsibility*, 220.

13   Gratton, "Race or Politics," *Journal of Policy History*, Vol. 30, No. 1 (Jan. 2018), 143.

14   Garraty, *Henry Cabot Lodge*, 145; "President Cleveland Veto's a Law Restricting Immigration," March 2, 1897, www.millercenter.org.

15   Garraty, *Henry Cabot Lodge*, 145.

16   Morris, *Edith Kermit Roosevelt*, 157; T. R. to HCL, May 12, 1895; Lodge, Lodge-Roosevelt Correspondence, Vol. I, 143.

17   T. R. to HCL, May 12, 1895, Lodge, Lodge-Roosevelt Correspondence, Vol. I, 143. Josephson, *The President Makers*, 49–50.

18   T. R. to HCL, May 18, 1895, Lodge, Lodge-Roosevelt Correspondence, Vol. I, 144.

19   Theodore Roosevelt, "Municipal Administration: The New York Police Force," *The Atlantic*, 1897. https://www.theatlantic.com/magazine/archive/1897/09/municipal-administration-the-new-york-police-.

20   Dalton, *Theodore Roosevelt*, 150; In Riis's memoir of his experiences with Roosevelt, the author describes what T. R. hoped these late-night patrols would accomplish. "Roosevelt wanted to know the city by night, and the true inwardness of the problems he was struggling with . . . One might hear of overcrowding in tenements for years and not grasp the subject as he could by a single midnight inspection with the sanitary police. He wanted to understand it all, the smallest with the greatest." Jacob A.

Riis, *Theodore Roosevelt the Citizen* (New York: MacMillan, 1912), 144; Morris, *The Rise of Theodore Roosevelt*, 504.

21 Harbaugh, *Power and Responsibility*, 84. Dalton, *Theodore Roosevelt*, 153.

22 Harbaugh, *Power and Responsibility*, 84. Dalton, *Theodore Roosevelt*, 153. T. R. to HCL, July 14, 1895, Lodge, Lodge-Roosevelt Correspondence, Vol. I, 149. In the same letter, Roosevelt also gleefully reported that many had become so hostile to his enforcement of the saloon closings that "several persons supposed to look like me have been followed at night by very unfriendly mobs!"

23 T. R. to HCL, July 20, 1895, Lodge, Lodge-Roosevelt Correspondence, Vol. I, 151. Morris, *The Rise of Theodore Roosevelt*, 516.

24 Edward Chalfant, *Improvement of the World: A Biography of Henry Adams, His Last Life, 1891–1918*, (New York: Archon Books, 2001), 93; Henry Adams was annoyed about making the trip to visit the continent. "Lord only knows what has induced the Senator from Massachusetts to go over with wife and sons to Europe, where he has not been these five- and- twenty years, and which he detests almost as much as I do; but go he will." Adams, *The Letters of Henry Adams, Vol. IV*, 291; In Lodge's reply about Roosevelt's activities as police commissioner, the senator wrote, "Once more in my opinion you are doing rightly, wisely and splendidly and building up a reputation and establishing a leadership from which I expect great fruits." HCL to T. R., July 24, 1895, Lodge, Lodge-Roosevelt Correspondence, Vol. I, 153.

25 Dalton, *Theodore Roosevelt*, 154–155; As the United States remained in the throes of the economic downturn, Lodge had decided to rent the family home on Nahant. With little cash on hand, it was the only way he could afford the visit to Europe. Upon hearing that Cabot had given a real estate broker access to the house to search for a summer renter, Anna Lodge was furious to hear of her son's plans. Writing Lodge she commented, "My heart stood still at the thought of what kind of stranger . . . might be wondering over that beloved house & among many sacred old time things & I at once determined to rent the house myself . . ." Lodge's mother ended up renting the house herself at a cost of $2,500.00, money Lodge then used for his European trip. Garraty, *Henry Cabot Lodge*, 156–157.

26 Henry Adams to Brooks Adams, July 19, 1895, Adams, *The Letters of Henry Adams, Vol. IV*, 299; Schriftgiesser, *The Gentleman from Massachusetts*, 129, 131; Garraty, *Henry Cabot Lodge*, 146; Josephson, *The President Makers*, 73; Zimmermann, *First Great Triumph*, 103.

27 HCL to T. R., July 24, 1895, Lodge, Lodge-Roosevelt Correspondence, Vol. I, 155; Zimmermann, *First Great Triumph*, 185; Widenor, *Henry Cabot Lodge and the Search for an American Foreign Policy*, 76; While Lodge enjoyed socializing among London's upper class, he found the British personally unappealing. "The miscellaneous assortment of British youths

and maidens who are here . . . are a weariness to me," he wrote Roosevelt. As one who also placed a high value on appearances Lodge, who attended countless formal affairs during his London stay, was unimpressed with the women he encountered. "They inherited the jewels & devised the dresses themselves," he said. Garraty, *Henry Cabot Lodge*, 157.

28   Garraty, *Henry Cabot Lodge*, 147; Zimmermann, *First Great Triumph*, 185.

29   Ibid. Lodge became acquainted with Luce when the admiral's son married one of his wife's sisters.

30   Zimmermann, *First Great Triumph*, 150–153; The idea of Hawaii being acquired by the United States created enormous excitement among Washington society. Hawaiian-themed parties were highly popular among the elite in the nation's capital. As the celebrants danced late into the night, orchestras, playing guitars and other native musical instruments sang one of the more popular songs of the day celebrating the demise of the "deposed island queen." "Come, Lilu-o-kalani, give Uncle Sam your little yellow hannie . . ." Henry Adams, not to be left out of the celebration, added a "four-hundred-pound Polynesian chief" to his network of the attractive and well connected. On one occasion, while still in his civil service role Roosevelt had the opportunity to meet the gentleman at Adams's home. "A polished gentleman," Roosevelt commented, "of easy manners, with an interesting undertone of queer barbarism." Morris, *The Rise of Theodore Roosevelt*, 468–469; Julius W. Pratt, *Expansionists of 1898: The Acquisition of Hawaii and the Spanish Islands*, (New York: Peter Smith, 1951), 200; Lodge and the other expansionists were also suspicious of the president when he requested permission from Congress for the British to lease a portion of the deserted island to connect a cable between Canada and Australia. Cleveland's request enraged Lodge who believed the president was allowing the British to get a foothold in the Pacific, thus putting London's interests above that of the United States. Pratt, *Expansionists of 1898*, 200; Lodge, as he wrote his mother, was always proud when his wife served as a hostess for an event at the Executive Mansion. "The President invited Nannie who was obliged to go to the White House to receive. She wore purple velvet and looked very well . . ."; Lodge, *The Lodge Women*, 121.

31   Garraty, *Henry Cabot Lodge*, 153.

32   Widenor, *Henry Cabot Lodge and the Search for an American Foreign Policy*, 70.

33   Widenor, *Henry Cabot Lodge and the Search for an American Foreign Policy*, 70, 73; Thomas, *The War Lovers*, 70; Zimmermann, *First Great Triumph*, 152.

34   Morrison, *The Letters of Theodore Roosevelt, Vol. I: The Years of Preparation*, 221–222; Zimmermann, *First Great Triumph*, 213–214, 222–223.

35   Ibid.

36   Morris, *The Rise of Theodore Roosevelt*, 528–529.

37   Ibid.

38   HCL to T. R., February 27, 1896, Reel 2, Lodge-Roosevelt Correspondence, MHS; Dalton, *Theodore Roosevelt*, 156.

39   HCL to T. R., February 27, 1896, Reel 2, Lodge-Roosevelt Correspondence, MHS; Dalton, *Theodore Roosevelt*, 156; T. R. to HCL, May 12, 1895, Lodge, Lodge-Roosevelt Correspondence, Vol. I, 143; HCL to T. R., August 10, 1895, Lodge, Lodge-Roosevelt Correspondence, Vol. I, 163; HCL to T. R., August 31, 1895, Lodge, Lodge-Roosevelt Correspondence, Vol. I, 169.

40   Dalton, *Theodore Roosevelt*, 156.

41   Brands, *T. R.*, 287; Dalton, *Theodore Roosevelt*, 156–157; Chanler, *Roman Spring*, 195.

42   Ibid.

43   Grondahl, *I Rose Like a Rocket*, 237; HCL to T. R., September 12, 1895, Lodge, Lodge-Roosevelt Correspondence Vol. I, 178.

44   Morris, *The Rise of Theodore Roosevelt*, 529; HCL to T. R., September 12, 1895, Lodge, Lodge-Roosevelt Correspondence, Vol. I, 174–175; In further comments to Lodge about his political future, Roosevelt believed his adversarial relationship made that idea almost impossible. "The chance for future political preference for me is just about such a chance as that of lightning striking." HCL to T. R., September 12, 1895, Lodge, Lodge-Roosevelt Correspondence, Vol. I, 176.

45   Morris, *The Rise of Theodore Roosevelt*, 529, 534. HCL to T. R., September 12, 1895, Lodge, Lodge-Roosevelt Correspondence, Vol. I, 175; Roosevelt wrote that so many within the NY GOP bureaucracy were frustrated by his behavior that "The Republican County Convention came within one ace of passing a resolution, which . . . disavowing all responsibility for me, and stating that the Republican Party had nothing to do with me." T. R. to HCL, October 11, 1895, Lodge, Lodge-Roosevelt Correspondence, Vol. I, 184.

46   HCL to T. R., September 22, 1895, Lodge, Lodge-Roosevelt Correspondence, Vol. I, 179; Dalton, *Theodore Roosevelt*, 156.

47   HCL to T. R., September 22, 1895, Lodge, Lodge-Roosevelt Correspondence, Vol. I, 179.

48   Ibid.

49   Morris, *The Rise of Theodore Roosevelt*, 530; T. R. to HCL, October 20, 1895, Lodge, Lodge-Roosevelt Correspondence, Vol. I, 192.

50   T. R. to HCL, October 29, 1895, Lodge, Lodge-Roosevelt Correspondence, Vol. I, 196.

51   Ibid.

52   Morris, *The Rise of Theodore Roosevelt*, 530.

53   T. R. to HCL, October 18, 1895, Lodge, Lodge-Roosevelt Correspondence, Vol. I, 189.

54 George H. Mayer, *The Republican Party 1854–1966*, (New York: Oxford University Press, 1967, second edition), 228; Garraty, *Henry Cabot Lodge*, 166.

55 Garraty, *Henry Cabot Lodge*, 166–167; HCL to T. R., February 27, 1896, Reel 2, Lodge-Roosevelt Correspondence, MHS; Thomas, *The War Lovers*, 141.

56 Ibid.

57 Thomas, *The War Lovers*, 118.

58 Brands, *T. R.*, 293.

59 T. R. to HCL, January 10, 1896, Lodge, Lodge-Roosevelt Correspondence, Vol. I, 208.

60 Morris, *The Rise of Theodore Roosevelt*, 538; T. R. to HCL, January 19, 1896, Lodge, Lodge-Roosevelt Correspondence, Vol. I, 210; Platt favored doing business on Sundays. During the day a number of the boss's lieutenants would assemble outside the boss's suite in an area aptly named "Amen Corner." In another play on Sunday as a day of worship, those like Lemuel Quigg and other political regulars who had weekly appointments were referred to as "Platt's Sunday School Class." Morris, *The Rise of Theodore Roosevelt*, 537.

61 T. R. to HCL, January 19, 1896, Lodge, Lodge-Roosevelt Correspondence, Vol. I, 210.

62 T. R. to HCL, February 16, 1896, Lodge, Lodge-Roosevelt Correspondence, Vol. I, 210; Brands, *T. R.*, 294; Letters from Theodore Roosevelt to Anna Roosevelt Cowles, 169.

63 Cowles, Letters from Theodore Roosevelt to Anna Roosevelt Cowles, 169.

64 William Safire, *Safire's Political Dictionary*, (Oxford: Oxford University Press, 2008), 237.

65 Robert Merry, *President McKinley: Architect of the American Century*, (New York: Simon & Schuster, 2017), 98–100; Gould, *Grand Old Party*, 120–123.

66 T. R. to HCL, July 14, 1896, Lodge, Lodge-Roosevelt Correspondence, Vol. I, 224; Garraty, *Henry Cabot Lodge*, 173.

67 Garraty, *Henry Cabot Lodge*, 173.

68 T. R. to HCL, July 30, 1896, Lodge, Lodge-Roosevelt Correspondence, Vol. I, 227.

69 Garraty, *Henry Cabot Lodge*, 174–175; Roosevelt described the speaking tour in a letter to Bamie. "The halls were jammed, people standing in masses in the aisles; and I have never in any other campaign seen such deep interest or noticed in the audience such interest desire to listen to full explanations of the question at issue." Cowles, *Letters from Theodore Roosevelt to Anna Roosevelt Cowles*, 194–195.

70 Morris, *The Rise of Theodore Roosevelt*, 572; T. R. to HCL, July 30, 1896, Lodge, Lodge-Roosevelt Correspondence, Vol. I, 226–227 and note on

bottom of 236; Morris, *The Rise of Theodore Roosevelt*, 573; Roosevelt viewed his time with Lodge on the campaign trail as "a real holiday." And found the experience "simply delightful." T. R. to HCL, July 30, 1896, Lodge, Lodge-Roosevelt Correspondence, Vol. I, 226–227.

71   T. R. to HCL, October 21, 1896, Lodge, Lodge-Roosevelt Correspondence, Vol. I, 237–238.

72   William McKinley, campaigns and elections, The Miller Center, www .millercenter.org.

73   Garraty, *Henry Cabot Lodge*, 176.

Chapter Eight: First among Nations

1   Brands, *T. R.*, 303; HCL to T. R., December 2, 1896, Lodge, Lodge-Roosevelt Correspondence, Vol. I, 241–242.

2   Brands, *T. R.*, 303.

3   HCL to Bellamy Storer, December 2, 1896, Reel 2 Lodge-Roosevelt Correspondence, MHS.

4   T. R. to HCL, December 4, 1896, Lodge, Lodge-Roosevelt Correspondence, Vol. I, 243–244.

5   HCL to T. R., December 7, 1896, Lodge, Lodge-Roosevelt Correspondence, Vol. I, 244–246. Garraty, *Henry Cabot Lodge*, 177.

6   HCL to T. R., December 7, 1896, Lodge, Lodge-Roosevelt Correspondence, Vol. I, 244–246.

7   HCL to T. R., December 7, 1896, Lodge, Lodge-Roosevelt Correspondence, Vol. I, 244–246; T. R. to HCL, December 9, 1896, Lodge, Lodge-Roosevelt Correspondence, Vol. I, 247.

8   HCL to T. R., January 21, 1897, Reel 2, Lodge-Roosevelt Correspondence, MHS.

9   HCL to T. R., March 8, 1897, Lodge, Lodge-Roosevelt Correspondence, Vol. I, 253–254.

10   HCL to T. R., March 8, 1897, Lodge-Roosevelt Correspondence, Vol. I, 253–254.

11   T. R. to HCL, March 22, 1897, Lodge, Lodge-Roosevelt Correspondence, Vol. I, 262.

12   John D. Long, *America of Yesterday: The Diary of John D. Long*, Lawrence Shaw Mayo, ed. (Boston: Atlantic Monthly Press, 1923), 147; Garraty, *Henry Cabot Lodge*, 178.

13   Long, *America of Yesterday*, 147. Garraty, *Henry Cabot Lodge*, 178.

14   Lodge, *The Lodge Women*, 105.

15   Garraty, *Henry Cabot Lodge*, 178–179.

16   Ibid.; "Theodore Roosevelt's Receipt from the Metropolitan Club Restaurant," Library of Congress Manuscript Division, www .theodorerooseveltcenter.org; John Knokey, *Theodore Roosevelt and the Making of American Leadership*, (New York: Skyhorse, 2015).

17   Morris, *Edith Kermit Roosevelt*, 165; Zimmermann, *First Great Triumph*, 185; Thomas, *The War Lovers*, 178; Brands, *T. R.*, 308.

18   Clay Risen, *The Crowded Hour: Theodore Roosevelt, the Rough Riders and the Dawn of The American Century*, (New York: Scribner, 2019), 28–30; Zimmermann, *First Great Triumph*, 250; Garraty, *Henry Cabot Lodge*, 180; Risen, *The Crowded Hour*, 41–42; Dalton, *Theodore Roosevelt*, 165.

19   Risen, *The Crowded Hour*, 28–30; Zimmermann, *First Great Triumph*, 250.

20   Garraty, *Henry Cabot Lodge*, 180; Risen, *The Crowded Hour*, 41–42; Dalton, *Theodore Roosevelt*, 165.

21   Ibid.

22   Garraty, *Henry Cabot Lodge*, 181–182.

23   Ibid.

24   T. R. to HCL, August 3, 1897, Lodge, Lodge-Roosevelt Correspondence, Vol. I, 268; Zimmermann, *First Great Triumph*, 239–240.

25   Risen, *The Crowded Hour*, 41.

26   Risen, *The Crowded Hour*, 41; Dalton, *Theodore Roosevelt*, 166; Garrity, "Young Men in a Hurry," 227–228.

27   HCL to T. R., August 19, 1897, Lodge, Lodge-Roosevelt Correspondence, Vol. I, 273; Zimmermann, *First Great Triumph*, 240.

28   Ibid.

29   T. R. to HCL, September 15, 1897, Lodge, Lodge-Roosevelt Correspondence, Vol. I, 276–277; Dalton, *Theodore Roosevelt*, 165.

30   HCL to T. R., September 27, 1897, Lodge, Lodge-Roosevelt Correspondence, Vol. I, 281.

31   HCL to T. R., September 28, 1897, Reel 2, Lodge-Roosevelt Correspondence, MHS; Lodge also asked Roosevelt about a potential appointment for a Lieutenant Commander Blocker "when the proper time comes." HCL to T. R., September 24, 1897, Reel 2, Lodge-Roosevelt Correspondence, MHS.

32   T. R. to HCL, November 5, 1897, Lodge, Lodge-Roosevelt Correspondence, Vol. I, 294.

33   Morris, *The Rise of Theodore Roosevelt*, 623; Garraty, *Henry Cabot Lodge*, 185.

34   Ibid.

35   Ibid.

36   Garraty, *Henry Cabot Lodge*, 186.

37   Ibid.; As Lodge later wrote about the order "I cannot conceive that any human being should criticize the department . . . I shall speak of the order issued by you [Captain A. S. Croninshield] and Mr. Roosevelt . . . as one of the wisest things that was done." Garraty, *Henry Cabot Lodge*, 186.

38   Brands, *T. R.*, 327–328; Zimmermann, *First Great Triumph*, 257.

39   Garraty, *Henry Cabot Lodge*, 188; Zimmermann, *First Great Triumph*, 258.

40   Garraty, *Henry Cabot Lodge*, 189.

41   Garraty, Henry Cabot Lodge, 189; Morris, *The Rise of Theodore Roosevelt*, 640; Brands, *T. R.*, 328–329.

42   Morris, *The Rise of Theodore Roosevelt*, 640; Worthington Chauncey Ford, *The Letters of Henry Adams, 1892–1918*, (Boston: Houghton Mifflin, 1938), 172–173.

43   Morris, *The Rise of Theodore Roosevelt*, 640; Winthrop Chanler, *Winthrop Chanler's Letters Collected by his Wife Margaret Terry Chanler*, (New York: Privately Printed, 1951), 68–69; Long, *America of Yesterday*, 186.

44   Garraty, *Henry Cabot Lodge*, 191.

45   Crowley, "Dear Bay," New York History, Vol. 53 No. 2, April 1972, 184–185.

46   Ibid.

47   Crowley, "Dear Bay," New York History, Vol. 53 No. 2, April 1972, 187; Garraty, *Henry Cabot Lodge*, 191.

48   T. R. to HCL, October 5, 1897, Reel 2, Lodge-Roosevelt Correspondence, MHS; Crowley, "Dear Bay," *New York History*, Vol. 53 No. 2, April 1972, 187; Garraty, *Henry Cabot Lodge*, 191.

49   Zimmermann, *First Great Triumph*, 273.

50   Ibid.

51   T. R. to HCL, May 19, 1898, Lodge, Lodge-Roosevelt Correspondence, Vol. I, 298.

52   HCL to T. R., May 24, 1898, Lodge, Lodge-Roosevelt Correspondence, Vol. I, 299–300.

53   Ibid.

54   T. R. to HCL, June 6, 1898, Lodge, Lodge-Roosevelt Correspondence, Vol. I, 303; T. R. to HCL, May 25, 1898, Lodge, Lodge-Roosevelt Correspondence, Vol. I, 301; Zimmermann, *First Great Triumph*, 274.

55   T. R. to HCL, June 10, 1898, Lodge, Lodge-Roosevelt Correspondence, Vol. I, 304–305.

56   Ibid.

57   T. R. to HCL, June 12, 1898, Lodge, Lodge-Roosevelt Correspondence, Vol. I, 309. Dalton, *Theodore Roosevelt*, 173; Brands, *T. R.*, 344.

58   HCL to T. R., June 15, 1898, Lodge, Lodge-Roosevelt Correspondence, Vol. I, 310.

59   T. R. to HCL, June 27, 1898, Lodge, Lodge-Roosevelt Correspondence, Vol. I, 314–315.

60   HCL to T. R., June 29, 1898, Lodge, Lodge-Roosevelt Correspondence, Vol. I, 316.

61   Crowley, "Dear Bay," *New York History*, Vol. 53 No. 2, April 1972, 186.

Chapter Nine: To the Top of the Pyramid

1   HCL to T. R., July 4, 1898, Lodge, Lodge-Roosevelt Correspondence, Volume I, 318; Lodge communicated his joy and his fears about Roosevelt, Bay, and Gus Gardner in a letter to Cecil Spring Rice.

2 HCL to T. R., July 6, 1898, Lodge, Lodge-Roosevelt Correspondence, Vol. I, 319–320.
3 Brands, *T. R.*, 361; "W. M. Laffan Dead of Appendicitis," *New York Times*, November 20, 1909, 11.
4 Ibid.
5 HCL to T. R. July 12, 1898. Lodge, Lodge-Roosevelt Correspondence, Volume I, 324; T. R. to HCL, July 31, 1898, Lodge, Lodge-Roosevelt Correspondence, Vol. I, 334; Edmund Morris, *The Rise of Theodore Roosevelt*, 695.
6 Ibid.
7 Morris, *The Rise of Theodore Roosevelt*, 692–693, 697; Brands, *T. R.*, 362; "Rough Riders Landed," *Washington Post*, August 16, 1898, 2; "The Rough Riders Land at Montauk," *New York Times*, August 16, 1898, 1; Duayne Draffen, "Roosevelt's Rough Ride Led to Montauk," *New York Times*, May 17, 1998, 14.
8 Ibid.
9 HCL to T. R., August 15, 1898. Lodge, Lodge-Roosevelt Correspondence, Vol. I, 337.
10 Morris, *The Rise of Theodore Roosevelt*, 698–699; Thomas Collier Platt, *The Autobiography of Thomas Collier Platt*, (New York, William Rickey and Co., 1910), 368.
11 Morris, *The Rise of Theodore Roosevelt*, 698–699; Platt, *The Autobiography of Thomas Collier Platt*, 368.
12 "Ex-Governor Black Dies at His Troy Home," *New York Times*, March 13, 1913, 13; Harold S. Gosnell, "Thomas C. Platt-Political Manager," *Political Science Quarterly*, Vol. 38, No. 3, September 1923, 445; Grondahl, *I Rose Like a Rocket*, 288.
13 "Ex-Governor Black Dies at His Troy Home," *New York Times*, March 13, 1913, 13; Gosnell, "Thomas C. Platt-Political Manager," *Political Science Quarterly*, Vol. 38, No. 3, September 1923, 445; Grondahl, *I Rose Like a Rocket*, 288.
14 Morris, *The Rise of Theodore Roosevelt*, 700; Castle Freeman Jr. "John Jay Chapman: Brief Life of a Neglected Critic," *Harvard Magazine*, January 1, 2001.
15 Morris, *The Rise of Theodore Roosevelt*, 701; Grondahl, *I Rose Like a Rocket*, 289; HCL to Thomas C. Platt, September 3, 1898, Reel 2, Lodge-Roosevelt Correspondence, MHS.
16 T. R. to HCL, September 4, 1898, Lodge, Lodge-Roosevelt Correspondence, Vol. I, 340.

387

17 Dalton, *Theodore Roosevelt*, 301.

18 HCL to T. R., September 8, 1898, Lodge, Lodge, Lodge-Roosevelt Correspondence, Vol. I, 343.

19 Platt, *The Autobiography of Thomas Collier Platt*, 369; M. F. Sweetser and Simon Ford, *How to Know New York City, a Serviceable Guide*, (New York: Kessinger Publishing, 1887), 98.

20 Morris, *The Rise of Theodore Roosevelt*, 708; Grondahl, *I Rose Like a Rocket*, 289; Platt, *The Autobiography of Thomas Collier Platt*, 369; Sweetser and Ford, *How to Know New York City*, 9; T. R. to HCL, September 19, 1898, Lodge, Lodge-Roosevelt Correspondence, Vol. I, 346.

21 HCL to T. R., September 23, 1898, Lodge-Roosevelt Correspondence, Vol. I, 348; HCL to T. R., September 12, 1898, Vol. I, Lodge-Roosevelt Correspondence, 344; Garraty, *Henry Cabot Lodge*, 87.

22 Ibid.

23 T. R. to HCL, September 28, 1898, Lodge, Lodge-Roosevelt Correspondence, Vol. I, 350; Grondahl, *I Rose Like a Rocket*, 291–293; Brands, *T. R.*, 366; Morris, *The Rise of Theodore Roosevelt*, 711; Dalton, *Theodore Roosevelt*, 274.

24 T. R. to HCL, September 28, 1898, Lodge-Roosevelt Correspondence, Vol. I, 350; Grondahl, *I Rose Like a Rocket*, 291–293;. Brands, *T. R.*, 366; Morris, *The Rise of Theodore Roosevelt*, 711.

25 Dalton, *Theodore Roosevelt*, 274.

26 HCL to T. R., October 14, 1898, Lodge, Lodge-Roosevelt Correspondence, Vol. I, 354; Morris, *The Rise of Theodore Roosevelt*, 715.

27 T. R. to HCL, October 14, 1898, Lodge, Lodge-Roosevelt Correspondence, Vol. I, 355.

28 Morris, *The Rise of Theodore Roosevelt*, 716.

29 Brands, *T. R.*, 368; Morris, *The Rise of Theodore Roosevelt*, 717.

30 Ibid.

31 T. R. to HCL, October 26, 1898, Lodge-Roosevelt Correspondence, Vol. I, 360. "Lodge on Campaign Issues," *New York Times*, October 25, 1898, 3.

32 T. R. to HCL, October 26, 1898, Lodge, Lodge-Roosevelt Correspondence, Vol. I, 360; HCL to T. R., November 3, 1898, Lodge-Roosevelt Correspondence, Vol. I, 361; Morris, *Edith Kermit Roosevelt*, 189.

33 Schriftgiesser, *The Gentleman from Massachusetts*, 180.

34 Garraty, *Henry Cabot Lodge*, 200.

35 Henry Adams, *The Letters of Henry Adams, Volume IV: 1892–1899*, 630; Schriftgiesser, *The Gentleman from Massachusetts*, 181; Despite the convivial atmosphere between Hay and Lodge the two strong-willed men continued to snipe at one another, all to the irritation of Henry

Adams. "The Senator, while agreeing in general approval of the Secretary of State's health, expresses an earnest wish that he would not look so exceedingly tired when approached on business at the department; while the Secretary with sobs in his voice assures me that the Senator gives him more trouble, about less matter, than all the governments of Europe, Asia and the Sulu Islands and all the Senators from the wild west and the Congressmen from the rebel confederacy. Tell me does patriotism pay me to act as a buffer state?" Henry Adams, *The Letters of Henry Adams, Volume IV: 1892-1899*, 635.

36   Garraty, *Henry Cabot Lodge*, 201–203; Henry Adams, *The Letters of Henry Adams, Volume IV: 1892-1899*, 659.

37   Garraty, *Henry Cabot Lodge*, 203; Henry Adams, *The Letters of Henry Adams, Volume IV: 1892-1899*, 670; Adams was perpetually complaining about the state of American politics, particularly as it concerned patronage and how Lodge and Mark Hanna were responsible. "There can be no executive efficiency while the Senate remains what it is," Adams stated that the current political climate where favoritism and back-room deals were the order of the day made it impossible for people of Adams's demeanor to succeed in the era's political environment. Henry Adams, *The Letters of Henry Adams, Volume IV: 1892-1899*, 646.

38   Garraty, *Henry Cabot Lodge*, 203.

39   T. R. to HCL, January 26, 1899, Lodge, Lodge-Roosevelt Correspondence, Vol. I, 390.

40   T. R. to HCL, December 27, 1898, Lodge, Lodge-Roosevelt Correspondence, Vol. I, 376.

41   Brands, *T. R.*, 370; HCL to T. R., December 31, 1899, Lodge, Lodge-Roosevelt Correspondence, Volume I, 377.

42   Brands, *T. R.*, 371.

43   Grondahl, *I Rose Like a Rocket*, 302–303, 318; Platt admitted he was pleased with the deference T. R. showed him but was also realistic that the governor was not someone who was easily controlled. "Roosevelt had from the first agreed he would consult me on all questions of appointments, Legislature or party policy. He religiously fulfilled this pledge, although he frequently did just what he pleased," Platt wrote in his memoirs. Grondahl, *I Rose Like a Rocket*, 307.

44   Grondahl, *I Rose Like a Rocket*, 325; Brands, *T. R.*, 378; T. R. to HCL, March 18, 1899, Lodge, Lodge-Roosevelt Correspondence, Vol. I, 396.

45   Grondahl, *I Rose Like a Rocket*, 327–328.

46   T. R. to HCL, April 27, 1899, Lodge, Lodge-Roosevelt Correspondence, Vol. I, 398.

47   Ibid., 399.

48   Ibid.; During the Lodges' trip they met Henry Adams who remained generally unhappy about his encounters with the public. "I am here

with the Lodges and a crowd of Americans unknown to me," Adams
crowed to Lizzie Cameron. "Why I came I do not know, except that Mrs.
Lodge brought me; nor do I know why or when or where I shall go."
Henry Adams, *The Letters of Henry Adams, Volume IV: 1892-1899,* 721.

49   Garraty, *Henry Cabot Lodge,* 203; Lodge, *The Lodge Women,* 126.

50   Garraty, *Henry Cabot Lodge,* 203; HCL to T. R., May 11, 1899, Lodge,
      Lodge-Roosevelt Correspondence, Vol. I, 400.

51   Garraty, *Henry Cabot Lodge,* 203. HCL to T. R., May 11, 1899, Lodge,
      Lodge-Roosevelt Correspondence, Vol. I, 401.

52   Morris, *The Rise of Theodore Roosevelt,* 739. "The Philippine-American
      War 1899–1902," Office of the Historian, www.history.state.gov.

53   Morris, *The Rise of Theodore Roosevelt,* 739–740; HCL to T. R., May 11,
      1899, Lodge-Roosevelt Correspondence, Vol. I, 400–401.

54   "Gov. Roosevelt in 1900 will not be a candidate for president," *New York
      Times,* June 30, 1899, 4.

55   Ibid.; T. R. to HCL, July 1, 1899, Lodge, Lodge-Roosevelt
      Correspondence, Vol. I, 404.

56   Morris, *The Rise of Theodore Roosevelt,* 741.

57   T. R. to HCL, July 1, 1899, Lodge, Lodge-Roosevelt Correspondence,
      Vol. I, 404.

58   Ibid.

59   Grondahl, *I Rose Like a Rocket,* 332.

60   T. R. to HCL, August 10, 1899, Lodge, Lodge-Roosevelt
      Correspondence, Vol. I, 417; T. R. to HCL, August 28, 1899, Lodge,
      Lodge-Roosevelt Correspondence, Vol. I, 418.

61   Ibid.

62   T. R. to HCL, August 28, 1899, Lodge, Lodge-Roosevelt
      Correspondence, Vol. I, 404.

63   T. R. to HCL, August 28, 1899, Lodge, Lodge-Roosevelt
      Correspondence, Vol. I, 404; Grondahl, *I Rose Like a Rocket,* 332; Miller,
      Theodore Roosevelt, 334.

64   HCL to T. R., December 7, 1899, Lodge, Lodge-Roosevelt
      Correspondence, Vol. I, 424; Morris, *The Rise of Theodore Roosevelt,* 741.

65   Ibid.

Chapter Ten: An Unhappy Choice

1   Mark Sullivan, *Our Times: The United States 1900–1925; Vol. I The Turn
      of the Century,* (New York: Charles Scribner's Sons, 1926), 97.

2   T. R. to HCL, December 11, 1899, Lodge, Lodge-Roosevelt
      Correspondence, Vol. I, 426; Morris, *The Rise of Theodore Roosevelt,* 741.

3   Ibid.

4   Morris, *The Rise of Theodore Roosevelt,* 749; Grondahl, *I Rose Like a
      Rocket,* 333.

5   HCL to T. R., December 19, 1899, Lodge, Lodge-Roosevelt
     Correspondence, Vol. I, 430–431.

6   T. R. to John Hay, July 1, 1899, Vol. I, Lodge, Lodge-Roosevelt
     Correspondence, 407.

7   HCL to T. R., December 29, 1899, Lodge, Lodge-Roosevelt
     Correspondence, Vol. I, 433.

8   Ibid.; Morris, *The Rise of Theodore Roosevelt*, 741; T. R. to HCL,
     December 29, 1899, Lodge, Lodge-Roosevelt correspondence, Vol. I, 434.

9   Grondahl, *I Rose Like a Rocket*, 341.

10   Margaret Leech, *In the Days of McKinley* (New York: Harper Brothers,
     1959), 530; Cong. Record, Vol. 33, 733–734.

11   Leech, *In the Days of McKinley*, 530; Cong. Record, Vol. 33, Part I,
     (Dec. 4, 1899–Jan. 10, 1900), 743–744.

12   Garraty, *Henry Cabot Lodge*, 203.

13   Lodge, *The Lodge Women*, 174.

14   Ibid., 172, 175.

15   Ibid.

16   Ibid., 176–177.

17   Garraty, *Henry Cabot Lodge*, 203; In mid-January, Henry Adams wrote
     Elizabeth Cameron that he had recently visited with Bay Lodge and
     noted that his secret engagement "seems to be quite public." Henry
     Adams, *The Letters of Henry Adams, Vol. V: 1899–1905*, (Cambridge,
     Mass.: Harvard University Press, 1988), 72. Hay's biographer writes
     "one wonders if the chronic friction between the senator and the
     secretary of state, ostensibly over treaties and the direction of foreign
     policy, was not exacerbated by the subtext of cuckoldry." Taliaferro, *All
     the Great Prizes*, 10.

18   Taliaferro, *All the Great Prizes*, 342–343.

19   Garraty, *Henry Cabot Lodge*, 211; Lodge, *The Lodge Women*, 129.

20   Garraty, *Henry Cabot Lodge*, 211.

21   Zimmermann, *First Great Triumph*, 426.

22   Garraty, *Henry Cabot Lodge*, 211.

23   Zimmermann, *First Great Triumph*, 426–427.

24   Ibid.; Garraty, *Henry Cabot Lodge*, 212–213; Adams lamented to Lizzie
     Cameron how disappointed he was about the reaction to the new treaty.

25   Lodge, *The Lodge Women*, 130.

26   Ibid., 134; Henry Adams came up with a new description of Lodge which
     he called "cabotin." The phrased defined Lodge as "a second-rate strolling
     actor" or a "political showman." Adams, *The Letters of Henry Adams,
     Vol. V: 1899–1905*, 96.

27   Lodge, *The Lodge Women*, 130; Emily Lodge describes the Adams
     view in the following manner: "no longer the Senator's mentor shows a
     combination of disdain and jealousy for his protégé, who was after all a

doer, who enjoyed imposing his will and who unlike Adams chose a more active life." Lodge, *The Lodge Women*, 134.

28   Michael Knox Beran, *Wasps: The Splendors and Miseries of an American Aristocracy*, (New York: Pegasus Books, 2021), 85; A note from Adams illustrates Lodge's sole devotion to politics by his attempt to arrange the appointment of a man Adams believed entirely unqualified to serve as Librarian of Congress. "Cabot went every day to the White House to press on McKinley an appointment which he knew to be exceedingly unfit, and which he did not want to have made, and which he knew would disgust his own wife and children as well as Hay and me and the Senate." Schriftgiesser, *The Gentleman from Massachusetts*, 189.

29   Simpson, "Henry Adams in the Age of Grant," *Hayes Historical Journal*, Vol. 8, No. 3, Spring, 1989, www.rbhayes.org; Taliaferro, *All the Great Prizes*, 341.

30   Beran, *Wasps*, 85.

31   Garraty, *Henry Cabot Lodge*, 223.

32   T. R. to HCL, January 22, 1900, Lodge, Lodge-Roosevelt Correspondence, Vol. I, 437; Harbaugh, *Power and Responsibility*, 132.

33   Grondahl, *I Rose Like a Rocket*, 336; Platt defended his argument about the need for Roosevelt to take the vice presidency in his autobiography. "I believed the death of Vice President Hobart had weakened the Republican Party, and that some strong, popular personality needed to be added to the ticket to be nominated in 1900; and I firmly believed that the virile personality of Mr. Roosevelt . . . would add great strength to the national ticket that year." Grondahl, *I Rose Like a Rocket*, 336.

34   HCL to T. R., January 25, 1900, Lodge, Lodge-Roosevelt correspondence, Vol. I, 439.

35   Grondahl, *I Rose Like a Rocket*, 341; Morris, *The Rise of Theodore Roosevelt*, 753.

36   HCL to T. R., January 27, 1900, Lodge, Vol. I, 439–440.

37   HCL to T. R., January 27, 1900, Lodge, Lodge-Roosevelt correspondence, Vol. I, 439–440.

38   T. R. to HCL, January 30, 1900, Lodge, Lodge-Roosevelt Correspondence, Vol. I, 442.

39   T. R. to HCL, February 2, 1900, Lodge, Lodge-Roosevelt Correspondence, Vol. I, 447; HCL to T. R., February 2, 1900, Lodge, Lodge-Roosevelt Correspondence, Vol. I, 444.

40   Brands, *T. R.*, 393.

41   Morris, *The Rise of Theodore Roosevelt*, 754–755.

42   Ibid.

43   T. R. to HCL, February 2, 1900, Lodge, Lodge-Roosevelt Correspondence, Vol. I, 447.

44   Ibid.

45   Morris, *The Rise of Theodore Roosevelt*, 757; Days earlier following an inquiry from Republican newspaper publisher and McKinley intimate H. H. Kohlsaat Roosevelt bluntly stated "the Vice Presidency was one of the few things I made up my mind it was not needful to write about. I am not going to take it on any account . . . It is the very last office I would want or care for. H. H. Kohlsaat, *From McKinley to Harding: Personal Recollections of Our Presidents*, (New York: Charles Scribner's Sons, 1923), 86.

46   Garraty, *Henry Cabot Lodge*, 204. Mrs. Lodge's obituary was on the front page of the *Boston Evening Transcript*, February 19, 1900, 1.

47   T. R. to HCL, March 8, 1900, Lodge, Lodge-Roosevelt Correspondence, Vol. I, 451.

48   Garraty, *Henry Cabot Lodge*, 204.

49   Garraty, *Henry Cabot Lodge*, 206; Widenor, *Henry Cabot Lodge and the Search for an American Foreign Policy*, 118.

50   Ibid.

51   Garraty, *Henry Cabot Lodge*, 206.

52   HCL to T. R., April 11, 1900, Lodge, Lodge-Roosevelt Correspondence Vol. I, 457–458.

53   Ibid.

54   HCL to T. R., April 16, 1900, Lodge, Lodge-Roosevelt Correspondence, Vol. I, 459.

55   HCL to T. R., April 19, 1900, Lodge, *Selections from the Correspondence of Theodore Roosevelt and Henry Cabot Lodge 1884–1918 Volume I*, 460; Chessman, "Theodore Roosevelt's Campaign Against the Vice-Presidency," *The Historian*, Vol. 14, No.2. (Spring 1952), 182.

56   HCL to T. R., April 19, 1900, Lodge, Lodge-Roosevelt Correspondence, Vol. I, 460; Chessman, "Theodore Roosevelt's Campaign Against the Vice-Presidency," *The Historian*, Vol. 14, No.2. (Spring 1952), 182.

57   Tom Lansford, *Theodore Roosevelt in Perspective*, (New York: Novinka Books, 2005), 56–57; There was also personal animosity between T. R. and Hanna. Before the Spanish-American War Theodore had used Hanna as an example of those individuals who were more concerned with making money than the nation's national interest. The two also had an unpleasant encounter at a GOP fundraising dinner when Roosevelt had shaken his fist at Hanna and exclaimed, "We will have this war for the freedom of Cuba, Senator Hanna, in spite of the timidity of the commercial interests." Hanna also found Roosevelt contemptible following his comment about McKinley's backbone being no better than a chocolate éclair. Brands, *T. R.*, 395.

58   Morris, *The Rise of Theodore Roosevelt*, 758.

59   Dalton, *Theodore Roosevelt*, 191.

60   T. R. to HCL, April 23, 1900, Lodge, Lodge-Roosevelt Correspondence, Vol. I, 461; Morris, *The Rise of Theodore Roosevelt*, 758.

61   Brands, *T. R.*, 394–395.

62   Morris, *The Rise of Theodore Roosevelt*, 760.

63   Leech, *In the Days of McKinley*, 531.

64   Morris, *The Rise of Theodore Roosevelt*, 760.

65   Dalton, *Theodore Roosevelt*, 191; Miller, *Theodore Roosevelt*, 340; Brands, *T. R.*, 397.

66   Ibid.

67   Miller, *Theodore Roosevelt*, 341; Morris, *The Rise of Theodore Roosevelt*, 762–765.

68   Theodore Roosevelt, *The Selected Letters of Theodore Roosevelt*, H. W. Brands, ed., (New York: Cooper Square Press, 2001), 242.

69   Scott Martelle, "Opinion: Like Teddy Roosevelt, Trump Wants to be the Bride at Every Wedding," *Los Angeles Times*, June 2, 2017, www.latimes.com.

70   Morris, *The Rise of Theodore Roosevelt*, 767; T. R. to HCL, June 25, 1900, Lodge, Lodge-Roosevelt Correspondence, Volume I, 465.

71   Morris, *The Rise of Theodore Roosevelt*, 768–769.

72   T. R. to HCL, June 25, 1900, Lodge-Roosevelt correspondence, Vol. 465.

73   Schriftgiesser, *The Gentleman from Massachusetts*, 193; In an account of Roosevelt's nomination by journalist Arthur W. Dunn: When Roosevelt's supporters expressed their belief that accepting the vice presidency was the equivalent of committing suicide, Lodge responded by saying "political suicide? I cannot imagine any more effective method of accomplishing such a result than by declining a nomination for the second highest office in the land when tendered by the Republican Party." Arthur Wallace Dunn, *From Harrison to Harding: A Personal Narrative, Covering a Third of a Century, 1888–1921*, (New York: G.P. Putnam, 1922), 338.

Chapter Eleven: Rendezvous with Destiny

1   Garraty, *Henry Cabot Lodge*, 214.

2   Morris, *The Rise of Theodore Roosevelt*, 768.

3   HCL to T. R., June 29, 1900, Lodge, Lodge-Roosevelt Correspondence, Vol. I, 467.

4   HCL to T. R., June 29, 1900, Lodge, Lodge-Roosevelt Correspondence, Vol. I, 467–468; Taliaferro, *All the Great Prizes*, 389–390.

5   HCL to T. R., June 29, 1900, Lodge, Lodge-Roosevelt Correspondence, Vol. I, 467–468.

6   Ibid., 468.

7   Dalton, *Theodore Roosevelt*, 194; Morris, *The Rise of Theodore Roosevelt*, 769; Roosevelt had a tenuous relationship with the Republican Party. During the 1896 campaign T. R. believed that the party was "a precious fortress of stability." T. R. and Lodge viewed the Democrats as ideological opponents who once in power would initiate "radical change . . . The crooks and the

criminals, the anarchists and the socialists . . . it had to be defeated." Blum, *The Republican Roosevelt*, 12.

8   Dalton, *Theodore Roosevelt*, 194.

9   Lodge, *The Lodge Women*, 180–181; In a report on the couple's wedding featured in the *Boston Evening Transcript*, the article noted that the marriage that occurred on August 18, 1900, was "a surprise to their wide circle of friends who had expected the event to take place at Bar Harbor early next month." "Quietly Married at the Advent," *Boston Evening Transcript*, August 20, 1900, 10.

10   Lodge, *The Lodge Women*, 180–183.

11   HCL to T. R., August 27, 1900, Reel 3, Lodge-Roosevelt correspondence, MHS; While Roosevelt had expressed surprise at the marriage, Lodge quickly came to view the event in a positive light. "Thank you for your kind words about Bay." (Earlier T. R. had commented that "Bay really has a touch of genius in him and we cannot hold genius to the lines to which we hold more common place people.") "Whatever his manner of getting married he has made a most fortunate choice, in my opinion, and I hope it will develop him." HCL to T. R., August 30, 1900, Lodge, Lodge-Roosevelt Correspondence, Vol. I, 475; T. R. to HCL, August 28, 1900, Lodge-Roosevelt Correspondence, Vol. I, 474.

12   "Governor Roosevelt in Denver," *New York Times*, September 26, 1900, 8; Dalton, *Theodore Roosevelt*, 195.

13   Harbaugh, *Power and Responsibility*, 140.

14   T. R. to HCL, August 28, 1900, Lodge, Lodge-Roosevelt Correspondence, Vol. I, 474; T. R. to HCL, November 9, 1900, Lodge-Roosevelt Correspondence, Vol. I, 479.

15   "Party's Duty," *Boston Sunday Globe*, November 11, 1900, 9.

16   Garraty, Henry Cabot Lodge, 214.

17   Ibid.

18   Ibid., 215.

19   Taliaferro, *All the Great Prizes*, 391, 394; In further comments about Lodge, Hay viewed the Senator as a ruthless bureaucratic infighter. "He is not unfriendly to me personally," Hay told White, "But neither you nor I would weight a feather weight with him, as against any selfish advantage. He would cut my throat or yours for a favorable notice in a newspaper." Hay also held low regard for the Senate and those who occupied it. "You may work for months over a treaty," Hay wrote Henry White, "and at last get everything satisfactorily arranged and send it into the Senate, [where] it is met by every man who wants to get a political advantage or to satisfy a personal grudge, everyone who has asked for an office & not got it, everyone whose wife who may think mine has not been attentive enough—and if they can muster one third of the Senate + one, your treaty is lost without any reference to its merits." Taliaferro, *All the Great Prizes*, 369.

20 "Table Gossip," *Sunday Boston Globe*, March 3, 1901, 38; "Inauguration of Roosevelt," *Boston Evening Transcript*, March 4, 5.

21 "Looking Ahead—Republicans Planning for 1904," March 3, 1901, *Boston Globe*, 3.

22 Ibid.

23 Brands, *T. R.*, 407; T. R. to HCL, March 27, 1901, Lodge-Roosevelt Correspondence Vol. I, 484–485; Dalton, *Theodore Roosevelt*, 196.

24 Brands, *T. R.*, 408.

25 Brands, *T. R.*, 407; T. R. to HCL, March 27, 1901, Lodge, Lodge-Roosevelt Correspondence, Vol. I, 484–485; Dalton, *Theodore Roosevelt*, 196.

26 T. R. to HCL, March 27, 1901, Lodge, Lodge-Roosevelt Correspondence, Vol. I, 484–485; HCL to T. R., March 30, 1901, Lodge, Lodge-Roosevelt Correspondence, Vol., I, 486–488.

27 Dalton, *Theodore Roosevelt*, 197.

28 T. R. to HCL, March 29, 1901, Lodge, Lodge-Roosevelt Correspondence Vol. I, 486; HCL to T. R., March 30, 1901, Lodge, Lodge-Roosevelt Correspondence, Vol. I, 488; HCL to T. R., April 4, 1901, Lodge, Lodge-Roosevelt Correspondence, Vol. I, 488; Dalton, *Theodore Roosevelt*, 727.

29 T. R. to HCL, April 10, 1901, Lodge, Lodge-Roosevelt Correspondence, Vol. I, 489. "A Successful Celebration," *Buffalo Review*, May 21, 1901, 4; Dalton, *Theodore Roosevelt*, 198.

30 "Senator Lodge's Speech," *Buffalo Review*, May 21, 1901, 4.

31 HCL to T. R., June 17, 1901, Lodge, Lodge-Roosevelt Correspondence, Vol. I, 492.

32 Dalton, *Theodore Roosevelt*, 198.

33 Ibid.

34 Dalton, *Theodore Roosevelt*, 199; T. R. to HCL, June 22, 1901, Lodge, Lodge-Roosevelt Correspondence, Vol. I, 495.

35 Brands, *T. R.*, 411; T. R. to HCL, August 20, 1901, Lodge, Lodge-Roosevelt Correspondence Vol. I, 497–498.

36 Brands, *T. R.*, 411; T. R. to HCL, August 20, 1901, Lodge, Lodge-Roosevelt Correspondence, Vol. I, 497–498.

37 Dalton, *Theodore Roosevelt*, 199; Brands, *T. R.*, 411.

38 Ibid.

39 T. R. to HCL, September 9, 1901, Lodge, Lodge-Roosevelt Correspondence Vol. I, 499.

40 Ibid., 501.

41 Brands, *T. R.*, 412–413; T. R. to HCL, September 9, 1901, Lodge-Roosevelt Correspondence, Vol. I, 501–502.

42 HCL to T. R., September 12, 1901, Lodge, Lodge-Roosevelt Correspondence, Vol. I, 502.

43 Lodge to Roosevelt, September 19, 1901, *Selections from the Correspondence of Theodore Roosevelt and Henry Cabot Lodge 1884–1918 Vol. I,* 504–505.

44 Beatty, *The Age of Betrayal*, 23–25; Kate Bacon, "Dark Side of the Gilded Age," *The Atlantic*, June 2007, www.atlantic.com.
45 Ibid.
46 Dalton, *Theodore Roosevelt*, 200–201; Brands, *T. R.*, 414.
47 Ibid.; Brands, *T. R.*, 415–416.
48 T. R. to HCL, September 23, 1901, Lodge, Lodge-Roosevelt Correspondence, Vol. I, 506.
49 Theodore Roosevelt, "The Strenuous Life," April 10, 1899, Voices of Democracy: A U.S. Oratory Project, www.voicesofdemocracyumd.edu; Dalton, *Theodore Roosevelt*, 420.

Chapter Twelve: The Changing of the Guard
1 Adams, *The Letters of Henry Adams, Vol. V*, 291.
2 Ibid., 300.
3 Garraty, *Henry Cabot Lodge*, 221; HCL to T. R., September 15, 1901, Theodore Roosevelt Institute, Dickenson State University.
4 HCL to T. R., September 15, 1901, Theodore Roosevelt Institute, Dickenson State University.
5 Ibid. Garraty, *Henry Cabot Lodge*, 222; Widenor, *Henry Cabot Lodge and the Search for an American Foreign Policy*, 127; Taliaferro, *All the Great Prizes*, 409.
6 Garraty, *Henry Cabot Lodge*, 222.
7 HCL to T. R., October 17, 1901, Lodge-Roosevelt Correspondence, Vol. I, 506; Brands, *T. R.*, 426.
8 T. R. to HCL, October 11, 1901, Reel 3, Lodge-Roosevelt Correspondence, MHS.
9 HCL to T. R., October 17, 1901, Lodge, Lodge-Roosevelt Correspondence, Vol. I, 506–507.
10 Dalton, *Theodore Roosevelt*, 215.
11 Ibid.
12 Ibid., 216.
13 HCL to T. R., October 19, 1901, Theodore Roosevelt Institute, Dickenson State University.
14 T. R. to HCL, October 28, 1901, Lodge, Lodge-Roosevelt Correspondence Vol. I, 510.
15 HCL to T. R., December 3, 1901, Lodge, Lodge-Roosevelt Correspondence, Vol. I, 512–513. Brands, *T. R.*, 427–428.
16 Brands, *T. R.*, 427–428.
17 Arthur Wallace Dunn, *From Harrison to Harding*, 261.
18 Ibid., 357.
19 Brands, *T. R.*, 546; Roosevelt, *Autobiography*, 352; Widenor, *Henry Cabot Lodge and the Search for an American Foreign Policy*, 128–129; Roosevelt's longtime friend, *Outlook* editor Lyman Abbott, wrote that the two

men's political views were only similar in foreign policy and that Roosevelt initially "looked up to Lodge as his adviser and leader." The author continues that over time as Roosevelt became more self-assured "their positions were gradually and perhaps unconsciously reversed and Roosevelt grew to be the leader while Lodge became the follower and disciple." Lyman Abbott, "More Rooseveltiana," *The Outlook*, April 29, 1925, 645–646.

20   Garraty, *Henry Cabot Lodge*, note, bottom 222.

21   O'Toole, *The Five of Hearts*, 362; John Hay, *Letters from John Hay and Extracts from Diary, Vol. III*, (Washington: Clara Hay, 1908).

22   Ford, *Letters of Henry Adams 1892–1918*, 365–366.

23   Ibid.; Morris, *Edith Kermit Roosevelt*, 231.

24   Ford, *Letters of Henry Adams 1892–1918*, 366.

25   Ibid.

26   Widenor, *Henry Cabot Lodge and the Search for an American Foreign Policy*, 121.

27   Garraty, *Henry Cabot Lodge*, 222.

28   Notes like the following were typical of those sent from the White House to Henry Cabot Lodge. "The President requests me to state that he and Mrs. Roosevelt will call at your house at 3:30 o'clock this afternoon, and would like very much to have you go riding with them." George M. Cortelyou to HCL, November 20, 1901, Reel 3, Lodge-Roosevelt correspondence, MHS; Other letters of a more intimate nature include the following from President Roosevelt about the poor of state of Theodore Roosevelt Jr.'s health. "Ted has double Pneumonia and is critically ill. It is too early as yet to speculate to the chances for his recovery . . . When he is clear in his own mind he is so plucky and good humored and thoughtful for others that I think his chances are better than they otherwise would be." T. R. to HCL, July 10, 1902, Reel 3, Lodge-Roosevelt Correspondence, MHS.

29   Garraty, *Henry Cabot Lodge*, 224; John A. Garraty, "Holmes Appointment to the U.S. Supreme Court," New England Quarterly, Vol. 22, No. 3, Sept. 1949, 291–292.

30   HCL to T. R., June 5, 1902, Lodge, Lodge-Roosevelt Correspondence Vol. I, 516.

31   Garraty, "Holmes Appointment to the U.S. Supreme Court," *New England Quarterly*, Vol. 22, No. 3, Sept. 1949, 293.

32   Garraty, *Henry Cabot Lodge*, 224.

33   "Holmes Appointment to the U.S. Supreme Court," *New England Quarterly*, Vol. 22, No. 3, Sept. 1949, 293–294.

34   "Downes V. Bidwell—182 U.S. 244, 21S. ct. 770 (1901), Law School Case Brief, www.lexisnexis.com; Doug Mack, "The Strange Case of Puerto Rico," *Slate*, Oct. 9, 2017, www.slate.com; Garraty, "Holmes Appointment to the U.S. Supreme Court," *New England Quarterly*, Vol. 22, No. 3, Sept. 1949, 294.

35   Garraty, "Holmes Appointment to the U.S. Supreme Court," *New England Quarterly*, Vol. 22, No. 3, Sept. 1949, 295.

36   Garraty, "Holmes Appointment to the U.S. Supreme Court," *New England Quarterly*, Vol. 22, No. 3, Sept. 1949, 295.

37   Brands, *T. R.*, 440; T. R. to HCL, July 10, 1902, Lodge, Lodge-Roosevelt Correspondence, Vol. I, 517–519; Mark Sullivan, *Our Times the United States 1900–1925: Vol. III Pre War America*, (New York: Charles Scribner's Sons, 1930), 7.

38   Garraty, *Henry Cabot Lodge*, 224.

39   Garraty, "Holmes Appointment to the U.S. Supreme Court," *New England Quarterly*, Vol. 22, No. 3, Sept. 1949, 295.

40   Garraty, *Henry Cabot Lodge*, 224.

41   Ibid., 224–225.

42   "Norman on Henry Cabot Lodge as the Boss of Washington," *Boston Sunday Post*, June 8, 1902, 16.

43   Ibid.

44   Brands, *T. R.*, 546; "Norman on Henry Cabot Lodge as the Boss of Washington," *Boston Sunday Post*, June 8, 1902, 16.

45   HCL to T. R., Aug. 9, 1902, Lodge, Lodge-Roosevelt Correspondence, Vol. I, 524.

46   HCL to T. R., Aug. 9, 1902, Lodge, Lodge-Roosevelt Correspondence, Vol. I, 524. T. R. to HCL Aug. 11, 1902, Lodge-Roosevelt Correspondence, Vol. I, 525.

47   Garraty, *Henry Cabot Lodge*, 222.

48   Harbaugh, *Power and Responsibility*, 151; Garraty, *Henry Cabot Lodge*, 226.

49   Garraty, *Henry Cabot Lodge*, 226.

50   Ibid.; William Jennings Bryan, *The Commoner Condensed, Vol. II*, (Lincoln, Neb.: Jacob North & Co., 1903), 321.

51   Harbaugh, *Power and Responsibility*, 156; Leroy G. Dorsey, "Theodore Roosevelt and Corporate America 1901–1909: A Re-Examination," *Presidential Studies Quarterly*, Vol. 25, No. 4, (Fall 1995), 725–726.

52   Brands, *T. R.* 435–436. "The Northern Securities Case," Theodore Roosevelt Center, Dickinson State University, www.theodore rooseveltcenter.org.

53   Brands, *T. R.*, 448–449; "Mrs. Lodge Sponsor," *Boston Globe*, Aug. 22, 1902, 12.

54   "President in Boston Today," Unknown date and publication, "Photographs and Clippings of President Roosevelt's Visit, Nahant & Lynn, 1902," Essex National Heritage Area.

55   "Mayor Shepard Sees the President and Mrs. Henry Cabot Lodge Off from Lynn for the Lodge Villa at Nahant," *Boston Globe*, Aug. 25, 1902, 1. "At Nahant Line," *Lynn Item*, undated, "Photographs and Clippings of President Roosevelt's Visit, Nahant & Lynn, 1902," Essex National Heritage Area.

56 "When the President Comes," *Boston Evening Transcript*, Aug. 15, 1902, 1.
57 "Roosevelt in Lynn," *Boston Evening Transcript*, Aug. 25, 1902, 5.
58 "Nahant and Lynn," unknown date and publication, "Photographs and Clippings of President Roosevelt's visit, Nahant & Lynn, 1902," Essex National Heritage Area.
59 Ibid.
60 Brands, *T. R.*, 451.
61 Ibid., 452.
62 Ibid., 453; HCL to T. R., Oct. 22, 1902, Lodge, Lodge-Roosevelt Correspondence, Vol. I, 528–529.
63 HCL to T. R., Sept. 22, 1902, Lodge, Lodge-Roosevelt Correspondence, Vol. I, 528–529.
64 Ibid.
65 HCL to T. R., Sept. 25, 1902, Lodge-Roosevelt Correspondence, Vol. I, 530.
66 T. R. to HCL, Sept. 27, 1902, Lodge-Roosevelt Correspondence, Vol. I, 532–533; Harbaugh, *Power and Responsibility*, 171.
67 Harbaugh, *Power and Responsibility*, 171; Susan Berfield, "The Coal Strike that Defined Theodore Roosevelt's Presidency," Smithsonian, July 15, 2020, www.smithsonianmag.org
68 Ibid.
69 Harbaugh, *Power and Responsibility*, 174; HCL to T. R., Oct. 5, 1902, Lodge, Lodge-Roosevelt Correspondence, Vol. I, 537.
70 Harbaugh, *Power and Responsibility*, 176; T. R. to HCL, Oct. 7, 1902, Lodge, Lodge-Roosevelt Correspondence, Vol. I, 538.
71 Ibid.
72 HCL to T. R., Oct. 11, 1902, Lodge, Lodge-Roosevelt Correspondence, Vol. I, 539.
73 Harbaugh, *Power and Responsibility*, 177.
74 "Launching the Corsair," *New York Times*, Dec. 13, 1898; Berfield, "The Coal Strike that Defined Theodore Roosevelt's Presidency," *Smithsonian*, July 15, 2020, www.smithsonianmag.org.
75 T. R. to HCL, November Oct. 17, 1902, Lodge, Lodge-Roosevelt Correspondence, Vol. I, 541.
76 Harbaugh, *Power and Responsibility*, 180–181.
77 Ibid.

Chapter Thirteen: A Delicate Balance
1 Adams, *The Letters of Henry Adams*, 398.
2 HCL to T. R., October 20, 1902, Lodge, Lodge-Roosevelt Correspondence, Vol. I, 542.
3 Schriftgiesser, *The Gentleman from Massachusetts*, 207.
4 "Last Speeches on President's List," *New York Times*, June 4, 1903, 1; T. R. to HCL, June 6, 1903, Theodore Roosevelt Center, Dickinson

University. "A Miners Story," E-History, The Ohio State University, www. ehistory.osu.edu.

5   HCL to T. R., June 10, 1903, Reel 4, Lodge-Roosevelt Correspondence, MHS.

6   Ibid.

7   T. R. to HCL, May 23, 1903, Lodge, *Selections from the Correspondence of Theodore Roosevelt, and Henry Cabot Lodge 1884–1918 Vol. II*, (New York: Charles Scribner's Sons, 1925), 17; HCL to T. R., May 21, 1903, Lodge, Lodge-Roosevelt Correspondence, Vol. II, 14.

8   Schriftgiesser, *The Gentleman from Massachusetts*, 212.

9   "Friction in Philippines," *New York Times*, April 11, 1902, 3.

10   Morris, *Theodore Rex*, (New York: Random House, 2002), 97, 99; Garraty, *Henry Cabot Lodge*, 209.

11   Garraty, *Henry Cabot Lodge*, 210; Ford, *Letters of Henry Adams 1802–1918*, 371.

12   Garraty, *Henry Cabot Lodge*, 244.

13   Ibid.

14   Ibid.

15   Harbaugh, *Power and Responsibility*, 189; HCL to T. R., Feb. 17, 1903, Lodge, Lodge-Roosevelt Correspondence, Vol. II, 2; "Personal and Confidential," March 25, 1903, Lodge-Roosevelt Correspondence Vol. II, 5.

16   HCL to T. R., June 23, 1903, Lodge, Lodge-Roosevelt Correspondence, Vol. II, 33; Garraty, *Henry Cabot Lodge*, 246.

17   T. R. to HCL June 29, 1903, Lodge, Lodge-Roosevelt Correspondence, Vol. II, 37; HCL to T. R., July 1, 1903, Reel 4, Lodge-Roosevelt Correspondence, MHS.

18   Garraty and Lodge, "Henry Cabot Lodge and the Alaskan Boundary Tribunal," *New England Quarterly*, Vol. 24, No. 4, Dec. 1951, 475.

19   Ibid.

20   Garraty, *Henry Cabot Lodge*, 250; Schriftgiesser, *The Gentleman from Massachusetts*, 210; While in London Lodge attempted to convince the British Foreign Secretary, Lord Lansdowne, to appoint Cecil Spring Rice as secretary to the British Embassy in Washington. Lodge made the request on two occasions but was unable to arrange the diplomat's transfer. While Spring Rice appreciated the gesture he was heavily involved in matters in St. Petersburg and little interest in leaving. Gwynn, *The Letters and Friendships of Cecil Spring Rice: A Record, Vol. I*, 370–371.

21   Garraty and Lodge, "Henry Cabot Lodge and the Alaskan Boundary Tribunal," *New England Quarterly*, Vol. 24, No. 4, Dec. 1951, 484; T. R. to HCL, Oct. 5, 1903, Lodge, Lodge-Roosevelt Correspondence, Vol. II, 66; T. R. to HCL, Aug. 16, 1903, Lodge, Lodge-Roosevelt Correspondence, Vol. II, 45.

22   HCL to T. R. July 30, 1903, Lodge, Lodge-Roosevelt Correspondence, Vol. II, 42; Garraty and Lodge, "Henry Cabot Lodge and the Alaskan

Boundary Tribunal," *New England Quarterly*, Vol. 24, No. 4, Dec. 1951, 476; Harbaugh, *Power and Responsibility*, 190–191.

23   T. R. to HCL, Oct. 12, 1903, Lodge, Lodge-Roosevelt Correspondence, Vol. II, 69; Garraty and Lodge, "Henry Cabot Lodge and the Alaskan Boundary Tribunal," *New England Quarterly*, Vol. 24, No. 4, Dec. 1951, 494; Schriftgiesser, *The Gentleman from Massachusetts*, 207.

24   Dalton, *Theodore Roosevelt*, 254–255.

25   Ibid.

26   Ibid.

27   "Panama as an Issue Pleases Mr. Lodge," *Cincinnati Inquirer*, Jan. 6, 1904, 7; "Senator Lodge's Speech," *Brooklyn Eagle*, June 6, 1904, 6; "Our Course in Panama," *Washington Post*, Jan. 6, 1903, 4.

28   "Panama as an Issue Pleases Mr. Lodge," *Cincinnati Inquirer*, Jan. 6, 1904, 7.

29   Adams, *The Letters of Henry Adams, Vol. V*, 538.

30   Dalton, *Theodore Roosevelt*, 256; Morris, *Theodore Rex*, 307; Adams, *The Letters of Henry Adams*, Vol. V, 538.

31   Brands, *T. R.*, 489–490.

32   HCL to T. R., September 29, 1903, Lodge, Lodge-Roosevelt Correspondence, Vol. II, 61.

33   Ibid.; Brands, *T. R.*, 491–492.

34   Brands, *T. R.*, 491–492.

35   During a speech at New York's Union League Club, Root referred to the president "as the greatest conservative force for the protection of property and our institutions in the city of Washington." Brands, *T. R.*, 502.

36   Morris, *Theodore Rex*, 332.

37   HCL to T. R., June 25, 1904, Reel 4, Lodge-Roosevelt Correspondence, MHS.

38   Ibid.

39   Ibid.; Dalton, *Theodore Roosevelt*, 262.

40   HCL to T. R., June 25, 1904, Reel 4, Lodge-Roosevelt Correspondence, MHS.

41   Ibid.

42   Dalton, *Theodore Roosevelt*, 262.

43   HCL to T. R., June 25, 1904, Reel 4, Lodge-Roosevelt Correspondence, MHS; Dalton, *Theodore Roosevelt*, 262; Morris, *Theodore Rex*, 335.

44   T. R. to Nannie Lodge, June 28, 1904, Reel 4, Lodge-Roosevelt Correspondence, MHS.

45   Harbaugh, *Power and Responsibility*, 227.

46   HCL to T. R., July 17, 1904, Reel 4, Lodge-Roosevelt Correspondence, MHS.

47   Dalton, *Theodore Roosevelt*, 265.

48   T. R. to HCL, November 9, 1904, Lodge, Lodge-Roosevelt Correspondence, Vol. II, 107; Brands, *T. R.*, 513; Morris, *Theodore Rex*, 364.

49   Dalton, *Theodore Roosevelt*, 267–268; Morris, *Edith Kermit Roosevelt*, 280–281.

50   T. R. to Nannie Lodge, November 10, 1904, Reel 4, Lodge-Roosevelt Correspondence, MHS; HCL to T. R., Nov. 15, 1904, Reel 4, Lodge-Roosevelt Correspondence, MHS.

51   Dalton, *Theodore Roosevelt*, 269–270; Harbaugh, *Power and Responsibility*, 235.

52   Dalton, *Theodore Roosevelt*, 269–270.

53   Garraty, *Henry Cabot Lodge*, 225.

54   Dalton, *Theodore Roosevelt*, 295; T. R. to HCL, Oct. 15, 1904, Theodore Roosevelt Center, Dickinson University.

55   T. R. to HCL, September 23, 1905, Reel 4, Lodge-Roosevelt Correspondence, MHS; HCL to T. R., September 26, 1905, Reel 4, Lodge-Roosevelt Correspondence, MHS; Adams continued to criticize Roosevelt, describing his management of the presidency as "confusion." The historian believed that the President's frenetic personality was responsible for using "his friends up with frightful rapidity." Concluding T. R. was a self-centered individual, Adams believed that for all his apparent closeness with Lodge it would just be a matter of time before Roosevelt "shall whack Cabot over the skull." Adams, Ford, *Letters of Henry Adams, Vol. II*, 454.

56   Simpson, "Henry Adams in the Age of Grant," Hayes Historical Journal, Vol. 13, No. 3, Spring 1989, www.rbhayes.org.

57   Dalton, *Theodore Roosevelt*, 271.

58   Brands, *T. R.*, 546.

59   Blum, *The Republican Roosevelt*, 74.

60   Ibid., 74–75; George E. Mowry, *The Era of Theodore Roosevelt 1900–1912*, (New York: Harper & Brothers, 1958), 198.

61   "Lodge Calls for Action," *Boston Evening Transcript*, Jan. 21, 1905, 6.

62   "Lodge For a Rate Court," *New York Times*, Jan. 21, 1905, 5.

63   Mowry, *The Era of Theodore Roosevelt*, 198–199. "Roosevelt Plan Would Increase Rates," Feb. 10, 1905, *New York Times*, 1.

64   Harbaugh, *Power and Responsibility*, 236–237; T. R. to HCL, May 24, 1905, Reel 4, MHS.

65   HCL to T. R., June 3, 1905, Lodge, Lodge-Roosevelt Correspondence, Vol. II, 129; Schriftgiesser, *The Gentleman from Massachusetts*, 216; Garraty, *Henry Cabot Lodge*, 227.

66   T. R. to HCL June 5, 1905, Lodge-Roosevelt Correspondence, Reel 4, MHS; In a note to the president Henry Adams praised Roosevelt's ability as a negotiator proclaiming him as "the best herder of Emperors since Napoleon." Adams to T. R., Nov. 6, 1905, Adams, *The Letters of Henry Adams, Vol. V*, 719.

67   Taliaferro, *All the Great Prizes*, 415, 536–543.

68   Ibid., 542; Hearing of Hay's death from John E. Lodge, Adams, distraught over the loss of his closest friend, could find nothing positive to say about the diplomat's legacy. "The newspapers may take their turn, and then the biographers can go to work. In a week he will be forgotten, and in fifty years another public, if there is still a public, will fabricate some sort of figure of him for the few score of people who still read history. At the rate we go I doubt exceedingly if anyone will care a straw." Adams, *The Letters of Henry Adams, Vol. V,* 682.

69   President Roosevelt viewed Hay as possessing qualities that made him ideal for public life. However, Roosevelt had an ambivalent relationship with his secretary of state. Since both men were well read, strong willed, lovers of conversation, and individuals who relished being at the center of power it is not surprising that their rapport was complicated. Both also believed that United States was destined to become a leader among the community of nations. As Hay's biographer John Taliaferro writes, the secretary often found Roosevelt's "impetuous outbursts" annoying. But the two men got on well. The secretary enjoyed Roosevelt's enormous vitality and enthusiasm, while Roosevelt was comforted by being in the company of a man who had known his late father. Unfortunately, as was so frequently the case with T. R. his ego often got the better of him. Following Hay's death Roosevelt confided to Lodge that Hay's tenure as secretary was less than impressive. "Of course, what I am about to say I can only say to a close friend. But in actual work I had to do the big things myself, and the other things I always feared would be badly done or not done at all." The president also took full credit for negotiating the agreement regarding the building of the Panama Canal. "I got the treaty in right shape only by securing the correction of all the original faults." Taliaferro, *All the Great Prizes,* 390, 415–419, 421; T. R. to HCL July 11, 1905, Lodge-Roosevelt Correspondence, Reel 4, MHS.

70   Dalton, *Theodore Roosevelt,* 279–281, 288; Henry Adams believed that between Lodge and Roosevelt, Root would accomplish little as secretary of state. Adams also blamed Lodge for being partially responsible for Hay's death. "The Senate killed Hay. Our friend Cabot helped murder him, consciously as possible, precisely as though he had put strychnine in his drink; but I always insisted to Hay that it was his own fault. He kept himself there knowing he was being killed." Adams believed that Hay was slowly done in by his inability to deal with the amount of interference of politics on foreign affairs and the strong partisanship that existed within the Republican-held Senate. Adams, *The Letters of Henry Adams, Vol. V,* 689; Vacationing with the Lodges, Adams continued to reminisce to Lizzie Cameron about Hay and rage over his disdain for Cabot. "I cannot venture myself any longer with Cabot. He has become physically repulsive to me." Adams also wrote that Nannie understood

his feelings. "If I told Cabot that he is personally and physically loathsome to me, like Gussie Gardner, he would not understand what I meant, but she would; and that is certainly what I should tell him if my temper for a single instant gave way to the senile irritability of my sixty-eight years." Adams to Cameron, July 16, 1905, Adams, *The Letters of Henry Adams, Vol. V,* 693.

71 Dalton, *Theodore Roosevelt,* 291.

Chapter Fourteen: The Gathering Storm

1 Dalton, *Theodore Roosevelt,* 291.
2 Harbaugh, *Power and Responsibility,* 161–162.
3 Ibid.; Louis Menard, "Decisions, Decisions," *The New Yorker,* July 3, 2005, www.thenewyorker.com; In commenting about the relationship with Roosevelt, Holmes believed the President resented the jurist for what Holmes referred to as "a political departure, (or, I suspect more truly, couldn't forgive anyone who stood in his way.)" Harbaugh, *Power and Responsibility,* 161–162.
4 HCL to T. R., Oct. 4, 1905, Reel 4, Lodge-Roosevelt Correspondence, MHS.
5 Mowry, *The Era of Theodore Roosevelt,* 201.
6 Harbaugh, *Power and Responsibility,* 246.
7 T. R. to Lyman Abbott, Feb. 23, 1906, Lodge, Lodge-Roosevelt Correspondence, Vol. II, 212–213.
8 T. R. to Lyman Abbott, Feb. 23, 1906, Lodge, Lodge-Roosevelt Correspondence, Vol. II, 213.
9 T. R. to Nannie Lodge, March 11, 1906, Reel 5, Lodge-Roosevelt Correspondence, MHS; Brands, *T. R.,* 546.
10 Ibid.
11 Brands, *T. R.,* 547; Blum, *The Republican Roosevelt,* 95–97; Schriftgiesser, *The Gentleman from Massachusetts,* 217; *Congressional Record,* Vol. 40, Part 3 (Feb. 3, 1906, to Feb. 26, 1906), 2414–2423.
12 Dalton, *Theodore Roosevelt,* 296.
13 Garraty, *Henry Cabot Lodge,* 227–229; Dalton, *Theodore Roosevelt,* 298.
14 Dalton, *Theodore Roosevelt,* 296; "John Ellerton Lodge 1876–1942 First Director of the Freer Gallery of Art," www.asia.si.edu.
15 Dalton, *Theodore Roosevelt,* 296.
16 Ibid.; T. R. to HCL, Oct. 2, 1906, Reel 5, Lodge-Roosevelt Correspondence, MHS; HCL to T. R., Oct. 4, 1906, Reel 5, Lodge-Roosevelt Correspondence, MHS.
17 HCL to T. R., Aug. 8, 1906. Reel 5, Lodge-Roosevelt Correspondence, MHS; HCL to T. R., Aug. 11, 1906. Reel 5, Lodge-Roosevelt Correspondence, MHS.
18 David M. Tucker, "Justice Horace Harmon Lurton: The Shaping of a National Progressive," *American Journal of Legal History,* Vol. 13, No. 3,

July 1969, 227–228; "Horace H. Lurton 1910–1914," *Supreme Court Historical Society*, www.supremecourthistory.org.

19 HCL to T. R., Sept. 14, 1906, Reel 5, Lodge-Roosevelt Correspondence, MHS; Tucker, "Justice Horace Harmon Lurton: The Shaping of a National Progressive," *The American Journal of Legal History*, Vol. 13, No. 3, July 1969, 227–228.

20 HCL to T. R., Sept. 14, 1906, Reel 5, Lodge-Roosevelt Correspondence, MHS.

21 Ibid.

22 T. R. to HCL, Sept. 4, 1906, Lodge, Lodge-Roosevelt Correspondence, Vol. II, 228.

23 HCL to T. R., Sept. 10, 1906, Lodge, Lodge-Roosevelt Correspondence, Vol. II, 229.

24 Tucker, "Justice Horace Harmon Lurton: The Shaping of a National Progressive," *The American Journal of Legal History*, Vol. 13, No. 3, July 1969, 229; The president also wanted to discuss the issue further with Taft to his lack of knowledge of "constitutional import." Morris, *Theodore Rex*, 462. Lurton's candidacy was not helped by a letter from fellow Tennessee lawyer, Newton Hacker, who described the jurist as "a Southern Democrat, dyed in the wool, and on all questions of a purely political character, he would most likely be swayed by his early predilections." Tucker, "Justice Horace Harmon Lurton: The Shaping of a National Progressive," *The American Journal of Legal History*, Vol. 13, No. 3, July 1969, 229; Roosevelt was so concerned with being thorough on the issue that he consulted three Supreme Court justices in making his final decision. The consultation involved five days of meetings with Taft, Elihu Root, and four senators (of which Lodge was probably one) leading to Moody's name being dropped to the press on October 24. Morris, *Theodore Rex*, 464. When Lurton was appointed to the court by President Taft in 1910, the Southerner confirmed Lodge's low opinion of his judicial philosophy by his poor four-year tenure. Dalton, *Theodore Roosevelt*, 292.

25 T. R. to HCL, Oct. 16, 1906, Reel 5, Lodge-Roosevelt Correspondence, MHS.

26 HCL to T. R., Oct. 25, 1906, Lodge, Lodge-Roosevelt Correspondence, Vol. II, 255.

27 Ibid., 256; Dalton, *Theodore Roosevelt*, 292; Harbaugh, *Power and Responsibility*, 347.

28 HCL to T. R., Oct. 25, 1906, Lodge-Roosevelt Correspondence, Vol. II, 256.

29 HCL to T. R., Oct. 18, 1906, Lodge, Lodge-Roosevelt Correspondence, Vol. II, 249.

30 T. R. to HCL, Oct. 1, 1906, Lodge, Lodge-Roosevelt Correspondence, Vol. II, 239.

31   T. R. to HCL, Oct. 2, 1906, Lodge, Lodge-Roosevelt Correspondence, Vol. II, 240.

32   HCL to T. R., Nov. 7, 1906, Lodge, Lodge-Roosevelt Correspondence, Vol. II, 259. "Hughes Is Elected," *Brooklyn Citizen*, Nov. 7, 1906, 1.

33   HCL to T. R., Nov. 7, 1906, Lodge, Lodge-Roosevelt Correspondence, Vol. II, 259.

34   Brands, *T. R.*, 567–572; Dalton, *Theodore Roosevelt*, 321–322.

35   Dalton, *Theodore Roosevelt*, 322–323.

36   Brands, *T. R.*, 587–588; Dalton, *Theodore Roosevelt*, 321.

37   Ibid.; Goodwin, *The Bully Pulpit*, 513–514.

38   Brands, *T. R.*, 591–592; Dalton, *Theodore Roosevelt*, 322–323; The "Gridiron Club," www.theodorerooseveltcenter.org/Research/Digital -Library/Record libld=030142; During Roosevelt's remarks the president shook his fist at Foraker and declared, "Some of those men were bloody butchers; they ought to be hung . . . It is my business and the business of nobody else . . ." Dalton, *Theodore Roosevelt*, 322.

39   T. R. to HCL, June 22, 1907, Reel 5, Lodge-Roosevelt Correspondence, MHS.

40   HCL to T. R., June 25, 1907, Reel 5, Lodge-Roosevelt Correspondence, MHS; "Say Brownsville Men Were Rioters," *New York Times*, July 26, 1907, 1; James A. Tinsley, "Roosevelt, Foraker and the Brownsville Affray," *Journal of Negro History*, Vol. 41, No. 1, Jan. 1956, 49.

41   Ibid.

42   T. R. to HCL, Sept. 27, 1906, Reel 5, Lodge-Roosevelt Correspondence, MHS; "Joseph B. Foraker," Ohio History Central, www .ohiohistorycentral.org.

43   HCL to T. R., July 1, 1907, Reel 5, Lodge-Roosevelt Correspondence, MHS.

44   Brands, *T. R.*, 594.

45   Goodwin, *The Bully Pulpit*, 395.

46   Brands, *T. R.*, 595. Historian H. W. Brands argues that as Roosevelt found his policy disagreements with Senator Lodge increasing, he turned to Taft who was less likely to push back on Roosevelt, particularly in decisions that might adversely affect the Republican Party; Goodwin, *The Bully Pulpit*, 395.

47   William Manners, *T. R. and Will: A Friendship that Split the Republican Party*, (New York: Harcourt, Brace & World, 1969), 46–47.

48   Manners, *T. R. and Will*, 46–47.

49   Schriftgiesser, *The Gentleman from Massachusetts*, 227–228. Root was Roosevelt's choice as well. "I would rather see Elihu Root in the White House than any other man now possible, he said. I have told several men recently that I would walk on my hands and knees from the White House to the Capitol to see Root made President. He couldn't be elected there is too much opposition to him on account of his corporate connections."

Oscar King Davis, *Released for Publication: Some Inside History of Theodore Roosevelt and his Times*, (Boston: Houghton Mifflin, 1925), 54.

50 Harbaugh, *Power and Responsibility*, 351–352; T. R. to HCL, June 27, 1907, Reel 5, Lodge–Roosevelt Correspondence, MHS.

51 Garraty, *Henry Cabot Lodge*, 258; Harbaugh, *Power and Responsibility*, 354.

52 Ibid.

53 Garraty, *Henry Cabot Lodge*, 258; HCL to T. R., Sept. 19, 1907, Reel 5, Lodge-Roosevelt Correspondence, MHS; Dalton, *Theodore Roosevelt*, 332.

54 HCL to T. R., Aug. 12, 1907, Reel 5 Lodge-Roosevelt Correspondence, MHS.

55 Ibid.; Dalton, *Theodore Roosevelt*, 330–331; John R. Moen and Ellis W. Tallman, "The Panic of 1907," *Federal Reserve History*, www .federalreservehistory.org.

56 HCL to T. R., Aug. 16, 1907, T. R. Center Dickinson University; Dalton, *Theodore Roosevelt*, 330–331.

57 HCL to T. R., Nov. 7, 1907, Reel 5, Lodge-Roosevelt Correspondence, MHS; Roosevelt was more optimistic, writing: "The net result is much better than it was four years ago or eight years ago, before the two last presidential elections." T. R. to HCL, Nov. 7, 1907. Lodge, Lodge-Roosevelt Correspondence, Vol. II, 284.

58 Garraty, *Henry Cabot Lodge*, 258; Brands, *T. R.*, 597.

59 HCL to T. R., Sept. 24, 1907, Reel 5, Lodge-Roosevelt Correspondence, MHS.

60 Brands, *T. R.*, 618–619; Garraty, *Henry Cabot Lodge*, 257.

61 Ibid.

62 Brands, *T. R.*, 626; Garraty, *Henry Cabot Lodge*, 260; Gould, *Grand Old Party*, 167; Goodwin, *The Bully Pulpit*, 564.

63 Ibid.

64 "Day's Work at the Convention," *Boston Globe*, June 18, 1908, 3.

65 Ibid.; Garraty, *Henry Cabot Lodge*, 260; In further discussing his convention experience Lodge wrote, "I also brought the ovation which I wanted you to have at the right time and in the right way . . . the great cheering in the middle of my speech was the finest recognition that I ever saw given in a convention." Lodge, whose sister had passed away months earlier, had come to Chicago listless and depressed. However, all that changed upon his arrival in Chicago. "The convention acted on me like a powerful stimulant. It took me out of myself and I have come back here feeling extraordinarily well and better than I have felt for many weeks." HCL to T. R., June 22, 1908, Reel 5, Lodge-Roosevelt Correspondence, MHS; Harbaugh, *Power and Responsibility*, 356; Dalton, *Theodore Roosevelt*, 339.

66 T. R. to Nannie Lodge, June 19, 1908, Reel 5, Lodge-Roosevelt Correspondence, MHS.

67   Ibid.; Roosevelt also communicated to Lodge how pleased he was with
      his friend's speech and his ability to keep the crowd under control.
      "Personally, it was of course to me a matter of very great importance that
      it should be my closest friend, the man whom everybody recognized as
      speaking for me, who required the convention to guard my honor to
      respect my good faith. It would have been a great mistake had you made
      any extended illusions to me . . . You said exactly what was right, neither
      to little nor too much, and you said it exactly as I should have wisht to
      have it said; I do not recall any speech at any nominating convention
      which . . . attracted such widespread and practically unanimous
      approval." T. R. to HCL, July 19, 1908, Lodge, Lodge-Roosevelt
      Correspondence, Vol. II, 303.
68   T. R. to Nannie Lodge, June 19, 1908, Reel 5, Lodge-Roosevelt
      Correspondence, MHS; Garraty, *Henry Cabot Lodge*, 262.
69   Gould, *Grand Old Party*, 154–155.

Chapter Fifteen: Return to the Arena
1   Garraty, *Henry Cabot Lodge*, 263. T. R. to Charles Washburn, Jan. 8,
     1915, Reel 6, Lodge-Roosevelt Correspondence, MHS; Lodge found it
     curious that Taft seemed uninterested in reappointing his fellow Ohioan
     James R. Garfield. Following a visit with Taft in Augusta, Georgia,
     Lodge realized that "Mrs. Taft and his brother, Henry, and no doubt
     some others of his family circle, were continually urging him to get
     rid of every Roosevelt appointment, to cut loose from the Roosevelt
     administration and the Roosevelt policies which alone had made his
     nomination and election possible . . . the result was the ruin of the Taft
     administration and the division and defeat of the Republican Party."
     HCL to Charles Washburn, March 6, 1915, Reel 6, Lodge-Roosevelt
     Correspondence, MHS.
2   HCL to Charles Washburn, March 6, 1915, Reel 6, Lodge-Roosevelt
     Correspondence, MHS; Archie Butt and Lawrence F. Abbott, *The Letters
     of Archie Butt: Personal Aide to President Roosevelt* (Garden City, N.Y.:
     Doubleday, Page and Company, 1924), 271.
3   Garraty, *Henry Cabot Lodge*, 263; Following a visit with Taft in Augusta,
     Georgia, Lodge informed Roosevelt that the President-elect had "the
     intention" "to get rid of every person who might keep President Taft
     in touch with the Roosevelt influence." In John Garraty's biography of
     Lodge, the author argues that Lodge wrote these recollections in 1915.
     While one of Taft's biographers contends that Lodge was responsible for
     beginning Roosevelt's feud with Taft, Garraty contends that if Lodge
     did not write about his conversation with Roosevelt in 1909 perhaps,
     he was trying to prevent a breach from occurring. Manners, *T. R. and
     Will*, 72–73; Garraty, *Henry Cabot Lodge*, 264–265; According to Lodge

biographer Karl Schriftgiesser, following a meeting with Taft in Augusta, Georgia, the senator, according to Taft's secretary Archie Butt returned to the White House and informed Roosevelt "that none of the present cabinet would remain . . . that it was evidently the intention to get rid of everybody who might keep President Taft in touch with Roosevelt's influence." Butt thought little of the Bostonian. "Lodge is so hopelessly selfish that if the Tafts did not kowtow to him he would delight in making trouble between them and the Roosevelts." Schriftgiesser, *The Gentleman from Massachusetts*, 236.

4   HCL to T. R., end of March 1909, Lodge, Lodge-Roosevelt Correspondence, Vol. II, 330; T. R. to Nannie Lodge, March 22, 1909, Reel 5, Lodge-Roosevelt Correspondence, MHS; Patricia O'Toole, *When Trumpets Call: Theodore Roosevelt After the White House*, (New York: Simon & Schuster, 2005), 17.

5   Archie Butt, *Taft and Roosevelt: The Intimate Letters of Archie Butt, Military Aide, Volume I*, (New York: Doubleday Doran & Company, 1930), 496–497.

6   HCL to T. R., end of March 1909, Lodge, Lodge-Roosevelt Correspondence, Vol. II, 332; HCL to T. R., April 29, 1909, Reel 5, Lodge-Roosevelt Correspondence, MHS.

7   Ibid.

8   Gould, *Grand Old Party*, 174–175.

9   Ibid.

10   HCL to T. R., end of March 1909, Lodge, Lodge-Roosevelt Correspondence, Vol. II, 332; Dalton, *Theodore Roosevelt*, 356.

11   Garraty, *Henry Cabot Lodge*, 269; "Bigelow and His Tuckernuck Retreat," *Yesterday's Island, Today's Nantucket*, Vol. 37, No. 10, June 28–July 4, 2007.

12   Garraty, *Henry Cabot Lodge*, 269; Crowley, "Dear Bay," 193.

13   Ibid.

14   Garraty, *Henry Cabot Lodge*, 270.

15   Ibid.

16   Ibid., 271; Lodge, *The Lodge Women*, 249.

17   Lodge, *The Lodge Women*, 249.

18   Ibid.

19   Ibid.

20   Lodge, *The Lodge Women*, 250–251.

21   Ibid., 252–253.

22   Lodge, *The Lodge Women*, 252–253, 269; In a letter to Corinne Roosevelt, Nannie wrote of Lodge's ability to carry forward with his life and work despite the tragic loss of Bay. "But thank Heaven Cabot has the quality of absorption in whatever he is doing & the power to contend the utterances of life's set prize, & so he stayed in to win or lose, but in any case to do his best." Lodge, *The Lodge Women*, 290.

23   Lodge, *The Lodge Women*, 252–253, 255, 262–263.

24   Ibid.; Carol J. Singley, "Wharton, Edith, 1832–1937," Walt Whitman Archive, www.whitmanrchive.org.

25   Lodge, *The Lodge Women*, 259–260.

26   Ibid.

27   Ibid.; Henry Adams was also strongly affected by Bay's passing. "I cannot pretend to say or do anything that would make this mortal blow easier to bear," Adams wrote to Nannie in the last few days of August. "You have so much left you and so much to do for them! You are not alone! [Bay] was the best and finest product of my time and hopes . . . You have lived and will continue to live in him." Lodge, *The Lodge Women*, 254–255; Even in that dark moment of grief, Henry Adams in a condolence note to Cabot could not help but include his views on the darkness he believed was engulfing society. "I look around, over the whole field of human activity, and [with Bay's loss] I can see no one else to offer a ray of light." Cecil Spring Rice, serving the British Foreign Office in Stockholm, recalled the uniqueness of Bay's mind and the special nature of his character. "I think he was the sort of stuff in the middle ages would have made a great saint or a great heresiarch—I dare say we have no use for such people now; I wonder if he found he was born out of his time or that ours was not a world for him." Stephen Gwynn, *The Letters and Friendships of Cecil Spring Rice: A Record Vol. II*, (Boston: Houghton Mifflin, 1929), 142. The letter never mentioned Bay's death and the Lodges considered it one of the valuable notes they received, rereading it continuously. Lodge, *The Lodge Women*, 269.

28   Lodge, *The Lodge Women*, 258–259; In encountering Nannie soon after Bay's death, Adams commented that "Nannie looks . . . uncommonly shaky in the hands and head," and Lizzie Cameron wrote of "being shocked" by Nanny's "weakness. Even her voice trembles and she looks terribly." Lodge, *The Lodge Women*, 272.

29   HCL to T. R., Oct. 20, 1909, Reel 5, Lodge-Roosevelt Correspondence, MHS.

30   HCL to T. R., Nov. 30, 1909, Reel 5, Lodge-Roosevelt Correspondence, MHS; Garraty, *Henry Cabot Lodge*, 273.

31   Davis, *Released for Publication*, 93; Lodge's criticism about Taft's lackadaisical attitudes was also reflected by the president's personal secretary Major Archie Butt. "So much in the President's character can be explained by his complacency," Butt wrote in late 1909. "He believes that many things left to themselves will bring about the same results as if he took a hand himself in their settlement. He acts with promptness and vigor when he has got to act, but he would rather delay trouble than seek it. Of course that is just the opposite view of one which would be taken by President Roosevelt." Archie Butt, *Taft and Roosevelt*, 202.

ENDNOTES

32 Edmund Morris, *Colonel Roosevelt,* (New York: Random House, 2010), 32–33; Dalton, *Theodore Roosevelt,* 357; Brands, *T. R.,* 667; Harbaugh, *Power and Responsibility,* 383.

33 HCL to T. R., Jan. 15, 1910, Lodge, Lodge-Roosevelt Correspondence, Vol. II, 358.

34 T. R. to HCL, April 11, 1910, Lodge, Lodge-Roosevelt Correspondence, Vol. II, 367; Harbaugh, *Power and Responsibility,* 387.

35 T. R. to HCL, April 11, 1910, Lodge-Roosevelt Correspondence, Vol. II, 370. While Roosevelt wished the best for Taft, he was emphatic in informing Lodge that "I most emphatically desire that I shall not be put in the position of having to run for the Presidency, staggering under a load which I cannot carry, and which has been put on my shoulders through no fault of my own."

36 HCL to T. R., April 19, 1910, Lodge, Lodge-Roosevelt Correspondence, Vol. II, 374; Garraty, *Henry Cabot Lodge,* 275; O'Toole, *When Trumpets Call,* 85.

37 T. R. to HCL, April 11, 1910, Reel 6, Lodge-Roosevelt Correspondence, MHS; Garraty, *Henry Cabot Lodge,* 276.

38 Garraty, *Henry Cabot Lodge,* 275; HCL to T. R., April 25, 1910, Reel 6, Lodge-Roosevelt Correspondence, MHS; Schriftgiesser, *The Gentleman from Massachusetts,* 234.

39 HCL to T. R., April 25, 1910, Lodge, Lodge-Roosevelt Correspondence, Vol. II, 374; Garraty, *Henry Cabot Lodge,* 276.

40 Garraty, *Henry Cabot Lodge,* 277; T. R. to HCL April 27, 1910, Lodge, Lodge-Roosevelt Correspondence, Vol. II, 378–379; Garraty, *Henry Cabot Lodge,* 275.

41 T. R. to HCL, May 5, 1910, Lodge, Lodge-Roosevelt Correspondence, Vol. II, 380.

42 Harbaugh, *Power and Responsibility,* 387–388; T. R. to HCL, May 5, 1910, Lodge, Lodge-Roosevelt Correspondence, Vol. II, 380; Harbaugh, *Power and Responsibility,* 388.

43 Morris, *Edith Kermit Roosevelt,* 361.

44 O'Toole, *When Trumpets Call,* 94; Butt, *Taft and Roosevelt,* 419–420.

45 T. R. to HCL, Aug. 17, 1910, Reel 6, Lodge-Roosevelt Correspondence, MHS.

46 Butt, *Taft and Roosevelt,* 419–420; T. R. to HCL, Aug. 17, 1910, Reel 6, Lodge-Roosevelt Correspondence, MHS. "Major Archibald Butt," April 16, 1912, *New York Times,* 4.

47 HCL to T. R., May 25, 1910, Reel 6, Lodge-Roosevelt Correspondence, MHS; T. R. to HCL, Aug. 1, 1910, Reel 6, Lodge-Roosevelt Correspondence, MHS; Determined to stick to supporting general party principles, Roosevelt believed that any expression of strong support for Taft would alienate much of the progressive element that he continued

to view the President in high regard. "The Taft people have been wild that I should come out in a flaming general endorsement of the Taft Administration, which would be bitterly resented by most of my staunchest friends. The greatest service I can render to Taft, the service which beyond all others will tend to secure his renomination and to make that renomination of use, is to try to help the Republican Party to try to win at the polls this Fall . . ." T. R. to HCL, July 19, 1910, Lodge, Lodge-Roosevelt Correspondence, Vol. II, 385–386.

48   Morris, *Edith Kermit Roosevelt*, 367.

49   T. R. to HCL, Aug. 10, 1910, Lodge, Lodge-Roosevelt Correspondence, Vol. II, 387–388; HCL to T. R., July 20, 1910, Reel 6, Lodge-Roosevelt Correspondence, MHS.

50   O'Toole, *When Trumpets Call*, 97.

51   HCL to T. R., July 20, 1910, Reel 6, Lodge-Roosevelt Correspondence, MHS; O'Toole, *When Trumpets Call*, 102; Morris, *Edith Kermit Roosevelt*, 367.

52   Davis, *Released for Publication*, 199, 202.

53   O'Toole, *When Trumpets Call*, 103–104; Harbaugh, *Power and Responsibility*, 390–391.

54   Ibid.; "United States v. E. C. Knight (1895)," The Supreme Court: Landmark Cases, www.pbs.org.

55   HCL to T. R., Sept. 5, 1910, Lodge, Lodge-Roosevelt Correspondence, Vol. II, 389–390.

56   "Roosevelt States His Creed," *Boston Evening Transcript*, Sept. 1, 1910, 3; O'Toole, *When Trumpets Call*, 104.

57   "Roosevelt States His Creed," *Boston Evening Transcript*, Sept. 1, 1910, 3.

58   Ibid.; O'Toole, *When Trumpets Call*, 105–106; HCL to T. R., April 19, 1910, Reel 6, Lodge-Roosevelt Correspondence, MHS.

59   HCL to T. R., Sept. 5, 1910, Lodge, Lodge-Roosevelt Correspondence, Vol. II, 388–389.

60   Garraty, *Henry Cabot Lodge*, 285; O'Toole, *When Trumpets Call*, 105.

61   T. R. to HCL, Sept. 12, 1910, Reel 6, Lodge-Roosevelt Correspondence, MHS; Garraty, *Henry Cabot Lodge*, 285.

62   Gould, *Grand Old Party*, 180.

63   Brands, *T. R.*, 680.

64   HCL to T. R., Nov. 13, 1910, Lodge, Lodge-Roosevelt Correspondence, Vol. II, 395; T. R. to HCL, Nov. 11, 1910, Lodge, Lodge-Roosevelt Correspondence, Vol. II, 394; O'Toole, *When Trumpets Call*, 112.

65   Dalton, *Theodore Roosevelt*, 369; Garraty, *Henry Cabot Lodge*, 285.

66   Garraty, *Henry Cabot Lodge*, 281; "Lodge Reviews His Public Record," *Boston Evening Transcript*, Jan. 4, 1911, 18.

67   Jonathan Stahl, "The Controversy Over the Direct Elections of Senators," April 8, 2016, National Constitution Center, www.constitutioncenter.org.

68   HCL to T. R., Feb. 6, 1911, Reel 6, Lodge-Roosevelt Correspondence, MHS.
69   O'Toole, *When Trumpets Call*, 125; Brands, *T. R.*, 683–684.
70   Garraty, *Henry Cabot Lodge*, 282.
71   Ibid., 286; Gould, *Grand Old Party*, 180–181.

Chapter Sixteen: A Chorus of Disapproval

1   Garraty, *Henry Cabot Lodge*, 286.
2   Ibid.; HCL to T. R., Feb. 6, 1912, Reel 6, Lodge-Roosevelt Correspondence, MHS.
3   HCL to T. R., Feb. 6, 1912, Reel 6, Lodge-Roosevelt Correspondence, MHS.
4   Ibid.
5   Ibid.
6   Dalton, *Theodore Roosevelt*, 378–379; O'Toole, *When Trumpets Call*, 147–148.
7   Ibid.
8   HCL to T. R., Nov. 13, 1910, Lodge, Lodge-Roosevelt Correspondence, Vol. II, 395.
9   Dalton, *Theodore Roosevelt*, 208–209. Brands, *T. R.*, 668.
10   HCL to T. R., Feb. 24, 1912, Lodge, Lodge-Roosevelt Correspondence, Vol. II, 423–424.
11   Garraty, *Henry Cabot Lodge*, 288–290.
12   Ibid.
13   Garraty, *Henry Cabot Lodge*, 291.
14   Adams, *The Letters of Henry Adams, Vol. VI*, 517; O'Toole, *When Trumpets Call*, 152–153.
15   T. R. to HCL, March 1, 1912, Lodge, Lodge-Roosevelt Correspondence, Vol. II, 424–425; Phillip C. Jessup, *Elihu Root, Volume II, 1905–1937*, (Hamden, Conn.: Archon Books, 1964), 179.
16   Adams, *The Letters of Henry Adams, Vol. VI*, 527.
17   Garraty, *Henry Cabot Lodge*, 292.
18   Schriftgiesser, *The Gentleman from Massachusetts*, 258; T. R. to Lodge, April 23, 1912, Reel 6, Lodge-Roosevelt Correspondence, MHS; Garraty, *Henry Cabot Lodge*, 293.
19   HCL to T. R., March 1, 1912, Reel 6, Lodge-Roosevelt Correspondence, MHS.
20   Ibid.
21   Brands, *T. R.*, 712; Dalton, *Theodore Roosevelt*, 401.
22   Ibid.
23   Brands, *T. R.*, 713–714.
24   Gould, *Grand Old Party*, 187–189.
25   Ibid.; "Lodge Comes Out for Taft," *Boston Globe*, June 24, 1912, 1; Morris, *Edith Kermit Roosevelt*, 381.

26 Gould, *Grand Old Party*, 187–189; "Lodge Comes Out for Taft," *Boston Globe*, June 24, 1912, 1; Morris, *Edith Kermit Roosevelt*, 381.

27 Garraty, *Henry Cabot Lodge*, 293.

28 Adams, *The Letters of Henry Adams, Vol. VI*, 487.

29 Garraty, *Henry Cabot Lodge*, 293.

30 "Makes Appeal to Idealists," *Boston Globe*, Aug. 17, 1912, 2; "Taft Gaining, Says Lodge," *Boston Globe*, September 26, 2012, 5; Dalton, *Theodore Roosevelt*, 401.

31 Dalton, *Theodore Roosevelt*, 401.

32 Ibid.

33 Christopher Klein, "When Teddy Roosevelt Was Shot in 1912, a Speech May Have Saved His Life," *History*, October 12, 1912, www.history.com; "Theodore Roosevelt Shot in Milwaukee," *This Day in History*, 1912, www.history.com.

34 HCL to Edith Roosevelt, Oct. 16, 1912, Lodge, Lodge-Roosevelt Correspondence, Vol. II, 425; HCL to T. R., Oct. 17, 1912, Reel 6, Lodge, Lodge-Roosevelt Correspondence, Vol. II, 426; T. R. to HCL, Oct. 28, 1912, Reel 6; Lodge, Lodge-Roosevelt Correspondence, Vol. II, 426.

35 Morris, *Edith Kermit Roosevelt*, 389–390.

36 Morris, *Colonel Roosevelt*, 265; T. R. to HCL, Dec. 31, 1912, Lodge, Lodge-Roosevelt Correspondence, Vol. II, 428; HCL to T. R., Jan. 2, 1913, Lodge, Lodge-Roosevelt Correspondence, Vol. II, 429.

37 Morris, *Colonel Roosevelt*, 273; HCL to T. R., April 22, 1913, Lodge, Lodge-Roosevelt Correspondence, Vol. II, 436.

38 HCL to T. R., April 22, 1913, Lodge, Lodge-Roosevelt Correspondence, Vol. II, 436.

39 Morris, *Colonel Roosevelt*, 273; Garraty, *Henry Cabot Lodge*, 294.

Chapter Seventeen: A Common Enemy

1 Garraty, *Henry Cabot Lodge*, 294.

2 Ibid.

3 Ibid.

4 Henry Cabot Lodge, *The Senate and the League of Nations*, (New York: Charles Scribner's Sons, 1925), 2; "New Regime Starts Well," *Boston Globe*, March 13, 1913, 10.

5 Morris, *Colonel Roosevelt*, 283–284; "Wilson and Race," President Wilson House, www.woodrowwilsonhouse.org; Richardson, *To Make Men Free*, 225.

6 Garraty, *Henry Cabot Lodge*, 297; Lodge thought for a man who had studied political science, the new president seemed to understand little of the details of how legislation was crafted and approved. "It is intolerable here just now waiting about while the Democratic majority struggles for six weeks to with the tariff bill," Lodge wrote T. R. in June 1913. "I

have not liked my summers in Washington when I have had plenty to do, but a summer with nothing to do but stand around is irritating to the extreme." HCL to T. R., June 25, 1913, Lodge, Lodge-Roosevelt Correspondence, Vol. II, 437; Garraty, *Henry Cabot Lodge*, 297.

7   Schriftgiesser, *The Gentleman from Massachusetts*, 259; Morris, *Edith Kermit Roosevelt*, 398; T. R. to HCL, Sept. 17, 1913, Lodge, Lodge-Roosevelt Correspondence, Vol. II, 438. As Lodge communicated to Roosevelt during his convalescence, other than "scarlet fever at the age of fifteen I do not remember ever being kept in bed by illness, although I have been shut up in the house now and then with a cold and have had an occasional attack of indigestion, but for fifty years, as I look back on it, I have had extraordinarily good health." In discussing his condition, the senator described the level of pain as so severe that "I hope that there is no pain for human beings worse than which ensued." HCL to T. R., Nov. 7, 1913, Reel 6, Lodge-Roosevelt Correspondence, HCL.

8   Morris, *Colonel Roosevelt*, 273; HCL to T. R., Sept. 2, 1913, Reel 6, Lodge-Roosevelt Correspondence, MHS.

9   H. W. Brands, *Woodrow Wilson* (New York: Times Books, 2003), 44–46.

10   Brands, *Woodrow Wilson*, 45–46.

11   HCL to T. R., Sept. 2, 1913, Reel 6, Lodge-Roosevelt Correspondence, MHS; Garraty, *Henry Cabot Lodge*, 300–301.

12   HCL to T. R., Sept. 2, 1913, Reel 6, Lodge-Roosevelt Correspondence, MHS.

13   Brands, *T. R.*, 734–735.

14   HCL to T. R., Sept. 2, 1913, Reel 6, Lodge-Roosevelt Correspondence, MHS.

15   T. R. to HCL, Dec. 12, 1913, Lodge-Roosevelt Correspondence Vol. II, 443–444; Candice Millard, *The River of Doubt: Theodore Roosevelt's Darkest Journey*, (New York: Broadway Books, 2005), 1–3.

16   HCL to T. R., April 6, 1914, Lodge, Lodge-Roosevelt Correspondence, Vol. II, 445.

17   Ibid.

18   Ibid.

19   Morris, *Edith Kermit Roosevelt*, 405; Morris, *Colonel Roosevelt*, 358.

20   HCL to T. R., May 4, 1914, Reel 6, Lodge-Roosevelt Correspondence, MHS; O'Toole, *When Trumpets Call*, 264–265.

21   Brands, *Woodrow Wilson*, 47–48.

22   Ibid.

23   HCL to T. R., Dec. 7, 1914, Reel 6, Lodge-Roosevelt Correspondence, MHS; Theodore Roosevelt, "Our Responsibility In Mexico," *New York Times*, Dec. 7, 1914, 1.

24   T. R. to HCL, Dec. 8, 1914, Lodge, Lodge-Roosevelt Correspondence, Vol. II, 449–450.

ENDNOTES

25   O'Toole, *When Trumpets Call*, 259.
26   Lodge, *The Lodge Women*, 304–308; O'Toole, *When Trumpets Call*, 260–261.
27   Garraty, *Henry Cabot Lodge*, 305; O'Toole, *When Trumpets Call*, 263; Morris, *Colonel Roosevelt*, 373.
28   Ibid.
29   Garraty, *Henry Cabot Lodge*, 307; HCL to T. R., Jan. 15, 1915, Lodge, Lodge-Roosevelt Correspondence, Vol. II, 451–452; As Lodge biographer John Garraty observes, Lodge believed Wilson was part of a conspiracy involving a small group of professors who were indirectly supporting Berlin due to the intellectual connection with central European culture. Garraty, *Henry Cabot Lodge*, 307.
30   HCL to T. R., Jan. 20, 1915, Lodge, Lodge-Roosevelt Correspondence, Vol. II, 452. Morris, *Colonel Roosevelt*, 397; T. R. to HCL, Feb. 6, 1915, Lodge, drafts of Lodge-Roosevelt edited correspondence, 520, MHS; HCL to T. R., Feb. 11, 1915, Lodge, drafts of Lodge-Roosevelt edited correspondence, 522, MHS; T. R. to HCL, Feb. 18, 1915, Lodge, drafts of Lodge-Roosevelt edited correspondence, 520, MHS; Dalton, *Theodore Roosevelt*, 458.
31   HCL to T. R., Jan. 20, 1915, Lodge, Lodge-Roosevelt Correspondence, Vol. II, 452; Morris, *Colonel Roosevelt*, 397; T. R. to HCL, Feb. 6, 1915, Lodge, drafts of Lodge-Roosevelt edited correspondence, 520, MHS; HCL to T. R., Feb. 11, 1915, Lodge, drafts of Lodge-Roosevelt edited correspondence, 522, MHS; T. R. to HCL, Feb. 18, 1915, Lodge, drafts of Lodge-Roosevelt edited correspondence, 520, MHS.
32   Dalton, *Theodore Roosevelt*, 456.
33   Ibid.
34   HCL to T. R., Feb. 19, 1915, Lodge-Roosevelt Correspondence, Reel 6, MHS.
35   Garraty, *Henry Cabot Lodge*, 309.
36   Ibid., 310–311; HCL to T. R., Feb. 19, 1915, Lodge-Roosevelt correspondence, Reel 6, MHS; HCL to T. R., Feb. 22, 1915. Lodge, drafts of Lodge-Roosevelt edited correspondence, 525, MHS; HCL to T. R., Feb. 22, 1915, Lodge, drafts of Lodge-Roosevelt edited correspondence, 526, MHS.
37   T. R. to HCL, Feb. 22, 1915, Lodge, drafts of Lodge-Roosevelt edited correspondence, 526, MHS.
38   David Pietrusza, *TR's Last War: Theodore Roosevelt, The Great War and a Journey of Triumph and Tragedy*, (Lanham, Md.: Rowman and Littlefield, 2018), 39.
39   Garraty, *Henry Cabot Lodge*, 315.
40   O'Toole, *When Trumpets Call*, 276–277; T. R. to Nannie Lodge, June 1, 1915, Reel 6, Lodge-Roosevelt Correspondence, MHS.

41   T. R. to Nannie Lodge, June 1, 1915, Reel 6, Lodge-Roosevelt correspondence, MHS.

42   Garraty, *Henry Cabot Lodge*, 317–318.

43   HCL to T. R., June 4, 1915, Reel 6, Lodge-Roosevelt correspondence, MHS.

44   T. R. to HCL, June 15, 1915, Lodge, drafts of Lodge-Roosevelt edited correspondence, 529, MHS; Brands, *Woodrow Wilson*, 61–62.

45   HCL to T. R., June 25, 1915, Reel 6, Lodge-Roosevelt correspondence, MHS.

46   Garraty, *Henry Cabot Lodge*, 316.

47   HCL to T. R., June 25, 1915, Reel 6, Lodge-Roosevelt correspondence, MHS.

48   T. R. to HCL, June 29, 1915, Lodge, drafts of Lodge-Roosevelt edited correspondence, 532, MHS.

49   Brands, *T. R.*, 757–758; HCL to T. R., September 25, 1915, Lodge, drafts of Lodge-Roosevelt edited correspondence, 536. MHS.

50   HCL to T. R., Sept. 25, 1915, Lodge, drafts of Lodge-Roosevelt edited correspondence, 536. MHS.

51   Lodge, *The Lodge Women*, 316.

52   Ibid., 319.

53   Ibid., 318.

54   Ibid., 319; In Corrine Roosevelt's memoir, she described Nannie as "beautiful, brilliant, exquisite in her delicate individuality, in her intellectual inspiration, in her fine humor and sense of values—her beautiful head like a rare cameo, her wonderful gray-blue eyes looking out under dark, level brows, she remains one of the pictures most treasured in the memories of the Roosevelts." Corrine Roosevelt Robinson, *My Brother Theodore Roosevelt*, (New York: Charles Scribner's Sons, 1921), 286.

55   T. R. to HCL, Oct. 2, 1915, Reel 108, Lodge Papers, MHS; In that same condolence note Roosevelt wrote: "What I am about to say will seem to you . . .comfortless; yet Edith and I both felt that there could be, for Nannie herself, no happier fate than to die as she did, in the fullness of time, her duties done and all her vivid charm undiminished." T. R. to Lodge, Oct. 20, 1915, Reel 108, Lodge Papers, MHS.

56   T. R. to Lodge, Oct. 20, 1915, Reel 108, Lodge Papers, MHS; Lodge, *The Lodge Women*, 320; In a condolence note to Lodge on Sept. 28 Henry Adams wrote of his deep sorrow at Nannie's passing. "I could say a great deal—volumes—but you know it all. You have got to endure what I have endured for thirty years, and I can make it no easier. My only comfort then was to be told over and over, how much I had lost—as though I did not know it better than anybody; and I can say no more to you now. . . ." Adams, *The Letters of Henry Adams, Vol. VI*, 702.

57   Lodge, *The Lodge Women*, 320.

58   HCL to T. R., Feb. 8, 1915, Lodge, drafts of Lodge-Roosevelt edited correspondence, 521, MHS; T. R. to HCL, May 8, 1915, Lodge, drafts of Lodge-Roosevelt edited correspondence, 528, MHS.

59   Mayer, *The Republican Party*, 339.
60   T. R. to HCL, Feb. 6, 1915, Lodge, drafts of Lodge-Roosevelt edited correspondence, 520, MHS; HCL to T. R., HCL, Feb. 8, 1915, Lodge, drafts of Lodge-Roosevelt edited correspondence, 521, MHS.
61   HCL to T. R., June 25, 1915, Reel 6, Lodge-Roosevelt Correspondence, MHS.
62   HCL to T. R., July 5, 1915, Reel 6, Lodge-Roosevelt Correspondence, MHS; T. R. to HCL, Nov. 27, 1915, Lodge, edited drafts of Lodge-Roosevelt correspondence, 539, MHS.
63   HCL to T. R., Dec. 2, 1915, Reel 6, Lodge-Roosevelt Correspondence, MHS.
64   Garraty, *Henry Cabot Lodge*, 323.
65   HCL to T. R., Dec. 4, 1915, Lodge, edited drafts, Lodge-Roosevelt Correspondence, 541, MHS; T. R. to HCL, Dec. 17, 1915, Lodge, edited drafts, Lodge-Roosevelt Correspondence, 542. MHS.
66   Brands, *Woodrow Wilson*, 49–51.
67   "Wilson Outlines the Nation's Defenses," *New York Times*, Nov. 5, 1915, 1.
68   HCL to T. R., Dec. 20, 1915, Lodge, edited drafts, Lodge-Roosevelt Correspondence, 545, MHS; Harbaugh, *Power and Responsibility*, 481; HCL to T. R., Feb. 1, 1916, Lodge, edited drafts, Lodge-Roosevelt Correspondence, 554–556, MHS; Garraty, *Henry Cabot Lodge*, 320; T. R. to HCL, Feb. 4, 1916, Lodge, edited drafts, Lodge-Roosevelt Correspondence, 558, MHS.
69   HCL to T. R. Feb. 1, 1916, Lodge, edited drafts, Lodge-Roosevelt Correspondence, 557, MHS.
70   HCL to T. R. Feb. 9, 1916, Lodge, drafts, edited Lodge-Roosevelt Correspondence, 565, MHS.
71   Harbaugh, *Power and Responsibility*, 478.

Chapter Eighteen: The Final Battle

1   Harbaugh, *Power and Responsibility*, 481–482.
2   HCL to T. R., Jan. 11, 1916, Lodge, edited drafts, Lodge-Roosevelt Correspondence, 548, MHS.
3   HCL to T. R. Feb. 9, 1916, Lodge, edited drafts, Lodge-Roosevelt Correspondence, 567–568, MHS.
4   HCL to T. R. Feb. 9, 1916, Lodge, edited drafts, Lodge-Roosevelt Correspondence, 568, MHS.
5   Morris, *Colonel Roosevelt*, 454–455.
6   Ibid., 448–449; O'Toole, *When Trumpets Call*, 291–292.
7   Morris, *Colonel Roosevelt*, 453–454; Garraty, *Henry Cabot Lodge*, 321–322.
8   Garraty, *Henry Cabot Lodge*, 321–322.
9   Morris, *Colonel Roosevelt*, 455–456; Garraty, *Henry Cabot Lodge*, 324.
10   Harbaugh, *Power and Responsibility*, 485–486; O'Toole, *When Trumpets Call*, 294.

11   Harbaugh, *Power and Responsibility*, 486.

12   Ibid.

13   Ibid.; John A. Garraty, "T. R. On the Telephone," *American Heritage*, Dec. 1957, Vol. 9, No. 1.

14   Ibid.

15   John D. Merrill, "Lodge Talked of as Possible Compromise," *Boston Globe*, June 9, 1916, 12.

16   Harbaugh, *Power and Responsibility*, 486; Garraty, *Henry Cabot Lodge*, 324–325; "Roosevelt Suggests Name of Lodge as Compromise," *Boston Globe*, June 10, 1916, 8.

17   O'Toole, *When Trumpets Call*, 296; A letter submitted to the Progressive National Committee suggesting Lodge stated the following: "In view of the conditions existing I suggest the name of Senator Lodge of Massachusetts. He is a man of the highest integrity, of the broadest national spirit and of the keenest devotion to the public good . . . He has not only a wide experience in public affairs, but a peculiarly close acquaintance with the very type of questions now most pressing for settlement . . ." Schriftgiesser, *The Gentleman from Massachusetts*, 280–281.

18   HCL to T. R., June 14, 1916, Reel 7, Lodge-Roosevelt Correspondence, MHS.

19   Ibid.

20   Ibid.

21   O'Toole, *When Trumpets Call*, 299.

22   Morris, *Colonel Roosevelt*, 460–461; Dalton, *Theodore Roosevelt*, 467–468.

23   Garraty, *Henry Cabot Lodge*, 326.

24   Ibid.; Gould, *Grand Old Party*, 207–208.

25   Garraty, *Henry Cabot Lodge*, 332–333; HCL to T. R., Jan. 26, 1917, Reel 7, Lodge-Roosevelt Correspondence, MHS; Dalton, *Theodore Roosevelt*, 474–475.

26   HCL to T. R., Jan. 26, 1917, Reel 7, Lodge-Roosevelt Correspondence, MHS; Garraty, *Henry Cabot Lodge*, 332; Morris, *Colonel Roosevelt*, 475; O'Toole, *When Trumpets Call*, 304–305.

27   HCL to T. R., Feb. 13, 1917, Reel 7, Lodge-Roosevelt Correspondence, MHS; T. R. to HCL, Feb. 20, 1917, Reel 7, Lodge-Roosevelt Correspondence, MHS.

28   HCL to T. R., Feb. 22, 1917, Reel 7, Lodge-Roosevelt Correspondence, MHS; T. R. to Lodge, Feb. 28, 1917, Lodge, edited Lodge-Roosevelt Correspondence, 592, MHS; O'Toole, *When Trumpets Call*, 306; HCL to T. R. March 2, 1917, edited Lodge-Roosevelt Correspondence, 593, MHS.

29   T. R. to Lodge, Feb. 28, 1917, Lodge, edited Lodge-Roosevelt Correspondence, 592, MHS.

30   O'Toole, *When Trumpets Call*, 306.

31   T. R. to HCL, March 2, 1917, Lodge, edited Lodge-Roosevelt Correspondence, 595, MHS.

32   Brands, *T. R.*, 779.

33   Morris, *Colonel Roosevelt*, 481; "Would Strike at Once," *New York Times*, March 21, 1917, 1; "War On Says Union League," *The Sun*, March 21, 1917, 1.

34   T. R. to HCL, March 22, 1917, Lodge, edited Lodge-Roosevelt Correspondence, 601, MHS; T. R. to Newton D. Baker, March 19, 1917, Reel 7, Lodge-Roosevelt Correspondence, MHS.

35   HCL to T. R., March 23, 1917, Reel 7, Lodge-Roosevelt Correspondence, MHS; T. R. to Newton D. Baker, March 19, 1917, Reel 7, Lodge-Roosevelt Correspondence, MHS.

36   Morris, *Colonel Roosevelt*, 481–482; T. R. to HCL, March 24, 1917, Lodge, edited Lodge-Roosevelt Correspondence, 603, MHS.

37   Morris, *Colonel Roosevelt*, 483.

38   "Lodge and Wilson Make Up," *Boston Globe*, April 3, 1917, 5.

39   HCL to T. R., April 4, 1917, Lodge-Roosevelt Correspondence, 604, MHS; Garraty, *Henry Cabot Lodge*, 333.

40   Bill Lamb, "Alexander Bannwart," Society for American Baseball Research, www.sabr.org.

41   HCL to T. R., April 4, 1917, edited Lodge-Roosevelt Correspondence, 604, MHS.

42   Ibid.; Lamb, "Alexander Bannwart," Society for American Baseball Research, www.sabr.org; "Senator Attacks Constituent," United States Senate Historical Office, www.senate.gov. There is some debate over who struck the first blow. According to Lodge's biographer Garraty, the senator went back and forth in his description of the event. Later in a formal statement Cabot recalled that he had struck first.

43   HCL to T. R., April 4, 1917, edited Lodge-Roosevelt Correspondence, 604, MHS; T. R. to HCL, April 6, 1917, edited Lodge-Roosevelt Correspondence, 606, MHS; Adams, *The Letters of Henry Adams, Vol. VI*, 749.

44   "Live Tips and Topics," *Boston Globe*, April 3, 1917, 7; In addition the fight made the front page of the *Boston Globe*. The publication entertained its readers by portraying Lodge and Bannwart in two squares with "in this corner" written underneath including their name and age. "Senator Lodge Right There with The Punch," *Boston Globe*, April 2, 1917, 1; Another newspaper drew a cartoon with Lodge in boxing trunks with the headline OUR NEW WHITE HOPE; Garraty, *Henry Cabot Lodge*, 333.

45   Brands, *T. R.*, 780–783.

46   T. R. to Newton D. Baker, April 23, 1917, Lodge, edited Lodge-Roosevelt Correspondence, 617, MHS.

47   HCL to T. R., April 23, 1917, Reel 7, Lodge-Roosevelt Correspondence, MHS.

48   Eric Trickey, "Why Teddy Roosevelt Tried to Bully his Way on to the World War I Battlefield," *Smithsonian*, April 10, 2017, www .smithsonianmag.org; Lodge was delighted when the "Roosevelt Amendment" passed the Senate. "It was, as you may suppose, a very great pleasure to me, and the deepest kind of personal satisfaction," Lodge

wrote following the passage of the measure. HCL to T. R., April 30, 1917, Lodge, edited Lodge-T. R. Correspondence, 632, MHS.

49 HCL to T. R., May 25, 1917, Lodge, edited Lodge-T. R. Correspondence, 636, MHS; O'Toole, *When Trumpets Call*, 313.

Chapter Nineteen: Twilight

1 HCL to T. R., Aug. 14, 1917, Lodge, edited Lodge-T. R. Correspondence, 638, MHS; T. R. to HCL, Aug. 15, 1917, Lodge, edited Lodge-T. R. Correspondence, 639, MHS.

2 HCL to T. R., Aug. 14, 1917, Lodge, edited Lodge-T. R. Correspondence, 638, MHS; T. R. to HCL, Aug. 15, 1917, Lodge, edited Lodge-T. R. Correspondence, 639, MHS; Garraty, *Henry Cabot Lodge*, 337.

3 HCL to T. R., Sept. 17, 1917, Reel 7, Lodge-Roosevelt Correspondence, MHS.

4 O'Toole, *When Trumpets Call*, 320.

5 HCL to T. R., March 5, 1918, Lodge, edited Lodge-Roosevelt Correspondence, 647, MHS; H. W. Crocker III, "The Roosevelt Sons in World War I," History on The Net, www.historyonthenet.com; O'Toole, *When Trumpets Call*, 320; Morris, *Edith Kermit Roosevelt*, 412.

6 Brands, *T. R.*, 786; Garraty, *Henry Cabot Lodge*, 339.

7 Garraty, *Henry Cabot Lodge*, 339.

8 Ibid., 340.

9 Morris, *Colonel Roosevelt*, 505–508.

10 Edith Roosevelt to HCL, Feb. 16, 1918, Reel 7, Lodge-Roosevelt Correspondence, MHS.

11 HCL to T. R., Nov. 5, 1917, Reel 7, Lodge-Roosevelt Correspondence, MHS.

12 Ibid.

13 Brands, *Woodrow Wilson*, 89.

14 Ibid.

15 Garraty, *Henry Cabot Lodge*, 340; Lodge, *The Senate and the League of Nations*, 94.

16 Garraty, *Henry Cabot Lodge*, 340.

17 O'Toole, *When Trumpets Call*, 67.

18 Ibid., 345; Burton, *Cecil Spring Rice: A Diplomat's Life*, 204–205.

19 Chalfant, *Henry Adams: His Last Life 1894–1918*, 524.

20 Garraty, *Henry Cabot Lodge*, 340; John M. Cooper Jr., *The Warrior and the Priest: Woodrow Wilson and Theodore Roosevelt*, (Cambridge, Mass.: Harvard University Press, 1983), 326–327.

21 Dalton, *Theodore Roosevelt*, 503.

22 Morris, *Colonel Roosevelt*, 529.

23 HCL to T. R., July 26, 1918, Library of Congress, Theodore Roosevelt Papers, Series I, Letters and Related Material 1759–1919, https://www.loc.gov/.

24 "Quentin Kept Policeman on Beat," *Washington Post*, undated, 1918, Reel 7, Lodge-Roosevelt Correspondence, MHS.
25 Garraty, *Henry Cabot Lodge*, 341.
26 "Lodge Demands a Dictated Peace Won by Victory," *New York Times*, Aug. 24, 1918, 1.
27 Ibid.; HCL to T. R., Aug. 31, 1918, Reel 7, Lodge-Roosevelt Correspondence, MHS.
28 O'Toole, *When Trumpets Call*, 395–396.
29 Garraty, *Henry Cabot Lodge*, 341; HCL to T. R., Oct. 7, 1918, Lodge, Edited Lodge-Roosevelt Correspondence, 659, MHS.
30 T. R. to HCL, Oct. 24, 1918, Reel 7, Lodge-Roosevelt Correspondence, MHS.
31 O'Toole, *When Trumpets Call*, 398. Garraty, *Henry Cabot Lodge*, 342.
32 Ibid.; Gould, *Grand Old Party*, 214–215.
33 Garraty, *Henry Cabot Lodge*, 343.
34 Morris, *Colonel Roosevelt*, 544–545; HCL to T. R., Nov. 18, 1918, Lodge, Edited Lodge-Roosevelt Correspondence, 666, MHS.
35 Morris, *Colonel Roosevelt*, 547.
36 HCL to T. R., Nov. 26, 1918, Lodge, Edited Lodge-Roosevelt Correspondence, 672, MHS.
37 Morris, *Colonel Roosevelt*, 547–548.
38 Ibid.
39 Ibid.
40 Ibid.
41 Ibid.
42 HCL to T. R., Dec. 23, 1918, Lodge, edited Lodge-Roosevelt Correspondence, 676, MHS; Conversation with Laura Cinturati, museum technician, Sagamore Hill National Historic Site, June 30, 2022.
43 Corinne Roosevelt-Robison to HCL, Jan. 6, 1919, Reel 7, Lodge-Roosevelt Correspondence, MHS; HCL to Edith Roosevelt, Jan. 6, 1919, Reel 7, Lodge-Roosevelt Correspondence, MHS.
44 "Simple Funeral of Colonel Roosevelt," *Boston Globe*, Jan. 8, 1919, 8.
45 "Lodge and Congress Honor Roosevelt," *New York Times*, Feb. 10, 1919, 6; "Gave Life to Service," *Washington Post*, Feb. 10, 1919, 3; "Roosevelt Extolled Throughout World Eulogy at Solomon Services," *New York Herald*, Feb. 10, 1919, 1; Morris, *Edith Kermit Roosevelt*, 436.
46 "Lodge and Congress Honor Roosevelt," *New York Times*, Feb. 10, 1919, 6.
47 Garraty, *Henry Cabot Lodge*, 349.
48 Ibid., 346.
49 Ibid.
50 Ibid., 347.
51 Ibid., 352–353; "Classic Senate Speeches: Constitution of the League of Nations," Feb. 28, 1919, www.senate.gov.

ENDNOTES

52 Garraty, *Henry Cabot Lodge*, 352–353; "Classic Senate Speeches: Constitution of the League of Nations," Feb. 28, 1919, www.senate.gov.
53 Brands, *Woodrow Wilson*, 109–110.
54 Ibid., 118–119.
55 Ibid., 119–120.
56 Ibid., 127–128; John Milton Cooper, "The Last Time America Turned Away from the World," *New York Times*, Nov. 21, 2019, www.nytimes.com.
57 Garraty, *Henry Cabot Lodge*, 418–420.
58 Ibid.
59 Ibid., 423–424.
60 Ibid., 424. There is no comment about Lodge's passing from Edith Roosevelt's biographer Sylvia Jukes Morris, who contends that T. R.'s widow had never forgotten his betrayal in not supporting her husband in 1912. Morris, *Edith Kermit Roosevelt*, 462.

Sources
1 Garraty, *Henry Cabot Lodge*, 420–421.
2 Ibid.
3 Ibid.; Morris, *Edith Kermit Roosevelt*, 436.
4 HCL to Edith Roosevelt, Feb. 12, 1924, Reel 7, Lodge-Roosevelt Collection, MHS; HCL to Edith Roosevelt, May 31, 1924, Reel 7, Lodge-Roosevelt Collection, MHS.

INDEX

Blair House, 207
Bliss, Cornelius, x, 127
Boone, Daniel, 104
Boston Christ Church, 15
Boston Daily Advertiser, 69–70
Boston Evening Transcript, 34, 262, 264
Boston Globe, 48, 72, 180, 276, 304, 310–311
Boston Herald, 59
Boston Sunday Post, 200
Boswell, Charles M., xix
Boswell, James, 15
Brands, H. W., 218
Bristow, Benjamin, x, 22
Brookline Unitarian Church, 18
Brown, Alfred Hodgdon, 251
Brown, John, 262
Brunswick Hotel, 61, 225
Bryan, William Jennings, x, xxi, 121–123, 151, 168, 175–178, 204, 246, 279, 282–291
Bryce, James, 75
Buchanan, James, 289
Buffalo Review, 182
"Bull Moose Party," 275–276, 295
Bulloch, Martha, xv, 4
Butler, Benjamin F., 39
Butler, Nicholas Murray, 171
Butt, Archibald "Archie," x, 248, 259

C

Cabot, George, 28, 30, 106
Cambridge University, 11–12, 17
Cameron, Elizabeth "Lizzie" Sherman, x, 78–79, 92, 96–97, 101–103, 135, 148–149, 162, 177, 195–196, 210–212, 217, 252–253, 273
Cameron, J. Donald, 78–79, 92
Carnegie, Andrew, x, 225
Carnegie Hall, 146, 321

Carow, Edith, xv, 68–69, 73–75. *See also* Roosevelt, Edith
Carranza, Venustiano, x, 297
Cedric, 214
Chanler, Margaret, 57
Chanler, Winthrop, x, 135, 173, 191, 278
Chapman, John Jay, x, 143–145
"Charter of Democracy, The," 269
Chicago Tribune, 49–50
Children's Aid Society, 4
Chinese Exclusion Act, 36
Christ Church, Boston, 15
Christ Church, Oyster Bay, 278, 324
Civil Service Commission, 83–91, 98–101, 110, 120, 128
civil service reform, 21–23, 26, 32–36, 61, 67, 82–91, 150
Civil War, 4, 9–11, 15, 20, 25, 29, 34–35, 45, 80, 119, 279
Clayton, Powell, 45–48
Clayton-Bulwer Treaty, 160–161, 179
Cleveland, Grover
  as governor, 32
  as president, x, 66, 77, 80–81, 99–101, 107–109, 113–114
  as presidential nominee, 50, 54–62
  speeches by, 80
  views on, 50, 54–62, 66, 80–81, 113–114, 212
coal strike, 204–210. *See also* mining industry
Coleridge, Samuel Taylor, 231
Columbia Law School, 26–27
Columbia University, 292
Conkling, Roscoe, x, 12, 25
Converse, Elisha S., x, 34–35
Coolidge, Calvin, 328
Coolidge, Thomas Jefferson, 242
Cooper, James Fenimore, 8, 113
corporate power, xxvii, 25–30, 95, 146, 164, 170, 194–211, 228–246, 261–271, 280–284

Foss, Eugene N., xii, 264
Fourteen Points, 317, 320–321
Fourteenth Amendment, 88
Franchise Tax Bill, 151
Franco-Prussian War, 16
Frémont, John C., xx

G
Gardner, Augustus "Gus," xii, 99,
   135, 158, 206, 210, 273, 286,
   291–292, 315–318
Gardner, Constance Lodge, 99,
   158–160, 215
Garfield, James A., xii, 34, 36, 41,
   44, 270
Garfield, James R., xii, 247
Garraty, John, 16, 94, 133, 289
"Garryowen," 245
General Electric Company, 102
George, Henry, 71, 73
Gilbert and Sullivan, 44
Gilded Age, 21, 185
Gilpatrick Hotel, 277
Gould, Jay, 30
Grand Pacific Hotel, 43
Grant, Ulysses S., xii, 21–23, 25, 34
Gray, Horace, xii, 197–200
"Great Fraud of 1876," 25
Great Railroad Strike, 185
Greeley, Horace, xii, 21–22
Guild, Curtis Jr., 237
Guiteau, Charles J., xii, 36

H
"Half-Breeds," 25
Halford, Elijah W., 83
Hall, Anna Rebecca, xv, 98
Hamburg, 248
Hamilton, Alexander, 28, 64
Hancock, Winfield Scott, xii, 36
Hanna, Marcus A., xii, xxii, 121–122,
   169–173, 187, 219
Harbaugh, William, 209

Harding, Warren G., xii, 312
Harper's Magazine, 94
Harper's Weekly, 48
Harriman, E. H., xii, 202, 220, 244
Harrison, Benjamin, 80–83, 85–91,
   98–100, 107, 240
Harvard Law School, 310
Harvard University, xxii, 11–19, 23,
   28, 30, 39, 55, 93–94, 182, 292
Hasty Pudding Club, 11, 18
Hawley, Joseph, xix–xx, xxiii
Hay, Clara Stone, xii, 78, 92, 95–96
Hay, John, xii, 4–5, 78–79, 92–97,
   127, 148, 160–163, 170, 179,
   191–195, 213, 224–227
Hayes, E. B., 77
Hayes, Rutherford B., xiii, 11–12,
   24–26, 78
Haymarket Square, 185
Hay-Pauncefote Treaty, 161
Hearst, William Randolph, xiii, 133,
   236–237
Hepburn, William, 226
Hepburn Act, 226, 232
Herakles, 250
"Hero of San Juan Hill," xxi
Hero Tales from American History, 104
Hess, Jacob, 27
Hewitt, Abram S., 71, 73
Higginson, Henry Lee, xiii, 17, 130,
   211, 243
Higginson, Thomas W., 55
Hill, James J., xiii, 202
Hitt, Robert R., 220
Hoar, George F., 148
Hobart, Garret, xiii, 127, 153–155,
   158
Hohenberg, Sofie, Duchess of, xvi,
   286
Holmes, Oliver Wendell Jr., xiii, 56,
   61, 197–200, 229–230, 233–235
Hoover, Herbert, xiii, 290
Hotel Walton, 171

INDEX